Consciousness

The study of consciousness is recognized as one of the biggest remaining challenges to the scientific community. This book provides a fascinating introduction to the new science that promises to illuminate our understanding of the subject.

Consciousness covers all the main approaches to the modern scientific study of consciousness, and also gives the necessary historical, philosophical and conceptual background to the field. Current scientific evidence and theory from the fields of neuropsychology, cognitive neuroscience, brain imaging and the study of altered states of consciousness such as dreaming, hypnosis, meditation and out-of-body experiences is presented. Revonsuo provides an integrative review of the major existing philosophical and empirical theories of consciousness and identifies the most promising areas for future developments in the field.

This textbook offers a readable and timely introduction to the science of consciousness for anyone interested in this compelling area, especially undergraduates studying psychology, philosophy, cognition, neuroscience and related fields.

Antti Revonsuo is Professor of Cognitive Neuroscience at the University of Skövde, Sweden, and Professor of Psychology at the University of Turku, Finland. He has been conducting research on consciousness since the early 1990s and has directed an undergraduate degree programme on consciousness studies since 1997. He is best known for his evolutionary–psychological theory of dreaming, the threat-simulation theory.

Consciousness

The science of subjectivity

Antti Revonsuo

 Psychology Press
Taylor & Francis Group

HOVE AND NEW YORK

Published in 2010
by Psychology Press
27 Church Road, Hove, East Sussex BN3 2FA

Simultaneously published in the USA and Canada
by Psychology Press
270 Madison Avenue, New York NY 10016

*Psychology Press is an imprint of the
Taylor & Francis Group, an
Informa business*

© 2010 Psychology Press

Typeset in Futura and Century Old Style by
RefineCatch Limited, Bungay, Suffolk
Printed and bound in Great Britain by
TJ International Ltd, Padstow, Cornwall
Cover design by Jim Wilkie
Cover image: © The Gallery Collection/Corbis

This publication has been reproduced with
paper manufactured to strict environmental
standards and with pulp derived from
sustainable forests.

*British Library Cataloguing in Publication
Data*
A catalogue record for this book is available
from the British Library

*Library of Congress Cataloging in
Publication Data*
Revonsuo, Antti.
  Consciousness : the science of
  subjectivity / Antti Revonsuo.
    p. cm.
  Includes bibliographical references and
  index.
  1. Consciousness.   I. Title.
  BF311.R395 2010
  153 – dc22   2009031336

ISBN: 978–1–84169–725–3 (hbk)
ISBN: 978–1–84169–726–0 (pbk)

To all my students,

– past, present, and future

Contents at a glance

Contents

CONTENTS

3   The conceptual foundations of consciousness science   69

Part two

List of figures

Introduction

Consciousness and its place in the scientific view of the world

To study consciousness is to study a deep mystery about ourselves. It is to study the nature of our *existence,* but not the kind of existence that physics and the other sciences study because they study the *objective* existence of atoms, galaxies, oceans, cells, time and space, among other things. To study consciousness is to study the fundamental nature of our *personal* existence, our *subjective* existence, our life as a sequence of subjective experiences. In this new field of science, we want to understand ourselves not only as entities that are alive and behave or interact with their environment, like bacteria or trees or dragonflies do, but also as beings who directly *experience* or *feel* or *sense their own existence*, who are alive in a sense fundamentally different from the ordinary biological notion of "being alive".

Being alive as a conscious subject is something much more than being alive in the purely objective biological sense. A conscious being is not merely alive in the sense of realizing a collection of physiological processes and capacities (such as growth or self-replication) that separate biological organisms from nonliving physical systems. A conscious being is *mentally, internally* alive. Unlike physical objects and simple biological organisms, a being who possesses a conscious mind also senses or feels or experiences its own existence. To crystallize this idea: A conscious being has an *internal psychological reality,* a *mental life* consisting of subjective experiences, with a *stream of consciousness* flowing within. The inner stream of subjective experience, which is directly present for us and continuously revealing itself to us, is consciousness.

Consciousness as the seat of our subjective experiences is the mystery to be solved by science. In particular, it is the very phenomenon to be described and explained by the science of consciousness, which is why we may call this new science by the name "The Science of Subjective Experience", or "The Science of Subjectivity" as in the subtitle of this book.

This book is an invitation to the mystery of consciousness and an introduction to the new science that specifically enquires into the mystery. We will try to understand what kind of challenge consciousness poses to current science and we will review the modern scientific approaches to the study of consciousness. Whether or not they will ultimately be successful in solving or removing the mystery of consciousness may be too early to tell.

Be that as it may, it is clear that a new field, specifically concentrating on consciousness, is urgently needed. The already existing fields that study the mind or the brain have ignored consciousness. Psychology, behavioural science, cognitive science and cognitive neuroscience have avoided consciousness or have been reluctant to put subjective experience into the focus of their research programmes. Those fields of study are more interested in such things as behaviour, representation, information processing, neural activity and other perfectly *objective* phenomena that are fundamentally different from subjective mental life. Therefore, a fresh start is required in order to scientifically zoom in on the subjective stream of experience, or consciousness itself. But what exactly is such a science all about? Do we have a clear enough idea of consciousness to approach it scientifically? What *is* our "inner mental life", the "subjective psychological reality"? Perhaps we need some clarification of this at the outset.

A person's subjective psychological reality contains all the experiences one has at any particular moment. It consists of different perceptual experiences, such as seeing colours, shapes and visual objects, located within a perceptual space extending in all directions. It contains auditory experiences whose sources are perceived to be located in the space around you. It contains smells and tastes, such as the sweet fragrance experienced when deeply sniffing a rose, eyes closed (as in the cover image of this book). Furthermore, it contains feelings, emotions and bodily experiences; you perceive and feel your body as being a part of the world around you, but you also experience your body from the inside, as a three-dimensional, living, feeling, moving entity whose behaviour you can control at will. You have a mental space where thoughts are entertained, where internal images pass by, memories are relived and where you feel the pull of desires. Taken together, these experiences – the perceptual, the bodily and the mental – form the contents of your subjective psychological reality.

Experiential events are fleeting. They are directly and vividly present in consciousness only briefly, only for a few seconds perhaps. The contents of the stream of experience flow ever onwards. The patterns of experience change all the time, some only gradually, some abruptly, but they never cease to move on. Yet, there seems to be a persisting subject – or perhaps the underlying mental "space" of experience itself – that never changes. Underneath the ever-changing patterns in the restless stream of experience there is the stable riverbed that unifies these experiences into a single inner world, thus forming a single unified psychological reality, the *world-for-me*, a spatial unity and a temporal continuity of consciousness and self that transcends the short-lived and changeable contents that come and go.

The flow of subjective experiences constitutes our conscious life as we know it. We know not exactly when it first started flowing, but ever since the beginning it has been going on, save for brief pauses during the night in deep sleep when even the faintest dream images cease to exist. We know not when it will come to an end, to a final moment of consciousness, or even if it ever will. "Is there life after death?" should be rephrased as "Will there still be a subjective psychological reality going on for me after death?" or "Will some sort of flow of subjective experiences continue for me even after my body and my brain are no longer alive in the biological sense of the word?" These are ultimate – and challenging – questions, and the answers depend on the discoveries to be made in the science of consciousness.

Why is consciousness considered a "mystery"? After all, we know consciousness intimately from the inside, it is the most natural thing there is for us and it is ever present in our lives. Of course, in that sense there is no mystery at all about consciousness. In fact, there is nothing in the world that we would be acquainted with better than the subjective experiences vividly present for us all the time. The problem, the absolute mystery, is elsewhere: we do not know how to fit consciousness together with the world-view of science. Physics and the other natural sciences describe a world where particles, force fields, atoms, molecules, stars and planets exist in an objective way and causally interact with each other. So far as we know, none of the things thoroughly described and explained by the sciences has an inner psychological reality, a stream of subjective experiences. Thus, despite all the amazing progress in physics, chemistry, biology and neuroscience, science remains incapable of describing – or even acknowledging the existence of – an inner subjective life. No matter how carefully we study the physics, chemistry and biology of an animal, the empirical evidence we acquire does not in any objective manner reveal whether the animal in some way feels or senses its own existence – whether it has an inner subjective psychological reality or not – nor, if it does, what its subjective experiences are like – what it would be *like* to *be* that animal and to see the world through its eyes.

At present we have no idea how our inner life could be explained in harmony with the world-view of the natural sciences. In that world-view, there is nothing that even remotely resembles our subjective lives. On the contrary, the scientific picture of the world is in many ways directly in conflict with our subjective experience. The physical universe as a whole is a giant, stagnant object in four-dimensional space–time where the dimensions of space and time all exist in one piece and nothing ever "happens". Past, present and future are simply different parts of the temporal dimension that coexist with each other and are equally fixed. The universe as described by physics has no particular moment of "now" that would be unique, in that only there do events flow forward, and behind it the past is fixed and before it the future lies wide open. The universe as described by the natural sciences includes no subjective qualities such as those that characterize each and every one of our experiences: colours, tastes, tones, pains, odours, feelings. The world as described by science consists of spatiotemporal causal structures, physical entities at microscopic (forces, particles, waves, fields) and macroscopic levels (planets, galaxies) and laws and mechanisms that can be described objectively and quantitatively.

By contrast, our subjective psychological reality is a forward-moving stream of qualitative experiences, located at a particular time and place in the physical universe, always happening in the "here and now" and taking place within a particular person's mind (or brain). How can such a thing exist in the physical universe? Is it something over and above the physical – something other-worldly, a spiritual bubble, a wandering soul – that has become attached to a biological organism inside the physical world? Somehow this small drop of precious soul-stuff seems to blow an inner mental life into the organisms it inhabits, to live a life through them and to see the world through their eyes. Is that the way we are – tiny drops of magical soul-stuff trapped inside material human bodies that are located inside the giant physical machinery of the universe? If such a spiritual view of ourselves seems to be out of the question, then is our consciousness just some kind of complex physical or biological mechanism in our bodies? Is our precious inner world simply made out of quite ordinary, slimy and boring brain-stuff with no other-worldly magical souls involved?

As these profound questions suggest, the science of consciousness is about our very existence. What kind of beings are we really – our selves, our souls, if you like – in the final analysis? What is consciousness? Who or what is the "subject" or the "self" who "has" my conscious experiences? What are our thoughts, experiences and memories *made of*? What about moments of intense joy, happiness, beauty and awe, when we seem to reach a higher consciousness, full of meaning: are they only fleeting electrochemical symphonies played by billions of neurons in harmony, or perhaps glimpses of an other-worldly mental realm, entirely beyond matter? Are we, our inner selves, something spiritual, soul-like; could our subjective life thus survive bodily death? Could our consciousness perhaps be reborn in some other life-form, so that after death there would be an inner life once again for us, though in a form unlike the present one?

The answers to these rather fundamental questions depend on what the science of consciousness will find out about our subjective psychological reality and about its physical seat, our brain!

The contents of this book

We have now defined the science of consciousness as *the science whose task it is to describe and explain our subjective psychological reality* – the inner stream of subjective experience. Although this branch of science is brand new, it has deep philosophical, historical and conceptual roots. In this book, we will first get acquainted with the foundations on which the science of consciousness is built. Having a grasp of the foundations will help us to understand how the science of consciousness originated and where it stands now.

We will first review the philosophical foundations of this field. In philosophy, questions about the ultimate nature of existence are put forward, such as: What kind of stuff is the universe ultimately made of – is it entirely composed of physical matter or is there something else besides? What is our subjective psychological reality – our consciousness – ultimately made of? Is it physical or nonphysical? How does the subjective psychological reality relate to the objective physical reality?

Questions like the above are *metaphysical* or *ontological* questions in philosophy. In Chapter 1 we will outline the major philosophical theories that offer mutually exclusive answers to the questions concerning the ultimate nature of consciousness and the relation between consciousness and the rest of the world, especially the brain. Although the philosophical discussions have been going on for centuries, the final solutions to them remain open and the problems remain as acute as ever. Thus, philosophical discussions of the ultimate nature of consciousness are a necessary and integral part of the science of consciousness.

Although the science of consciousness in its modern form emerged only recently (during the 1990s), the study of consciousness has its roots deep in the history of psychology. In fact, it is possible to fully understand the current situation only by exploring the historical development of psychological science. We will find that, at one time, psychology actually defined itself as the science of the conscious mind, but later on it had a total change of heart. As a result of the radical turn of the tides, scientific psychology flatly rejected the study of consciousness. This sinister history is the main reason why experimental psychology during the last 50 years never became the science of consciousness (but rather the science of behaviour, or the science of cognition). The initiative for establishing the science of consciousness anew was taken in philosophy and cognitive neuroscience instead. In Chapter 2 we will learn about the many surprising twists and turns that the study of consciousness went through between the 1870s and the 1990s – during the roughly 120 years before the emergence of the current "new wave" of consciousness research.

The first task for any branch of science is to describe, clearly and systematically, the phenomena it aims to explain. Otherwise we would not really know what it is we are trying to explain, nor could we recognize and test whether our explanations are successful or not. Thus, long before there were proper astronomical or biological theories, astronomers, botanists and "natural historians" had made observations and described, meticulously and systematically, the unchanging constellations and the wandering planets in the sky, and countless species of flora and fauna found even in the remotest corners of the Earth. They had also developed systematic definitions and concepts for recognizing and labelling natural phenomena, so that the scientists could communicate clearly with each other about their observations of the relevant phenomena.

Hence, one of the first tasks for the science of consciousness is to produce a set of basic definitions and concepts that help the researchers to communicate their findings and theoretical ideas in a clear and systematic manner. Unfortunately, at this early stage of consciousness science, much controversy and confusion still remains concerning the most accurate and useful ways to define the phenomena that are to be explained. We will however try to steer clear of the conceptual confusions. I will therefore introduce the most fundamental concepts and try to define them as clearly as possible. That is the task before us in Chapter 3. In the rest of this book, the concepts defined there will serve as the conceptual framework, in the light of which we will survey the empirical findings and theories of consciousness.

After the foundations have been explained and clarified, the book then moves on to the four central domains of consciousness science: *neuropsychology and consciousness*; *neural correlates of consciousness*; *theories of consciousness*, and *altered states of consciousness*. In the first section on neuropsychology we will learn what happens to consciousness as a result of brain injury or neurological deficit. Depending on the location of the damage, different aspects of consciousness may be lost or at least radically and permanently altered. These surprising alterations and dissociations constitute an important line of evidence on the internal structure and unity of consciousness. They also provide us with evidence concerning the brain mechanisms involved in the realization of particular aspects of consciousness. In the second section on the neural correlates of consciousness we learn how the modern methods of cognitive neuroscience, such as functional magnetic resonance imaging (fMRI) and electroencephalography (EEG), can be used to collect evidence on the neural mechanisms of consciousness, and what the evidence shows so far. The third section reviews the most significant theories of consciousness that have been put forward recently by philosophers, psychologists or neuroscientists. There, we will try to understand what it is that a theory of consciousness should explain, and we will evaluate how far in this task the already existing theories can take us. The fourth and final section focuses on altered states of consciousness as another important source of evidence for the science of consciousness. There, we study altered states of consciousness such as sleep, dreaming, hypnosis, meditation and higher states of consciousness such as flow or peak experiences and mystical experiences. These fascinating forms of consciousness may reveal aspects and mechanisms of subjectivity that could never be reached by just studying the paradigmatic "normal" waking state.

Higher states of consciousness lead us to a more practical question: What should we *do* with our consciousness? Is it possible to reach higher forms or states of consciousness that would make our subjective existence in this (sometimes boring or depressing) physical universe more bearable? How could we enhance states of consciousness that are positive and meaningful? Happiness and subjective well-being are states of consciousness that make subjective existence worthwhile. The science of consciousness might thus consider allying itself with the emerging new sciences of happiness and subjective well-being that focus on the *positive* qualities of our subjective existence – higher consciousness – and how to reach and cultivate such states.

All in all, this book offers an invitation to ponder a deep and awesome mystery from a scientific point of view; it is a basic introduction to the new science that attempts to solve one of the oldest and most difficult scientific (and philosophical) problems. If this new science one fine day proves to be successful, we will finally come to understand what the place of our mental life is in the physical world. And if the present book proves to be successful in *its* task, the reader will come to understand the very basics of this new, fascinating branch of science and, hopefully, will learn to appreciate the beauty and depth of the mystery – as well as catch a glimpse of the possible scientific solutions to it.

A cautionary note on the approach to consciousness taken in this book

In the book you will be reading, I have made an attempt to present the science of consciousness as a wide, multidisciplinary field where philosophy, psychology and neuroscience become seamlessly intertwined and entangled with each other. Still, I have selectively included only the topics that I personally see as the core of the science of consciousness and I have left out some others that seem more peripheral. Thus, the reader should bear in mind that this book does not cover everything that has been discussed in the enormously broad field of consciousness studies, and even the things that it does cover are presented in a simple and straightforward manner, often stepping rather quickly over the many complex controversies between different standpoints in the field. I felt a straightforward style of writing that emphasizes clarity, brevity and breadth of coverage to be a necessary feature for an introductory book to a field often plagued by deep and complex philosophical and empirical controversies and much conceptual confusion.

I have attempted to present the materials from a relatively neutral standpoint that allows the reader to formulate his or her own opinion. Still, I do realize that a totally neutral way of even so much as just defining consciousness is impossible, and therefore some philosophical and theoretical choices and biases that are my own are, at places, unavoidable and rather obvious. To get a perspective that is independent of my biases, I recommend the reader to refer back to the original sources that are given in the References at the end of the book and the Further Reading lists at the end of each chapter.

The field of consciousness research is teeming with different and usually squarely opposing approaches, but it would not be possible to give all the different viewpoints and arguments an equal amount of space and attention and still end up with a readable textbook. Thus, although I attempt to give a neutral "bird's eye view" to the field, the current book is at least implicitly reflecting my own vision of the science of consciousness. This view is not universally accepted by all consciousness researchers, but then nor is any other view. In case the reader happens to be curious about my own explicit standpoint in the philosophy and science of consciousness, I give a brief account of it in the Epilogue of this book, and a thorough presentation with all the relevant background and sources can be found in my earlier monograph, *Inner Presence* (Revonsuo, 2006).

The present book has gradually taken form over the years as I have taught undergraduate and postgraduate courses on the mind–body problem, the history of psychology, the philosophy of science, the neuropsychology of consciousness, cognitive neuroscience, theories of consciousness and altered states of consciousness. Much of the groundwork for this book, as well as for my teaching, I have done by relying on a number of other texts, foremost among them being Farthing's (1992) excellent but somewhat dated and out-of-print book *The Psychology of Consciousness*. Other important books that I have used in teaching or that have otherwise had a great influence on my work are *The Nature of Consciousness*, edited by Block and others (1997), Hothersall's (2004) *History of Psychology, Fourth Edition*, Finger's (1994) *Origins of Neuroscience*, Churchland's (2002) *Brain-Wise, Studies in Neurophilosophy*, Gazzaniga et al.'s (2008) *Cognitive Neuroscience, The Biology of the Mind*, Blackmore's (2004) *Consciousness, An Introduction*, Velmans' and Schneider's edited volume (2007) *The Blackwell Companion to Consciousness* and the new two-volume *Encyclopedia of Consciousness* edited by Banks (2009).

I would greatly appreciate any feedback from the readers of this book, be they students, teachers, professionals in the field or lay readers. Your comments and suggestions would be invaluable to me, especially if ever I were to write a second edition where the inevitable shortcomings of the present one could be remedied.

Acknowledgements

This book is wholly inspired by my dear students. Teaching courses in consciousness and cognitive neuroscience for the past 10 years at the University of Skövde, Sweden, has given me the unique opportunity to interact with many bright students who are equally fascinated by consciousness as I myself am. During this time I have gradually realized how difficult it is to find easily readable, up-to-date undergraduate textbooks on consciousness that would describe the basic issues in a simple, clear and integrative manner. My goal was to write exactly such a book, for my students as much as for myself, as a helpful tool to introduce the field to the beginner. Whether or not this goal has now been met I must leave for my future students and other readers of this book to decide. I want to thank all my students in the Consciousness Studies Programme at the University of Skövde, Sweden: your endless curiosity – and your insightful but sometimes impossibly difficult questions – about consciousness have been invaluable to me. I hope I now have a better idea as to what needs to be explained in an introductory course on consciousness, and how it ought to be explained without any unnecessary philosophical complications or incomprehensible scientific jargon.

Over the years, there have been far too many colleagues and students involved in the fascinating discussions on consciousness to mention everyone here, but at the very least the following people I am not likely to forget as long as my consciousness has any lights on at all: Paavo Pylkkänen, with whom we originally put the Consciousness Studies Programme together; Anders Milton and Monica Bergman – among my first students in Sweden, now my fellow teachers; Karin Freidlitz and Daniel Labbe – the founding members of the unforgettable Skövde Mad Scientists' Society; Csengelle Dioszegi from the very first class of Consciousness Studies in 1997; Petri Kåhlman (no-one else has participated in so many of my courses!); Robin Brandt (never short of a few questions!); Almira Osmanovic (now graduate of the Karolinska Institute, Stockholm); Isabelle Clavenstam (thanks for the comments on the final manuscript!); all the other students who graduated or who participated in our Mini-conference on Consciousness, Spring 2009; and, finally, all the incredibly active first-year students in our new undergraduate programme that combines the science of consciousness with the (even newer) science of happiness.

The members of my Consciousness Research Group at the Centre for Cognitive Neuroscience, University of Turku, Finland, have contributed significantly to my knowledge on various aspects of consciousness, and furthermore have given useful comments on the manuscript of the book: thanks to our hypnosis expert Sakari Kallio (also known as F. A. Mesmer), Mika Koivisto (the world's leading expert on VAN!), Katja Valli (the relentless Threat Simulator), Mirja Johanson, Valdas Noreika, Niina Salminen-Vaparanta, Pilleriin Sikka (the craazzyy AWEsome), Levente Moro, Heidi Sederholm (FLOWENLIT Meditation Master) and Panu Helle.

Two of my former students have played a crucial role in putting the manuscript of this book together for publication – without their help this poor little book might have never come into being. Linda Laurila did brilliant work in drawing the illustrations, based only on the vague sketches that I had hastily penned on paper. Linda Bergström did an equally brilliant job with checking and finalizing the whole manuscript for submission to the publisher and in keeping me firmly on schedule as the deadline was approaching. My warmest thanks to both of you!

I enjoyed writing this book, but would not have been able to even consider such a project without support from: the Signe och Ane Gyllenbergs Stiftelse and the Academy of Finland (project 8110957, "Neurophilosophy of Consciousness" and project 8124623, "Neuroethics of Brainreading"); the School of Humanities and Informatics, University of Skövde, Sweden; and the Department of Psychology, University of Turku, Finland. They have provided me with the financial and institutional support that made the writing of this book possible, which I am happy to acknowledge most gratefully.

Antti Revonsuo
Turku, June 2009

Part one

Background to the science of consciousness

Chapter 1

The philosophical foundations of consciousness science

Introduction

In philosophy, the *mind–body problem*, or the relationship between the inner mental world and the external physical world, has been discussed for thousands of years. What is the human soul, or the mind, or consciousness? What is its relationship to the body, the brain or physical matter in general? In some theories, the nature of consciousness (subjective psychological reality) and the nature of the brain (objective physical, biological reality) are seen as fundamentally different: made out of very different kinds of basic stuff. That solution makes it all the more difficult to explain how the two could be in close causal interaction with each other. Alternatively, other theories assume that consciousness and the rest of reality are not tremendously different after all, but consist of the same basic stuff. The problem for the latter is to show how consciousness could be just the same as ordinary physical matter – or vice versa! In addition to the mind–body problem, the science of consciousness also has to face the *other-minds problem:* How can we *know* about other minds? We cannot directly perceive, detect or measure the presence of consciousness. We do not seem to have any scientific access to the subjective psychological realities of other creatures. Thus, are they beyond science altogether?

1.1 The first distinction: Dualism and monism

We will first divide the philosophical mind–body theories into two different categories, *dualistic* theories and *monistic* theories.

Definition of dualism

All dualistic theories say that the world (the universe as a whole) consists of two categorically different types of entity or substance. One of them is physical. This substance constitutes physical matter, energy, force fields, elementary particles and forces, and all the rest of the things that the physical sciences take as the fundamental building blocks of the universe. In the final analysis, the more complex physical systems, such as stars, mountains and trees, consist of the elementary physical entities.

The other substance is mental by nature. "Mental" is taken by definition to be something nonphysical, something entirely different from the physical rather than a part or a variety of the physical. It is less clear *what* the mental substance is supposed to consist of, but it seems natural to assume that, whatever it is, it must be the same sort of stuff that forms our subjective psychological reality. Thus, the mental stuff consists of subjective, qualitative states of consciousness located within the mental space where conscious events happen. It is directly present for us in our sensations, percepts, thoughts, emotions, images, as they are subjectively experienced in the stream of consciousness. Typically, the nonphysical substance is depicted as some kind of ghostly mind-stuff or soul-stuff that is independent of physical matter and even of the laws of nature that govern the physical realm. Soul-stuff is presumed to be beyond all objective physical measurements and observations, consisting perhaps of extremely fine, ethereal "soul-atoms" that are unlike any physical particles, or existing in a mental "soul-space", another dimension altogether that lies beyond the physical space–time.

Definition of monism

By contrast, all monistic theories say that the world (the universe as a whole) consists of only *one* type of substance. Different monistic theories, however, disagree about the ultimate nature of the fundamental substance. Some say that the universe is at bottom thoroughly physical (materialism or physicalism), whereas others say that the universe consists of nothing but mental substance across the board (idealism). Yet others claim that the universe is, at the rock bottom level, neither "mental" nor "physical" (neutral monism). We will return to these distinctions in due time. Now we will first explore dualistic theories of consciousness in more detail.

1.2 Dualistic theories of consciousness

Dualistic theories take it for granted that both physical matter and subjective consciousness are real phenomena that exist in their own right. Neither owes its existence to the other; they are both on an equal footing in the universe. They are just radically different kinds of stuff. This is one of the inviting characteristics of dualistic theories. They show due respect both to the external physical world – basically accepting all the physical sciences, as far as they go – and to our inner subjective world, saying that it is a reality of its own, beyond the physical one.

But dualistic theories also have some serious weaknesses. First, they have difficulty in telling us exactly what *kind* of stuff the nonphysical soul-stuff is supposed to be and where it is located in relation to physical space. They only tell us what it is *not*: it is not physical – it is nonphysical. But what is it to be nonphysical or immaterial? If our consciousness is based on nonphysical soul-stuff, then we need a testable scientific theory that describes and explains exactly what soul-stuff is, how it behaves and where it is to be found. Therefore, dualistic theories are not necessarily able to offer us terribly convincing answers to the ontological problem, enquiring about the basic nature of consciousness. What is worse, they are also in trouble when trying to answer the relational question: How exactly does the nonphysical soul-stuff *relate* to the physical world, especially to our bodies and brains?

If we know anything about the relationship between consciousness and physical reality, it is that those two realms seem to collaborate seamlessly whenever we perceive external objects or whenever we perform voluntary actions. On the one hand, the sensory organs in our bodies receive physical energy from the world and convert it to neural signals that in some way are transformed to subjective sensations and percepts in our inner psychological world. On the other hand, we formulate thoughts and plans and we experience desires and cravings in our consciousness. By a mere act of will we can make our physical muscles, limbs and bodies move through physical space, guided by our conscious will and intention. There seems to be a two-way interaction between consciousness and physical reality: first, the external world reaches into our consciousness, which thereby senses and perceives the world; second, our mind reaches out to the external world and thereby guides the behaviour of the body at will.

Usually dualistic theories are differentiated from each other on the basis of how they answer the relational question, or how exactly does the nonphysical soul-stuff relate to the physical world, especially to our bodies and brains? The three main alternatives are known as interactionism, epiphenomenalism and parallelism.

Interactionism

The main idea in interactionism is, as the name hints, that there is *two-way causal interaction* between the external physical reality and the subjective psychological reality, or brain and consciousness. In other words, physical stimuli in the external world (e.g. electromagnetic energy such as light) first hit sensory organs (such as the retina in the back of the eye), then the signal is transformed into neural impulses that travel to the brain, especially the visual cortex in the backside of the brain, and there at some stage, veiled in mystery, the physical brain activation gets in touch with the nonphysical soul-stuff or consciousness, thus causing us to have the subjective experience of seeing. This is the "bottom-up" causal pathway leading from physical input into conscious output. The "top-down" causal pathway (also called "mental causation") travels in the opposite direction, leading from conscious input (a thought, a desire or an intention to act) to physical output. To take an example, let us say you feel a sudden strong urge to eat chocolate. The desire is a conscious experience. It causes you to look around for the chocolate bar and then, when you spot it, causes your hand to reach towards the bar, grab it quickly, move it into your mouth and sink your teeth into it. A conscious experience thus caused physical changes, first in the brain and then in the neural messages travelling from the brain to the muscles and finally these changes created physical movements of your body.

Often in our everyday behaviour the bottom-up and top-down causal pathways form interactive sensorimotor loops. If you step on a thorn barefoot, the signals from your foot travel quickly to your brain and you experience the pain in your foot and a strong urge to stop the pain. Then you try to locate the source of the pain, you look and touch the sore spot and when you spot the thorn sticking painfully there you pull it out in relief. If you walk on a strawberry field, looking for ripe red strawberries, when you see one (as a result of neural activity in the bottom-up pathway from the retina to the visual cortex to consciousness) you reach out to pick it (as a result of activity in the top-down pathway, from conscious perception and desire to overt physical behaviour).

The causal interaction between the physical and the nonphysical realms seems to work rather smoothly. In fact, in our everyday behaviour we never even need to think about it. We just open our eyes and let the physical stimuli flow in, resulting in conscious visual experience. We use our physical bodies to carry out our intentions and desires and all this seems to work absolutely flawlessly. The problem is to explain *how* exactly two radically different realms – physical processes such as neural activity, and nonphysical qualitative vibrations of the soul such as our sensations, thoughts and desires – could interact at all, let alone so smoothly. That is, the interactionist approach owes us a scientific theory, at least a preliminary one, concerning the actual mechanisms that mediate between the two worlds.

Well, why does not the interactionist then provide us with a theory or a description of the mechanisms? The trouble is that the physical realm is *causally closed* and, respectively, the nonphysical realm is *causally inert* (at least with respect to the physical). The causal closure of the physical world means that physical events can only be causally influenced by other physical events, and are able to cause further events only of the purely physical kind, through mechanisms that are themselves nothing but physical. Causation requires mechanisms that have physical properties, such as mass, energy, force fields, physical motion through physical space, and so on. The causal inertia of consciousness means that our experiences, if they are thoroughly nonphysical, have to be unnecessary for any physical events to happen and in fact they must be inherently incapable of moving or influencing anything in the physical world whatsoever, including neural activities in our brain. If consciousness consists of ghostly soul-stuff, then, like the prototypical ghosts, it will simply slide through all material things without having any effects on them!

The problem that the dualist faces is this. To causally interact with the physical realm (such as the brain), a thing needs to have at least some physical properties. Thus, soul-stuff should have some physical properties after all if it is to have any impact on our brain activity. But for the dualist consciousness is by definition something nonphysical. How could something thoroughly nonphysical, something devoid of mass, energy, motion, gravity, spatial extension and location and all imaginable physical features, cause anything at all to happen in any objects of the physical world, such as the brain? How exactly does soul-stuff pull the physical strings in the brain to actualize a physical manifestation of its free will? This is a complete mystery. Unless a convincing scientific hypothesis of the mechanisms working between the soul and the brain can be put forward, interactionism remains pure metaphysical speculation that can only be afforded within philosophy, not playing any part in the empirical science of consciousness.

The problem of explaining the nature of the two-way interaction between consciousness and brain is not the only problem for interactionism, although it is perhaps the most difficult one. Other problems arise when we attempt to fit the dualist view of consciousness in the scientific world-view with all the other branches of empirical science, such as evolutionary history (phylogeny), individual development (ontogeny) and neuropsychology. At what point in evolution did the immaterial soul-stuff for the first time become causally attached to biological organisms? How and why did that happen if divine intervention is not allowed? When did the first living creature get a soul, turning into a conscious being that could "see the light" and feel its own existence? Presumably, before that grand moment in the history of life on Earth, every creature on this planet had been a totally nonconscious zombie, a mere biological mechanism without any inner mental life. A similar question can be asked with regard to a human fetus or baby: When, how and why does the soul-stuff make a connection to its developing brain? When does the baby "see the light" of subjective existence for the very first time?

Soul-stuff alone is supposed to be able to turn mere biomechanical zombies into conscious human beings with an inner subjective life. Thus, there is a pressing need to find the answers to the questions concerning the emergence of the inner life in evolution and child development. At the same time it is very difficult to pinpoint any stage either in evolutionary history or in individual development that would mark such a radical turning point, or any imaginable mechanism that could explain how it all happens. All the changes we can objectively determine along those paths seem to be purely physical, chemical and biological and seem to form a smooth, gradual continuum. The point at which a soul supposedly becomes attached to the brain would seem to involve, from the biological point of view, an arbitrary point along a continuum where an inexplicable force glues the soul and brain together.

One further problem for the dualist comes from neuropsychology. We know now a number of neurological disorders that somehow damage brain tissue or brain function and thereby lead to severe alterations in the person's consciousness and self. Due to brain damage, a patient can lose a part of the normal perceptual qualities or the perceptual space, experience alterations in the body image or even out-of-body experiences, lose the memories of an entire lifetime or change in temperament and personality as if becoming another person altogether. Thus, it seems as if the structure and the contents of the subjective psychological reality would be directly and absolutely dependent on the structure and the functions of the brain (for more details, see the section on neuropsychology and consciousness, Chapters 4–6).

If the nonphysical soul-stuff, however, is supposed to be entirely independent of physical brain-stuff, then how come the features of the soul (the consciousness and the self) of the person become irreversibly destroyed just by destroying small areas of the physical brain? According to dualism, should not the soul be able to continue its existence happily, without any problems whatsoever, entirely *without* a brain? Yet, all the empirical evidence we have from neuropsychology points to a regrettable fate that awaits us all: destroy the physical brain-stuff and you will thereby have destroyed the person and his consciousness for good. If dualism is to survive as a scientifically serious alternative, it needs to come up with a plausible theory of the neuropsychological deficits of the soul.

Cartesian dualism: The paradigm case of interactionism

Interactionism is probably better known as Cartesian dualism, which is undoubtedly the most famous philosophical theory of consciousness ever, first formulated by René Descartes (1596–1650). Descartes ended up with his theory of consciousness when he was examining the nature of human knowledge, in particular whether there is anything at all that we know with *absolute* certainty, beyond the shadow of a doubt.

He assumed, in his enquiry, the method of systematic doubt. He decided to doubt the validity of each and every statement that we normally take for granted in our everyday lives. Is it possible that the world we perceive through our senses is not how it seems to be? Is it possible that there is no such world, that it is just a hallucination or a dream? What about my own body as I perceive it: Could it also be just a hallucination? Why not? In our dreams we are often led to believe that there is a world and we are bodily present in that world, yet we later discover that all of it was only a hallucination. Such a world as we see in our dreams does not really exist.

How do we know that we are not in some kind of dream right now? Well, Descartes reasoned, we do *not* know it, at least not with any absolute certainty. Descartes speculated on the possibility that there is a powerful evil demon who can create complex hallucinations and delusions magically at will. If that should be the case, then it is possible that the poor Descartes has been fooled all along about the existence of the external world and even about the existence of his own body. Is there anything he could *not* have been fooled about, *ever*? Is there anything at all that he would still know with *absolute* certainty, despite all the elaborate scheming by the evil demon?

There is one thing that Descartes concluded and summarized in one of the most famous slogans in the history of philosophy: *Cogito, ergo sum*. I think, therefore I am. With this Descartes pointed to the fact that as long as there was any sort of thinking going on – no matter how delusional – any kind of subjective conscious experiences going on – no matter how misleading – then at least he himself as a *subject* of those thoughts and experiences must exist in order to *have* the thoughts and experiences. Even if it is all only a dream, the dream itself must consist of *something* that exists. And that something is necessarily a *mental* entity, not a physical one.

Thus, the demon can never deceive Descartes about his own existence – he cannot create a situation where Descartes as a subject of experience and thought does not exist at all, but yet would be deluded into experiencing something and thinking that he does exist. The total absence of thoughts and experiences – the total absence of an inner conscious life – entails the total absence of personal existence. Conversely, the presence of any thoughts or other mental experiences entails that a thinker of those thoughts or a subject of those experiences exists: I think, I experience – therefore, I exist.

Although we cannot be sure that material or physical objects exist out there – we might be just hallucinating all of it when we see trees, mountains or houses – we can yet be sure that our thoughts and experiences do exist. According to Descartes, we can conclude that our very being is thus intimately connected with those purely mental things. We are basically just minds or souls whose fundamental constituents are thoughts and conscious experiences. Descartes himself said that he is nothing more than a thing that thinks, that is, a "mind" or a "soul". The *substance* of the mental realm, or consciousness, *is* thought and experience. Descartes called this substance by the Latin name "*res cogitans*", "the substance that thinks". Under the label of "thinking" he included not only inner verbal speech (what we in our ordinary language call "thinking"), but also other mental experiences such as sensations, percepts, bodily experiences and feeling: more or less everything that we currently include under the notion of consciousness.

The mental substance is unlike physical matter, which Descartes called "*res extensa*" – literally, the substance that extends spatially. The mental substance by contrast has no spatial extension or location; it is a single unified soul that cannot be divided into parts like physical objects can. We are beings made of "*res cogitans*", we are conscious mental beings, thinking but unextended. Our physical bodies are unthinking things, but spatially extended ones: they are made of "*res extensa*". Therefore, our mind is fundamentally different from and independent of our body, and may continue its existence even without the lump of physical matter we consider to be our body.

Yet, according to Descartes, mind and body are in intimate connection, as if fused together. The mind or soul cannot be localized into any specific part of the body, but the causal connection between the two realms functions through the brain, in particular through a small gland called the pineal. Descartes knew about the sensory and motor nerves that seemed to mediate our sensations, perceptions and motor actions, therefore he regarded the pineal gland as a promising place for a channel between brain and soul. First, the pineal is located in the centre of the brain, which makes it ideal as the headquarters for controlling sensorimotor functions. Second, the pineal is unified, forming a single nucleus in the brain, unlike many others that exist in duplicate, one in each cerebral hemisphere. The anatomical unity of the pineal in the brain corresponds nicely with the mental unity of consciousness. Third, the pineal is located at the roof of the third brain ventricle. In medieval theories that reigned up until the times of Descartes, the soul was thought to be located in the fluids (in the form of "animal spirits") that fill up the brain ventricles, not in the neural tissues at all. In his theory, Descartes preserved the ancient idea that the fluids in the brain ventricles mediate the messages between the body, the brain and the soul. Vibrations of the pineal were believed to be transformed into vibrations of the fluids in the third ventricle, which were then conducted to the muscles as commands to move the extremities. Nerves were believed to be hollow tubes, like hydraulic water-pipes, that mediate distant causal effects to the muscles through changes of hydraulic pressure in the nerves. Stimulation of the sensory nerves, respectively, was believed to be conducted to the brain, to be transformed into vibrations of the fluids in the ventricles and thereby communicated to the pineal, which forwarded them to the soul.

This is Descartes' interactionistic dualism in a nutshell (see Figure 1.1). Although nearly 400 years has passed since he put forward these ideas, his theory continues to be debated and criticized in the recent literature on consciousness. Of course, there are very few scientists or philosophers today who defend something like interactionist dualism. Yet, no-one has been able to solve the problem of consciousness in terms of a nondualistic theory either, so Descartes is not any worse off than anyone else! We still do not have a scientific theory that would explain, once and for all, how the subjective psychological reality is connected with the objective physical and biological reality. Hence, dualism has not been defeated for good yet. It just *might* make a comeback. But if the nonphysical soul would make a comeback and be seriously considered as a scientific hypothesis, then we would have to revise our current scientific world-view quite a bit! Most scientists and philosophers, however, are not prepared to do that, thus they will try almost anything else first before they would consider a dualistic theory of consciousness. They also see no evidence whatsoever supporting dualism. Thereby dualism has become the very last resort, only acceptable if nothing else works.

Epiphenomenalism

Perhaps the gravest problem for interactive dualism is to explain *mental causation* or how the nonphysical soul-stuff causally influences physical brain activity so that our behaviour is guided by the mind. Epiphenomenalism represents a way to get rid of that problem: it denies the possibility of mental causation, the idea that events in consciousness have effects in the objective physical world. In other words, the non-physical mental reality cannot causally influence physical matter or brain activity. However, epiphenomenalism does allow causation the other way round: from the physical realm to the mental realm. Physical changes in the sensory systems and in the brain cause conscious events in our subjective psychological reality. Thanks to the unidirectional causation from external world to brain to consciousness, we consciously

Figure 1.1 Interactionist dualism

The figure depicts how brain and mind are in two-way causal interaction through time. First, brain activity has causal effects on consciousness (brain > consciousness causation, symbolized by the arrow pointing up). This happens for example when visual information arrives in the visual cortex and causes a conscious visual percept in the mind of the observer. Second, contents of consciousness within the same person's mind have causal effects on each other (consciousness > consciousness causation, symbolized by the arrow between the two clouds of consciousness). This happens for example when a conscious percept causes a conscious thought or an intention to act. Third, at least some contents of consciousness have causal effects on brain activity and thereby also on behaviour (consciousness > brain causation (or *mental causation*), symbolized by the arrow pointing down). This happens for example when a conscious intention to act causes changes in the motor cortex where behaviour is initiated

sense and perceive the world around us. Physical brain activity causes two types of things: further physical changes in the brain, which ultimately cause all our observable behaviour; and events in consciousness, such as sensations, percepts, thoughts, intentions, action plans. But the nonphysical events in consciousness have no causal powers whatsoever. They do not cause any changes in the brain nor do they cause any further conscious events in the mind. Conscious events are, causally, a dead end. They have been compared to immaterial shadows cast by physical brain activity, shadows that just hang around, or perhaps "above" brain activity, but do absolutely no work whatsoever and have no effects on anything (see Figure 1.2).

Thus, the strength of epiphenomenalism is that it can explain all human behaviour by purely physical causation. Physical stimulation causes physical brain states, which cause further physical brain states, which cause our observable

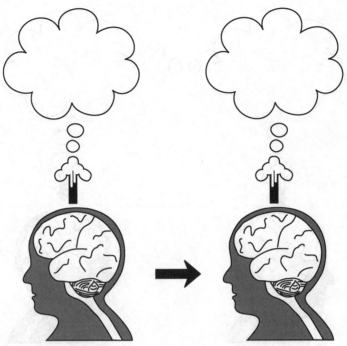

Figure 1.2 Epiphenomenalism

The figure depicts how brain and mind are only in one-way causal interaction through time. First, brain activity has causal effects on consciousness (brain > consciousness causation, symbolized by the arrow pointing up). This happens for example when visual information arrives in the visual cortex and causes a conscious visual percept in the mind of the observer. Second, the initial brain activity in the visual cortex causes further activities that spread to other cortical areas (purely physical causation between brain activities is symbolized by the black arrow pointing from left to right). The further brain activities have simultaneously further causal effects on consciousness (the second arrow pointing up). Consciousness itself has no causal effects on anything (there are no causal arrows originating from consciousness)

behaviour. And that is the whole story there is to tell in terms of scientific explanation. Objective causal mechanisms in the physical world, such as neuronal firing patterns in the brain, are sufficient to explain all aspects of human behaviour. As scientific explanations are basically nothing but detailed descriptions of the causal mechanisms that determine the behaviour of observable phenomena, we are blessed with a science of psychology (or cognitive neuroscience) that explains all the objective data we will ever have, by simply referring to fully physical (chemical, biological, neural, etc.) mechanisms. The nonphysical (mental, subjective, conscious) phenomena are not needed in the explanation of anything. They are *epi*-phenomena, mere secondary effects or side-effects of brain activity.

Unfortunately, getting rid of mental causation is a double-edged sword. Undoubtedly, the greatest weakness of epiphenomenalism is precisely the fact that it gives our mental life *no* active role at all in the world. Our streams of consciousness are mere shadows dragged along by the brain, and we ourselves as conscious beings are nothing more than passive onlookers whose existence makes no difference whatsoever to anything in the world. We are at best in for a joyride, helplessly floating in the stream of consciousness but under the illusion of having control of our behaviour or of having a free will to decide what to do next. In actual fact, we have no control whatsoever over anything and our conscious will is but a deception. We are like shadows that confuse themselves with the physical things whose shadows we are, believing that we are in control because the physical things change in perfect correlation with our experiences. The shadow cast by a hammer might believe that it is in control of the hammer's behaviour and causes the physical hammer to move and hit the nail and the physical nail to sink in. We make exactly the same mistake in believing that we, as conscious subjects, are in control of our own behaviour. The physical causes in the brain do all the work and our minds follow the physical causes like shadows.

The fatal problem here is that the view of ourselves as mere passive shadow-like observers is in stark conflict with our beliefs and direct experiences about ourselves. According to epiphenomenalism, all of the following statements are false: the feeling of thirst causes me to drink; the feeling of pain causes me to take an aspirin; my deliberate plans and careful considerations cause me to take one course of action rather than another; what I visually experience to be around me causally guides my behaviour; and so on. Our everyday experience about being in control, about our subjective psychological reality causally influencing our behaviour, is simply so strong that we are not prepared to give it up just like that. The view of ourselves as mere conscious puppets whose strings are attached to the brain of an otherwise nonconscious biomechanical zombie is very difficult to accept. On the contrary, we take ourselves as conscious human beings whose observable behaviour is largely determined by the mental events happening in our subjective psychological reality. We – our minds – *do* make a difference in the world and we *can* change the world by having our inner conscious life guide our external behaviour.

Therefore, it is hard to accept an epiphenomenalist view of ourselves. Our lives as conscious beings would be totally useless; we would be like helpless spectators locked in a giant virtual-reality movie theatre, forced to watch the movie without being able to influence its events.

Epiphenomenalism is rarely put forward as an explicit theory of consciousness. Rather, it is a position (or a trap) where many a theorist finds himself after painting himself into a corner by first putting forward a thoroughly physicalist theory of mind. The purely physicalist theory may nicely explain sensation, perception, cognition, action and behaviour as objective, nonconscious phenomena. Epiphenomenalism creeps in only after there is no explanatory role left for our inner conscious life. In the theory, all seems to work just perfectly even without an inner life. Hence, to give at least some kind of place to our subjective psychological reality in a physicalist theory, as a last resort consciousness is interpreted as an epiphenomenon that hangs somewhere above the physical, somewhere beyond all the objective neural and cognitive mechanisms that do all the real work. An epiphenomenon cannot interfere in any way with the physical workings of the "real" mechanisms, and therefore it can be easily added to the physical theory without changing anything else in the picture.

In the 1870s the British physiologist and philosopher Thomas Henry Huxley defended a neurophysiological version of epiphenomenalism. In the 1980s, the American linguist and cognitive scientist Ray Jackendoff (1987) defended a cognitive theory of consciousness that implied epiphenomenalism, and in the 1990s the Australian philosopher David Chalmers (1996) formulated a philosophical theory of consciousness that makes subjective experience explanatorily irrelevant and therefore his view at least approximates epiphenomenalism. Thus, epiphenomenalist theories are not difficult to find even in the modern wave of consciousness research. Certainly, they are much more common than interactionist theories. Yet, they are hardly any more convincing than interactionist dualism would be. The weakness of interactionism is that it cannot even begin to explain the mechanisms of mental causation, whereas the weakness of epiphenomenalism is that it flatly denies the existence of mental causation. As neither of these solutions is terribly convincing, perhaps we must look elsewhere for more credible theories.

It may be asked why epiphenomenalism should count as a variety of dualism at all. The principal reason is that all forms of epiphenomenalism postulate a mental realm that has no causal powers. Now, for something to be "real", or to "exist" in the way that science could take it as a physically "real" phenomenon whose existence can in some way be detected or empirically tested, it needs to have at least *some* causal powers. Otherwise, it would be totally impossible to ever detect or confirm either the presence or the absence of the postulated entity if its existence makes no difference whatsoever in the happenings of the physical world. A phenomenon without any causal powers cannot be detected objectively or empirically, because there is no way it could influence any physical measurements or instruments, no matter how sophisticated. Therefore, any theory that postulates causally powerless entities, by definition of the empirically or physically real, thereby postulates nonphysical entities. This makes epiphenomenalism a version of dualism.

However, the nonphysical entities postulated by an epiphenomenalist theory may be viewed either as composed of a fundamentally nonphysical *substance* or as nonphysical *properties* of physical things. The former kind of theory represents *substance dualism* and the latter is often called *property dualism*. In fact, most of the modern versions of epiphenomenalism are closer to property dualism than substance dualism. They suggest that certain types of neural activities or computations – or perhaps quantum phenomena going on in the brain – have epiphenomenal features or properties. Our subjective psychological reality, thus, would consist of those nonphysical features emerging from the physical features and activities of the brain. Property dualism coupled with epiphenomenalism may come fairly close to strong emergent materialism, a theory that we will explore in more detail in Section 1.3.

Parallelism

Causal interaction between the mental and the physical seems to be inexplicable in scientific terms. Epiphenomenalism gets rid of only one half of this problem by denying that the mental realm could causally influence the physical realm. But is it not equally mysterious how causal effects could go the other way around? How does neural activity in the brain get causal access to a nonphysical consciousness? The causal interface from the physical to the mental realm remains to be explained.

Parallelism bites the bullet and flatly denies that there are *any* causal relationships between the physical and the mental realms (see Figure 1.3). We are mistaken not only about our actions being caused by our conscious mental states but also about physical stimuli and consequent neural activities causing our sensations and percepts. Parallelism accepts that the external physical reality and our internal psychological reality are in total harmony and synchrony. But it is a mistake to explain the harmony of physical and mental events by referring to causation between them. There is merely a perfect *correlation* between the two realms. Now it is easy to confuse correlation with causation – we do it all the time, in fact. In the movies when we see a person talking or a window shattering we, at the same time, hear sounds that are in perfect synchrony with the visual events and therefore we automatically assume that the voice is *generated* by the visual images and their source is located where we see the images. In fact, the images projected on the screen of course have no causal effects that we could detect by hearing. However, there is a stereo soundtrack that is perfectly correlated and in harmony with the images. This correlation creates the *illusion* that the visual events cause the auditory events. But if the soundtrack becomes

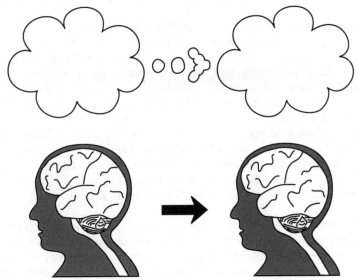

Figure 1.3 Parallelism

The figure depicts how brain and mind are in perfect synchrony through time, but not in any causal interaction with each other. Brain activity and contents of consciousness happen at the same time, in parallel. Brain activity only has causal effects on other brain activities, and contents of consciousness only have causal effects on other contents of consciousness. When a visual stimulus is presented, the initial brain activity relating to the stimulus causes further brain activities (purely physical causation between brain activities is symbolized by the black arrow pointing from left to right). Simultaneously, contents of consciousness have causal effects on each other (consciousness > consciousness causation, symbolized by the arrow between the two clouds of consciousness). This happens for example when a conscious percept causes a conscious thought or an intention to act

desynchronized with the images, then the illusion breaks down and we notice that the images and the sounds are causally independent of each other.

Thus, we can at least imagine that causal interaction between the mental and the physical could be an illusion brought about by perfect correlation and synchronization. But if the perfect correlation cannot be explained by causation, how can it be explained at all? The philosopher Gottfried Leibniz (1646–1716) believed in a pre-established harmony that synchronized events without actual causation between them. If the physical and mental worlds are fully deterministic so that everything that will happen in them is predetermined, then it is sufficient to push the "start" button simultaneously for both worlds and their harmony will be forever preserved. Just like in the movies: If the sequence of the images and the sequence of the sounds are perfectly determined in such a way that there will be a correlation at any given point, it is sufficient to start both tracks at the same time and keep them rolling at the same pace so that the perfect harmony between the two will automatically take care of itself.

There is just one small problem: How did the correlations in the two different worlds get established in the first place, and who in this case pushed both "start" buttons at exactly the same moment? Leibniz believed that God was responsible for this.

Occasionalism – a variety of parallelism – explains the mental–physical synchrony in a slightly different manner. According to this theory the harmony between the two worlds is not pre-established, but instead *separately* established for each event or occasion. God (or His will) is at work every time when two events need to be harmonized across the mental–physical boundary! If occasionalism is true, God must be very busy indeed with all the divine interventions required to make mind and matter go hand in hand!

The world-view of parallelism is based on theistic religious belief and divine intervention. In the modern scientific world-view, explanations or theories of consciousness based on religious ideas are out of the question. The problems created by parallelism are thus at least as big as the problems it gets rid of. Consequently, it is no wonder that parallelist theories are hard to come by in the modern science of consciousness.

We have now considered the major varieties of dualism: interactionism, epiphenomenalism and parallelism. Each has its strengths and its weaknesses. None of the theories seems even remotely plausible as a modern scientific theory of the relationship between consciousness and brain. Instead of dualism, perhaps some variety of monism fares better. Next, we will get acquainted with the major theories that deny dualism of brain and consciousness and instead take both as being made up of a single substance.

1.3 Monistic theories of consciousness

Monism was defined above as the doctrine that treats the whole universe, mind and brain included, as composed of one single type of basic substance. Monistic materialism or physicalism takes the basic substance to be physical matter, monistic idealism takes it to be soul-stuff or consciousness and neutral monism takes it to be neither – it is "something else" instead. Let us first review the major varieties of monistic materialism or physicalism.

Materialism (or physicalism) defined

The strength of materialism lies in the fact that it is firmly based on the natural sciences and the modern scientific view of the world. Whatever the best theories in physics, chemistry and biology say about the nature of physical matter, whether organic or inorganic, is taken for granted in materialism and taken to be the whole story about the world. Thus, in its explanation of consciousness, materialism cannot appeal to soul-stuff or divine intervention, or to anything else that seems to go beyond the realm of the empirical sciences.

But unfortunately in its strength also lie the seeds of its weakness. The main problem about the modern scientific world-view and about the natural sciences, including biology and neuroscience, is that they seem constitutionally incapable of describing or explaining consciousness, the subjective psychological reality that obviously does have a close connection to the brain. Hence, the challenge for materialistic theories is to explain *how consciousness fits in with the materialistic scientific picture at all!* The three principal lines of thought can be summarized as follows: (1) we are mistaken about consciousness – no such thing really exists at all, it is only an *illusion* created by confused everyday thinking or language; (2) consciousness is real but it is itself a fully physical thing, an *ordinary neurophysiological process* going on in the brain; (3) consciousness is real and physical, but it is a *very special type or a higher level of brain activity*, unlike any ordinary low level neurophysiological process we currently know about, even though the special, higher neurophysiological level of consciousness is completely *based* on lower level, ordinary neurophysiology.

Thought (1) is called "eliminative materialism", because it tries to eliminate the notion of consciousness from science. Thought (2) is known as "reductive materialism", because it tries to reduce consciousness to something else (ordinary neurophysiology) that science is better able to handle. Thought (3) is "emergent materialism", because it claims that entirely *new* types or higher levels of physical phenomena, such as subjective consciousness, can *emerge* from the complex organization of ordinary, lower level physical phenomena, such as neurophysiological processes in the brain. Next we will analyse each of these theories in more detail, paying particular attention to their strengths, weaknesses and overall plausibility.

Eliminative materialism

At first glance, denying the existence of consciousness might seem like an overly foolhardy move that is difficult to defend by any rational argument. However, eliminative materialists do have good reasons for proposing the elimination of consciousness from science. Their arguments are based on the history of science, which shows that several *other* phenomena *have* turned out to be illusions and were thus eliminated from science. Why not consciousness, too?

The most famous example comes from the history of chemistry. *Phlogiston* was believed to explain what happens when something burns. Phlogiston was assumed to be a mysterious substance that is released from the burning material when the heat and the flames are generated. However, when burning was studied carefully by the early chemists, nothing like phlogiston was ever found. Instead, it was discovered that burning involved a substance called "oxygen" that behaved in the opposite way to how phlogiston was believed to operate. Oxygen is taken from the surrounding air and becomes bound to the burning substance rather than being released from it. The oxygen theory of burning replaced the phlogiston theory and the substance called "phlogiston" was eliminated from science as something that does not really exist at all.

In the 1800s in astronomy, many astronomers believed they had detected a new planet called "Vulcan". (Of course, they were not referring to the fictitious home planet of Mr. Spock of *Star Trek*, but a real planet in our own solar system.) The gravitational effects of Vulcan could be seen in the orbit of another planet (Mercury), and reports of direct observations of the planet passing across the disk of the Sun started to appear. But with time the observations turned out to be inconsistent with any calculated orbit for the new planet, and it turned out to be impossible to predict when exactly the planet becomes observable. To escape all systematic observations, either the planet had to behave most erratically and unpredictably, or, alternatively, there simply *was* no planet out there behind the miscellaneous observations. Finally, the hypothesis that such a planet exists at all was discarded. Vulcan, a whole planet once believed to exist, was eliminated without mercy from the scientific world-view!

If chemical substances and entire planets can become eliminated, why not consciousness? Like phlogiston and Vulcan, consciousness is based on an extremely shaky theory. In fact, the "theory" it is based on is hardly a scientific theory at all, but rather a part of our unscientific folk-beliefs. It is a part of an intuitive and built-in theory that we humans come equipped with, variously called "*folk psychology*" or "*grandmother psychology*" or "*theory of mind*". All normally developed humans learn to use these theories as they grow up in social interaction with other humans. When we observe another human do something, say switch the light on in a dark room, we interpret the behaviour by projecting a conscious mind into the behaving system. Aha, he *wanted to see* what there is in the room and he *believed* that he can get the lights on by turning the switch, and now he is *looking around the room and seeing* its contents. Desires, beliefs and perceptions are conscious mental events we assume are going on inside the mind of the human, and these unobservable inner states explain why he behaves the way he does.

We learn to automatically "mentalize" or project a mind not only into our fellow humans but also into animals and robots, in fact any entities that show complex, autonomous behaviours. We easily mentalize autonomously moving machines, describing their behaviour with what they "try" or "want" to do, what they "perceive" or "believe" about their environment, and so on. When you see a computer-controlled autonomous vacuum-cleaner or lawn-mower going about its business all by itself, as if it was guided by a conscious mind, it is enormously difficult *not* to mentalize it!

The folk-psychological theory of mind behind all the mentalizing we engage in is *not* a *scientific* theory. It is only a quirk of human social perception, probably installed into the brain during our evolutionary history because it was useful for predicting the behaviour of others. There is no guarantee that folk psychology gives the *correct* picture of the mind. When applied to robotic vacuum-cleaners or lawn-mowers, it certainly does not! In fact, old folk theories in other domains, like biology and physics, have turned out to be grossly mistaken. They had to be given up when the actual scientific theories in those domains developed.

The eliminativist's argument is that in empirical science the folk-psychological theory shall go the same way as the folk biology and the folk physics have gone: down the drain. Now, the view that each person (and other complex systems) is inhabited by an inner soul or subjective psychological reality or consciousness is just a piece of faith in the folk-psychological theory. As the empirical sciences, especially cognitive neuroscience, make progress and newer and better brain imaging devices become available we will not find anything in the brain that corresponds to our naive ideas about an inner conscious life. The whole notion of consciousness will turn out to be unhelpful in describing the reality found in the brain, just like the notion of phlogiston turned out to be useless for a chemical theory of burning. We should eliminate consciousness from science and replace it with neuroscientific concepts. Future neuroscience will tell us how the brain works and how it guides our behaviour, but in that story no mention of "consciousness" or anything remotely resembling it will be necessary.

Not only is consciousness a purely folk-psychological concept, but it is also a hopelessly obscure notion. No-one seems to be able to define what "consciousness" refers to anyway. Different people have completely different ideas of "consciousness", thus there is not even a coherent conception of consciousness around. Such conceptual confusion will further guarantee that "consciousness" will never be "found" in the brain or anywhere else for that matter, nor will neuroscience need any vague concept like that in the final Grand Unified Theory of the brain.

The philosophers Paul and Patricia Churchland are probably the best-known representatives of eliminative materialism. In 1988, Patricia Churchland wrote in the spirit of eliminative materialism about the fate of consciousness in neuroscience: "[T]he various sciences of the mind–brain will likely converge upon unified explanations. Perhaps not of 'consciousness', for in the evolved framework that may have gone the way of 'caloric fluid' or 'vital spirit'" (Churchland, 1988, p. 301). Another eliminativist philosopher, Kathleen Wilkes, was even more explicit: "[T]he term 'conscious' and its cognates are, for *scientific* purposes, both unhelpful and unnecessary ... not bothering with 'consciousness' would not restrict research" (Wilkes, 1988, pp. 38–39). But such opinions were mostly voiced years before the rise of the modern science of consciousness in the 1990s. These days, it is much more difficult to find eager proponents of the outright elimination of consciousness, perhaps because there is already too much high-quality empirical research and scientific progress going on around the topic. In more recent writings, Patricia Churchland herself has left elimination behind and now cautiously defends the approach that consciousness is a natural phenomenon that can be investigated scientifically as well as introspectively (Churchland, 2002).

The main weakness of eliminative materialism lies in its sheer implausibility when the idea of elimination is applied to consciousness. Consciousness is quite different from theoretical notions in science, such as the substance phlogiston or the planet Vulcan. Consciousness is not a *hypothetical* entity that we have invented because it might nicely explain our observations of other people's behaviour. By contrast, it is the subjective psychological reality directly present for us every moment of our lives. Consciousness as an experiential reality directly before us constitutes *data* rather than *theory.* The data are there, plain to see for anyone, anytime.

Thus, to deny the existence of consciousness is not analogous to denying the existence of phlogiston, it is analogous to denying the data that constitute our evidence for burning: the heat, the flames and the smoke. Of course, if you turn a blind eye to the data and refuse to see that burning exists, then you need not explain burning. But unfortunately no-one is going to believe your "eliminativist" theory of burning. Denying the data that are plain for all to see is not going to convince anyone.

How can anyone take an eliminativist position seriously, let alone defend it? Here we have to go deeper into the background assumption concerning what "science" is and what constitutes "data". If we take the standard view of the physical sciences, only phenomena that can be observed objectively or publicly are regarded as sources of data. Our subjective psychological reality cannot be observed in any such way, only behaviour and brain activity can. Objective observations of the brain and behaviour do not reveal anything like consciousness – a subjective "world" of experience – anywhere inside us. Consciousness is revealed to us only from the first-person's point of view, where we as subjects have experiences in our own consciousness. The process of having experiences – the existence of consciousness – cannot be seen or detected by scientists or scientific instruments that observe us from the outside perspective.

The first person's point of view is not accepted as a valid source of data in the physical sciences, therefore it is possible to argue that subjective experiences are not a part of the overall scientific data that need to be explained by the sciences. Viewed from the third-person's objective point of view, consciousness (as data) does not exist, only behaviour and brain activity do; therefore it is easy, perhaps even necessary, to eliminate consciousness from science as an erroneous folk-psychological hypothesis.

Then again, the opponent of eliminativism can argue that we need not accept the third-person's point of view of the physical sciences as authoritative or all-inclusive. If consciousness, whose very existence – as Descartes showed – is beyond *any* doubt whatsoever, can nevertheless be denied by some type of science, then there is something seriously wrong with the science rather than with consciousness. The task of science is to faithfully describe and explain the world: how the world works and what sort of entities it consists of. If there are undeniable subjective phenomena in the world that cannot be captured through the objective standpoint of the physical sciences, then we need to revise the scientific standpoint so that it will not be blind to consciousness anymore. We need a science that admits and takes seriously the reality of the inner subjective world. The least science can do is to stop pretending that such a reality does not exist.

So the battle rages on, revealing perhaps the fundamental reason why science is in such difficulty with consciousness. Perhaps the nature of consciousness is inconsistent with the way in which we traditionally practice science. Perhaps the scope of our physical sciences is too narrow. Be that as it may, eliminative materialism fails to convince us that the problem of consciousness could be solved by simply ignoring it. The least that an eliminative materialist should do, if he wants to convince anyone, is to present the alternative, purely neurobiological and supposedly superior theory that opens our eyes to see how the actual reality works while discarding all reference to consciousness. In chemistry, everyone gave up phlogiston without further ado once the existence and function of oxygen was convincingly established. I suppose everyone would give up consciousness if the eliminativist presents a detailed, convincing theory that answers all our questions about the mind and the brain by replacing consciousness with something else. But before that kind of alternative explanation becomes available, eliminative materialism remains a desperate attempt to deny the problem rather than a fruitful solution to it.

Reductive materialism

Unlike eliminative materialism, reductive materialism at least accepts that conscious mental phenomena exist. We have not made a mistake concerning the *existence* of consciousness. Still, we certainly *have* committed an awful error in thinking that consciousness and brain are somehow two entirely *different* things. In fact, they are not. They are one and the same thing. The aim of reductive materialism is thus to argue that consciousness is itself just a commonplace physical entity or process in the brain, not unlike all the other physical entities and processes in the brain that we know about. Hence, we have only been mistaken about the basic nature of consciousness, not about its existence.

Consequently, reductive materialists accept that there are conscious sensations, perceptions, emotions, thoughts, and so on, going on inside our heads. There is a subjective psychological reality. Yet, reductive materialists deny that the subjective psychological reality is anything different from the brain as an objective neural reality. Our everyday idea that they are different is just an illusion. Consciousness *is* a brain process and nothing more. Consciousness is *identical* with a set of neural activity states. In other words, consciousness can be *reduced* to the brain.

The philosophers Ullin T. Place and J. J. C. Smart first formulated the modern idea of mind–brain reduction in the 1950s, connecting it with the more general reductionistic ideas that were popular in the philosophy of science in those days: Ernest Nagel's model of intertheoretic reduction and Carl Hempel's model of deductive-nomological explanation. More recently, Jaegwon Kim (1998, 2005) has reformulated the ideas of physicalistic mind–brain reduction so that it fits better together with what is actually going on in the biological sciences when something is explained. Although Kim defends a thoroughly physicalistic and reductionistic view of the mind, he in fact ends up with the fashionable view among philosophers nowadays that while the rest of the mental domain can be neatly reduced to the brain or "physicalized", consciousness alone escapes this fate and appears to be irreducible.

As in eliminative materialism, so in reductive materialism the arguments typically refer to the history of science. Theories that describe one type of phenomenon have sometimes been successfully reduced to more basic theories describing other types of phenomena. The supporters of reductive materialism hope that the same development will take place at the interface between neuroscience and psychology before long.

There are several cases to be found in the history of science where an old term, perhaps one originating in a folk theory and in everyday language, has been replaced by a more scientific term referring to the same thing but under a different description. The everyday notion of (visible) "light" has been replaced by the notion "electromagnetic radiation at certain wavelengths" (to which the human eye is sensitive). The everyday notion of "water" has been replaced by the chemical formula "H_2O". The notion of "heat" (or "temperature" in solid bodies) has been replaced by the notion of "mean kinetic energy of molecules". Thus, "light", "temperature" and "water" have turned out to be nothing but certain physical entities described and explained by a wider physical theory. "Light" can therefore be identified with a certain spectrum of electromagnetic energy, and "water" with a certain chemical substance. In a nutshell: "*water = H$_2$O*".

In philosophy of science, such *identity statements* ("*X = Y*") between entities of an old theory and entities of the new, more comprehensive theory, are deemed crucial steps in the reduction of the old theory to the new one. (Because of this, in philosophy, reductive materialism has also been called "identity theory" or "type-type identity theory".) The identity statements have also been called "bridge laws" or "bridge principles". This name refers to the fact that, say, "*water = H$_2$O*" is treated as a "law" (of nature) and this law or principle creates a bridge from an old, narrow conception to a more basic and more comprehensive theoretical conception of the entities involved. Once such bridges have been established, the old notions and the entire old theory can be discarded and all the phenomena once described by the old theory can now be described and explained in a more accurate manner in the context of the new, wider and more basic theory.

Reductive materialism as a theory of consciousness is based on the hope that what is true of theoretical developments somewhere in the physical sciences will be true of developments in the sciences in general, and at the interface between neuroscience and psychology in particular. The psychological theory and the description of conscious mental phenomena at the subjective psychological level are taken as the "old", narrow conception that should be reduced to the more basic and comprehensive scientific framework provided by the neurosciences (see Figure 1.4).

Conscious sensations, percepts and thoughts are described in the "old" folk-psychological theory with everyday language, such as "I see blue", "I feel pain" or "I thought that I must be dreaming". Although the mental events that these statements refer to are real and exist, they are not what they seem to us from our own subjective perspective. Instead, they are purely neural states. Each type of conscious mental event (e.g. seeing blue, seeing red, seeing green . . .) corresponds to or is identical with a certain type of neural activity, to be discovered by future neuroscience. Thus, if the reductive materialist's dreams come true, one fine day particular subjective experiences will be identified with particular neural states. Perhaps we will learn that the visual experience of seeing blue is really "*40 Hz neuroelectrical oscillations in cortical visual area V4*", the visual experience of seeing red is really "*42 Hz neuroelectrical oscillations in V4*" and the experience of seeing green is "*44 Hz neuroelectrical oscillations in V4*". Then we can replace the old-fashioned, inaccurate talk about subjective visual experiences with accurate scientific terms denoting neuroelectrical oscillations in the visual cortex.

The message of reductive materialism is that consciousness is not an *independent* or *autonomous* part or level of reality. Thus, it is not a genuine *psychological* reality at all; it is a thoroughly neurobiological reality that we have only mistaken as somehow especially psychological. Just like water is nothing over and above the chemistry of H_2O, and any mass of water can be reduced to a complex set of H_2O molecules without leaving anything "watery" out, consciousness is nothing over and above a

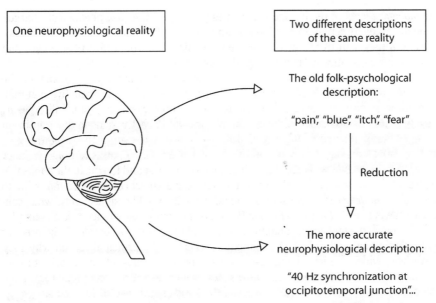

One neurophysiological reality

Two different descriptions of the same reality

The old folk-psychological description:

"pain", "blue", "itch", "fear"

Reduction

The more accurate neurophysiological description:

"40 Hz synchronization at occipitotemporal junction"...

Figure 1.4 Reductive materialism

Psychological concepts referring to conscious experiences and neurophysiological concepts referring to neural activities are simply two ways of describing one single neurophysiological reality. Future neuroscience will be able to connect the old, fuzzy folk-psychological concepts with new, accurate neurophysiological concepts, and thus reduce all descriptions of consciousness to descriptions of neurophysiology. Consequently, consciousness will have been reduced to the brain and the science of consciousness will have been reduced to a branch of neurophysiology

complex set of neural activities going on in our brain, thus it can be exhaustively reduced to that level without anything "psychological" being left out from the equation.

Eliminative and reductive materialism are often confused with each other, although they are manifestly different. It is understandable, though, why eliminative and reductive materialism might be confused with each other. They are similar in saying that what really exists is the brain and its neural activities. That is all there is when it comes to the description or explanation of the mind, too. In some sense, both try to get rid of the mind or a psychological level of reality while preserving only the neurophysiological and other levels described by neuroscience. Only the way in which they discard psychological reality is different. Eliminative materialism says that there is absolutely *no* real level of phenomena whatsoever in the world that would correspond to consciousness. Conscious mental phenomena are likened to such things as the canals of Mars, the Loch Ness monster, extraterrestrial visitors and garden-fairies. All of them are phenomena that many people believed in at one time or another but, with the advance of science, have turned out not to exist. By contrast, reductive materialism does not doubt the existence of consciousness, but rather accepts that when we have subjective conscious states we are in touch with something that really exists. It is just that we are mistaken in thinking that this thing exists at a separate, purely *psychological* level of reality and constitutes purely *psychological* phenomena that are fundamentally different from physical and neural phenomena. Instead, as science advances they will turn out to be some particular types of neural phenomena that have nothing specifically "psychological" about them.

On both accounts, it seems that a crucial aspect of ourselves – or maybe the very core of our self – is being thrown out or left unexplained. In reductive materialism this is perhaps not as equally obvious as in eliminative materialism. Still, it seems clear that to talk about neural firings, activations and deactivations in different brain areas or oscillatory synchrony in neural assemblies is not at all the same thing as talking about feelings of pain, sensations of colour, passionate emotions or inner thoughts – and never will be. What is being left out is, first and foremost, the subjective aspect of the conscious mental events. The subjective aspect concerns *what it is like* to *have* or to *undergo* such conscious events, what it *feels* like subjectively, what conscious life is like *for the subject* or *for the organism* that possesses a conscious mind.

Indeed, the subjective, qualitative aspect of mental life is completely ignored by both eliminative and reductive explanations. That is the principal reason why they have been widely criticized and discarded as hopeless philosophical theories of consciousness. In fact, the modern wave of consciousness research originated in the criticism against philosophical theories of the mind that denied or ignored subjective psychological reality. It seemed as if those theories were not even aware of how much they were missing, until in 1974 the philosopher Thomas Nagel, in his paper "What is it like to be a bat?", which later became a classic, showed that the then fashionable reductionistic philosophies of mind could not begin to explain nor even try to take into account the subjective, qualitative aspect of the mind: consciousness.

Microphysicalism: The ultimate reductionism

Reductive materialism about the mind is connected, in the philosophy of science, with a larger world-view that attempts to give a grand unified picture of the world. The idea is that all the sciences (or all scientific theories) that describe the different aspects of the natural world – physics, chemistry, biochemistry, biology, neuroscience – will, one fine day, be reductively connected to each other. That is, neuroscience will be reduced to cell biology and molecular biology, which will be reduced to biochemistry and chemistry, which will be reduced to physics, which will ultimately be reduced to microphysics describing the basic physical laws and building blocks of the physical universe: elementary particles, fundamental physical forces, quantum theory, and so on. This ultimate form of reductionism can be called *microphysicalism*. Its supporters (often physicists) believe that only the fundamental, bottom level of the physical universe "really" exists. All the rest is just a convenient illusion that we humans suffer from because we cannot directly perceive the fundamental microlevel, but only see a crude macroscopic image of it through our imperfect senses. Most of our current scientific theories are merely coarse approximations of the one true microphysical reality, but ultimately science could, at least in principle, get rid of such approximations and reduce everything to descriptions of the events at the elementary physical levels, the only true reality.

We can, however, argue against microphysicalism by pointing out that reductions to the ultimate level do not seem to take place even within the physical sciences themselves, let alone in biology, neuroscience or psychology. Somehow the special sciences seem to involve new types of laws or new kinds of entities and causal interactions that simply are not describable in the language of microphysics. Chemistry still exists as an independent science – it has not become just quantum physics. Cell biology still exists – it has not become just chemistry. A wholesale reduction does not look like a realistic possibility.

Furthermore, we can appeal, like Descartes, to the undeniable reality of our own subjective experiences. The subjective sensory-perceptual and cognitive-emotional reality that we experience in our consciousness does not even remotely look like anything that microphysics describes. Therefore, we can conclude that in the physical world there must be at least *one* higher level physical reality beyond pure microphysics, namely the subjective psychological reality that exists in its own right. The reality of consciousness cannot be dismissed as an illusion, because we cannot very well be deceived as to the existence of our own consciousness. That fundamental truth was established already by Descartes. Consciousness itself, as we experience it, cannot be just the result of some kind of coarse perception of the true microphysical reality, either. We do not "perceive" consciousness through our external senses like we perceive sticks and stones; we are directly in touch with the reality of consciousness as it is. Yet, consciousness, as it reveals itself to us directly, cannot be described or explained in microphysical terms – or at least we currently have no idea how it could. It surely does not look like lots of quantum wave functions or quarks or 11-dimensional strings dancing around, although physicists believe that the bottom level of the physical world consists of such exotic microentities. At the very least the microphysicalist owes us an explanation: How does he derive the experiential qualities and patterns of our consciousness from the microlevel physical theories? Only if that can be done will microphysicalism gain the credibility it now misses.

If consciousness is a natural part of the physical world, then microphysicalism cannot be the whole or the final truth about the physical world. What is even more worrying is that microphysicalism seems itself to stand on extremely shaky ground. The physical theories that describe the ultimate microlevels of reality are, to put it mildly, just utterly weird. They describe a reality wholly alien to our everyday experience, a reality of quantum effects where time, space, causality and even the whole notion of objective existence seem to dissolve. Why should we believe that only this ultimate bottom level of the universe "really" exists when it seems that its existence is in fact much less "real" than the existence of our everyday macroscopic world? It seems as if reality and existence themselves require more substantial temporal and spatial scales that cannot be found at the microphysical levels. Perhaps, in contrast to microphysicalism, the large-scale macroscopic world is in fact "more" real than the infinitesimal microworld whose existence and behaviour seem impossible to understand.

In conclusion, microphysicalism seems unhelpful when we try to understand what the conscious mind is or how it relates to the brain. The reality of brain and consciousness is so far removed from the microphysical scales of reality that it hardly pays off to even try to connect them at this point, and even if they could be connected somehow, it is very difficult to see how any genuine explanatory relationship could be established between them.

Eliminative materialism, reductive materialism and microphysicalism all seem

that's a shaky rebuttal

to take it for granted that consciousness, the subjective psychological reality, is *less* "real" than the underlying physical reality. They seem to work on the background assumption, most obvious in microphysicalism, that the world is ultimately a physical system that consists of simple, elementary physical entities and the basic laws of nature that govern their behaviour – all the rest is an illusion in the eye of the human beholder. In the long run, science should get rid of such illusions.

But, on second thoughts, perhaps the background assumption is wrong to begin with. Perhaps, on the contrary, the world is inherently a complex whole consisting of a layered structure where reality itself is expressed in consecutive levels of complexity, each higher level of course *based* on the lower ones but still forming a reality of its own, relatively independent of the lower levels. This idea is the starting point of the next theory that we will get acquainted with: emergent materialism.

Emergent materialism

The notion of "emergence" can be defined as follows: When entities of a certain type become organized in complex ways, engaging in sophisticated causal interactions and forming complex structural and functional wholes, entirely *new* types of phenomena or *new* kinds of properties, unlike those had by any of the parts of the system, may appear in the phenomenon as a whole. The new types of phenomena or properties are called *emergent*: they *emerge* from the lower level phenomena that did not possess them in isolation from the holistic system.

Not just any feature or phenomenon manifested by a large-scale system can be considered emergent, however. Genuine emergence implies *novelty*: something entirely new, entirely unlike anything at the lower level parts, comes into the world through emergence. Thus, if you take 1 kilogram (kg) of sand and add it to another similar pile of sand, you end up having a bigger and heavier pile of sand, but the new pile hardly gives us any surprises or gives rise to the emergence of new phenomena. The "novelty" of emergence implies something like unpredictability, surprise and perhaps even inexplicability. A new feature is deemed "unpredictable" if, taken what we knew about the lower level parts, we could not have predicted or calculated the kinds of features that were manifested by the higher level system. By contrast, we are totally taken by surprise to observe such new features of which the parts showed no trace. A new feature is "inexplicable" if we are not only surprised but thoroughly baffled by the new types of features, so that there seems to be no explanation as to why such features suddenly emerged out of the system. The emergence hence seems more or less mysterious to us.

Defined in this manner, emergence partly depends on our previous knowledge. If you do not know much about biology, it will seem to you like a miracle that out of an apparently dead, small acorn or a tiny sunflower seed, when combined with water, sunlight and ground, gradually emerges a huge, complex, beautiful living organism that does not resemble the original seed in any way at all.

Now it is easy to see why emergent materialism might describe the relationship between consciousness and the brain rather well. The brain is an enormously complex biological system consisting of lower level physical, chemical and neurophysiological entities engaged in multifarious causal interactions. In fact, for all we know the human brain may be the most complex physical system that exists in the whole universe. Within the confines of our skull, countless billions of neurons and synapses, neurotransmitter systems and neural firings are organized into one holistic unit. Therefore, if any physical system should have any emergent properties at all, perhaps the human brain is the number one candidate for housing genuine emergence, due to its incredible complexity. Emergent materialism thus states that although neurons and neural firings as such are totally devoid of consciousness, when billions of them are organized into a complex whole, as is the case in the human brain, entirely novel, unpredictable features such as subjective consciousness may emerge out of the large-scale neural activities (see Figure 1.5). In the current philosophy of mind, John Searle (1992, 1997) in particular argues for an emergentist view: "All of our conscious experiences are explained by the behaviour of neurons and are themselves emergent properties of the system of neurons" (1997, p. 22).

So far, so good. But the problems with emergent materialism start when we consider the relationship between emergence and explanation. Is it possible to have a scientific *explanation* of emergence that describes exactly *what* happens when the emergent properties come into being? It seems that supporters of emergent

Figure 1.5 Emergent materialism

When brain activities reach a high degree of complexity, a higher level of physical reality – consciousness – emerges. The higher level cannot be reduced to traditional neurophysiology, because it has higher level features (such as qualia) not present in any lower level neurophysiological systems. Still, even the higher level of consciousness is a purely physical phenomenon and a part of the material world. It is unclear whether the emergence of the higher level of consciousness can be explained by studying the brain. According to weak emergent materialism, explanation is possible. However, according to strong emergent materialism, we will never understand how the higher level of reality comes about from the brain

materialism do not agree on this question. Consequently, we should distinguish between two different forms of emergent materialism: *weak* and *strong*. In a nutshell, the former says that emergence can be explained while the latter denies this.

Weak emergence

Weak emergent materialism points to the history of science, especially to the relationships between various scientific disciplines. There was a time, not so long ago, when the different branches of the natural sciences, namely physics, chemistry and biology, each existed in theoretical isolation from each other. This was because it was impossible to explain chemical properties in terms of physical ones, or biological properties in terms of chemical ones, although it seemed clear that chemical properties must emerge from physical ones and biological properties must emerge from chemical ones. However, during the 20th century, the gaps between these sciences were removed. With the advent of a model of the internal structure of the atom, the periodic table of chemical elements and the development of particle and quantum physics, it has become possible to understand how the physical laws operating on the microlevel physical entities and structures ultimately govern the chemical world. They determine which elements form compounds with which others, and why. It has even become possible to predict or calculate what the properties of an entirely new chemical compound will be like prior to observing it in reality.

In a similar vein, although "life" seemed to be a unique and mysterious feature of biological organisms, now it has become possible to explain how living organisms can be put together by combining lower level (nonliving) chemical and biochemical constituents into complex systems. We now understand the basic mechanisms that make a living organism tick – it has become possible to explain "life" by referring to the microlevel, nonliving parts of biological organisms.

When we look around in the sciences, weak emergent materialism seems to work almost everywhere. First, some puzzling holistic phenomena are identified and their correlation to the lower level is described. At this early point, the correlation seems like a mystery: We do not understand, at first, how the two seemingly different types of phenomena could be connected by a mechanism. Gradually their relationship is revealed as based on immensely complex, multilevel mechanisms that work between the two types of phenomena. Finally, the mechanisms can be described in so much detail that the original mystery vanishes and we come to understand how the new types of higher level phenomena emerge from the lower level parts. In fact, the sciences at large seem to be organized into a hierarchical system of theories or models that describe the world at different levels of complexity. Physics is at the bottom level, then chemistry, biochemistry, molecular biology, cell biology, physiology, and so on. The structure of science seems to reflect the structure of reality itself: Reality seems to be a layered system consisting of successive levels, and each level requires a specialized science to study and describe what is going on at that level. The relationships between levels may at first seem mysterious, but later on we discover the principles that connect different levels. Thereby we come to understand how the higher level emerges from the lower level.

Weak emergent materialism says that the relationship between consciousness and the brain is just business as usual in the sciences. Consciousness just happens to be now at the frontiers of our understanding, but inevitably the problem will dissolve in a similar manner as the earlier problems have dissolved in the history of science. A hundred years ago most biologists believed that "life" was something fundamentally different from ordinary physical processes and thus supported some sort of dualistic theory of life (also called "vitalism"). This theory is analogous to the dualistic theories of consciousness we have already explored above. Today, all biologists know that "life" is just a complex physical process that requires no nonphysical forces or entities whatsoever. There is no deep mystery anymore about what "life" is in the biological sense of the word. A single-cell organism is alive. The emergent property of "being alive" can be exhaustively explained by the causal processes going on at the bio-physical, biochemical and molecular levels.

In a similar vein, there seems to be a deep mystery about consciousness and its relation to the brain. However, the mystery is just an illusion created by our current ignorance of the neural mechanisms that constitute consciousness. Once we reveal and describe the underlying mechanisms, the sense of mystery will vanish into thin air and we will feel that we fully understand how consciousness emerges from the brain, just like we already understand how the feature of "being alive" emerges from the complex microlevel organization of biological organisms.

All that sounds very promising, of course, but we may ask: How does weak emergence in the end differ from a sophisticated reductive explanation? Will not sub-jective consciousness disappear in the process in just the same way as it would disappear in a straightforward reduction of consciousness to the brain? And if it does not disappear, how can we say that it will have been genuinely explained? There is a fine line over here that weak emergent materialism tries to walk, between falling on the one side to the reduction and disappearance of consciousness and, on the other, to preserving consciousness as an inexplicable mystery.

Unfortunately, at this point the supporter of weak emergence cannot tell us how the mystery is going to be removed. All that can be offered right now is an optimistic piece of faith in the steady progress of science. The lack of any concrete solution leads to doubts over whether any such solution is forthcoming, ever. The pessimistic alternative that preserves the mystery of consciousness forever is our next topic.

Strong emergence

Weak emergent materialism is rather optimistic about the future developments of cognitive neuroscience. One day, cognitive neuroscience will be able to fully describe and explain consciousness so that all sense of mystery will vanish. Strong emergent materialism, by contrast, is less hopeful. It says that the inexplicability of the emer-gence of consciousness from the brain is not just due to the early stage of cognitive neuroscience – it is due to the fact that the relationship is inexplicable in principle. In other words, even if science one day is able to describe all the neural events in the brain exhaustively, and furthermore correlate the neural events with conscious events in the subjective psychological reality, we will forever lack an understanding of *why* those two realities correlate in the first place. Thus, we will never be able to discover the causal mechanisms that mediate between the two realms – we will never be able to describe any mechanisms that would explain how neural activity at the lower level turns into subjective experience at the higher level. It will seem to us like a magic trick, such as turning water into wine, or like the magical touch of King Midas, turning ordinary substances inexplicably into gold. There is no explanatory mechanism; "emergence" is just a name for a persistent mystery.

Supporters of strong emergent materialism point to the fundamental differences between the subjective psychological reality and the objective physical (or neural) reality. The former includes qualitative experiences that feel like something and exist only from the first-person point of view; the latter consists of physical entities and causal mechanisms that involve nothing subjective or qualitative about them and exist from the third-person point of view or objectively. Nothing we can think about or imagine could make an objective physical process turn into or "secrete" subjective, qualitative "feels". It is like trying to squeeze wine out of pure water: it is just not in there, and there can be no natural mechanism (short of magic) that could ever turn the former into the latter. The best we can reach is a theory stating that, yes, consciousness does emerge from the brain, and then to simply list all the correlations between these two realities: when brain activity of type Z occurs, then a conscious experience of type Q emerges, and so on. But that is where scientific explanation will have to end. We will never come to understand *how* the conscious features flow out of the brain activity, or *why* such subjective states should be created by the brain at all. Our own existence as subjective beings will remain a persistent mystery for science.

We can divide strong emergent materialism even further, based on what the *origin* of the mystery is supposed to be. One version blames it all on us, or rather on our incurable stupidity. Rather than "stupidity theory", however, it is called "cognitive closure": Humans are *cognitively closed* from the correct theory of the brain–consciousness relationship. There is no mystery out there in the world itself. The way in which consciousness emerges from the brain is a fully natural event with only natural causes; nothing supernatural or magical is involved. Unfortunately the theory that would describe how this entirely natural mechanism works is beyond human cognition altogether. Just like hamsters will never understand the theory of natural selection (they are cognitively closed in relation to it), or gorillas will never grasp quantum mechanics, we humans have limited cognitive capacities too. We hit the intellectual wall at the borderline between neuroscience and psychology: The correct explanatory theory is unreachable for us, and, even if handed to us on a silver plate by a higher extraterrestrial intelligence, what we could make of it would equal what hamsters could make of Charles Darwin's *Origin of Species* if a copy was placed in their cage.

The other version does not blame it on us but instead regards the universe itself as inherently mysterious. The mysterious universe theory suggests that perhaps there are hidden "levels" or "dimensions" of the physical universe, not described by our standard physics, and we can be directly in touch with those mysterious corners of physical space in our consciousness. These "mental" dimensions of the universe are still parts of the physical world and emerge from the more ordinary aspects of the physical, yet they are so entirely different from anything our physics is used to handling that for present-day science they would be categorized as "supernatural". According to this view, there is more to the world than we can see and more than even the best methods of the natural sciences can see. Therefore, science will never be able to describe or explain consciousness because consciousness exists at a plane of the universe that emerges from the physical but is inherently supernatural or mystical for physical science. It remains unclear whether any sort of scientific approach can get a grasp of that realm, certainly not any science we can currently imagine.

It may be difficult to distinguish strong emergent materialism from epiphenomenalism, because the most radical forms of emergence seem to go beyond the physical. The supernatural aspects of the mysterious universe theory would surely be regarded as nonphysical features of the known physical universe, thus slipping on the side of property dualism (discussed above in connection with epiphenomenalism).

Strong emergent materialism is also sometimes called *mysterianism* (Flanagan, 1992), first formulated by the philosopher Colin McGinn (1991). Mysterianism combines the idea that consciousness is a natural phenomenon or feature of the physical universe (which denies supernatural or dualistic theories) and the idea that no explanation of consciousness is or ever will be available to humans (the inevitable human stupidity or the cognitive closure argument).

Weak or strong emergence?

While weak emergent materialism is optimistic about the capabilities of science to explain consciousness in the long run and encourages further empirical research in cognitive neuroscience into the issue, strong emergent materialism discourages further research on the biological explanation of consciousness, considering it futile. At the very least, strong emergent materialism or mysterianism demolishes any hopes of ever resolving the issue within a traditional scientific framework.

On the basis of our current knowledge (or rather ignorance) it is impossible to choose between the weak and strong alternatives of emergent materialism, as they both try to predict the future course of science that no-one can know with any certainty at this point. All we do know is that the research has certainly not reached any ultimate limit yet. On the contrary, the empirical research that connects brain activity with conscious mental phenomena is only at the very beginning. Strong emergent materialism predicts that there will come a day when neuroscience and brain research have been completed and there is absolutely *nothing* new to be discovered about the biological mechanisms working in our brains – yet, we still will not have a clue as to how or why consciousness emerges from the biological processes in the brain. Weak emergent materialism, on the other hand, predicts that at the point when we reach complete understanding of the brain we will necessarily also possess a theory of consciousness that explains how subjective experiences emerge from biological brain processes and why their emergence simply *must* happen under the biological circumstances that exist in the living human brain.

Until then, the only thing we can do is to go on with the empirical research. If the history of science is any guide to be trusted in this matter, we will gain a totally new *kind* of understanding along the way, the kind of understanding that is impossible even to imagine now. The problem of consciousness will be seen in an entirely new light, and if we are lucky the problem will dissolve altogether – perhaps in a manner that does not fit into any of our current ideas of emergence and reduction.

Supporters of strong emergent materialism might not be happy with this kind of vision of the future. It has been said that some prefer an eternal mystery to its scientific solution, because it would be more exciting to live in a universe that contains genuine mysteries – especially concerning our own nature and origin. Science has already been able to remove many big mysteries, but will it be able to deal with this one as well? No doubt, the new science of consciousness is now needed to figure out how far we can go towards a solution to the mystery!

Summary of monistic materialism

The challenge for materialism is to find a place for subjective mental life in a world that consists of purely physical entities. Eliminative materialism flatly denies the reality of a subjective mental life: Consciousness is a misconception and therefore will have no place in the physical universe that science concerns itself with. Reductive materialism treats consciousness as a real but misunderstood phenomenon that will be relocated from psychology to neuroscience as we discover the neural entities that are identical with the subjective mental reality. We will come to see that consciousness was a neural (and therefore ordinary physical) entity all along; it has no features that go beyond its physical-neural base in the brain. Thus, both eliminative and reductive materialism try to get rid of the subjective and qualitative aspects of mind, by claiming either that such things are unreal to begin with or that their reality is not what we thought it to be; instead of being subjective and qualitative and thereby a special psychological reality, it is a purely neural reality, devoid of any fundamentally psychological qualities. Emergent materialism, by contrast, tries to widen our conception of the physical, by claiming that the physical world itself consists of levels of complexity and perhaps consciousness is a higher level of organization arising from the complex interactions of neural activities in the brain. But emergent materialism leaves it open whether we could ever explain or understand the mechanisms of emergence. At this point we have no idea, yet, how a subjective psychological reality could "emerge" out of neural firings. And strong emergent materialism predicts that we will never be able to understand what happens at the interface between the objective neural and the subjective psychological realities. If this pessimistic prediction holds, then emergent materialism hardly solves the brain–consciousness problem any more than postulating an immaterial soul-substance does. In both cases, merely a new name for an old mystery has been invented.

Despite its overwhelming popularity among philosophers and scientists, materialism has not been able to explain consciousness yet. This encourages us to search for alternative approaches to explain consciousness that do not accept the fundamental assumptions of materialism: that everything in the universe consists of physical-material entities and nothing else. This cornerstone of the modern scientific world-view may have to be questioned in the light of the problem of consciousness. Next, we will look at what the alternatives are for a thoroughgoing materialism and whether they could be defended with more success than materialism.

Idealism

The opposite of materialism, idealism, takes the mental reality of consciousness as the primary reality and treats physical matter as a mere illusion. All that exists, the entire universe, consists of nothing but conscious mental phenomena. The reality around us is all just like a dreamworld – seemingly solid and concrete, but in the final analysis merely a complex image in our consciousness (or perhaps, as in some more exotic varieties of idealism, in the mind of God).

Idealism might at first glance seem rather difficult to defend, because the objective reality of the physical world all around us seems just obvious. A closer look, however, reveals that the reality of the material world is not indubitable after all. Scientific theories that postulate physical entities such as atoms, molecules, cells, galaxies, elementary particles, physical forces, and the like, are in the final analysis all based on indirect observations. Some observations in science can be made relatively directly with the naked eye, but most others only very indirectly through complex research instruments and experimental designs. Nevertheless, our scientific world-view ultimately depends on the observations that scientists make about the physical world. A galaxy is a blurry spot of whiteness seen by looking into the telecope and a living cell is a pattern of contours and colours seen in a microscope – nothing "physical" in there, only patterns of subjective experience in the scientist's own conscious perception!

Every instance of observation necessarily involves conscious perception. To observe some physical thing is to have a conscious perceptual experience that is theoretically *interpreted as* representing or being causally modulated by a physical thing that is supposed to exist independently of our perception of it. Behind physical objects as they appear in our perception are assumed to be physical objects as they are in themselves. Yet, nobody has ever seen the physical world directly as it is in itself; we only get indirect evidence of its existence through our senses and perceptual images. Even the everyday objects we see around us are just bundles of organized sensations in our consciousness. We can never see behind the sensations, to directly grasp the molecules, atoms, electrons and quantum fields; yet we assume that somewhere behind the perceptual images in our consciousness there is the real physical world devoid of any subjective content, a world where only physical particles and forces exist.

It follows that there is not – nor could there ever be – *any* direct evidence about the existence of the physical world as it is in itself. All the evidence is indirect and only comes through our conscious experience – thus we have no absolute guarantee that any physical world even exists behind the conscious perceptions we have. Perhaps the idea of an independent, objective physical world out there is just an abstract theoretical hypothesis that we have constructed to account for the order and the systematic features in our sensation and perception. Perhaps all there is are the sensations and the perceptions themselves: We live in a dreamworld all the time but this dreamworld is highly organized and internally coherent, and it includes what appear to be physical objects.

The most famous idealist in philosophy is George Berkeley (1685–1753). He argued that only spirits (or conscious mental experiences) exist in the primary sense, and the essence of perceived (seemingly) physical things lies in *being perceived* – they have no independent existence. Also Descartes argued, in his evil demon argument, that it is in principle possible that we live in an illusory reality (like in the famous movie *The Matrix* where the everyday world turns out to be a hallucinatory virtual reality created by artificially stimulating the brain). Applied to the modern scientific world-view, idealism implies that the physical world of molecules, atoms, galaxies and quantum fields could merely be our imaginary interpretation to explain the in-themselves-invisible background causes of conscious perception. In all the percepts we have directly, only subjective qualities of experience are present: visual patterns of colour and light; tactile feelings of hardness, smoothness, softness; auditory patterns of sounds and voices. We normally think we see the external world directly "out there", but what we experience directly are only complex patterns of subjective experience that seem like a solid physical "world".

Thus, for all we know the physical could turn out to be a massive illusion after all! So, perhaps the physical, rather than the mental, should be eliminated from science, or at least reduced to patterns of conscious experiences – the only thing whose existence is beyond all doubts! *Phenomenalism* treats physical matter as something that is dependent on consciousness: Matter is a possibility of observation, nothing more. The idealist's famous slogan is: *To exist is to be perceived.* But we may ask: being perceived *by whom*? One extreme position in idealism says: by me. *Solipsism* is the view that only I exist – the whole world is just a dream going on in my own consciousness. Other people do not exist but as images in my mind, just as the people I encounter in my dreams have no independent existence of their own – they are creatures of my consciousness. Solipsism is hard to refute conclusively, but even harder to take seriously as a hypothesis about the world. Other forms of idealism do not deny the existence of other minds or persons. We live in a world of conscious experience, but the world is not contained in any single person's mind – perhaps it is a giant dream world in the mind of God.

At the smallest spatiotemporal scales, physical matter itself seems to behave in ways difficult to comprehend from a purely "objective" standpoint. Quantum mechanics involves several paradoxes where the spatiotemporal, physical features of physical entities seem to be defined at least partly by whether or not those entities are being observed. The most famous thought experiment in quantum physics concerning the role of the observer in defining physical reality is known as Schrödinger's Cat; if quantum physics is correct (and remember that it is considered the most powerful physical theory we have), whether the cat in this imaginary experiment is alive or dead seems to be determined by whether the cat has been observed by someone's conscious perception! As long as the cat remains inside a box and its state is not observed by anyone, the poor creature is (according to the Copenhagen interpretation of quantum theory) in a weird indeterminate state called superposition that contains both possible states at the same time – in some ghostly manner, Schrödinger's Cat is *both* dead *and* alive! But let someone glimpse into the box, and immediately the one and only fate of the animal is sealed.

Therefore, idealism cannot be ruled out yet, for all we know, some form of idealism might begin to gain further support any day from the most advanced physical science we have!

Neutral monism

Both materialism and idealism encounter deep problems. For materialism, it is difficult to find a place for consciousness; for idealism, it is difficult to find a place for physical matter. Thus, perhaps there is something wrong with the basic starting points of these positions. Perhaps it is a mistake to think that the world, at bottom, must be either totally material or totally mental. The truth might rather lie somewhere in the middle. Neutral monism argues that this is in fact the case. The universe is, at bottom, neither mental nor physical, but consists of a substance that is even more fundamental than either of those, or perhaps of a substance that somehow includes both in some primitive form.

Double-aspect theory states that the fundamental substance includes both a mental and a physical aspect, and therefore the world contains both mental and physical phenomena. They are not categorically different from each other; they are just different kinds of manifestations of the basic substance of the universe. When the basic substance engages in events and objects of the world, it takes either a mental form or a physical form.

The double-aspect theory of mind and matter is often compared to the particle–wave duality in quantum physics. At the quantum level, the quantum entities are neither particles nor waves. When the causal effects of quantum entities such as electrons or photons are registered or measured by scientific instruments, however, they always manifest themselves either as particles or as waves, but never as both at the same time. And when nobody is looking or observing them, they exist in a "neutral", indeterminate form that is neither particle nor wave, or perhaps both at the same time. In the case of consciousness and brain, when the subject observes his or her own consciousness it shows itself in the form of phenomenal experiences, but when an external observer looks at the very same brain from an external perspective only neural structures and electrochemical activities can be seen. The first-person perspective and the third-person perspective to consciousness cannot be taken at the same time by the same observer. And it may be a mistake to treat either of the perspectives as primary or more fundamental. In modern consciousness research, the British psychologist Max Velmans (1991, 2009) has developed this sort of a double-aspect view: First-person and third-person perspectives of the brain–mind are complementary and mutually irreducible, and the explanation of consciousness requires both.

Panpsychism is the view that everything (physical) in the universe – every last molecule, atom and elementary particle – also contains a conscious or mental ingredient. The mental and the physical are like two sides of a coin: one cannot be had without the other. In panpsychism, the physical and mental features coexist all the time in all physical entities. In double-aspect theory, the neutral substance manifests itself in either physical or mental forms, but is not manifesting both features everywhere simultaneously – the brain is a special case.

Gustav Fechner (1801–1887), a scientist who played a decisive role in the early scientific study of consciousness (see more about his scientific work, called psychophysics, in Chapter 2), was by his philosophical approach a panpsychist. In his view, the world is composed of a hierarchy of minds or souls. Plants, animals, planets, stars and galaxies all possess varying degrees of consciousness. The whole universe is penetrated by countless conscious minds; inner subjective life flows all around us – humans are not lonely, faint flames of phenomenal light in a vast universal nonconscious darkness. On the contrary, above the individual human consciousness there is the collective consciousness of the whole human race; above that there is the unified consciousness of the entire biosphere of the planet Earth, above that there is the consciousness of the solar system, the galaxy and, finally, the absolutely universal consciousness. Although each human consciousness is, from its own point of view, isolated from others and confined to its own little phenomenal world, at the higher levels an individual consciousness is but a tiny element in the higher planetary, galactic and universal consciousness. Fechner was extremely serious and convinced about this world-view – so much so that he wrote an entire book just about the souls of plants!

Proto-panpsychism has been recently introduced into the philosophy of consciousness by the philosopher David Chalmers. According to this variety of panpsychism, everything physical contains not a full-blown conscious mind but only an extremely simple and elementary form of consciousness (called proto-consciousness). In ordinary physical particles and objects the conscious elements are so simple that we would not even recognize them as instances of consciousness, but in the human brain they are amplified and organized into a complex system of conscious mental states.

The philosopher Galen Strawson in 2006 published a powerful defence of panpsychism, trying to show that it is the most plausible solution to the problem of consciousness. He first dismisses elimination and reduction of consciousness, because we simply cannot deny the existence of experience, although some desperate modern philosophers of mind surely have tried to do so – Strawson (2006, p. 5) calls the denial of subjective experience *"the strangest thing that has ever happened in the whole history of human thought"*! Then he dismisses all forms of weak emergence, because he believes that wholly nonexperiential physical phenomena simply cannot give rise to experiential phenomena. Strong emergence he considers absurd, because it involves a belief in something like supernatural magic going on within the physical world. Thus, the only even remotely plausible alternative that is left is what he calls micropsychism, a form of panpsychism. According to this idea, microlevel physical phenomena must themselves be intrinsically experiential. If that is true, then weak emergence begins to make sense again, because it seems quite reasonable to assume that macroexperiential phenomena (our sensations and perceptions) might arise from microexperiential phenomena – the elemental experiential features in all physical matter and energy – through complex organization. As experience is involved everywhere and all along from the very lowest physical levels upwards, it need not be magically created from nonconscious physical ingredients at any particular level of organization.

Neutral monism and panpsychism gain some credibility from the fact that we do not really know what the fundamental *intrinsic* nature of the physical is. Physical sciences can only describe the abstract mathematical and formal features of physical entities – their spatiotemporal structure and the laws of physical forces and motion – but remain silent about the inner nature of those entities. That is why physics is full of mathematical equations: We only know that there is *something* out there that behaves according to the equations, but we do not know whether it is internally like the qualities of lived conscious experience, or like dark, dead bits of completely insentient stuff. Therefore, we have no scientific grounds for claiming either that the physical must be totally different in nature from consciousness or that it must be similar to it. For all we know (and for all physics can tell us), the physical *could* just as well have an intrinsic nature or aspect that corresponds to subjective qualitative experience. We do not know what the physical is, but we do know with absolute certainty what the fundamental, inner nature of consciousness is: subjective qualitative experience. Maybe that is what the physical is made out of too! Perhaps the entire physical world consists, at the bottom level, of simple qualities of experience. When we measure and describe them from the outside perspective, they appear as "electrons", "photons" and the like. But maybe in this case we should not judge the book by the cover – the cover may look purely physical, but perhaps the contents are experiential!

Functionalism

Functionalism is not usually classified as a variety of neutral monism, but in some ways this is the most appropriate category because functionalism identifies consciousness neither with physical matter nor with an immaterial soul-substance. Instead, functionalism regards the essence of mind to be in an abstract domain of complex *causal relationships* between any given entities. For functionalism, a mental state is defined by *a set of relations* rather than by the material or immaterial nature of the entities that realize the relationships. The nature of the material components that implement the pattern of relations is irrelevant. Thus, in principle, identical functional relations could be realized in a neural system and in a soul-stuff system. However, functionalists are usually also materialists, therefore they believe that in practice the functional relations are realized in the physical matter that biological organisms (or digital computers) are made of.

A mental state is a *function* of an information-processing system. A function is defined in terms of the relations between the inputs to the system and the outputs the system produces: input–output transformations. Our behaviour, too, can be characterized in terms of input–output relations: if I see a ball approaching rapidly (perceptual input), I will reach out my hand to grasp it (behavioural output); if I feel an oncoming headache (input), I will take a painkiller (output); if I see my train arriving (input), I approach the correct platform (output). A sensory perceptual input to the mind is being transformed to a behavioural output. These mental input–output transformations should be describable exactly and formally, as computations or algorithms (mathematical equations) that the brain (or the mind) uses to determine what output to produce in response to any given input (see Figure 1.6).

This is exactly how the digital computer works: it transforms inputs (e.g. signals from the keyboard) according to exact rules (the program that runs) to outputs (the "behaviour" of the computer, often reflected on the display). Originally, the fact that functionalism can explain how digital computers manage almost humanlike intelligent "mental" feats was considered a strength of the theory. The relationship between the computer's software (program) and its hardware (the physical machine) was thought to be analogical or even identical with the relationship between mind and brain. Thus, mind was regarded as an abstract functional creature like a computer program. According to functionalism, the mind is not dependent on the brain, because the same abstract functional structure that constitutes my mind could in principle be programmed into a computer and thereby the computer would come to have "artificial intelligence" or a humanlike intelligent mind. A further pleasant consequence of this

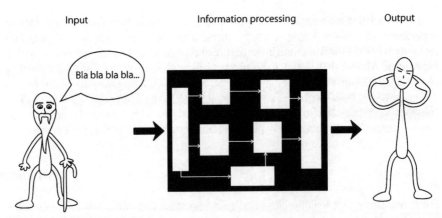

Input   Information processing   Output

Bla bla bla bla...

Figure 1.6 Functionalism

According to functionalism, the mind (the big black box) consists of information-processing functions similar to computer programs. The mind takes in sensory information as input (e.g. words in spoken language), the information is processed at many different stages (depicted by the smaller white boxes inside the big black box), each stage or box conducts its own specific type of information processing (e.g. attention, recognition, memory, action planning) and then the mind produces behaviour as its output (in this case, covering the ears to not hear what is being said). The functionalistic description of the mind can be given without even mentioning the brain, because the functions of the mind exist at an abstract level of description, independent of the neurophysiology of the brain

view was that it should be possible to liberate the mind from the confines of the mortal body by copying it into a computer or robot or another brain. Thus, functionalism (at least some of the more radical forms of it, such as computationalism and "strong artificial intelligence") promised a kind of immortality for the human mind. Your mind need not die with your brain: its abstract functional structure, its essence – your essence – could be saved and programmed to some other system, a computer or a robot, for example. Then you would become that other system (or it would become you). This theory sounds almost like paradise found: the benefits of an immortal soul without any of the metaphysical problems of Cartesian dualism (Section 1.2).

If it sounds too good to be true, that is exactly what it turned out to be. Initially, in the 1950s and 1960s, functionalism and the computer metaphor of the mind gained much support in cognitive science and philosophy of mind. However, in the 1980s it was getting more and more obvious that functionalism is incapable of describing the human mind, because it leaves something out. One of the most important things it ignores is – surprise, surprise! – consciousness. Functionalism gives no account of the subjective and qualitative reality we experience in our consciousness. In fact it seems that it *cannot* give any account of it because the subjective "feel" and the qualitative features of the mind do not seem to be "functional" in that they cannot be described in terms of input–output transformations of information. Consider the fragrance of a fine perfume, a burst of joy, a point of light in darkness: How could these qualitative experiences be nothing but transformations of input information to output behaviour? How could we write a computational algorithm or equation that captures the experiential content of these states? Conscious experiences do not consist of input–output relationships, therefore they are not describable at all by functionalism. In a functionalist framework, there seems to be no place for consciousness. Functionalism may work well in the case of the real computer or a simple nonconscious neural system, because they have no conscious experiences anyway. But humans have a subjective psychological reality, and if your theory of mind leaves it out it cannot be a terribly convincing theory of mind.

Several philosophical arguments that proved to be fatal were put forward against functionalism. Many of them pointed out that functionalism suffers from two problems directly related to consciousness: *absent qualia* and *functional zombies*. Qualia are the subjective qualitative features of the conscious mind, and they present a problem for functionalism because it cannot give any account of them nor even acknowledge that such features exist. These features are absolutely essential for consciousness, yet completely beyond a functionalist characterization of the mind. Consequently, a complete but purely functionalistic theory of the mind would not even mention qualia, because they cannot be characterized functionally. Thus, functionalism cannot explain the conscious mind. The absence of qualia in functionalism leads to the second problem. Even if one day we manage to build intelligent computational systems that satisfy fully a functionalist criterion of having a humanlike mind – they process information as we do, and they behave and give intelligent responses in the same manner as we do – we will have built mere *nonconscious zombies*: complex systems with incredible capacities for information processing and sensorimotor input–output transformation, but totally devoid of subjective consciousness (more about these in Chapter 3, Sections 3.1 and 3.2).

Functionalism was the dominating theory of mind in the 1970s and 1980s (with a number of influential defenders, such as Hilary Putnam, Jerry Fodor and Daniel Dennett), but the growing problems with consciousness (pointed out by several other famous philosophers, such as John Searle and Ned Block) were among the main reasons for the downfall of functionalism in the 1990s, when the modern science of consciousness emerged. Although some types of functionalism are still relatively popular in the philosophy of mind, only few people take the doctrine seriously any more as the final solution to the mind–body problem.

1.4 Why the mind–body problem will not go away

The "Explanatory Gap" and the "Hard Problem"

As we have observed above, an amazing number of different philosophical theories have been put forward to solve the problem of consciousness. Yet, so far none of the proposed solutions has been entirely successful. The problem remains with us, and now philosophers have tried to identify its core: *Why* exactly is the problem so frustratingly difficult? Is there something special about consciousness that sets it apart from everything else that science obviously can handle? Nowadays the hard core of the mind–body problem is discussed under the labels the *"Explanatory Gap"* (coined by Levine, 1983, 1993) and the *"Hard Problem"* (coined by Chalmers, 1996). The Hard Problem is, in its most general form, the problem that we do not have the slightest idea how *any* physical system could *ever* produce or give rise to *any* subjective, qualitative experiences. In particular, we are totally in the dark about how neurons, neural activities or anything physical going on in the brain could do the trick.

The Explanatory Gap illustrates further why the Hard Problem is so hard – why the explanation of consciousness is not going to happen in the same way as the typical explanation of physical things usually happens. The explanation of how hydrogen and oxygen molecules, when put together in a particular manner, necessarily produce water molecules is intelligible. The explanation for why water is liquid when the temperature is between 0 and 100 °C is transparent: in this condition, the molecules can freely roll over each other, whereas in lower temperatures they cannot and water becomes ice. There are no incomprehensible mysteries here.

But phenomenal experiences in our subjective psychological reality seem to be utterly different from the physical or neural properties in the objective biological reality of the brain. To count as a genuine explanation, the connection between subjective experience and objective brain activity should be made equally transparent and intelligible as the explanation of liquidity in terms of the behaviour of water molecules. But how could any imaginable combination of neural activities add up to phenomenal experiences with a lawlike necessity that would be plain for us to see and understand?

An explanation of subjective conscious phenomena in terms of objective biological phenomena just does not seem to work, because any imaginable connection between a particular subjective experience and a particular neuronal activity seems wholly arbitrary and nonexplanatory: How or why should *this* particular neural activity give rise to just *this* particular quality of experience? Even if we find out that neural activity of type Z *invariably* gives rise to phenomenal experience of type Q, and even if it would be an unshakable law of nature that $Z \Rightarrow Q$, we would still not understand *why* the connection between Z and Q exists or *what it is based on* or *how it works*; we would only know *that* such a connection exists. The arrow from Z to Q could equally well read: "and here a miracle happens". Any attempt at an explanation of the connection between the physical and the phenomenal realms falls headlong into a bottomless chasm: the unbridgeable Explanatory Gap.

Subjectivity

Properties that can be described and explained can be observed publicly and objectively: Given the proper technical equipment, basically anyone can make an observation or a measurement concerning, say, the firing of neurons in the brain. The fact that there are neurons firing in the brain, and that they are firing at a certain rate or frequency, is an objective fact. The neural phenomenon exists independently of whether we observe it or not, and its existence can be confirmed or disconfirmed through measurements and observations, in many different ways, by different people independently of each other. This constitutes the status of neural firing as an objective fact about the world.

Phenomenal consciousness is different (for a definition of phenomenal consciousness, see Chapter 3, Section 3.1). The fact that you feel euphoric, or there is a pain in your tooth, or you are having a vivid dream experience of flying through the air, is subjective. No-one apart from yourself can observe or have those experiences, nor can anyone else absolutely confirm or disconfirm their existence or know their experiential quality as you do. Even if we scan your brain activity with the latest brain scanning technology, we will at best only see patterns of neural or metabolic activity in the brain; through objective measurements, we will not see anything even remotely resembling your experiences. The experiences exist only for a single person, you, from your first-person's perspective, in your subjective psychological reality.

The problem is that science builds exclusively on a third-person's objective perspective. Only entities that can be somehow studied from that perspective are treated as "real". Physical entities can be observed by anyone either directly with sense organs or indirectly through their effects on research instruments; they have causal powers and they fulfil specific causal roles in the physical world; and they consist of other physical properties or entities, so that large-scale entities can be decomposed to microlevel entities. Phenomenal consciousness does not seem to obey these principles. It cannot be observed either directly or with the help of any research instruments such as functional brain imaging (at least not with any currently available research instruments). Phenomenal features or the qualities of experience do not seem to be analysable into causal or functional roles, which is exactly why functionalism never got a grip of consciousness. And the qualitative features of experience – such as whiteness, painfulness, sweetness, softness, happiness – do not seem to be composed of lower level microscopic physical entities such as neurons or molecules. Thus, it seems impossible to have a theory of the brain from which an explanation of consciousness would follow in a natural manner, for the brain can be fully described in objective physical, chemical and biological terms just like any other purely physical system, but such a description in no way leads to or includes an explanation of the qualitative, subjective features of consciousness.

Even worse is to come. Not only is the objective approach unable to explain consciousness, but it seems unable to acknowledge its very existence! If we stick firmly to the third-person's physicalist point of view on the world, the qualities of phenomenal experience seem to vanish altogether. The colours we experience – blueness, greenness, redness, yellowness, whiteness, blackness – as subjective qualities are nowhere to be found in the physical world. They are not properties of electromagnetic radiation in the so-called visible wavelengths. The radiation consists of photons in different wavelengths of energy, not of photons painted with different experiential colours. In the electromagnetic energy to which our eyes are sensitive (i.e. visible light), there is nothing even remotely resembling our experience of colours as far as our physical theories of electromagnetism can tell. The same goes for other qualities of experience. In NaCl (common salt), there is nothing constituting the "salty" quality that we taste in our phenomenal consciousness. Chemically, NaCl is just a simple molecule; it contains no tastes hidden inside.

If the qualities of experience are not in the physical stimuli out there, perhaps they can be found in the brain activities inside us. Certainly, tasting NaCl (or seeing a colour) does *correlate* with specific changes in brain activity. But to measure or describe the neural changes does not equate to finding out about the salty quality of the experience. Some specific neurons in the brain can be described as firing in a specific way when we taste salt or when we experience blueness in our visual field, but as far as neuroscience can tell there is nothing qualitatively blue or salty in the neural activities. We simply have no idea how the qualities of experience come about or why they correlate with specific neural activities rather than others. It is the Explanatory Gap all over again – subjectivity simply does not seem to fit into the objective world of science.

What is it like to be a bat?

In a famous article, the philosopher Thomas Nagel (1974) posed the above question by using animal consciousness (or in general *alien* consciousness) as his example. More specifically, he put forward the most famous question in modern consciousness studies: *What is it like to be a bat?* What is life like for a bat as a subjective conscious being? Will science ever be able to tell us? He first pointed out that none of the (then) available and popular theories of mind (reductionism, behaviourism and functionalism) could even begin to answer this question. They simply ignore the whole question. Thus, it seems that although science will one day be able to give a full description of bat behaviour, anatomy, physiology and neuroscience, and cognitive information processing in the bat brain, we still would have no idea of what it is like to be a bat. To figure that out, a third-person approach is insufficient. Thus, Nagel asked if there might be any way around this problem so that we could reach the *subjective point of view* of the bat. He tried out three alternatives as thought experiments.

First, *imitation:* What if I followed closely the life of bats in their natural habitat and started to imitate a bat way of life. I would hang upside down in the attic during the day and hunt for flying insects for food with an echolocation radar system during the night. Unfortunately, that kind of adventurous field research would not get us very far. I would only find out what a miserably poor imitation of bat behaviour would feel like for a human being (probably extremely awkward and unnatural), not what it feels like for the bat to be a bat (presumably perfectly simple and natural).

Second, what about *shared experiences* between humans and bats? Both species can feel pain, hunger, thirst, cold, warm, and so on. But this would not work either. Surely the bat's psychological reality is as rich as the human's, although the two realities are qualitatively very different, and of course the bat's reality mostly focuses on representation of rather different things in the world than the human conscious mind does. The bat's conscious mind probably represents other fellow bats in the colony, the best flight routes to food and mates, the typical shapes and flight patterns of edible flying insects and mortal threats for bats from larger deadly predators. Thus, only concentrating on the experiences of pain, hunger, thirst, cold and warm would leave out most things of the bat's world, just as it leaves out most of the human subjective world. If aliens from another planet came to Earth and modelled our consciousness by only taking into account those kinds of experiences, we would protest that they still have no idea of what it is like to be a conscious human being. The bat would protest similarly against us, if it could.

The third suggestion Nagel considers is to be *gradually transformed* (by using some future technology) into a bat and then back into a human. Apart from the sobering fact that such a transformation is technically beyond our wildest dreams, even if we had it at hand, it probably would not solve the problem of knowing what it is like to be a bat. Before becoming the bat, the foolhardy consciousness scientist would not yet know what it is like. While being the bat, our heroic explorer would know, but unfortunately would also be constitutionally incapable of communicating that knowledge to anyone. The bat the scientist has now become would not remember that it was supposed to gather and later communicate scientific data about bat consciousness, or even have any idea that the whole experience is in fact a scientific experiment. We could just as well try to interview any ordinary bat right now with results as meagre as with the transformed bat. And when the backward transformation is completed, our explorer very likely would be unable to recall or verbally describe what it was like to be a bat. We have all been fetuses, experienced our own birth and spent months in a cradle as babies, yet we have no idea anymore what it was like to be a fetus, a newborn or an infant. What was our conscious experience like? Was it clear and distinct, or blurred and chaotic? How did we perceive our own tiny body, how did we feel about our parents, did we have *any* idea what was going on? We just do not know – and the transformation from a human fetus or baby to an adult human is significantly less radical than the imagined transformation from a human being to a bat.

Future science and consciousness

Thus, Nagel ends up with the pessimistic conclusion that science will probably never find out what it is like to be a bat. Such knowledge is beyond all imaginable research instruments or measurements, and even if it was not, it would still remain beyond human language and concepts and therefore in principle be indescribable by any human science. In agreement with Nagel, many current philosophers hold that the problem of consciousness will remain with us forever, even if neuroscience and cognitive science make progress in other ways. Even a perfected cognitive neuroscience would not be able to tell us what it is like to be a bat, or why and how neuronal activity brings about conscious experiences.

Then again, at least some philosophers and many neuroscientists are more optimistic about the prospects for a true explanatory science of consciousness. They point out that scientific progress is impossible to predict and that future breakthroughs are impossible to foresee before their time comes. Therefore, what philosophers can and cannot imagine today will have no consequences whatsoever to the future of science. The history of science shows that before major scientific breakthroughs were actually made (say, relativity theory, quantum mechanics or DNA and genetics), philosophers and scientists were utterly unable to imagine them.

Whether consciousness can be explained or not, the neurosciences of the distant future will in any case be like unimaginable science-fiction for us, just like 21st-century genetics and molecular biology would have seemed like magic for any 19th-century biologist.

Philosophical problems and consciousness

As is by now obvious, the empirical science of consciousness will have to deal with some of the most challenging philosophical problems related to the *nature* of the mind (ontology) and to our ability of *knowing* or *finding out* about the mind (epistemology). First, the *mind–body problem* can only be solved by presenting a theory that answers the question: What is consciousness and how is it related to the brain? This is an ontological problem. Second, the *problem of other minds*, by contrast, is an epistemological problem, and asks: How can we ever know anything about the consciousness of other beings? How could we objectively determine which animals are conscious and which are not? How could we decide whether computers, robots and perhaps some of our fellow humans are really conscious beings or only nonconscious zombies? How could we find out what it is like to be another type of conscious being? To solve the problem of other minds, we should develop research instruments that objectively detect consciousness. By pointing the "consciousness-metre" to any creature, a light turns on, with green meaning "consciousness detected – this creature has a subjective inner life" and red meaning "consciousness not detected – this creature is dead, deeply unconscious or a zombie". Finally, to solve the "What is it like to be a bat?" problem, we should have methods that not only *detect* the *presence* of consciousness, but are able to *describe its quality* in detail. Perhaps the ideal consciousness-scanner of the distant future will present another creature's consciousness for us in some kind of virtual-reality simulation where our own consciousness temporarily mimics the phenomenal form and contents of the alien consciousness (for more about this idea, see Revonsuo, 2006).

Chapter summary

We have explored the main philosophical theories of consciousness. *Dualistic* theories say that consciousness and physical matter are fundamentally different. According to *interactionism*, brain and consciousness engage in bidirectional causal interaction back and forth; according to *epiphenomenalism* there is only one-way causation from brain activity to consciousness, but consciousness itself has no causal powers; and according to *parallelism*, conscious events and brain events have no causal connections but they nevertheless proceed in perfect harmony to create the illusion of causation. *Monistic* theories say that consciousness and physical matter are basically the same stuff. *Monistic materialism* is divided into *eliminative* materialism (consciousness is an illusion and does not really exist: the whole concept should be rejected), *reductive* materialism (consciousness is nothing over and above some type of brain activity) and *emergent* materialism (consciousness is a higher level of organization in the brain, dependent on brain activity but not reducible to it). *Neutral monism* states that both physical matter and consciousness are based on stuff that is more fundamental than either matter or consciousness. *Idealism* is the view that everything is basically made out of mental stuff or conscious experience. *Functionalism*, which is perhaps the most influential modern philosophical theory of mind, does not identify consciousness with any particular kind of stuff, either mental or physical, but with abstract causal or computational or input–output relations, which can be realized in basically *any* kind of stuff as patterns of causal roles – consciousness or mind is *software*, like a computer *program*, not hardware, like a computer made of physical parts or a brain made of biological parts.

In spite of all these attempts to solve the philosophical problem of consciousness, the mystery surrounding it remains. The *Hard Problem* says that we have no idea how or why any physical system should produce conscious experiences, and the *Explanatory Gap* refers to the impossibility of forming any intelligible bridge from physical or neural features of the brain to the qualitative features of consciousness, even if we can show that those features always are associated with each other. Finally, Thomas Nagel's famous argument in "What is it like to be a bat?" shows that science probably cannot ever tell us much about the subjective conscious life of bats or other nonhuman creatures, because the subjective facts characterizing an alien mind cannot be captured through any objective scientific means or expressed and communicated in human concepts.

Further reading

Beckermann, A., Flohr, H., & Kim, J. (Eds.) (1992). *Emergence or reduction?* Berlin: Walter de Gruyter.

Block, N., Flanagan, O., & Güzeldere, G. (Eds.) (1997). *The nature of consciousness: Philosophical debates*. Cambridge, MA: MIT Press.

Broad, C. D. (1925). *The mind and its place in nature*. London: Routledge & Kegan Paul.

Chalmers, D. (1996). *The conscious mind*. Oxford: Oxford University Press.

Kim, J. (1998). *Mind in a physical world*. Cambridge, MA: MIT Press.

Kim, J. (2005). *Physicalism, or something near enough*. Princeton, NJ: Princeton University Press.

Levine, J. (1983) Materialism and qualia: The explanatory gap. *Pacific Philosophical Quarterly*, *64*, 354–361.

Levine, J. (1993). On leaving out what it's like. In M. Davies & G. W. Humphreys (Eds.), *Consciousness* (pp. 121–136). Oxford: Blackwell.

Nagel, T. (1974). What is it like to be a bat? *Philosophical Review*, *83*, 435–450.

Pauen, M., Staudacher, A., & Walter, S. (Eds.) (2006). Special issue on epiphenomenalism. *Journal of Consciousness Studies*, *13* (1–2).

Searle, J. (1992). *The rediscovery of the mind*. Cambridge, MA: MIT Press.

Skribna, D. (2005). *Panpsychism in the West*. Cambridge, MA: MIT Press.

Velmans, M. (2009). *Understanding consciousness* (2nd ed.). Hove, UK: Routledge.

Brief discussion questions

1   In your opinion, what is the most plausible mind–body theory and what is the least plausible? Why? In the classroom, arrange a voting and rank the theories from least to most plausible. Discuss the reasons that you have for supporting or resisting each theory.

2   Do you think that the Hard Problem and the Explanatory Gap will be solved by science in the future? If not, why not? If yes, how could it happen and when: within 10 years, 50 years, 100 years or in the distant future?

3   Imagine worlds where different mind–body theories are true: in each world, the

mind–body problem has been solved for good, and thus one or another theory has been established as scientific fact. What would life be like in a world where: Cartesian dualism turned out to be true; epiphenomenalism is a fact; weak or strong emergent materialism is established as fact; panpsychism has been confirmed and physical matter is teeming with subjective experience; or where idealism has defeated materialism? How would the different solutions change people's attitudes towards life and death?

Chapter 2

The historical foundations of consciousness science

Introduction

The modern scientific study of consciousness may at first glance appear to be a brand new branch of science that surfaced suddenly during the 1990s. In fact, the historical roots of the science of consciousness go much deeper than that. The first wave of the science of consciousness flourished already back in the late 1800s. We will now trace the developments of the science of consciousness from those early days to where we stand today.

2.1 The 1800s: From philosophy to experimental science of consciousness

Up until roughly the 1850s, human consciousness was conceived of as a Cartesian soul: nonphysical by nature, without spatial extension or location in physical space and intrinsically unified or undividable. The soul, by its very nature, was taken to be beyond scientific observation or measurement. Therefore, there could be no such thing as a science of consciousness.

Phrenology

The Cartesian dualistic line of thought was gradually discarded during the 19th century. First, in the early 1800s, phrenologists like Franz Joseph Gall (1758–1828) argued that the human mind can be divided into several different faculties and each of them is located in a particular part of the brain. They also held the modern scientific view that the human mind is a biological phenomenon to be investigated by science, not an immaterial soul to be pondered only by metaphysics and philosophy. However, the phrenological theory concerning the nature of the faculties or subsystems of the mind, their correlation with brain location, shape and size and with the external shape of the skull, turned out to be catastrophically mistaken.

Phrenologists produced anatomical drawings and busts of the human head where the skull was divided into tens of different regions that were named with more or less obscure psychological terms describing what were supposed to be universal psychological characteristics, such as "Secretiveness", "Love of Animals", "Desire for Liquids", "Sense of the Terrific" and "Intuition", to mention just a few of the most curious mental faculties invented by the phrenologists. Their location on the skull surface pointed to the brain regions directly below where the psychological features were taken to reside. The analysis of an individual person's psychological profile was based on the assumption that the prominence of the various shapes and regions of the skull reflected the size of the corresponding brain area, which in turn reflected the strength of the psychological feature in the person.

Phrenology, as it was practiced in the 19th century, developed into a flourishing pseudoscience rather than an academic psychological science. Phrenologists offered an analysis of one's personality and future prospects based on measurements of the size and shape of the skull. The resulting mumbo-jumbo was not very different from the astrological horoscopes that we have seen in more recent times.

Phrenological terminology and theory became widely popularized and a part of the contemporary culture and literature. For example, Dr. Mortimer in the Sherlock Holmes books is a phrenology enthusiast who at one point reveals to the detective that he would like to have a cast of Holmes' skull in his collection (until the original becomes available) (Hothersall, 2004).

Although often ridiculed as just a crazy fad, phrenology did contain some scientifically valuable ideas, especially when placed in its historical context. First, it was the inaugural scientific approach that argued for a strictly biological view of the mind, to replace the purely philosophical and religious dualism that had reigned for centuries. Second, it was the first theory to suggest that the mind is divisible into several different, functionally specialized subsystems. In this respect it was just like modern cognitive psychology. Third, it proposed that each subsystem is taken care of by a localized and specialized brain area, which is the same idea that underlies modern cognitive neuropsychology. Some of the subsystems named in the phrenological maps were actually similar to modern ideas about functional specialization in the human cortex: Specialized brain areas for language, verbal memory, colour processing, form processing, calculation, planning and humour can be found in some of the phrenological maps as well as in the models and images of the mind–brain in modern neuropsychology and cognitive neuroscience. Of course, the phrenological maps were not based on any proper theory, any reliable empirical data or any valid measurements, unlike the modern brain localization results. Thus, even though some of the phrenological labels still make a bit of sense, in phrenology the localization of functions to the brain was no better than pure guesswork.

Psychophysics

The first scientific measurements and theory of consciousness were put forward by the physicist Gustav Fechner in 1860. He called his approach *psychophysics*. Fechner managed to connect aspects of the subjective psychological reality (sensory experiences) to physical measurements and quantities. His observations and theories are still considered valid, and there still exists a branch of experimental psychology called psychophysics where research is based on the legacy of Fechner.

Fechner realized that specific contents of subjective experience can be generated by presenting specific physical stimuli to an observer. By carefully controlling the physical features of the stimuli, the experimenter could indirectly manipulate and control the content of the observer's consciousness. Fechner was particularly interested in the *intensity* of stimulation and its relation to subsequent subjective sensations. Intensity is a feature that characterizes the physical stimulus: A tone can be physically louder (i.e. the signal has more physical energy) than another one and a weight physically heavier than another. The physical intensity can be exactly and objectively measured. Also the subjective experience generated by the stimulus varies along the dimension of intensity: Sounds are heard as louder or weaker and weights feel heavier or lighter.

Fechner set out to study the relationship between the objective physical measure of intensity and the subjective phenomenal feel of intensity. He made several groundbreaking scientific observations. He realized that at very low physical stimulus intensities no subjective experience whatsoever was created in the mind. These he called *negative sensations*. At some point, when the physical stimulus is made stronger, it becomes just barely noticeable by the subject. The borderline stimulus is called the *just noticeable stimulus* and it marks the division between present and absent sensations (or *sensitivity*). Two sensations can be subjectively alike or different. The *minimum difference of stimulus magnitude* that can be noticed is called the *just noticeable stimulus difference* and it is the basis of stimulus discrimination.

Fechner found that physical stimulus magnitude was not directly or linearly correlating with the subjective intensity of stimulation. The *just noticeable difference* (JND) between two physical stimuli depends on their absolute magnitude: the larger the absolute magnitude of the two stimuli to be compared, the larger the physical difference between them has to be before we subjectively experience them as different. We might be able to feel the 100 g difference between two weights of 1.0 kg and 1.1 kg, but not between 10.0 kg and 10.1 kg, for example.

Fechner formulated a mathematical function or law that describes the relation between physical stimulus and subjective experience (also known as the *Weber–Fechner Law*), according to which subjective sensation is a logarithmic function of physical intensity.

2.2 Introspectionism: The first scientific psychology of consciousness

Wilhelm Wundt and the birth of psychological science

Fechner's approach to the objective measurement of consciousness was taken further by another German scientist, Wilhelm Wundt (1832–1920). In the 1800s, there was a general agreement that "psychology" is the study of conscious experience; therefore, psychology was self-evidently regarded as the science of consciousness. Wundt is regarded as the father of the experimental science of psychology. He founded the first laboratory of experimental psychology in Leipzig, Germany, in 1879, where he and his many students applied the experimental methodology invented by Fechner to a much wider set of conscious mental phenomena than just sensations.

Because psychology was the study of consciousness or immediate experience, there was a special method for psychology: *introspection*. This method has provided the name for the first scientific approach to experimental psychology from the 1860s to the 1920s: *introspectionism*.

For Wundt and his followers, the method of introspection consists simply of *having* experiences, carefully *attending to* them and subsequently *verbally describing* them. Thus, no "inner sense" or "inner perception" is needed to "observe" the contents of one's mind. Wundt's introspective laboratory experiments were carefully planned and controlled. Introspection was applied along with other methods, such as measurement of manual reaction time. The subjects who participated in the experiments were highly trained so that they would be able to give detailed and reliable descriptions of their conscious experiences.

At the theoretical level, Wundt viewed consciousness as an entire *field* of experiential elements. The elements were not passive, atomic qualities that combined through a mechanical mental chemistry, as his follower Titchener believed, but according to Wundt the elements of consciousness were ongoing processes or events that were actively synthesized by the mind to complex contents of consciousness or ideas. The field of consciousness where the experiential events occur is divided into a centre and a periphery by the focus of attention. In the centre, the elements were synthesized to larger wholes and perceived clearly. Wundt called this process *apperception*. As opposed to apperception, the experiential events going on in the field outside the centre were only *apprehended*, that is, experienced only vaguely (Leahey, 1980).

Wundt's views are, in hindsight, surprisingly modern. Nowadays we talk about focal selective attention and the process of binding elementary perceptual features to coherent perceptual objects – cognitive processes that seem to be not so far from Wundt's idea of apperception. Wundt furthermore held a rather holistic idea of consciousness, believing that the simple elements of consciousness are synthesized into holistic units by attention. The most important follower of Wundt, Edward Titchener (1867–1927), held a more atomistic view of consciousness.

Titchener and structuralism: The atoms of consciousness

Titchener was a student of Wundt and did his PhD studies in Leipzig in the early 1890s. After that he moved to America and stayed there at Cornell University for the rest of his life. Titchener developed introspectionism to its most radical form, known as *structuralism*.

According to Titchener, mind is the stream of mental processes that we experience subjectively. This stream flows from birth to death. Mind is the sum total of mental processes experienced by an individual during his whole lifetime whereas *consciousness*, by Titchener's definition, is the sum of mental processes that make up my experience right *now*. Consciousness is thus like a time-slice or a cross-section of mind: it constitutes the mind of any given present time.

The tasks of psychology as the science of the mind and consciousness are, according to Titchener, the following:

1   To analyse mental experience into its simplest components.
2   To discover how these elements combine to more complex mental contents and to figure out the laws followed by the combination of elements.
3   To describe the connection between mental experiences and physiological or bodily processes.

The name of Titchener's approach to psychology, structuralism, derives from the fundamental assumption behind his science: Consciousness has an *atomistic structure* that, at bottom, consists of *simple elements.* Titchener wrote in 1896 (p. 13):

> The first object of the psychologist, therefore, is to ascertain the nature and number of the mental elements. He takes up mental experience, bit by bit, dividing and subdividing, until the division can go no further. When that point is reached, he has found a conscious element.

Titchener got inspiration from the success in the physical sciences of a similar atomistic and analytic strategy. He referred to chemistry as a kind of model for the science of psychology. "Ideas" or complex mental processes are like chemical compounds; "sensations" or the simple mental elements are like chemical elements that cannot be further analysed to simpler parts:

> The idea is a compound; it consists of a number of elemental processes, travelling side by side in consciousness: it therefore resembles the compound bodies analysed in the chemical laboratory. But the sensation resists analysis, just as do the chemical elements oxygen and hydrogen. It stands to the idea as oxygen and hydrogen stand to water.
>
> (Titchener, 1896, pp. 27–28)

Titchener developed the use of introspection in laboratory experiments into a fine-tuned, sophisticated skill that only proficient, highly experienced subjects were able to do properly:

> Be as attentive as possible to the object or process which gives rise to the sensation, and, when the object is removed or the process completed, recall the sensation by an act of memory as vividly and completely as you can
>
> (Titchener, 1896, p. 33)

An introspective report should be formulated and given only *after* the original experience has gone, so as not to disturb the natural course of the experience. "Introspective examination must be a *post mortem* examination" (p. 34), as Titchener put it.

The introspective report should, however, not simply describe the experience as such. This kind of descriptive introspection would not yet give us the elements of consciousness. In order to get at the elements, *analytic introspection* should be applied, which decomposes the experience into its simplest parts. A contemporary of Titchener, Oswald Külpe, described analytic introspection in this way:

> We must first of all subject the whole of conscious content to an exact analysis, and determine the ultimate elements of which it is composed ... The only analogous elements in natural science are those of chemistry ... And just as the chemical element is a certain substance that resists further analysis, so are the simple contents of psychology experiences in which no parts are further distinguishable.
>
> (Külpe, 1895, p. 19)

In laboratory experiments conducted by the structuralists, Fechner's psychophysical principles were applied. Thus, to study how many different elementary colour sensations there are, two entirely similar spectra of colours were thrown on the wall. They were observed through two narrow slits. The observer's task is to take a look at a colour in the first specturm and then move the second slit across the second spectrum to find an indistinguishable colour and then a minimally different colour. Every "just different" colour is a conscious element. Titchener estimated that we have about 700 + 150 + 30,000 qualities of visual sensation: 700 just different degrees of lightness between black and white, 150 just different spectral colours and about 30,000 just different combinations of colour and lightness.

This, in a nutshell, was the research programme of structuralism. It had several strengths: Structuralism attempted to connect psychology to the natural sciences both metaphysically and methodologically. The metaphysical idea of atomism was directly inspired by chemistry and physics. The methodological laboratory approach was directly inspired by the natural sciences (Titchener, 1896, p. 35): "The psychological experiment does not differ in any essential respect from the experiments of the other sciences – physics, physiology, etc."

Thus, psychology as the science of consciousness tried to be as objective and as scientific as possible, given that its object of study was the conscious mind that could not be sampled or measured directly or publicly. Yet, Titchener was convinced that the difference between psychology and the other sciences was only minor. The results of the psychological experiments were in principle replicable in other observers and in other laboratories, so everyone could in principle check the results by himself – the results were, if not public, at least intersubjectively verifiable.

Still, structuralism did not lead to converging results from different laboratories. Two grave disagreements between different laboratories (Titchener's and Külpe's) in particular hinted at some fundamental problems in the methodology of analytic introspection. One debate was over the number of the elements of consciousness. According to Titchener's results there were, altogether, more than 42,415 elements (1896, p. 67). Külpe's laboratory, however, reported a significantly smaller number of elements, around 11,000. Contradictory results are not unusual as such in science – they are the rule rather than the exception. But in this case there seemed to be no way to settle whose results were closer to the truth. There was no independent way to establish whose introspections were flawed and whose were correct. Each laboratory had trained its own subjects to use introspection in a particular way, which probably guaranteed that they perceived, analysed and consequently experienced and reported even the very same stimuli in a different manner.

Another similar quarrel was created around the question of "imageless thought". Külpe's laboratory announced that in experiments where the task required problem solving and where the goal was to observe thought processes directly as they happened, the subjects reported some sort of thought-like experiences that involved no concrete images (words, pictures) whatsoever. This was in direct conflict with Titchener's (and Wundt's) theory, according to which the contents of consciousness necessarily involve images of some sort: Imageless thought is an impossibility. Again, it was hopeless to try to resolve the quarrel through further experiments. Titchener's subjects reported, when replicating the experiment, that they did not have any imageless thoughts, whereas Külpe's subjects continued to report such things. The experiment itself was likely to invoke what we would today regard as unconscious cognitive processing, but in those days the mind was equated with consciousness. Outside the sphere of consciousness there could not be any mind or mental process, only physiological, non-mental processes. Therefore, an unconscious but mental process was inconceivable for Titchener and Wundt, because it was in direct conflict with their deepest philosophical background assumptions concerning what the mind is and what it is not.

These internal disagreements were among the most important reasons for the downfall of introspectionism. At least as important were the attacks from the outside, from new, rising research programmes within psychology. They ranged from approaches that considered psychology as the science of consciousness but did not share the atomistic view of the mind that was so essential to structuralism, to approaches that totally discarded consciousness.

William James and the stream of consciousness

While Wundt represented a strictly German approach to the study of the mind, Titchener was his leading disciple in the Anglo-American world. William James (1842–1910), however, has become the most prominent figure in the history of intro-spectionist psychology. James is regarded as the grandfather of modern conscious-ness studies. His classical work, the two-volume *Principles of psychology* (1890/1950), is still among the best works, if not *the* best, on consciousness that has ever been written by any scientist or philosopher.

William James' views about psychology as the science of "Mental Life" were importantly different from those of Wundt and Titchener. James disliked at least two aspects of the Wundt–Titchener approach: its reliance on endless, painstaking experimentation in the laboratory and its atomistic view of consciousness. James was well aware of Wundt's work and had visited his laboratory, but did not find that kind of mechanistic laboratory psychology of consciousness appealing:

> Within a few years what one may call a microscopic psychology has arisen in Germany, carried on by experimental methods, asking of course every moment for introspective data ... This method taxes patience to the utmost, and could hardly have arisen in a country whose natives could be *bored*.
>
> (James, 1890/1950, Vol. 1, p. 192)

James emphasized the worth of integrative theory over detailed laboratory experimentation; he thus regarded the theoretical fruits delivered by the laboratory approach as meagre. Furthermore, James opposed the atomistic view of conscious-ness that was embedded in the German approach to psychology and was even more pronounced in British Associationism, held by famous British philosophers such as David Hume and John Stuart Mill. Titchener's structuralism was the combination of these two atomistic traditions and therefore was directly opposed to the Jamesian view. James criticized the view that psychology should start with sensations, the simplest mental facts for both associationism and structuralism. James argued that such things as "simple sensations" do not exist:

> No one ever had a simple sensation by itself. Consciousness, from our natal day, is of a teeming multiplicity of objects and relations, and what we call simple sensations are results of discriminative attention, pushed often to a very high degree.
>
> (James, 1890/1950, Vol. 1, p. 224)

For James, consciousness is a holistic, dynamic, ever-changing stream of experience. James used the word "thought", as in "stream of thought", but by "thinking" he meant "consciousness": "*I use the word thinking . . . for every form of consciousness indiscriminately*" (Vol. 1, p. 224).

> Consciousness, then, does not appear to itself chopped up in bits. Such words as "chain" or "train" do not describe it fitly as it presents itself in the first instance. It is nothing jointed; it flows. A "river" or a "stream" are the metaphors by which it is most naturally described. *In talking of it hereafter, let us call it the stream of thought, of consciousness, or of subjective life.*
>
> (James, 1890/1950, Vol. 1, p. 239)

The stream of subjective life shows, however, some sort of internal structure. But its structure is not that of a fixed compound built out of elementary atoms, but a dynamically flowing structure where clear images appear at the centre of attention, always surrounded by a more vague background that colours the experience with a myriad of echoes from past experiences, relations to memories and other present experiences, and future expectations.

> Every definite image in the mind is steeped and dyed in the free water that flows round it. With it goes the sense of its relations, near and remote, the dying echo of whence it came to us, the dawning sense of whither it is to lead. The significance, the value, of the image is all in this halo or penumbra that surrounds and escorts it, – or rather that is fused into one with it . . .
>
> (James, 1890/1950, Vol. 1, p. 255)

For James, the existence of states of consciousness is the most fundamental fact for the science of psychology, a fact that cannot be doubted. The method of investigation for studying these facts scientifically is introspective observation:

> *Introspective Observation is what we have to rely on first and foremost and always.* The word introspection need hardly be defined – it means of course the looking into our own minds and reporting what we there discover. *Every one agrees that we there discover states of consciousness.*
>
> (James, 1890/1950, Vol. 1, p. 185)

William James was thus a representative of the introspectionist era in the history of psychology, but his background assumptions about consciousness and mind were very different from the then-dominating structuralism. In some sense, James' views about consciousness and his critique of atomism make him an ally to Gestalt psychology, a German school of psychological thought that seemed to become the next big thing in German psychology after Wundt.

2.3 The fall of introspectionism as a science of consciousness

The heyday of introspectionism was reached around the early years of the 20th century, when all the leaders of this era, Wundt, Titchener and James, reached the peaks of their careers and dominated psychology in Europe and America. But a turn of the tides was just around the corner: In Germany, a new movement called Gestalt psychology arose, opposing especially Wundt's and Titchener's structuralism. Furthermore, outside experimental laboratory psychology, Freud's view of the mind as essentially unconscious in nature started to gain foothold all over the place. In America, behaviourism called into question the scientific and philosophical basis of the introspectionist approach to psychology in general.

Gestalt psychology: Consciousness is holistic, not atomistic

Gestalt psychology was founded by three Germans whose names became identified with the approach: Max Wertheimer, Kurt Koffka and Wolfgang Köhler. This approach grew in the 1910s and 1920s to a significant position in Germany. But unfortunately politics interfered with the further development of German psychology and science. In 1933 all Jews working in German universities were expelled, and the remaining professors were soon required to start their lectures with a Nazi greeting. Thus, by 1935 the leaders of the Gestalt psychology movement had escaped from Nazi Germany to America, where they never gained the same kind of leading position in the academic world as they had held in Germany. In the USA Gestalt psychology persisted under the shadow of behaviourism up to the 1960s when the last surviving member of the three founders, Wolfgang Köhler, died.

Gestalt psychology criticized structuralism for its atomistic view of consciousness and argued for a holistic conception. Consciousness, the world of subjective experience, is also for the Gestalt psychologists the primary reality that the science of psychology is supposed to investigate. But this reality is not built up from tiny, localized pieces of simple sensations by combining them like pieces of a mosaic. The way that localized sensations are experienced in fact depends on the entire surrounding context. The smaller parts thus depend on the whole, rather than the whole being built up out of independent localized atoms of sensation. Gestalt psychology thus rejects the "mosaic hypothesis" of introspectionism:

> The most fundamental assumption of Introspectionism is therefore this: true sensory facts are local phenomena which depend upon local stimulation, but not at all upon stimulating conditions in their environment.
>
> (Köhler, 1947, p. 95)

> ... "sensory experience in a given place depends not only on the stimuli corresponding to this place, but also on the stimulating conditions in the environment ... this is the view held by Gestalt Psychology".
>
> (Köhler, 1947, p. 93)

Gestalt psychology also criticized introspectionist methodology, analytic introspection, as an unnatural and artificial way of relating to our psychological reality, leading to a sterile and isolated science of psychology that does not study the psychological reality where people in fact live their lives:

> Thus, if his [the introspectionist's] attitude were to prevail, such experiences as

form the matrix of our whole life would never be seriously studied. Psychology would observe and discuss only such experiences as are, to most of us, forever hidden under the cover of merely acquired characteristics. Even the best Introspectionist is not aware of his true sensory facts unless he assumes his special attitude, which – fortunately for him – he drops when leaving the psychological laboratory. So far removed from common experience is his true sensory world that, if we should ever learn its laws, all of them together would not lead us back to the world we actually live in.

(Köhler, 1947, p. 85)

In modern psychological vocabulary, this argument criticizes the *low ecological validity* of the introspectionist research programme because the laboratory results seemed to have little meaning for or application to everyday life.

For Gestalt psychology the psychological reality to be studied is the natural sensory-perceptual world that is directly present for us as a unitary whole. The consciousness to be studied by psychology is the everyday holistic perceptual world we see all around us, not a set of elementary sensations hidden deep somewhere behind the everyday perceptions and only uncovered through painstaking experimental procedures and analysis in the psychological laboratory.

According to the Gestalt view of perception, patterns of stimulation give rise to complex holistic experiences in the unitary field of consciousness. We see holistic objects in the perceptual field around us and we see our own body in the centre of the field. All the contents of our experience, including our own body, are phenomenal objects in consciousness, not the real physical objects somehow directly perceived, as we take them in our everyday thinking:

Our view will be that, instead of reacting to local stimuli by local and mutually independent events, the organism responds to patterns of stimuli to which it is exposed; and that this answer is a unitary process, a functional whole, which gives, in experience, a sensory scene rather than a mosaic of local sensations.

(Köhler, 1947, p. 103)

... "my body", before which and outside of which the phenomenal objects are perceived, is itself such a phenomenal object along with others, in the same phenomenal space, and that under no circumstances may it be identified with the organism as the physical object which is investigated by the natural sciences, anatomy and physiology.

(Köhler, 1929/1971, p. 130)

The dynamically structured unified field of consciousness corresponds to the accompanying brain events: "Experienced order in space is always structurally identical with a functional order in the distribution of underlying brain processes ... Units in experience go with functional units in the underlying physiological processes" (Köhler, 1947, pp. 61–63).

This is the famous *principle of psychophysical isomorphism*, the mind–brain theory held by the Gestalt psychologists. According to this principle, the structure of conscious perceptual experience is directly (isomorphically) mapped into some physiological process in the brain. The field of phenomenal consciousness is based on (or perhaps identical to) a holistic electrical field in the brain:

> Under no circumstances has the phenomenal object anything to do with the place in physical space where the "corresponding" physical object is located. If it has to be localized at all at some point in physical space, then obviously it belongs most properly to that place in the brain where the directly corresponding physiological process takes place.
>
> (Köhler, 1929/1971, p. 128)

Although Gestalt psychology rejected the atomistic view of consciousness held by structuralism, they shared with Wundt and Titchener the conviction that psychology is the science of the conscious mind. It is the task of psychology to reveal the principles and laws that the conscious mind follows and to connect the conscious mind to the underlying physiological reality, the brain. By contrast, behaviourism, which replaced both introspectionism and Gestalt psychology, rejected the conscious mind altogether.

Behaviourism: How consciousness became taboo in scientific psychology

The leading approach in experimental psychology from the 1920s to the 1950s was behaviourism. Its founder, John B. Watson (1878–1958), attacked introspectionism for the first time in 1913 in a famous paper where he argued that consciousness cannot be an object of study in a scientific psychology. Watson's idea of science was based on two views about the nature of science called positivism and empiricism. According to these philosophical ideologies, science should be based only on the directly and publicly observable. Theoretical concepts that refer to unobservable entities cannot be allowed. No metaphysical speculations can be allowed either. Consciousness or subjective experience cannot be publicly observed and it cannot be understood in purely physical terms, therefore it cannot be a part of any science. Talk about consciousness and subjective experience in psychology is no better than the obscurantist talk about "soul" in philosophy. Both "consciousness" and "soul" are beyond all scientific measurement; they remain mere metaphysical speculations. Thus, psychology should, according to Watson, discard all reference to consciousness and reject all psychological concepts (such as sensation, perception, volition, desire, thought, emotion) that have a subjective component to them. In this way, psychology could finally become as objective as the natural sciences.

Watson also criticized introspectionist psychology for its methodological weakness and for the impossibility of studying animals or small children because they cannot deliver introspective verbal reports about the contents of their minds. Therefore, psychology should only study the objectively observable behaviour of organisms, whether animal or human, and the correlations that exist between objective physical stimuli and objective physical behaviour of organisms (see Figure 2.1). Psychology does not study what is going on *inside* the organisms – whatever there is, such things simply go outside the scope of psychology. There are two ways in

Stimulus   Organism: Behaviour
                                 The black box

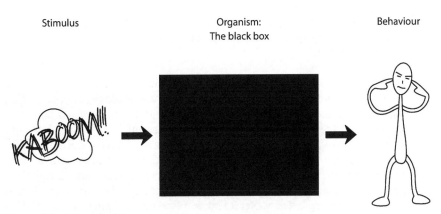

Figure 2.1 Behaviourism

The mind and the brain of the behaving organism are of no interest or relevance to behaviourism. The behaving human or animal is treated as a black box whose insides are not studied by
psychology. Psychology is the science of the externally observable behaviour, especially about
the relationships between the objective physical stimuli and the consequent behaviour

which the inside of the organism might be studied, but neither of them is a part of
psychology. First, the researcher can open up the skull of the organism and make
observations of the anatomy and physiology of the brain. But that kind of investigation concerns purely biological, physiological facts – whatever we might find in the
brain, it is no concern of the science of psychology. Second, the researcher can turn to
his internal subjective experiences. But as introspection is unreliable and states of
consciousness not publicly observable, saying anything about them is, again, of no
concern to scientific psychology. At most, it might amount to speculative metaphysics,
but that is not psychology – it is not even science!

We will not go any deeper into behaviourism in this book. It is sufficient to
know that behaviourists categorically rejected consciousness and mind from scientific psychology; according to them, psychology is the science of behaviour, not the
science of the mind, and certainly not the science of our subjective conscious life. It
is not entirely clear whether behaviourists believed that consciousness does not
exist at all or only that its existence is of no relevance to scientific psychology. Be
that as it may, it is largely due to the legacy of behaviourism that there was
virtually no serious research on consciousness going on in psychology until the late
1980s. "Consciousness" and "introspection" became widely dreaded taboos in
psychology, and this pitiful attitude to consciousness by and large was hanging
around at psychology departments long after behaviourism had withered and its
successor, cognitive science, had taken its place as the dominating approach in
psychology.

Psychology as a science of consciousness thus largely originated in the German
academia, beginning with Fechner and Wundt and continuing to Gestalt psychology.
The American approach (apart from William James), from behaviourism to functionalism and cognitive science, redefined psychology and removed consciousness from
its scope. Kurt Koffka, one of the fathers of Gestalt psychology who moved from

Germany to the USA, reflected that the intellectual climate was very different in these two countries, the German approach being more philosophical and the American approach more practical:

> There can be no doubt that the intellectual climates of Germany and the United States are widely different ... In America, the climate is chiefly practical; the here and now, the immediate present with its needs, holds the centre of the stage, thereby relegating the problems essential to German mentality to the realm of the useless and nonexisting. In science this attitude makes for positivism, an overvaluation of mere facts and an undervaluation of very abstract speculations, a high regard for science, accurate and earthbound, and an aversion, sometimes bordering on contempt, for metaphysics that tries to escape from the welter of mere facts into a loftier realm of ideas and ideals.
>
> (Koffka, 1935, p. 18)

It is fascinating to speculate on how the history of psychology would have looked, and in particular what the fate of the psychology of consciousness would have been, had the original German approach to consciousness not been largely demolished and forgotten due to the political and historical turmoil that eventually led to the Second World War.

Freud's critique of consciousness

So far we have focused on the history of consciousness in the context of purely academic psychology. But consciousness was surely discussed also outside the laboratory-based, experimental psychological science. In psychiatry and clinical psychology, the interest was not in the basic sensory-perceptual processes, but in altered states of consciousness such as dreams, hypnosis and states of consciousness relating to mental or neurological disorders. Sigmund Freud (1856–1939) studied these kinds of altered conscious states in his patients, which might at first glance suggest that he must also have contributed to psychology as the science of consciousness. But in fact Freud turned out to contribute greatly to the dismissal of consciousness from psychology. His influential theory of the mind gave consciousness only a minor role, and he openly opposed the introspectionists' idea that the mind is to be equated with the *conscious* mind and the Wundtian idea that the notion of "unconscious mental life" involves a contradiction in terms. Instead, Freud was convinced that the explanation of abnormal mental states or psychopathology could never be done in terms of the purely conscious mind:

> As long as psychology disposed of this problem by the verbal explanation that the "psychic" is the "conscious", and that "unconscious psychic occurrences" are an obvious contradiction, there was no possibility of a physician's observations of abnormal mental states being turned to any psychological account.
>
> (Freud, 1900/1950, p. 461)

By contrast, Freud proposed that the unconscious mental life is the most important and the original form in which the mind exists – consciousness is pure icing on the cake:

> The physician and the philosopher can meet only when both acknowledge that "unconscious psychic processes" is "the appropriate and justified expression for an established fact." The physician cannot but reject, with a shrug of his shoulders, the assertion that "consciousness is the indispensable quality of the psychic" ... the unconscious must be accepted as the general basis of the psychic life. The unconscious is the larger circle which includes the smaller circle of the conscious; everything conscious has a preliminary unconscious stage, whereas the unconscious can stop at this stage, and yet claim to be considered a full psychic function.
>
> (Freud, 1900/1950, pp. 462–463)

Furthermore, the method of introspection cannot be used to probe the depths of the unconscious mind: it is an *unobservable* for the subject himself whose mind it constitutes! Its existence and characteristics can only be inferred through associations, behaviours, dreams and other indirect expressions by an external observer, the physician:

> For a single intelligent observation of the psychic life of a neurotic, a single analysis of a dream, must force upon him the unshakable conviction that the most complicated and the most accurate operations of thought, to which the name of psychic occurrences can surely not be refused, may take place without arousing consciousness ... The physician must reserve himself the right to penetrate, by a process of deduction, from the effect on consciousness to the unconscious psychic process.
>
> (Freud, 1900/1950, p. 462)

The unconscious mind has a two-level structure:

> There are two kinds of unconscious. Both are unconscious in the psychological sense; but in our sense the first, which we call Unconscious, is likewise incapable of consciousness; whereas the second we call Preconscious because its excitations, after the observance of certain rules, are capable of reaching consciousness ... We described the relations of the two systems to each other and to consciousness by saying that the system Preconscious is like a screen between the system Unconscious and consciousness.
>
> (Freud, 1900/1950, p. 465)

What of consciousness, then? In Freud's theory, it was viewed as a relatively uninteresting internal sensory mechanism that merely registers experiential qualities: "What role is now left, in our representation of things, to the phenomenon of consciousness, once so all-powerful and overshadowing all else? None other than that of a sense-organ for the perception of psychic qualities" (Freud, 1900/1950, p. 465). Freud's theory of the mind served to shift the interest of psychiatrists and clinical psychologists away from consciousness, because the true mental reality was way beyond (or deeply beneath) the superficial conscious mind.

Watson's behaviourism and Freud's psychoanalysis rose quickly to power in their respective fields, in fact almost simultaneously in the 1920s. The last bastion of the original Wundtian introspectionism, represented by Titchener at Cornell University, fell in 1927, as Titchener died from a brain tumour at the age of 60. There were no young, enthusiastic structuralists or introspectionists to continue Titchener's and Wundt's work. Consequently, consciousness had suddenly fallen on truly hard times all over the different branches of psychology. The Great Crash hit consciousness around the same time it hit Wall Street in 1929, but, as we will see, the Great Depression of consciousness lasted up until the 1990s!

2.4 From cognitive science to the science of consciousness

Cognitive science: A science of mind, but devoid of consciousness

The cognitive approach to the study of the mind started to challenge behaviourism in the 1950s, rose to power during the 1960s and 1970s, but gradually weakened and changed after that, although it must be said that in some sense it is still an influential, perhaps even the dominating, paradigm in psychology but nowadays it is merged with a biological approach to the mind in cognitive neuroscience and evolutionary psychology.

Cognitive science rejected the view that psychology should only use terms that refer to publicly observable phenomena of physical stimulation and behaviour. By contrast, theoretical terms that refer to goings-on inside the behaving organism became acceptable once more. Thus, we may say that cognitive science, unlike behaviourism, was a science of the mind or a science of mental processes. Yet, cognitive science was not a science of consciousness nor a science of our subjective mental life. Instead, it was founded on the computer metaphor of the mind. The grand idea behind this was that the mind is just like a computer program, and the mind relates to the brain just like a computer program relates to the computer hardware. Just like computers, minds process and store information, take information as input and, after processing this information internally, produce output (some kind of response or behaviour). The mind in cognitive science was an information-processing system whose internal workings can be described and explained in the same manner as the operation of a computer program.

Thus, a cognitive theory of the mind refers to various stages of information processing that proceed inside the organism from input to output. The processing can be divided into several different functions that proceed sequentially. Each function can be decomposed into a set of sub-functions, which in turn can be decomposed to ever-simpler sub-sub-functions. Finally, all this boils down to a basic level of processing, which in principle is the same in the digital computer and the brain. In the digital computer, logical gates open and close, letting current flow through or not. This is the basis for the machine language that can be expressed in terms of a binary code of "1"s and "0"s. In the brain there are neurons, which were believed to function as kinds of logical gates, too, either firing a neural impulse or not, thus representing a basic binary code of the mind.

In philosophy, these doctrines are known as "computationalism" and "functionalism" (already discussed in Chapter 1, Section 1.3). The view of human beings embedded into the original computer metaphor was that of a mechanistic computer-robot that can behave in an intelligent manner due to the computer program running inside it. There is no stream of subjective life inside this mechanism – or if there is such a thing the cognitive theories remain silent about it. The cognitive mind is not a subjective conscious mind. There is nothing in a cognitive theory of the mind to tell us what kind of information processing becomes a part of consciousness and why.

According to cognitive science, we are nothing more than information-processing zombies. Thus, when it comes to describing and explaining consciousness, cognitive science was only a little better than behaviourism. And when it comes to connecting the mind with the brain, and psychology with the neurosciences, classical cognitive science was of no help either. In its original form, cognitive science regarded neuroscience as largely irrelevant to the study of the mind. According to functionalism, the computer program of the mind (i.e. the information processing that guides the organism's behaviour) can be exhaustively described at an abstract computational level, without ever mentioning the hardware (the physical computer or the biological brain) where the mind-program is running. The same program can run in different machines and is independent of any particular physical instantiation. To describe and explain the mind we should study the internal computational structure of the program, in which the intelligence of the program is embedded. Studying the brain will not tell us anything of interest about the mind.

The treatment that cognitive science gave to subjective consciousness and to brain and neuroscience paved the way to its own downfall. In the late 1980s, the philosophical literature was swarming with arguments to show that functionalism and computationalism cannot explain qualia (for a definition of qualia, see Chapter 3). In other words, that cognitive science cannot explain nor even take consciousness into account. Around the same time, psychologists and neuroscientists started to interact more and more, because it had become possible to see what happens inside the brain while a cognitive operation is going on inside the mind. Neuroscience could now offer the functional imaging tools to empirically connect mental phenomena to brain physiology. Thus, the doctrine that the mind could be understood without knowing anything about the brain was discarded, and *cognitive neuroscience* emerged. Its mission was to connect the mental levels of reality with the biological levels of reality. In cognitive neuroscience even aspects of the mind such as emotions and consciousness that were ignored in traditional cognitive science were now taken very seriously.

Phoenix rising: Emergence of the modern science of consciousness

The phoenix is a mythical bird that supposedly burned itself on a funeral pyre and rose from the ashes with renewed youth. The same pattern seems to apply to the psychological science of consciousness: burned to ashes in the first half of the 20th century, but rising with renewed vigour before the century was over. The ashes started to show signs of life already in the 1970s, but what rose from the ashes was not a bird, but a bat!

Without doubt, the most important paper in the modern history of consciousness studies was published in 1974 by the philosopher Thomas Nagel (remember the "bat" guy from Chapter 1, Section 1.4?). In his paper entitled "What is it like to be a bat?" Nagel showed, first, that the concurrent popular solutions to the mind–body problem have all failed and, second, that the reason for their failure is the problem of consciousness. Furthermore, he formulated the problem anew, in a way that captured the core idea so vividly that it could not be ignored any longer. According to his formulation, the problem of consciousness is the problem of describing and explaining the subjectivity of consciousness: what it feels like to *be* a conscious biological organism, what life is like *for* it, as experienced from its subjective point of view. Nagel came to the pessimistic conclusion that the facts describing consciousness are facts that cannot be captured by human concepts. Thus, the problem of consciousness might be inexplicable in the context of science.

Nagel's paper caused a growing uproar among philosophers, especially among those who had firmly believed that the dominating philosophical doctrines, such as functionalism and reductionism, are perfectly capable of explaining the mind. But other arguments soon followed, especially those that were targeted against functionalism and thereby against the basis of cognitive science, the computer metaphor of the mind. The general outline of these arguments was to take a complex computational system that is fully described and explained by functionalism and let it be so complex that it is capable of the same information-processing functions as a real human being. According to functionalism, such an artificial system should equal the human mind in every respect because it is functionally equivalent to a human mind and functions are the essence of mind. Now, the critics continued, these functionally equivalent systems do not seem to have any consciousness whatsoever. They are mere nonconscious robots or zombies. Therefore, consciousness – the subjective feelings, the qualities of experience – presented a severe problem for functionalism and showed that it cannot be the whole story or the correct story about how the mind works.

Another direction from which the problem of consciousness started to emerge to the awareness of scientists and philosophers was neuropsychology. First, there were the surprising studies on the *split-brain operation* in the 1970s. When the two cerebral hemispheres of epilepsy patients had been surgically separated from each other to treat the epilepsy, it appeared that after the operation each hemisphere had a consciousness of its own, isolated from any direct contact with the consciousness in the other hemisphere. These puzzling results triggered much debate and speculation about the nature of consciousness and self and their relation to the brain.

In the 1970s and 1980s, neuropsychologists discovered several new phenomena that again brought the problem of consciousness to the surface. *Blindsight* or visual perception without subjective visual experience is the most notable and surprising of them. When a neurological patient has suffered damage in the primary visual cortex, then he or she is blind in the region of the visual field that corresponds to the damaged area in the brain. The subject sees absolutely nothing there. Yet, the surprise was that when such patients were forced to guess (by pointing with their finger) where the invisible stimulus might be or how it might be moving across the blind visual field, their guesses were surprisingly accurate. Clearly, the pointing movement of the hand was guided by the visual information from the stimulus, but somehow that information seemed to bypass consciousness altogether. A similar phenomenon was found in neuropsychological patients with face recognition difficulties. Although the patients could not recognize any faces as familiar – the faces of friends, family members and celebrities look to them like faces they have never seen before – some measurable indirect reactions (such as galvanic skin responses, reaction times, EEG responses) showed that at some nonconscious level their brain still recognized the familiar faces and treated them differently from the unfamiliar ones. This phenomenon was called implicit (or covert) face recognition. Again, this pattern suggested that only the conscious level of information processing was damaged by the brain lesion, but that the nonconscious processing of the same information was intact. The neuropsychologists who studied these phenomena realized that they had struck on something that requires an explanation in terms of consciousness and a theory that describes the differences between nonconscious and conscious information processing in the brain. The philosophers who heard about these phenomena realized that the problem of consciousness cannot be solved just by sitting in the armchair and thinking about it – one has to be informed about all the relevant empirical facts and the new counter-intuitive neuropsychological findings as well. (For more about blindsight and other neuropsychological deficits of consciousness, see Chapters 4–6.)

Gradually, consciousness became the central topic of cross-disciplinary discussion. Books entirely devoted to the problem of consciousness started to appear, written by cognitive scientists, psychologists, philosophers, neuroscientists and, more and more, by people from different fields interacting with each other. Among the early books that served to define the new field of consciousness research were the following. In 1987, the cognitive scientist Ray Jackendoff published a book called *Consciousness and the computational mind*. It was an attempt to find a place for consciousness in a computational theory of the mind. In 1988, two extremely important books were published: Bernard J. Baars' book called *A cognitive theory of consciousness* and the anthology edited by Anthony Marcel and Eduardo Bisiach called *Consciousness in contemporary science*. The former drew together a lot of material from the cognitive sciences and also from neuroscience to outline the global workspace theory, a theory that explains what kind of cognitive system consciousness is and what type of information it processes. (For more on this theory, see Chapter 11 on theories of consciousness.) The latter book contained contributions from a variety of leading philosophers and researchers. The editors commented: *"Perhaps the hub of this book . . . is whether consciousness provides a problem for functionalism"* (Marcel & Bisiach, 1988, p. 6). Indeed, at that time it was the rapidly growing worry among many that the cognitive approach was turning out to be inadequate to solve the problem of consciousness.

The next wave of important books on consciousness was contributed by the philosophers Daniel Dennett (*Consciousness explained*, 1991), Colin McGinn (*The problem of consciousness*, 1991), Owen Flanagan (*Consciousness reconsidered*, 1992) and John Searle (*The rediscovery of the mind*, 1992). These philosophers represented rather different approaches to the problem, which made it clear that we are nowhere near a grand unified theory of consciousness. They, however, took into account the results of the empirical sciences and attempted to give philosophical interpretations to them and to find a place for consciousness in the scientific world-view. Furthermore, the influential neuroscientists Francis Crick and Christof Koch published a famous paper in 1990, arguing that the time was now ripe for neuroscience to attack the problem of consciousness. In psychology, the first modern textbook explicitly about the psychology of consciousness (Farthing, 1992) was published. The stage was thus set for the emergence of the science of consciousness.

The emergence of the new field cannot be timed with precision, but we may say that before 1990 no field called "consciousness studies" or "science of consciousness" existed but after 1995 such a field was already there. Crucial landmarks for the emergence of this field were the new peer-reviewed academic journals *Consciousness and Cognition* (launched 1992) and *Journal of Consciousness Studies* (launched 1994). Also, international conferences centring on consciousness were organized: the famous "Toward a Science of Consciousness" conferences in Tucson, Arizona, started in 1994 and have been going on biannually. The Association for the Scientific Study of Consciousness (ASSC) organized its first meeting in Claremont, California, in 1997 and annual meetings have been arranged ever since. Clearly, the new field had been formed and became organized by the turn of the millennium.

Although the science of consciousness is connected to a number of fields, it is perhaps most tightly connected to another new field that emerged almost simultaneously with it: cognitive neuroscience. This field tries to connect the psychological (or cognitive) reality to the biological reality – thus it is an attempt to get rid of another weakness of classical cognitive science, its neglect of neuroscience and the brain. The science of consciousness takes seriously the subjective phenomenal experience that cognitive science and functionalism were incapable of explaining, and cognitive neuroscience takes seriously the neural and biological basis of the mind, which cognitive science regarded as of little relevance for explaining how the mind works. Thus, by the 1990s the approach of classical cognitive science, based on functionalism and the computer metaphor of the mind, had been largely abandoned. The mind–body problem and the problem of consciousness had returned.

Around the turn of the millennium, consciousness and its relation to the brain was widely recognized as one of the biggest challenges – perhaps the deepest remaining true mystery – for science to unravel. Unlike behaviourism or cognitive science, the new wave of cognitive neuroscience and consciousness studies did not start out by first putting forward a definite philosophical view of what the mind must be like or what is allowed and what is not allowed to study, but were rather driven by more practical motivations. During the 1990s it had become possible to "see" into the living, conscious human brain by using functional brain imaging. This caused great excitement among neuroscientists and psychologists, and everyone wanted to see where the "seat of the soul" is in the brain or what happens in the brain when this or that happens in the mind. The philosophical worries were put to one side for a moment, and at least the empirical scientists simply wanted to check how far we can go by using this fancy new neuroimaging equipment. Words of warning, however, were issued from the philosophers' camp. Some said that neuroscience can never solve the problem of consciousness, others stated that consciousness is not located in the brain and therefore cannot be found there and others claimed that consciousness is to be explained at its own purely phenomenological level and neuroscience need not be involved.

Empirical neuroscientists took a straightforward empirical approach to the problem. They started to search for the neural correlates of consciousness and decided to worry about the philosophical issues later, if any remain. This is more or less the situation at this writing (June 2009): The empirical research proceeds rapidly, and the philosophers continue to quarrel over what exactly the results mean for the explanation of consciousness. Many exciting discoveries have been made, yet more await to be made. The problem, the mystery, is as deep as it ever was, but now at least almost everyone is willing to work on it.

Chapter summary

The history of the scientific study of consciousness is closely related to the history of experimental psychology. Experimental psychology started out in the late 1800s as the science of the conscious mind, with Fechner's psychophysics, Wundt's laboratory psychology, Titchener's analytic introspection as the method for consciousness science and structuralism as the doctrine about the nature of consciousness, William James' brilliant writings about consciousness and Gestalt psychologists' holistic views about perceptual consciousness as an electrical field in the brain. In the 1920s, experimental psychology made a radical turn towards behaviourism and rejected consciousness, whereas clinical psychology and psychiatry became totally enchanted by the Freudian unconscious mind, belittling the role of consciousness. Cognitive science and functionalism replaced behaviourism in the 1960s, but consciousness remained a taboo in psychology. In the late 1980s, consciousness started to make a comeback, and together with the rise of cognitive neuroscience the 1990s, saw the sudden emergence of the modern science of consciousness.

Further reading

Baars, B. J. (2003). The double life of B. F. Skinner: Inner conflict, dissociation and the taboo against consciousness. *Journal of Consciousness Studies, 10*, 5–25.

Finger, S. (1994). *Origins of neuroscience*. New York: Oxford University Press.

Freud, S. (1950). *The interpretation of dreams* (A. A. Brill, Trans.). New York: Random House. (Original work published 1900.)

Güzeldere, G. (1997). The many faces of consciousness: A field guide. In N. Block, O. Flanagan, & G. Güzeldere (Eds.), *The nature of consciousness: Philosophical debates* (pp. 1–67). Cambridge, MA: MIT Press.

Hothersall, D. (2004). *History of psychology* (4th ed.). New York: McGraw-Hill.

James, W. (1950). *The principles of psychology* (Vols. 1 and 2). New York: Dover. (Original work published 1890.)

Koffka, K. (1935). *Principles of Gestalt psychology*. New York: Harcourt, Brace & Co.

Köhler, W. (1947). *Gestalt psychology*. New York: Liveright.

Külpe, O. (1895). *Outlines of psychology*. New York: Macmillan.

Leahey, T. H. (1980). *A history of psychology*. Englewood Cliffs, NJ: Prentice-Hall.

Marcel, A. J., & Bisiach, E. (Eds.) (1988). *Consciousness in contemporary science*. Oxford: Oxford University Press.

Schwitzgebel, E. (2004). Introspective training apprehensively defended: Reflections on Titchener's lab manual. *Journal of Consciousness Studies, 11*, 58–76.

Titchener, E. B. (1896). *An outline of psychology*. New York: Macmillan.

Brief discussion questions

1   What does the history presented in this chapter tell us about the nature of scientific psychology? How should we define psychology? Is it the science of the mind, the science of behaviour, the science of cognition, the science of the brain, the science of consciousness or a combination of some of the above?

2   Introspection was discredited as unscientific by behaviourists and it still has a scientifically questionable reputation. Discuss what were the scientific strengths and weaknesses of introspectionism as a historical movement in psychology, and introspection as a data collection method in psychology. Should introspective methods be used in psychological science or not? If yes, how can they be used to guarantee good quality of data?

3   Have we learnt anything from history? Have psychology and related fields made progress so that our current approaches in the study of the mind and consciousness are in some sense better and on a firmer basis than the historical approaches were? Or should we expect radical turns of the tide again?

4   Do your own introspective experiment: Stare at a source of bright white light for a few moments (window, light bulb, etc.) and then close your eyes and pay attention to the colours of the after-images you see. What colours do you see? This phenomenon is called the Flight of Colours, and it was used in Titchener's laboratory to train introspective observers (Schwitzgebel, 2004). Unfortunately Titchener was quite clear that, to be a worthy laboratory introspectionist, the subject should report seeing a particular sequence of colours in the after-image (blue-green-yellow-red-blue-green). Untrained observers rarely see this, but observers trained in Titchener's laboratory did. It is unclear whether there really is a fixed sequence of colours or whether the subjects in Titchener's laboratory became biased during training because they knew what they were expected to see.

Chapter 3

The conceptual foundations of consciousness science

Introduction

Each and every branch of science needs its own vocabulary, a set of systematically organized, interconnected concepts that describe the flora and fauna of the relevant part of reality. In this chapter, we will try to figure out how the modern science of consciousness should describe its objects of study and why it has been so difficult to come up with a clear understanding of what "consciousness" refers to in the first place. If consciousness is not the same thing as behaviour or cognition or information processing, then the traditional concepts found in psychology and cognitive science are not sufficient for the science of consciousness. A new vocabulary for the science of consciousness is urgently required.

3.1 How to describe the subjective reality of consciousness

Science is an attempt to build models of the world that faithfully reflect reality and help us humans to systematize and understand what kind of phenomena there are in the world, how they are organized and related to each other and how they work. Reality at large seems to be hierarchically organized, a multilayered but interconnected whole. Thus, we have different kinds of conceptual systems – different branches of science – that are specialized in studying particular layers of the world. There is the purely physical world studied by physics, the chemical world of chemical elements and compounds studied by chemistry, the biological world of living entities investigated by biology, the neural world of the brain studied by neuroscience and, finally, the psychological reality studied by psychology.

The science of consciousness studies the reality of our conscious life – our psychological lives as streams of subjective experiences – and therefore we need a conceptual framework or a model that describes this reality. A science can only be as clear as the basic concepts and definitions it has to offer concerning the basic phenomena in the reality it investigates. The concept of consciousness is notoriously vague and ambiguous. There are many different usages and definitions of the concept of consciousness, especially in everyday language. Unfortunately a similar conceptual confusion has reigned also in the scientific study of consciousness, at least in its initial stages.

But now that the modern scientific study of consciousness has put some effort into defining what consciousness really is, it is possible to characterize the basic concepts needed to describe consciousness in a clear and unambiguous way. Of course, not everyone working in this new field would agree completely with the definitions and characterizations of consciousness presented here. Only time will tell if these are the definitions that will survive as the basic vocabulary of the science of consciousness in the long run. In any case, at this stage the concepts defined below form the very basics of the science of consciousness.

Phenomenal consciousness: The fundamental form of subjectivity

The notion of "phenomenal consciousness" refers to subjective experience as such. To be phenomenal is to be experienced, and to be experienced is to be included in a subjective psychological reality. To be present in a subjective psychological reality is to be something whose existence can be *felt* or *sensed* by the organism. Phenomenality is a property whose mere existence feels like something. But phenomenality is not one thing and the feeling another thing; rather, the existence of the phenomenal event is constituted by its feel. To be phenomenal is to exist as felt. Take away the feel of phenomenality and you take away phenomenality itself. The existence of a phenomenal property makes a difference to *what it is like to be* the subject in whose psychological reality the property appears.

Phenomenal consciousness as a whole contains all the subjective experiences or the "feels" we have at any given moment. Phenomenal consciousness is, at least metaphorically, like a wide field or sphere of experiences that are simultaneously present in the same person's subjective stream of consciousness. It includes sensations of light and darkness, of colours and sounds, of bodily feelings, emotions, desires and volitions, of internal mental images and inner speech passing through our minds. All this taken together delivers to us, at least in our normal waking state, an entire *dynamic sensory-perceptual world* in the centre of which we find our own selves, anchored to our body image. The typical global content of phenomenal consciousness thus takes the form of an *embodied self in a world*, with thoughts and images inside its head and with a first-person's perspective to the surrounding world.

Qualia

Phenomenality is experience, and experience by definition feels like something. What exactly an experience feels like is a matter of the *quality* of experience. Simple sensations have been regarded as the clearest examples of pure qualities of experience. Our phenomenal consciousness is teeming with different phenomenal qualities: blue, green, red; dark and light; pain and itchiness; saltiness and sweetness. One of the best characterizations of this fact was given by the philosopher Leopold Stubenberg (1998) in his book on qualia:

> At every moment of our waking and dreaming lives we are immersed in a sea of colours, sounds, smells, tastes, tickles, pains, and the like. Throughout our lives we are subject to a ceaseless barrage of such qualities. At every moment an abundance of such qualities confronts us. Nothing seems more obvious to me. Nothing seems more mysterious to me.
>
> (p. 18)

> It is in virtue of this fact that it is like something to be me . . . Without my qualia I am, as far as *I* am concerned, dead.
>
> (p. 24)

Philosophers in particular use the notion of "qualia" (singular "quale") to talk about phenomenal consciousness in its simplest, most basic form. Other aspects of the mind, perhaps even other aspects of consciousness, may be explicable by science, but qualia seem to escape physical explanation. And if qualia cannot be explained then neither can phenomenal consciousness, for phenomenal consciousness is nothing but the system in the brain–mind where qualia reside. Or perhaps it is nothing but the global, organized system that is *made up of* qualia. In any case, if there are no qualia, there can be no phenomenal consciousness. If there is no phenomenal consciousness, there is nothing that it is like to be the biological system. Without qualia, life is not like anything at all for the organism – it is dead inside, mentally empty, there is no subjective stream of psychological life within. The waters of the subjective stream of psychological life hence consist of qualia, flowing by in various organized patterns that make up the personal world we live in. When we exist as subjective beings at all, we are indeed immersed in a sea of experiential qualities.

The qualities of experience vary in intensity: The presence of a sound, a colour or a touch can be barely noticeable or extremely strong. They also have a location in our perceptual world: Whenever they occur, sounds, colours, touches and other qualities are felt in particular locations of the perceptual world. And they have duration: they appear in some conscious moment, stay for a while and then disappear from consciousness. Phenomenality thus seems to consist of qualities that appear at some point in perceptual space and time, showing some particular intensity or strength.

The state of being conscious and the specific contents of consciousness

To be conscious is to be in a state that *allows* subjective experiences (Figure 3.1), phenomenal "feels" or qualia to come about in the mind–brain of an organism. To be unconscious is to be in a state that does *not* allow any subjective experiences (Figure 3.2).

Consciousness understood as a *state* should not be confused with the particular *contents* of consciousness. The state that allows subjective experiences is not itself something we experience, rather, it is *a background condition* of the mind–brain that merely *enables* phenomenal consciousness.

The opposite of the state of being conscious is, of course, the state of being *unconscious*. When absolutely no contents of phenomenal consciousness at all can appear in our subjective psychological reality, when phenomenal consciousness is totally removed, then we are in the state of unconsciousness. The state of unconsciousness is not the experience of a subjective psychological vacuum or the experience of a dark black phenomenal space empty of all contents – it is simply *not an experience at all*, not even one of emptyness or blackness. When in this state, there is no subjective psychological reality for us. This nonexperiential state can be brought about by the deepest stages of sleep (NREM stage IV), severe drunkenness, anaesthetic agents used in surgery, epileptic seizures in the brain or serious head and brain injury that lead to coma or to a vegetative state.

Unconsciousness as a state can be defined as *a temporary background condition of the mind–brain that does not allow any subjective experiences to be brought about – there is a (typically) temporary but total absence of qualia*. During moments of unconsciousness, there is nothing that it is like to be the person or the brain that is in this state. Unconsciousness is not the presence of an unconscious experience, but the total absence of all phenomenal "feels"; the subjective stream of experience runs dry

Figure 3.1 Consciousness "on"

Consciousness as a state enables all different kinds of subjective experiences. It can be metaphorically depicted as a state where the internal phenomenal lights of the mind are "on"

Figure 3.2 Consciousness "off"

Unconsciousness as a state disables all subjective experiences. The unconscious state can be metaphorically depicted as a state where the internal phenomenal lights are "off" and consciousness is temporarily absent

and phenomenal consciousness ceases to exist for a moment (see more on the absence of consciousness in Section 3.2).

As opposed to the overall state of being conscious, particular *contents of consciousness* are *specific patterns of qualities that appear in phenomenal consciousness*: the visual experience of roundness and redness caused by a tomato in front of one's eyes; the tactile experience of sharpness caused by touching a needle; the sound caused by dropping a glass on a stone floor; the feeling of happiness or sadness felt in the mind and the body. In Figure 3.3, the contents of consciousness are dominated by a sudden excruciating pain localized in the foot.

The internal structure of phenomenal consciousness: Centre and periphery

At any given moment in our normal waking state, our phenomenal consciousness (also called primary consciousness; Farthing, 1992) is like a wide field or sphere containing a multitude of experiences. The field of phenomenal consciousness

Figure 3.3 Contents of consciousness

Specific conscious experiences, such as a sharp pain localized in a body part, form the particular contents of consciousness. They consist of patterns of qualia or experiential qualities that have intensity, temporal duration and spatial localization within the sphere of primary (phenomenal) consciousness

exhibits an internal centred structure in terms of the intensity, clarity, detail and organization of the qualities of experience. There is a single area in the field that forms the centre of consciousness. In the centre, the phenomenal qualities appear in their clearest form to us, their intensity appears stronger and their structure contains more detail (see Figure 3.4). In the centre of consciousness, different qualities of experience are bound coherently together to form complex spatiotemporal patterns that correspond to perceptual objects. Thus, in the centre of consciousness we may appreciate a multicoloured moving object that has a complex spatiotemporal structure and produces sounds as the object moves around (say, a colourful bird flying by). All these different qualities are coherently bound and kept together in our perceptual field to form a recognizable representation of an object, such as a bird.

Surrounding the centre of consciousness there is peripheral consciousness or the phenomenal background against which the centre is experienced. In the phenomenal background there is a nebulous, dynamic tapestry of more shadowy experiences that merely suggest the presence of various perceptual qualities or objects without representing them explicitly or clearly. The phenomenal background constitutes, as William James would have said, the free waters that flow around all the definite images in the stream of subjective experience. He also pointed out that definite images in consciousness "form but the very smallest part of our minds as they actually

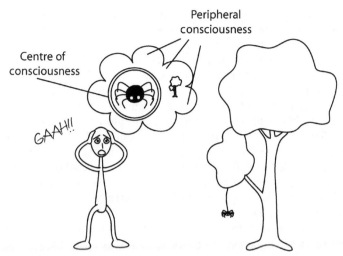

Figure 3.4 Primary consciousness

The sphere of primary (phenomenal) consciousness is divided into the centre of consciousness, surrounded by peripheral consciousness (or the phenomenal background). In the centre, defined by the spotlight of attention, contents have been selected into detailed processing. Consequently, they are experienced vividly and clearly. By contrast, the contents in the periphery are experienced only vaguely. In the figure, the small spider is selected into the centre of consciousness and experienced vividly and clearly, whereas the tree remains in the periphery, experienced only vaguely

live" (1890/1950, Vol. 1, p. 255). The phenomenal background is wide; it contains a multitude of vague images that surround the centre of consciousness both spatially and temporally. Every image is embedded within a spatial context, the background against which the image is experienced. But every definite image in the focus of consciousness also carries with it the dying echo of the immediately preceding images and the arising expectation of the next images to be appreciated: "The present image shoots its perspective far before it, irradiating in advance the regions in which lie the thoughts as yet unborn" (James, 1890/1950, Vol. 1, p. 256).

The borderline between the centre and the periphery is not sharp and may often go unnoticed in our everyday experiences. In everyday life we are usually under the impression that the perceptual world around us is equally clear and detailed everywhere. This, however, is an illusion brought about by the rapid shifts of attention within the field of consciousness.

The spotlight of selective attention is the name for the cognitive mechanism that separates the centre from the background in phenomenal consciousness. Wherever we turn the spotlight of our attention in the sphere of experience, there the nebulous mists of the phenomenal background immediately dissolve and reveal definite images. Therefore, it is impossible to catch the vagueness of the background introspectively, for any attempt to pay special attention to an aspect in the background will turn against itself – the background becomes the foreground and the vague phenomenal halo becomes the precise image. William James compared the paradoxical attempt to observe the vagueness of peripheral consciousness to the attempt to capture a snowflake crystal on a warm palm of the hand to observe more closely the structure of the flake, and also to the hopeless attempt to turn on the light "quickly enough to see how the darkness looks"! (James, 1890/1950, Vol. 1, p. 244).

A modern version of this paradox is known as the *"refrigerator light illusion"*. Whenever you open the refrigerator door the light is always on. But is it also on when the door is closed? If you try to check this by opening the door as quickly as possible, you will end up with the illusion that the light must always be on, even when you are not looking! That is how we end up with the illusion that the contents of consciousness are clear and vivid all over the perceptual field, even when we are not attending to them. It is impossible to see the vagueness of the phenomenal background directly. But in cognitive psychology it has been possible to devise experiments to show how much detail we see in the periphery, which is not terribly much – perceptual objects outside the centre seem to be represented as loose bundles of phenomenal features, bundles that may suggest the size, colour or form of an object but only very imprecisely. But when attention is directed to such vague bundles, they are immediately bound together to form definite images that represent definite objects in the world (Revonsuo, 2006).

In cognitive psychology, experiments on brief visual stimuli illustrate the interplay between phenomenal consciousness and attention. Cognitive psychologists, however, talk about iconic memory in this context rather than of visual consciousness. The concept of "iconic memory" refers to a brief storage of visual information. Its contents are extremely *rich*: it can hold practically complete visual information for a very short time (about 1 s); it holds information about the location, colour, size and shape of visual objects, but it does *not* contain information about the *category* or the *meaning* of the objects; it involves "visible persistence" or a *phenomenal trace* of the stimulus that has already physically disappeared; and its contents *decay rapidly* and only a small part of them can be verbally reported before the contents become fully erased. Yet, for a brief duration, *any* part of the contents is in principle accessible for reporting. Where attention is directed before decay, there the contents can be reported (Palmer, 1999; Sperling, 1960).

Iconic memory has been studied by briefly showing subjects a visual display with rich information (typically, several rows and columns of letters). After the display has disappeared, the subjects are able to report only about four or five letters, although they *claim to have seen all of them*. When a cue indicating the row of letters they should report is given immediately *after* the stimulus has disappeared, the subjects can report letters from *any* row at all. This shows that *all* of the information *was briefly available* for selective attention and report.

These observations suggest that the total contents of iconic memory match the contents of momentary phenomenal consciousness in vision: both consist of a wide field rather than a narrow spotlight. Furthermore, the contents of the reportable part of iconic memory match the contents of selective attention or the centre of consciousness, and thus also the contents of the ensuing reflective consciousness. Most importantly, the experiments establish that *there is more in the phenomenal visual field at any moment than what can be reported or attended to*. The nonreportable contents in the phenomenal background form, nonetheless, a significant portion of the total contents of consciousness as they are phenomenally present for the subject, at least briefly.

Although the results of iconic memory experiments clearly support the distinction between attention and consciousness, the relationship between these two concepts remains fuzzy, even controversial in the current discussions on consciousness (Block, 2007; Lamme, 2003, 2004).

Attention and consciousness

The concept of "attention" is very popular in cognitive psychology and neuroscience. Much research has therefore been done on attention, its different forms and its cognitive and neural mechanisms. By contrast, cognitive scientists have not traditionally used the concept of "consciousness" (or its synonym "awareness") at all, probably because of the lingering taboos of behaviourism and because the computer metaphor and functionalism (the philosophy behind cognitive science) cannot handle subjective experience. Therefore, the concept of attention has sometimes almost replaced the concept of consciousness, and the underlying suggestion is that perhaps consciousness is nothing over and above attention. If that were the case, then no separate concept of consciousness would even be needed, nor would we need a new field that studies consciousness, as there already is a strong cognitive tradition where attention is studied.

Thus, we should state clearly how "attention" and "consciousness" differ from each other and why the study of attention is not automatically the study of consciousness (Koivisto, Kainulainen, & Revonsuo, 2009). Attention refers to the *selection of some information for further, more detailed processing*. Attention *amplifies* some signals and *filters out* others. By contrast, consciousness refers to subjective experience. Now, attentional selection and conscious experience are often correlated – the contents selected by the spotlight of attention typically form the clearest experiences in the centre of consciousness and the objects of further processing in *reflective* consciousness (more about reflective consciousness in a moment).

However, attention and consciousness can also be dissociated from each other. Attentional amplification or filtering of information can take place at levels of sensory information processing that are outside or before consciousness, that is, attention can operate at nonconscious levels of processing in the brain. For example, an emotionally significant word or image can draw attention and cause a larger response in the brain even if it is shown so briefly that it cannot be consciously seen at all.

Conversely, subjective experiences can take place outside the spotlight of attention. In visual perception, the spotlight of focal selective attention operates across the entire visual field of subjective experiences. When you search for a familiar face in a big crowd, the spotlight of attention moves from face to face serially, whereas the entire phenomenal background representing the extent of the crowd consists of more vague phenomenal contents – an unrecognizable visual mass of faces and people – outside the spotlight of selective attention.

The division of phenomenal consciousness to a centre (defined by selective attention) and a periphery (all that remains outside the centre, thus defined by absence of selective attention) implies that there are at least some kinds of less clear phenomenal experiences outside attention. If there were not, the whole notion of peripheral consciousness or the phenomenal background would be senseless.

The periphery of consciousness is, however, covered by another form of attention called *spatial attention*. If the perceptual space where a stimulus falls does not receive any spatial attention at all, then the stimulus (and the whole space) will not enter even peripheral consciousness and will not be experienced at all. As we will see later in the section on neuropsychology (in Chapters 4 and 5), patients whose spatial attention mechanisms in the brain have been damaged lose large parts of perceptual space from consciousness without even realizing that anything is missing. They are unaware of external stimuli and sometimes of their own body parts if the stimuli reside in the neglected space. It seems as if in these patients the field of phenomenal consciousness has become restricted to only one half of the perceptual space, but the patients themselves do not experience anything missing. It is impossible for them to see or conceive of the conscious space that is no longer there and realize that it has been lost.

Change blindness and inattentional blindness

Recent experiments have also cast doubt on whether even normal observers can see anything outside the spotlight of selective attention. The surprising phenomena known as change blindness and inattentional blindness suggest that whatever remains outside the spotlight cannot be seen – or that if it was vaguely experienced in some way, at least it cannot be later recalled or reported.

Imagine that for a couple of seconds or so you briefly see a photograph depicting some complex scenery, say, some people in front of historical buildings and monuments, with trees, flowers and grass in the background. You seem to have a momentary visual experience of the landscape with all its colours and details. After the picture disappears, a bright white background is flashed for a fraction of a second, after which the same picture reappears but you are told that there is some fairly big difference between the first and the second picture. Would you be able to see the difference? Most people believe they would, but in actual fact it is extremely difficult to notice if one tree, building, person, shadow, cloud or some other object has disappeared, shifted its location or been inserted. This astonishing failure to detect even large changes in successive visual displays is called *change blindness* (CB) (Simons & Rensink, 2005).

To notice a change, one has to locate attention *exactly* at the object that is changing. Normally our visual system follows the transient cues that draw attention to the location of change and thus we automatically detect the change. If between the two pictures there is no mask (such as the white flash), then it would be a piece of cake for our visual system to notice the difference. We simply become immediately aware of how a building, person or tree disappears or appears in the picture, because the location of the change reveals itself. But when the location of the change is masked from selective attention, we are just flabbergasted when being told that a large change has occurred in the picture. For us it looks just like the same picture, and it may take several trials before one can finally detect the change. Once one has detected the change, it is difficult *not* to see it every time when the pictures change – now it looks really conspicuous.

Imagine that you are given the following task: A cross is presented briefly on a computer screen and your task is to decide which is longer, the vertical or the horizontal line. You perform this task obediently for a few trials and then after one trial you are unexpectedly asked by the experimenter whether you saw anything *else* appear on the screen during the previous trial. During the last trial, an additional object was displayed somewhere near the cross for several hundreds of milliseconds, but it may well be that when you are asked about it you have no idea that there was anything else there besides the cross itself (Mack & Rock, 1998). This failure to report unexpected stimuli, irrelevant to the primary task but appearing in the same display with the target stimuli, has been called *inattentional blindness* (IB). Depending on the visual and semantic features and the precise location of the unexpected stimulus, IB is found in 25–75% of subjects. IB-like phenomena also occur in more natural visual environments. As the famous experiment *Gorillas in Our Midst* (Simons & Chabris, 1999) shows, when we are intensively focusing our attention on a basketball that is being passed from player to player, we may even fail to notice that someone in a gorilla suit walks across the playing ground!

Furthermore, magicians often utilize inattentional blindness and change blindness in their magic tricks (without actually knowing anything about the science behind those phenomena) when they amaze us by making objects disappear into thin air in front of our very eyes. Now it is possible to show in detail how such tricks manage to fool our perceptual consciousness by misdirecting our attention at the critical moment of the trick elsewhere, thereby making us blind to, say, seeing that the magician in fact drops the "disappearing" object to his lap from the hand we are not currently attending to (Kuhn & Findlay, in press).

How should these surprising failures to report what appear to be clearly visible stimuli (IB) or conspicuous changes in stimuli (CB) be interpreted? There are two conflicting ways to interpret them. The first identifies the contents of consciousness with the contents of the spotlight of selective attention; the second points to failures in visual memory rather than to the poverty of visual phenomenology.

The first interpretation of CB and IB proposes that we are not aware of *anything* beyond the spotlight of focal attention, that is, *there are no visual experiences outside the spotlight of attention*. We are under the refrigerator light illusion – it seems to be always on, but in fact it is always off when we are not looking! Likewise, we are under an illusion that we see (and experience) everything in the visual field all of the time, but in reality we see things only if we attend to them; the things to which we do not attend are not actually seen at all, they are only potentially seen (for a critical analysis of this position, see Tye, 2009).

A less radical variety of this view states that there is the phenomenal background surrounding the spotlight of attention. However, regions of the background that are not currently visited or sampled by attention are only very briefly, roughly and vaguely representing the contents of the corresponding regions of the stimulus field. Thus, if nothing happens in the background stimulus field that would immediately draw the spotlight of attention to itself, the corresponding phenomenal field will not be updated and therefore the new stimulus does not affect the phenomenal background in any way that would allow a recognition of the change to take place.

The relationship between attention and consciousness is rather complex, because there are several types of consciousness and several types of attention. But we could summarize the relationship in the following way: Total lack of spatial attention to a region of perceptual space probably implies total absence of phenomenal consciousness to all stimuli in that region. The paradigm example of this is the neuropsychological syndrome neglect (to be discussed in Chapter 4). Total absence of the spotlight of selective attention from a stimulus implies that the stimulus cannot be selected for further processing in reflective consciousness (see below) and thus cannot be described or reported either. Change blindness and inattentional blindness are incontestable evidence for this.

The phenomenal background in primary consciousness – the vague experiences surrounding the spotlight – thus consists of those stimuli that receive at least some spatial attention but remain outside the spotlight of attention.

Next we will see what happens to the contents in the centre of consciousness, the contents that have been selected for further processing by the spotlight of attention.

Reflective consciousness

The centre of consciousness, defined by where focal selective attention falls or is directed to in the field of consciousness, also functions as a gateway to higher levels of conscious processing. The contents in the centre of consciousness are not only experienced more clearly than the background, but they can also enter into complex cognitive processing that goes on in what is called reflective consciousness.

In reflective consciousness, cognitive operations are carried out that take the images in the centre of phenomenal consciousness as input and allow them to access a wide variety of other cognitive mechanisms. Thus, the phenomenal images can be named, recognized or used to guide behaviour. In everyday language we call the mental phenomena going on in reflective consciousness "thoughts", "judgements", "beliefs", "naming", "conceptualization", "action plans", and so on. Philosophers might say that reflective consciousness takes phenomenal images as input and produces propositional mental contents as output. They are contents that can be expressed by a proposition, or a sentence expressing some state of affairs (such as "X is Y").

This may sound awfully complex and abstract (not to mention boring), but in fact it is something very familiar to us, something that is constantly going on in our minds. Let us take a practical example: Imagine that you bite something that is too hard for your teeth and you feel a sudden sharp pain in your tooth that continues as a dull ache afterwards. As the feeling of pain first emerges, the pain experience immediately finds its way into the centre of consciousness. After a couple of seconds perhaps, your reflective consciousness starts labelling and evaluating the experience in terms of propositional thoughts. The thoughts take the pain experience as their object and reflect upon it, therefore this form of consciousness is called "reflective consciousness".

The propositional thoughts that arise might be along the following lines:

- Autsch, What a pain! I hope I didn't break my tooth . . .
- It feels awful . . . Should I call my dentist or will this go away on its own . . .?
- The tooth must be broken and the nerve exposed or something . . . I will have to get an appointment with my dentist, and quickly!

Here is how reflective consciousness operates, formulating "thoughts about" the experience in phenomenal consciousness:

- Autsch, What a pain! [*Naming or categorizing the experience as "pain"*]
- I hope I didn't break my tooth . . . [*Formulating a possible causal explanation for the experience and expressing a desire that this explanation would not turn out to be true*]
- It feels awful . . . [*Naming and evaluating the quality and intensity of the experience*]
- Should I call my dentist or will this go away on its own . . .? [*Formulating possible future scenarios*]
- The tooth must be broken and the nerve exposed or something . . . [*Categorizing the probable cause of the experience*]
- I will have to get an appointment with my dentist, and quickly! [*Formulating an action plan*]

Thus, reflective consciousness is nothing abstract or unfamiliar – it mostly consists of the "inner speech" that we hear whispering in our "mind's ear" as our own thoughts, silently speaking with our own voice to ourselves (see Figure 3.5).

Reflective consciousness is obviously very different from pure phenomenal consciousness. The wide sphere of pure phenomenal consciousness consists of patterns of qualities that we would call sensations, percepts, emotional experiences and feelings and sensory-perceptual images. All this variety of pure phenomenal experience occurs in complex, ever-changing dynamic patterns across a phenomenal field with a vivid but limited centre that restlessly changes position against a wide phenomenal background.

Reflective consciousness, by contrast, consists mostly of auditory-linguistic images that have a phenomenal surface (i.e. how they feel like in terms of their

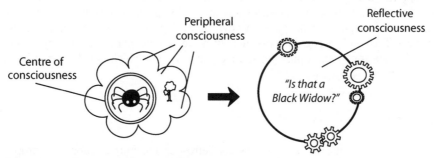

Figure 3.5 Reflective consciousness

The contents in the centre of consciousness (or in the spotlight of attention) are rapidly subjected to higher cognitive processing where the contents can be thought about, named, evaluated, verbally reported or acted upon. Reflective consciousness operates with concepts and language, formulating thoughts about our experiences in silent inner speech. In this case, the reflective thoughts try to evaluate, name and classify the creature that has been consciously perceived, to figure out how dangerous it may be

heard or imaginary auditory qualities) but, more importantly, they also possess *semantic content*: they are propositions, symbolic expressions that refer to things outside of themselves – say, to experiences in phenomenal consciousness. Just like the spotlight of selective attention that picks the contents of phenomenal consciousness for further processing is serial and limited in its capacity (we cannot have several different clear and vivid contents of consciousness in the spotlight at exactly the same time), reflective consciousness also is *serial* and *limited in its capacity* – we cannot formulate several explicit, completely independent trains of thought at the same time. On the other hand, the results or outputs provided by selective attention and reflective consciousness have wide access to our belief systems, our plans and our actions. Thus, the contents of selective attention and reflective consciousness largely determine the overall course and the current goals of our voluntary behaviour. Reflective consciousness has direct access to all voluntary output mechanisms. We can express our beliefs, judgements or action plans in many different ways: verbally, by pointing, by deliberately choosing a particular course of action, and so on.

"Access consciousness" (Block, 2001) is another closely related term that refers to the type of consciousness that is dependent on selective attention and goes beyond pure phenomenal consciousness. The name emphasizes the wide-ranging availability or access of the attended contents of consciousness to other cognitive systems, such as action, long-term memory, planning or verbal report. Reflective consciousness and access consciousness can be regarded as talking about the same, selective-attention-dependent, cognitive stage of consciousness, only emphasizing slightly different aspects of it.

A purely cognitive concept that refers roughly to the same system as "reflective consciousness" is "working memory". Working memory is a cognitive mechanism that contains active information in many forms, such as phonological. Its subsystem, the "central executive", guides selective attention on the basis of voluntary choices and goals. In many respects the functions of working memory match with those of reflective consciousness. However, the concept of "working memory" originates from a cognitive theory of the mind, based on the computer metaphor, and has not been put forward as a theory of consciousness in the first place. Therefore the relation of this cognitive construct to our subjective psychological reality remains somewhat unclear. Textbooks of cognitive psychology, however, contain detailed descriptions of working memory from a purely cognitive point of view, which is not covered in the present book.

Introspection

Reflective consciousness is necessary for introspection. Introspection is a process where we choose to focus our attention on particular contents of phenomenal consciousness and then formulate a verbal report concerning the experience. The essence of introspection could thus be defined in the following way: When we engage in introspection we choose particular contents of phenomenal consciousness and focus our attention on them. We furthermore name or conceptualize (some aspects of) the experience, or formulate a verbal report with the intention of recording or communicating the contents of our experience.

There are three different forms of introspection that should not be confused with each other (Farthing, 1992) but only one of them is a potentially useful method for the scientific study of consciousness:

1 *Analytic introspection.* This is the type of introspection used by Edward Titchener's school called "structuralism" in the history of psychology (see Chapter 2 for details). It is based on an atomistic theory of the structure of consciousness. The goal is to analyse an experience into its simplest phenomenal elements: pure, isolated sensations or qualia. This method led to diverging results from different laboratories and to criticisms against the atomistic view embedded in it. The supposed "atoms" of experience were merely artificial constructions that existed only as a result of the method to investigate them, not independently of them. It has been rejected ever since the days of structuralism (however, painters may still use something like analytic introspection when they need to dissect the patterns of light and colour in a scene and transform them into patterns of oil paints or watercolours on a canvas, to capture the likeness of the visual experience).

2 *Interpretive introspection.* This type of introspection we use naturally every day when we try to interpret or explain our own choices, actions, emotions and other experiences. If we make a choice between different alternatives (say, when choosing between different products in the supermarket) and need to explain our choice (to ourselves or to others), we always come up with a plausible-sounding story that explains why we preferred one alternative over the others. However, empirical observations from both normal healthy subjects and from certain neuropsychological syndromes have made it clear that our plausible-sounding stories are often mere post hoc rationalizations that keep up the appearance, for ourselves as well as for others, that we are in charge and we always know what we are doing and why we are doing it. In reality, our choices may be determined by factors we are completely unaware of, yet, we believe we know why we acted or felt in a certain way. Thus, interpretive introspection does not yield reliable knowledge of the true causes of our actions, and therefore is suspect as a method for studying them. It may give us more information of the mechanisms that construct coherent belief systems for us and keep up a positive self-image by self-justification and by reducing an unpleasant mental state called cognitive dissonance. Pathological cases of *confabulation* are especially illuminating, because they reveal how misguided somebody's beliefs about himself might be and yet how resistant to correction such delusions often are. We will investigate such cases in more detail in the section on disorders of self-awareness (Chapter 6).

3 *Descriptive introspection.* This is the kind of introspection that is still useful as a scientific method. Here, the only task of the subject is to try to describe, with his or her own words and in everyday language, the experiences that are occurring right now (or that just occurred a moment ago) in phenomenal consciousness. The purpose is simply to make a record of and to communicate to others the contents of phenomenal experience in just the way they were experienced.

Descriptive introspection is widely used. The clearest example of its usage is found in dream research where subjects wake up from sleep (or are woken up in a laboratory) and their task is to give a verbal introspective report of the contents of the dream experiences they were having just prior to waking up. At home, the subjects use the *diary method* and write their dreams down, immediately after waking up, in a dream diary. In the laboratory, the subject's dream report is given orally, immediately after waking the subject up from sleep with a sound signal. The oral narrative is recorded. The instructions given to subjects participating in dream research and other introspective tasks underscore that the subject is supposed to report absolutely *everything* that he experienced, *exactly* as he experienced it, without leaving anything out and without adding anything. *The truth, the whole truth and nothing but the truth!*

Introspective reports as scientific data: Can we trust them?

But how sure can we be that we actually *are* getting the truth about the subject's conscious experiences? Descriptive introspection has its problems as a method for gathering data. The first problem is *forgetting*: As the report is formulated only after the experience is gone, on the basis of the memory traces it has left behind, it is in principle possible that parts of the experience were never properly encoded into memory or were already forgotten by the time the report was formulated and therefore were never described in the report. The second problem is *reconstruction*: As the weak, scattered memory images of the dream are called back to consciousness in a disorganized order, the subject might construct a different sequence of events than in the original experience. Third, the subject might fill in the missing gaps by *confabulating* or *inferring* plausible sounding scenarios that make the dream seem more coherent and story-like than it ever was originally. Fourth, even if clearly recalled, the *verbal description* of some experiences might be very difficult or even impossible. There may be some experiences in the dream that are so bizarre or unusual that there are no words in ordinary language to describe them – such experiences are called *ineffable*. Fifth, there is the *creation of artificial experiences through observation*. The intention to observe and the process of observation of one's experiences might change the experiences from what they would have been naturally. The task of reporting one's dreams might actually change one's sleeping patterns or even directly influence the content of dreams, so that the dreams that are experienced and reported are not the same dreams as the same subject would have had that night if not participating in the study at all. If a subject is taken to the laboratory to sleep, the first night in particular is usually not good because the subjects have difficulty falling asleep and many of the dreams are nightmarish anxiety dreams about the laboratory environment (or about the mad scientists in their white coats chasing the dreamer!). Later, when the subjects get used to the environment, they sleep better. Sixth, if the subject knows what the researchers hope or expect to see in the results, this *experimental demand* might work as a *suggestion* to dream more about such things or to report such things in more detail than other things, thus there may be a *bias* in the results to the direction the researchers would like to see. Seventh, some subjects may be inclined to *censor* some of their experiences, especially those of a sexual or violent nature, so as not to embarrass themselves in front of the researchers. This problem may be overcome by guaranteeing total anonymity in the research so that it is not possible to know who has reported which dream (but unfortunately in the sleep laboratory this arrangement is not feasible). Finally, whatever the subjects report, *there is no way in which the accuracy of the reports could be independently checked or verified*. As dream experiences are subjective events in phenomenal consciousness, we cannot objectively measure or record them, nor check how closely the report reflects the real dream – we have to rely on the report alone.

However, we may have more confidence in the results if the same *types* of results occur again and again in data from different subjects and different groups who have reported their dreams without knowing about each other. Thus, although the accuracy of any single dream report might be suspect for any of the reasons mentioned above, the systematic statistical patterns in large amounts of data from different subjects, populations and laboratories probably reflect the overall patterns of experience that tend to occur in people's dreams. It would be rather implausible to claim that none of the experiences reported in tens of thousands of reports actually ever took place and that none of the patterns found in the results are real. As with any other scientific data, dream reports are not 100% accurate – there is always some "noise" that partly obscures the "signal" – but we have no reason to believe that all or most of the reports would be worthless.

When we take these problems carefully into account and try to minimize them, descriptive introspection can be safely used as a method to collect data about the contents of phenomenal consciousness. In fact, descriptive introspection is rather widely used in psychological research. Many kinds of interviews and questionnaires ask about the subject's past or present experiences. The *Experience Sampling Method* is the flagship of modern introspection. It is also known as the "beeper" method. Subjects carry a beeper in their pockets and are beeped at random intervals. Whenever they hear the beep, their task is to give an immediate introspective (or retrospective) report: to describe what was going on in their subjective psychological reality just before they heard the beep. With this method, it has been possible to study how happy people feel in different everyday situations and when they are most likely to experience the state called "flow" – a higher state of consciousness where there is total engagement, absorption and everything else disappears from awareness.

The "thinking-out-loud" method (or direct introspection) uses direct online introspective reporting during a task. For example, the subject is given a problem to solve or is asked to let his or her mind just wander, but anything that happens in consciousness (especially the verbal inner speech in reflective consciousness) should be verbally expressed aloud. The thoughts are recorded and later analysed. The problem with this method is that *having* an experience and *reporting* the experience easily interfere with each other, because it is very difficult to do both at the same time.

Furthermore, even in psychological laboratory experiments, subjects are often instructed to respond on the basis of their subjective experience (sometimes, however, they are instructed to just guess between two alternatives even if they did not see the stimuli – this is called the *forced-choice* task). The researcher presents a stimulus and the subject is supposed to respond to the stimulus, perhaps by reporting how he or she experienced it, if at all. Such responses are usually given by pressing a key on a computer keyboard or mouse. Even though this all seems very objective, the keypresses are equivalent to subjective introspective reports whose propositional content has been fixed beforehand: pushing one key means, say, "I saw something red" whereas pushing another key means "I didn't see anything", and so on. Pressing the key in such cases is based on reflective consciousness and introspection, although experimental psychologists still carefully avoid using these words to describe what is going on in the experiment, because of the heritage of behaviourism that turned such words into taboos in psychology.

Self-awareness

Self-awareness is a special form of reflective consciousness. The following things are necessary for self-awareness:

1   In *phenomenal consciousness*, there must be *a self-related experience*: an experience specifically related to the body image or to other aspects of the person who is having the experiences.

2   In *long-term memory*, there must be a *self-concept* and a *self-representation*. Usually these form a vast memory system called "autobiographical memory", the entire life-history of the person, as remembered by the person himself. Further, self-representation involves semantic or factual knowledge about oneself, such as personality, future plans, social status, physical outlook, and so on.

3   In *reflective consciousness*, the two first components must meet, that is, an experience currently in phenomenal consciousness must become connected to the activated self-representation in long-term memory. When these two components are combined, self-awareness arises in reflective consciousness. When we see an image reflected from the mirror and realize that the image depicts "me", then we are self-aware. The image is seen as located somewhere out there beyond one's own body, yet it is understood that the body seen *out there* in the mirror is actually "my" body, the body of the person right *here*. Only very few animals in fact are capable of this kind of self-recognition (chimps, bonobos, orangutans, possibly gorillas, dolphins, elephants and, outside these few mammal species, magpies have so far been successful). The rest of the conscious beings in the animal kingdom simply *have* experiences, but they are never capable of construing in their little minds the idea of a *temporally continuous self* who *owns* those experiences (see Figures 3.6 and 3.7).

In more detail, self-awareness means the ability to understand or think that *this* experience *right now* is actually had by a person or self who is *continuous in time*, has had many other experiences in the past and will hopefully have many further experiences in the future. To be self-aware is to understand that *this* experience now is *my own* experience – it belongs to the same temporally continuous self that I have a lot of old memories about and knowledge about in storage. The type of consciousness related to self-awareness has also been called "extended consciousness". Such a notion refers in particular to extension through time, as opposed to phenomenal consciousness that is always anchored to the present moment. An ability called "mental time travel" is closely related to self-awareness. With self-awareness, we can take a trip back to our own personal past and relive in autobiographical memories the events that

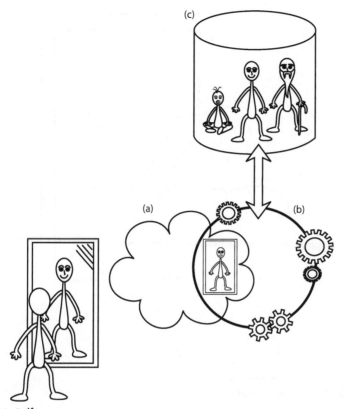

Figure 3.6 Self-awareness

Mirror self-recognition requires self-awareness. When you recognize yourself in the mirror, you see an image of your body in the mirror. This image is experienced in your primary (phenomenal) consciousness as any other object visually perceived (a). Then it is subjected to higher cognitive processes in reflective consciousness (b). In your long-term memory (c), your self-representation and your autobiographical memory are activated and self-related information is accessed and subjected to reflective processing. In reflective consciousness, the present self-related experience (image in mirror) and the self-representation from memory are brought together. The two sources of information are matched together in the recognition "That is me!", implying self-awareness. At the same time this new self-related information may change the self-representation in long-term memory, for example, to get an updated memory image of what exactly I look like these days

have happened to us in the past. Also, we can plan or imagine what might happen to us tomorrow or in the future.

Although our physical bodies and our phenomenal experiences are, as such, always stuck in the present moment, self-awareness coupled with mental time travel can free us from the confines of the prison cell of the present. People who suffer from severe amnesia have difficulty with mental time travel and seem unable to see themselves either in the past or the future: their experience and their self exist in the

Figure 3.7 Mirror self-recognition

In the animal kingdom, at least chimpanzees, orangutans, bonobos, elephants and dolphins can recognize themselves in the mirror, thus showing at least rudimentary self-awareness. Gorillas, however, have not usually passed the mirror test, apart from the gorilla Koko who has been raised by humans and can communicate with humans using sign language

present only. Thus, deficits of long-term autobiographical memory might actually lead to the narrowing down of self-awareness.

Another case in psychology where the distinction between phenomenal consciousness and self-awareness is central comes from the science of happiness. There, the concept of happiness (or *subjective well-being*) is defined as the function of two components: the *affective* components or how many positive and negative emotions you feel over time; and the *cognitive* components or how you evaluate your life (life satisfaction). The positive and negative emotional states can be best measured by the beeper method: asking people at random intervals to report how they feel right *now*. We get representative samples of their emotional lives. If positive, pleasant emotional states are clearly more frequent than negative ones, then the person enjoys overall affective happiness. However, the cognitive components require the involvement of self-awareness. They are measured by asking people to evaluate how satisfied they are overall with their lives, or to what extent they have achieved or are about to achieve their important goals in life. This requires mental time travel in both directions. Once, long ago, our past self had goals and aspirations, started various projects and made crucial choices, so that one day our future selves would be happy. Life satisfaction is about seeing our lives as temporally continuous and evaluating where we are in this long journey wherein we reach towards our goals, set in the distant past by a past self, to be enjoyed in the (hopefully not-too-distant) future by a future self. If, in this reflection, we see that we have made progress on several fronts, then we evaluate our lives positively and enjoy high levels of life satisfaction or cognitive happiness.

The two components can be dissociated from each other. Think about the vain hedonist who enjoys lots of momentary pleasures (high affective happiness in phenomenal consciousness) but whose life is empty of long-term projects: he is just drifting from moment to moment without any progress towards important goals – he does not even have such goals (thus resulting in low life satisfaction). The opposite example is the suffering artist who sacrifices everything for his art, believing that he thereby contributes something good, beautiful and of eternal value to the world. As he sees his masterpiece slowly unfolding, he makes progress towards his most significant life goal and his life satisfaction peaks. At the same time he is poor, isolated and ignored, enjoying few emotional pleasures but suffering from many pains, which brings low affective happiness. True happiness seems to require both emotional (momentary) feelings of positive emotions in phenomenal consciousness and positive evaluations of one's life in reflective consciousness and self-awareness.

3.2 Concepts to describe the absence of consciousness

We also need concepts that refer to things that lack consciousness. There are two concepts that are often used indiscriminately: *unconscious* and *nonconscious*. Here we will define them so that there is a clear difference between them.

Unconscious

"Unconscious" refers to *temporary* absence of consciousness from some entity (a memory, a person) that can, at least potentially, also exist in a conscious state. For instance, information in our long-term memory can exist either in an unconscious form or, when activated and retrieved to mind, in a conscious form. In fact, most of the memory traces in our autobiographical memory are, at any single moment, in an unconscious form. But we can recall them back into consciousness by will. We can choose to think about what happened last summer, what happened when we graduated from school or when we had our first kiss. Any memory trace can magically be called back, and then it turns into mental images in phenomenal consciousness. We see images of the scenes, hear the voices, feel the touches and perhaps even smell faint traces of the scents that were present then. Then the memory trace exists in a conscious form. Similarly for the state of the entire person: An anaesthetized person is temporarily unconscious, but the state of consciousness returns after the surgery.

There are many different types of unconscious information in the brain. Episodic and autobiographical memories contain information about the events in our own personal past. Semantic memory contains more general information about the facts, concepts and words that we have learned. Unconscious information differs also as to the ease with which it can be retrieved to consciousness. Information about significant recent events and very familiar names, places or objects is readily retrievable to consciousness, whereas events in our distant past or words in a language we learned years ago and never used may be nearly irretrievable.

Nonconscious

"Nonconscious" refers to the *permanent* absence of consciousness from any entity, but especially such entities that might in some way resemble conscious beings due to their intelligent behaviour or information content. For example, in our brains there is also a lot of purely nonconscious information. It is the type of information that never did and never will exist in a conscious state. Some types of nonconscious memory contain information about motor programmes and skills – information about how much and in which order different muscle groups should be activated when riding a bicycle or hitting a tennis ball. We have no conscious access to such information: We cannot retrieve information about the muscles or the motor programmes to consciousness, only about how it feels to carry out such programmes. Similarly, our brain regulates and monitors at a nonconscious level several physiological factors, such as body temperature, hormonal levels, blood pressure, and so on. But even more deeply nonconscious information lies in our brain – information about whose existence we have no idea at all through any of our subjective experiences. The biological information encoded in the DNA of our brain cells is exactly that type of nonconscious information. The informational contents of DNA molecules cannot be retrieved or activated inside the brain in such a way that they or their immediate consequences would be experienced as some kind of mental content or as patterns of phenomenal experience in consciousness. Therefore, the genetic information contained in our brain cells is a prime example of nonconscious information.

Present-day robots and computers are mechanisms that represent information from their environment and on the basis of that information and their internal programs they guide their behaviour in complex and intelligent ways. Yet, they are nonconscious. We have no reason to believe that they would enjoy any kind of phenomenal experiences. The engineers who built and programmed them surely did not make any attempt at giving them subjective experiences. Our robots and computers are merely immensely complex pocket calculators that mechanically compute and represent huge amounts of nonconscious information. Inside these systems, there is no phenomenal consciousness, no qualities of experience and no subject with an inner mental life (unless, of course, panpsychism happens to be true – but in that case *everything* has consciousness, even my pocket calculator does and so does my pocket!).

Zombies

Nonconscious beings that mimic conscious beings in their behaviour and information processing – or may pose as conscious beings – are called "zombies". This term originates from voodoo culture. "Zombie" in that context is a person raised from the dead through black magic and turned into a mindless slave of its master. Thus, originally "zombies" were understood to be beings who have no mind or will of their own, a kind of "living dead", but who nevertheless were able to follow orders and carry out tasks. Yet, they did not look like normal people, nor were they posed as such. The voodoo zombies were grim, monstrous creatures that looked more like walking corpses with a blank face than like living human beings (Figure 3.8).

In a famous horror film from the 1950s, *The Invasion of the Body Snatchers*, people looked and behaved perfectly normal but they had turned dead inside – they had no feelings, emotions and perhaps no phenomenal consciousness anymore. This comes very close to the notion of "zombie" in the current philosophy of consciousness. The definition of zombie in philosophy is: Zombie is a being that is *externally indistinguishable from a normal human being* but has *no phenomenal consciousness* whatsoever. A zombie is a nonconscious being, a creature or mechanism that has no stream of subjective life. If we ask the question "What is it like to *be* a zombie – is there

Figure 3.8 Zombie

Depicted here is a classical voodoo zombie or "living dead" in the horror genre. These zombies are supposed to be mindless creatures raised from the dead, and they usually have evil intentions towards the living. Zombies in philosophy do not look like this at all, because the philosopher's zombie looks exactly like a normal human being but is devoid of consciousness and therefore also is a mindless creature

something that life is like *for* a zombie?", the only correct answer is "No, there is nothing that it's like to be a zombie, nothing that life is like for it. It is a mentally dead creature." Yet, from the outside it looks exactly the same as a normal human being. It walks and talks and smiles and looks you in the eye.

Originally, the notion of zombie in philosophy was invented as a thought experiment to test our ideas about consciousness. Can we separate consciousness from behaviour? Can we imagine a being that lacks consciousness but has all that belongs to human external appearances and behaviours? It seems we can grasp the notion of such a creature rather easily, and that some of our present-day robots and computers already are capable of mimicking human behaviour so well that the day may not be far in the future when zombies – or something near enough – become a technological reality.

Zombies have become important tools for testing theories of mind, such as behaviourism and functionalism. Before the emergence of consciousness studies, several arguments in philosophy were targeted against those doctrines by using zombies as thought experiments. The logic of the arguments is approximately the following: Take a proposed theory of mind such as behaviourism, functionalism, cognitive science, etc. and describe creatures or systems or information-processing mechanisms that totally fulfil the requirements of the theory for passing as a human mind. Thus, if the background theory is correct, the creature should be equivalent to a human being in its psychological reality. Now, the big question is: Are the systems that fulfil the theory conscious beings, do they have an internal subjective mental life or are they mere nonconscious zombies that only keep up the appearances of being conscious but inside there are no qualities of experience anywhere to be found? Unfortunately for functionalism and computational cognitive science, those theories turned out to describe zombie psychology rather than the psychological reality of conscious human beings. That is, those theories had very little to say about subjective, qualitative consciousness. Therefore, if we build a system according to the theories of functionalism or cognitive science, we may as well end up with building a zombie. Or at least the theory says nothing about how to distinguish a zombie from a conscious human being, and therefore says nothing at all about consciousness.

The classical zombie arguments were fatal nails to the coffin of functionalism and convinced many that if we want to explain consciousness and the human conscious mind, then functionalism or computational cognitive science cannot be the answer. Later on, the zombie arguments have been developed even further. It has been suggested that it would be possible to imagine even a *neurobiological zombie*: a *biologically* perfect copy of a normal human being, but still a zombie that lacks consciousness.

The conceivability of a neurobiological zombie is questionable. It might be that it seems conceivable only because we do not yet understand the nature of those biological brain processes that make up consciousness. The neurobiological zombie could be compared to imagining a "zombie cell": a cell that is a perfect molecule-by-molecule copy of a biological living cell, yet lacks the property of "being alive". In the 1800s, that kind of thought experiment would have sounded reasonable, but now that we know that "life" in the biological sense of the word is nothing over and above the biochemical processes carried out by the micromechanisms in the cell, we understand that a "zombie cell" could not exist or that it could exist only in a world where "being alive" consists of something more than physical and chemical processes. It would require a dualistic conception of life (called "vitalism"): a nonphysical "life-force" that has to be added to all the biochemical processes before they become "truly" alive.

In a similar vein, a neurobiological zombie may be impossible in our world. If consciousness is a higher level of biological organization in the brain, then duplicating the brain automatically duplicates consciousness. If, on the other hand, consciousness turns out to be some kind of dualistic mind-dust that exists independently of the brain, then it is possible to imagine a fully normal brain in a fully normal body with fully normal human behaviour, but all this in the absence of the mind-dust that delivers the subjective stream of experience. Belief in a neurobiological zombie thus requires resort to at least some version of dualism. Therefore, most scientists working currently on the problem of consciousness would deny the possibility of neuro-biological zombies, whereas several philosophers seem to think that such a creature is perfectly conceivable.

The concept of zombie as a metaphor for a complex behavioural system devoid of consciousness has spread from philosophy to other areas of consciousness research. For example, in *neuropsychology* such perceptual systems that take in sens-ory information, process it outside of consciousness and are able to guide behaviour based on purely nonconscious processing are sometimes called "zombie systems" or "the zombie within". This is because they appear to be complex, intelligent behavioural systems, but at the same time we know that they work in total internal darkness, without any qualitative subjectivity involved in their operation. Also, the question of *animal consciousness* is sometimes formulated with the help of the notion of zombie: We may ask which living organisms are mere zombies and which are serious candidates for possessing phenomenal consciousness and thus feeling their own existence.

3.3 Alternative definitions and usages of the concept of "consciousness"

In this book "consciousness" is anchored to its core meaning as subjective phenomenal experience, or as the presence of qualitative "feels" for a subject. The other central notions, such as "reflective consciousness" and "self-awareness", have been built on the ground provided by the notion of "phenomenal consciousness". The absence of consciousness and its metaphoric image, the zombie, is defined by the absence of subjective experience.

This way of defining the concept of consciousness is by no means the only way, not even inside the field of consciousness studies. In the following, we analyse some alternative definitions for "consciousness" and try to understand how they differ from the notion of consciousness as subjective experience.

Consciousness defined as the ability to respond to stimulation

In clinical medicine, "consciousness" is defined as the ability to respond to external stimulation. To be conscious, according to this definition, is to be able to respond appropriately when particular stimuli are presented. There are a few standardized stimuli that are typically used: calling the patient's name, touching the patient's hand or asking the patient to clench a fist, asking the patient to open or to close eyes, causing pain and observing if the patient responds to the painful stimuli in some way. The overall "level" of consciousness is calculated on the basis of these types of responses: If the patient responds appropriately to all stimuli, then he is fully conscious, but if he responds to none of them, he is deeply unconscious or in a coma.

Ability to respond has no necessary condition to phenomenal consciousness. We can easily imagine that a patient responds to some stimuli fully automatically, although there are no conscious experiences caused by the stimulus, or any conscious experiences present at all. The opposite is also true: We can easily imagine that the patient does not give any responses to any stimuli, yet that he has vivid inner experiences, either related or unrelated to the currently present stimuli.

Therefore, it would be much more accurate to talk about "responsiveness" than "consciousness" in this context. The patient may lose or regain external responsiveness, but whether he is in a (phenomenally) conscious or an unconscious state is another matter, determined not by external responses as such but by whether his brain is capable of supporting qualities of experience.

Consciousness defined as the ability to represent information from the external world

When consciousness is defined as representation of the objects of the external world, the paradigm example of consciousness is taken to be perception. According to this definition, to be conscious is to be conscious *of something* or to be *aware of* something. This can be further analysed in terms of representation and information: To be aware of an object X in the world is to receive information through the senses from that object and to consequently represent internally that object – to have an internal representation of X. Something in the brain–mind is an internal representation of X if the occurrence or the level of activity of the representational vehicle (say, neural firings in the brain) reliably covaries with or indicates the presence of X currently in the perceiver's environment.

Again, definition of consciousness in terms of "awareness of" and representation has no necessary connection to subjective experience. There are lots of representations of external stimuli in our sensory organs and in our brains, but most of them are not coupled with any subjective experiences at all. Thus, they are totally nonconscious forms of representation. Conversely, there are lots of subjective experiences going on in our minds that bear no representational relationship to the current external environment. Dream experiences are a prime example of totally hallucinatory experiences that do not correspond with the external stimulus environment at all. Therefore, representation and "awareness of" something should not be confused with phenomenal consciousness. To represent something is merely to carry information about it, regardless of whether that information is experienced or not. To be phenomenally conscious is for there to be subjective phenomenal qualia present in the mind, regardless of whether the qualitative patterns carry any information about anything external to them or not.

Consciousness defined as wakefulness

Sometimes consciousness is defined in terms of wakefulness. This definition is in fact like a combination of the two definitions criticized above: representation of and responsiveness to the environment. According to this idea, to be conscious is to be aware of oneself and one's surroundings, and to be able to respond to and interact with the environment. The same counter-examples apply as above. For example, dreaming takes place when we are asleep as opposed to awake. Dreams are subjective experiences during sleep that do not represent the environment. Dream experiences are hallucinatory, stimulus-independent and internally generated in the brain, but still they are vivid phenomenal experiences, often equally as vivid and clear as perceptual experiences during wakefulness. Thus, dreams are a form of phenomenal consciousness. Wakefulness may be necessary for accurate conscious perception of the environment to take place, but it is not a necessary requirement for the presence of phenomenal consciousness as such.

Consciousness defined as access to output systems, control of behaviour or behavioural interactions with the world

Functionalists in particular try to reduce consciousness to some input–output function or causal role in the control of behaviour. Along the functionalist lines of thought, consciousness has been defined as "access consciousness". Access refers to the output function of conscious information: Consciousness is the type of information that accesses many other cognitive systems – motor systems – and thereby also is able to guide or control external behaviour, especially verbal reports about the contents of (reflective) consciousness. According to the functionalist definition, then, conscious information is only the information in the brain that fulfils the access function. "Access" refers to global informational access, especially the access to output systems within the human cognitive system.

If consciousness is identified with the global access function of information, the ability to report the contents of consciousness verbally or to respond externally to stimuli is at least implied as necessary for consciousness, because "access" generally means access to output systems. Furthermore, the access definition of consciousness reduces consciousness to a certain type of information processing (or input–output function) and hence suffers from all the same problems as functionalism does as a theory of consciousness. It leaves out qualia, and it rejects the possibility that there could be pure phenomenal consciousness that is independent of selective attention, reflective consciousness, verbal report or control of output mechanisms.

Consciousness and awareness

The concepts of "consciousness" and "awareness" are often used interchangeably, as in "visual consciousness" and "visual awareness": both refer to conscious experiences in the visual modality. "Awareness", however, is more often used in connection with externally triggered, stimulus-related perceptual consciousness, as in "awareness of a stimulus". Consciousness (phenomenal) as such refers simply to the direct presence of subjective experiences, but awareness of a stimulus refers to an entire process of conscious perception wherein an external physical stimulus first physically affects our sensory receptors and then triggers neural responses that travel to the brain, where cortical mechanisms analyse the content of the stimulus and cause a subjective experience that internally represents the external stimulus. To be aware of something thus presupposes that there is some kind of perceptual object out there, behind the experience, and that our conscious experience represents that object; therefore we are "aware of" the object and have a conscious experience of the object.

"Awareness" may also mean roughly the same as the reflective consciousness of and the ability to report a specific content of consciousness. For example, "phonological awareness" requires the ability to pay selective attention to single phonemes in words, and thus take phonemes as objects in reflective consciousness and name them. If one can do this, then one can report what is the first or the last phoneme of a word – and precisely such tests are used to measure phonological awareness. In general, "X awareness" is the ability to apply reflective consciousness to entities of type X, when such entities appear in phenomenal consciousness. Thus, self-awareness is the ability to apply selective attention and reflective consciousness to self-related experiences, such as the mirror image reflecting one's own bodily self.

Chapter summary

We have defined several concepts that refer to consciousness as the subjective mental life that we experience:

- *Phenomenal consciousness* is subjective experience as such, necessarily involving "qualia" or the qualitative character of subjective experience.
- *State and contents of consciousness* refer to consciousness as a general background state that allows specific contents of subjective experience to appear in our minds. A human is either in the conscious state or in an unconscious state (some borderline cases also exist, however, such as drowsiness and the minimally conscious state following after coma).
- *Structure of phenomenal consciousness.* Subjective experiences are clearest in the centre of consciousness, defined by the spotlight of selective attention, which is surrounded by a periphery or a phenomenal background of more vaguely defined experiences.
- *Reflective consciousness.* In reflective consciousness, we formulate conscious thoughts that are about our other experiences and use these thoughts and judgements to guide our behaviour.
- *Introspection* is a form of reflective consciousness. In descriptive introspection, we formulate verbal descriptions of our subjective experiences to communicate our experiences to outsiders.
- *Self-awareness* is a form of reflective consciousness where we connect our current experiences with our internal self-representation and realize that the experience is our own experience, the experience of a self or person who is continuous in time.

- *Unconscious* and *nonconscious* information is processed or encoded in the brain without any subjective experiences being associated with them. Unconscious information can, however, become conscious information – it is potentially conscious – whereas nonconscious information is not even potentially conscious.
- *Zombies* are a metaphor for complex, intelligent behavioural systems that operate in the total absence of consciousness, without any subjective experiences being involved.
- *Confusing usages of consciousness.* In some contexts, consciousness is defined in terms of "behavioural responsiveness", "wakefulness", "alertness", "internal representation of the world" or "awareness/perceptual representation of a stimulus", but these definitions are confusing because they bear no necessary relationship to subjective experience.

Further reading

Banks, W. B. (Ed.) (2009). *Encyclopedia of consciousness* (Vols. 1 and 2). San Diego, CA: Academic Press.

Block, N. (2001). Paradox and cross purposes in recent work on consciousness. *Cognition*, *79*, 197–219.

Chalmers, D. J. (1996). *The conscious mind.* Oxford: Oxford University Press.

Dainton, B. (2000). *Stream of consciousness.* London: Routledge.

Farthing, W. G. (1992). *The psychology of consciousness.* New York: Prentice-Hall.

Metzinger, T. (1995). The problem of consciousness. In T. Metzinger (Ed.), *Conscious experience* (pp. 3–37). Thorverton: Imprint Academic.

Revonsuo, A. (2006). *Inner presence.* Cambridge, MA: MIT Press.

Taylor Parker, S., Mitchell, R. W., & Boccia, M. L. (Eds.) (1994). *Self-awareness in animals and humans.* New York: Cambridge University Press.

Brief discussion questions

1 How many different definitions or usages of "consciousness" are there (in this book and elsewhere)? Make a list of as many definitions as you can think of. Which ones are clear and useful for the scientific understanding of consciousness, and which are obscure and confusing?

2 Identify and describe situations where you have:

(i) pure phenomenal consciousness (no reflection, no self-awareness; only vivid experiences);

(ii) a lot of reflective consciousness (constant inner speech commenting on your ongoing experience);

(iii) mental time travel to your personal past and future.

Describe from your own experience the differences between these types of consciousness and discuss them with others in the class.

3 Are zombies conceivable in principle?

(i) Is it conceivable that a system (say, a robot) could look and behave externally exactly as a normal human being, including flawless speech, normal emotional expressions etc., and yet not have any phenomenal consciousness? If yes, explain why; if no, why not?

(ii) Is it conceivable that a system (say, a robot) could look and behave externally exactly as a normal human being, including flawless speech, normal emotional expressions etc., *and* also have exactly similar brain and body as a normal human being, and yet not have any phenomenal consciousness? If yes, explain why; if no, why not?

Part two

Central domains of consciousness science

I. Neuropsychology of consciousness

Introduction: What are the central domains of consciousness science?

In the first part of this book, we have learned about the philosophical, historical and conceptual background from which the modern science of consciousness has emerged. Now we are ready to proceed to the central domains that are covered by the science of consciousness: (I) *neuropsychology of consciousness*; (II) *neural correlates of consciousness*; (III) *theories of consciousness*; (IV) *altered states of consciousness*. The key findings from these areas have more or less defined the modern scientific studies on consciousness – they form the very core of its empirical database.

The evidence in consciousness science comes from several different sources. As in any branch of science – and in particular in cognitive neuroscience – we aim to find *converging evidence* from multiple different sources, that is, evidence that all points in the same direction. When we investigate the relationship between consciousness and brain, the most direct evidence comes from two sources: (1) studies on neuropsychological patients who have suffered a brain lesion that affects some aspect of consciousness; and (2) laboratory measurements of natural brain activity (functional brain imaging) or artificial stimulation of the brain in normal subjects when specific conscious phenomena happen in their minds in a controlled manner. The converging evidence, as we shall see, shows that particular areas of the brain are concerned with particular aspects of consciousness. If a certain well-specified part of the brain is damaged, the damage leads to a certain type of loss or distortion of subjective experience. If the same part is artificially stimulated in a healthy subject, changes in the same kind of experience are reported by the subject. And when a subject engages in a task that calls for this type of consciousness, brain activity is seen in the same area where damage wipes that aspect of consciousness away.

All this empirical evidence from multiple sources should be explained by a theory of consciousness. Theories of consciousness are not hard to find in the current literature – almost everyone in the field seems to have his or her own theory – but it is questionable whether any theory explains all of the data we already have, or even a substantial part of it. We will explore the major theories of consciousness and try to evaluate their explanatory success.

In the final section of Part two, we explore altered states of consciousness where subjective experiences are different from the normal waking state. Altered states reveal the full richness of human experience, because in altered states it is possible to have experiences that go far beyond those we ever have during the normal waking states. Some altered states, such as dreaming, are familiar to all of us, whereas others, such as out-of-body experiences and mystical states, may seem bizarre and mysterious. The science of consciousness should, however, take all the different kinds of altered states of consciousness seriously, because they may reveal aspects of consciousness that we would never find out about by focusing only on the normal waking state.

Chapter 4

Neuropsychological deficits of visual consciousness

Introduction: The unity of visual consciousness

In our everyday experience, visual consciousness seems to consist of a single, unified visuospatial world in which we see a multitude of different objects located in three-dimensional space. Each object consists of a unique combination of different visible features, such as colour, shape and motion, coherently bound together into a single package: the object as we perceive it. Thus, our visual world appears to have *global spatial unity* (the unity of the overall visual space where the objects seen are located) and *local unity* (the unity of each separate object that is perceived). All this unity and coherent organization of the perceptual world is perfectly natural and totally effortless for us. We simply open our eyes and the visible world appears immediately before our eyes, as solid and real as anything we could ever imagine.

Therefore, in our everyday thinking, we take the perceptual world in our visual consciousness to be identical with the external physical world itself, as if we could perceive the physical world directly. Yet, we know that we do not perceive it directly. There is no radar beam of consciousness flowing out from our brain and touching the physical objects, thus making us conscious of them. On the contrary, light (or electromagnetic radiation in the visible wavelengths) must first be reflected from the physical environment and then it must strike our eyes and the retina at the back of the eye, so that the signal is transformed there into neural bioelectrical activity that is transmitted to the visual cortex. After complex neural processing that we do not fully understand, the visible world of consciousness is constructed somewhere inside the brain and we thereby have subjective visual experiences: We consciously see the world. The perceptual world as we experience it is the *final* link in a complex causal chain where the external physical world and the light reflected from it are the *first* link. Our visual consciousness is several steps removed from the stimulus objects in the external world.

Thus, our consciousness presents to us a perceptual *model* of the world, not the world itself but a kind of virtual reality created by our brain. It is the brain's best guess as to what is out there.

The indirect nature of conscious vision becomes obvious when we meet neuropsychological patients whose visual world has been permanently altered. Although there is nothing wrong with their eyes – the visual information is received and processed quite normally in their visual sensory organs – their brain cannot put together the visual world in the normal manner. Therefore, they see a rather different world. Sometimes it is quite difficult to understand what their visual world is like, because it has become so strange that words cannot describe it.

In the neuropsychology of consciousness, philosophical questions about consciousness are all over us. We bump into the problem of other minds and alien consciousness: Will science ever tell us *what it is like to be* a patient with a damaged brain and a distorted consciousness? And we gain fascinating insights into the mind–body problem when brain damage reveals surprising connections between different parts of the brain and different aspects of consciousness.

Neuropsychological deficits – localized damage of brain tissue – may wipe out or distort aspects of the subjective experience of seeing, changing the patient's visual world in most peculiar ways. If we could specify the way in which the subjective experience has been changed or lost and the precise location where the brain is damaged, then we could propose the hypothesis that the damaged parts of the brain are normally necessary for constructing the type of contents of consciousness that has now been lost for the patient.

In the following we will make an attempt to understand how brain damage alters the subjective experience of seeing. Whatever the alterations are like, they will tell us something about the way in which the brain normally manages to construct the world we consciously see around us.

4.1 Cerebral achromatopsia: Colour qualia vanish without a trace

The visual world is a world of coloured objects and surfaces. The blueness of the sky, the greenness of the grass and the trees, the redness of the setting sun – we attribute the colours we see to the external physical objects, as if the colours in our experience would be out there in the world. But in fact they are not, they are features of our experience, although they are externalized so that they seem to be out there beyond our bodies and minds. Somehow our brain constructs a sensory-perceptual world that is qualitatively coloured. Somehow it manages to localize the colours *out there*, on the surfaces of external objects beyond our body and brain, although the brain where the colours are generated is *in here*.

The qualitative colours are productions of the brain, which is easy to accept knowing that it is quite possible to see vivid colours independently of any direct sensory contact with the external physical world. One of the strongest pieces of evidence comes from dream research, where systematic studies of dream content have shown that most dreams are experienced in colours. In our dreams, the colours also seem to be out there, on objects external to our own body, but of course the whole dream must be happening in our brain. Thus, during dreaming the brain constructs a phenomenal world that contains similar colour qualities as the perceptual world does during waking perception. A coloured visual world can exist in consciousness, in the absence of any sensory input. Thus, the existence of colour experience must depend only on what is simultaneously going on in the brain.

If phenomenal colour experiences are only directly dependent on internal brain processes, then they should be vulnerable to some type of brain damage that strikes at the neural mechanisms necessary for colour construction. That indeed is the case in a neuropsychological disorder known as "achromatopsia". Literally, it means No-Colour-Vision (a/chromat/opsia). This condition is profoundly different from ordinary "colour blindness", which is caused by the lack of certain types of wavelength-sensitive cells in the eye. In ordinary colour blindness the wavelength signals from red and green stimuli are similar to each other when they reach the brain. The brain never learns to attach a consistently different colour quality to, say, tomatoes and grass, because there is no difference between the colour signals these two objects elicit in the eyes and the brain. The eyes cannot discriminate the so-called "red" wavelengths from the so-called "green" wavelengths. It is a genetically based disorder of sensory wavelength discrimination.

By contrast, achromatopsia is a disorder where a person who has seen the world in colours all his life suddenly loses colour vision completely because of damage in the visual cortex of the brain. There is nothing wrong with the eyes or with the sensory wavelength discrimination: they work fine. Nor is there necessarily any other perceptual or cognitive deficits present. There is only a lack of colour qualities in visual consciousness. The perceptual visual world is still there, but somehow it is horribly changed into a greyscale world of murky black-and-white objects drained of colours. Many objects that previously were seen as vividly coloured now appear unrecognizable in their dark greyish form.

The most illustrative achromatopsic patient case in neuropsychology was described by the famous neurologist Oliver Sacks. This case was special not only because of selective achromatopsia of the whole visual field, but also because of his thorough acquaintance with colours as a professional painter. Thus, he was probably more vividly aware of what he had lost than any other achromatopsic patient had ever been. Along with the colour experiences, he had lost a central part of his identity:

> It had gradually come upon him, during this time, that it was not merely colour perception and colour imagery that he lacked, but something deeper and difficult to define. He knew all about colour, externally, intellectually, but he had lost the remembrance, the inner knowledge, of it that had been part of his very being . . . It was as if his past, his chromatic past, had been taken away, as if the brain's knowledge of colour had been totally excised, leaving no trace, no inner evidence of its existence behind.
>
> (Sacks, 1995, p. 10)

> But black and white for him was a reality, all around him, 360 degrees, solid and three-dimensional, twenty-four hours a day . . . neither "grey" nor "leaden" could begin to convey what his world was actually like. It was not "grey" that he experienced, he said, but perceptual qualities for which ordinary experience, ordinary language, had no equivalent.
>
> (Sacks, 1995, p. 8)

Achromatopsia may be unilateral or bilateral. In the unilateral form (also called hemiachromatopsia), the damage is in the colour area of the visual cortex in only one hemisphere of the brain, the left or the right. This leads to the curious situation that one half of the visual world is normally coloured whereas the other half is completely devoid of colours. There is a sharp borderline in the middle of the visual field, between the phenomenally coloured half and the greyscale half-world. This shows that each side of the brain is capable of producing all the colour qualities independently of the other, but each side can only "paint" one half of the visual world with the colours it has. Furthermore, the left visual cortex paints the right side of the visual field, and vice versa – the damage in the brain is always on the opposite side in relation to the missing colours. This is because the information from the left visual field crosses over to the right cerebral cortex, and vice versa. In the bilateral condition, similar damage affects both cerebral hemispheres and therefore the entire visual world is devoid of colour. Incidentally, the lack of colours in visual dream experiences sometimes reported by healthy subjects may resemble temporary achromatopsia: The colour areas of the visual cortex may not be fully activated during sleep to produce colours normally.

The location of the damage leading to achromatopsia can be characterized with precision. The area is called V4 or the colour area. Converging evidence from functional brain imaging shows that the same area becomes active in the normal brain when coloured as opposed to black-and-white stimuli are presented. Thus, we now know which areas in the visual cortex are necessary for the production of colour qualities. Yet, we have no understanding of *how* the brain does the trick. How are the neurophysiological activities in this area transformed into phenomenal colour experiences in a subject's consciousness? What are the underlying neural mechanisms, in physical or neurobiological terms, that correlate with or bring about the phenomenal qualities? The answers to these questions would go a long way in solving the Explanatory Gap, or perhaps in showing that it is unsolvable.

4.2 Visual agnosia: Loss of coherent visual objects

In a healthy brain the elementary phenomenal qualities, such as colours and contours, are carefully organized by the brain to form coherent perceptual wholes, the three-dimensional objects that we see all around us. The visual qualities that make up an object typically include such things as colour, brightness, surface structure, three-dimensional shape and specific location and distance in space from the observer. These features are bound together into one tight package of information that, in perceptual consciousness, simulates or represents the distant physical object from which the physical electromagnetic signals (light waves) were reflected. The perceptual world surrounding us in our conscious experience is mostly made up of such coherent packages of information, laid out in the perceptual space around us.

This kind of visual experience of a world of coherent objects comes to us so effortlessly that we hardly ever realize that it must be an enormous accomplishment for the visual brain to be able to produce such a representation of the world at all. If specific areas of the visual cortex cannot function properly, the visual world becomes a field of disintegrated qualities: different colours, different degrees of brightness, small pieces of contour haphazardly distributed across the visual field. The coherent packages of information – visual objects – are lost. There are no visual objects anymore, only a chaos of disorganized visual features. Perceptual objects become unrecognizable by the visual experience they produce. By contrast, touching the same objects can still lead to normal recognition, because touch information and visual information are processed in different brain areas.

Something like this happens in visual agnosia. The most severe form is known as *apperceptive agnosia*. Patients suffering from it cannot make any sense out of the visual qualities they see. Even simple visual forms and objects such as a ball or a book have become unrecognizable. This is demonstrated by the patients' helpless behaviour if they have to rely on vision alone. They cannot name or number the objects directly before their eyes. They cannot draw copies of them that would resemble the model. They have difficulty in finding their way around objects in a room and they may bump into pieces of furniture. Yet, the patients are not blind. Neither have they lost their visual acuity, in the manner that a short-sighted person (without glasses) has. The patients can still see fine visual detail but the problem is that *the details do not add up to coherent objects*!

Somewhat milder forms of visual agnosia are called *associative agnosia* or *integrative agnosia*. These patients also have great difficulty in recognizing objects, but they see a bit more than patients with apperceptive agnosia do. They seem to see at least small pieces of coherent contour of objects or parts of objects, but still they cannot see the object as a unified whole. They can, surprisingly, draw recognizable copies of line drawings of objects, although they cannot recognize the objects depicted or their own copies! They manage to produce the copies by applying a "line-by-line" copying strategy where they focus on one part of the contour at any one time, but they never see the picture as a whole. Thus, they have no idea what it is that they are copying, nevertheless outsiders with normal vision can recognize what their drawings represent! Typically, the patients can also draw recognizable images from memory, although they themselves cannot recognize them after they have drawn them.

There is a special type of agnosia called *prosopagnosia* that in some way resembles the above cases but is restricted to the perception of faces only. Some patients with such face recognition difficulties have reported that they can see all the *parts* of the face, such as the eyes, eyebrows, lips, nose, and so on, but they *cannot put them together*! The parts just jump around incoherently without settling into a coherent representation of a face. Some patients with face recognition difficulties do not see even the parts of faces, and faces for them appear like empty ovals without any features. Prosopagnosic patients with difficulty seeing faces as faces have damage to the early stages of face recognition, the stage that normally produces the coherent visual image of a face.

The above cases vividly demonstrate that the binding or integration of visual qualities to coherent packages of information is an essential function of the visual brain. It is impossible to recognize the objects around us if all we have in consciousness is a collection of disorganized visual qualities. The cortical areas that seem to be specialized in producing coherent object and face representations for visual consciousness can be localized with the help of data from lesion locations in the visual cortex of agnosic patients as well as from functional brain imaging of the healthy brain in response to coherent visual images.

Although the cortical locations necessary for unified visual consciousness have been discovered and explored in cognitive neuroscience, we still do not understand the mechanisms that actually put the representations together and deliver the results to consciousness. All we know is that the information characterizing one single object is distributed in several different places across the cortex. Therefore, there must be some mechanism that binds the information together.

The *binding problem* is the problem of understanding how the distributed pieces of information are put together in the brain for the unity of conscious perception. A solution to the binding problem will reveal the mechanisms responsible for the unity of consciousness.

4.3 Semantic dementia: Loss of the meaning of objects

There is much more to the visual consciousness of objects than just binding the basic visual features together into a coherent three-dimensional shape. The perceptual world of objects in which we live our lives is a world of *meaningful* objects – things that are not merely coherent patterns of visual qualia, but representatives of particular *categories* of objects. The coherent packages of information in our visual consciousness are not only *seen* immediately, effortlessly, but moreover they are *recognized as* trees, houses, birds, clouds, persons, chairs, tables, dogs and cats. How different the perceptual world would look if the objects around us lost their meaningfulness! It would be an alien world full of objects whose nature is unknown to us and whose identity or function we could only guess at.

The cognitive mechanism that attaches meaningfulness to perceived objects is called *semantic memory*. It is the part of our long-term memory that contains all the conceptual and factual knowledge we possess about the world. The information in semantic memory allows us to recognize, say, different animals as representatives of different types or species: dogs, cows, horses, camels, zebras, tigers, frogs, otters, lions, camels, mice, giraffes; birds, butterflies, bees, bugs, and so on. Our perceptual world contains numerous different kinds of animals that can be distinguished using the semantic-conceptual categories in our semantic memory. Of course, some people have a richer semantic memory than others; still, everyone can distinguish the most common types of animals from each other.

Semantic dementia is the name of a disorder where this kind of detailed knowledge is selectively lost. Other aspects of cognition, perception, memory and intelligence are preserved, but the semantic knowledge or the meaningfulness of words and objects is gradually lost. At advanced stages semantic dementia usually leads to an Alzheimer type of general cognitive decline, but in the first stages the patients merely seem to lose the fine-grained factual and conceptual knowledge of different kinds of objects, such as different species of animals.

Thus, when shown pictures or names of the above-mentioned animals, a patient with semantic dementia may not be able to tell anything about them or define what they are. Typically, the patients respond to such tasks by saying: "Well, it is some kind of animal, but I am not sure what". Or they might resort to using the only animal categories that they have left in their semantic memory, thus calling all the above animals either "cats" or "dogs". Such categories usually are spared because they have been learned first in childhood (this is the "first in – last out" principle in progressive neuropsychological disorders).

One patient responded in the following manner when he was shown different words and asked to define what they meant (Hodges, 2003):

Deer:	They're owned by farmers, in the fields of course, we shave their fur off . . . or is it a sheep? Do we do that too, with deer? I'm not sure.
Ostrich:	Is it an animal, don't know what kind . . . I never see it in [the supermarket].
Zebra:	I've no idea what it is.
Seahorse:	I didn't know they have horses in the sea.
Trumpet:	Yes, I do seem to remember the word trumpet. If only I had a dictionary I could tell you what it is.

The same patient also misinterpreted everyday objects and therefore his interactions with objects were sometimes bizarre. For example, he put sugar into a glass of wine and orange juice on his lasagne.

The perceptual world of objects thus becomes impoverished of meaningfulness and resembles the simple world of a child, with only a few different kinds of things, and lots of things and words whose meaning escapes understanding or becomes fuzzy. Total loss of semantic memory while other cognitive capacities are still preserved has not been reported. It would most likely make the whole world look like an alien planet inhabited by an extraterrestrial civilization. The flora and fauna would look strange or unrecognizable and the technological artefacts inexplicable. Perhaps something like that happens in advanced semantic dementia, but then the patient's cognitive capacities are already widely affected and he is most likely unable to describe his experiences anymore.

4.4 Simultanagnosia: Loss of the phenomenal background

The perceptual objects we see are not only coherent and meaningful packages of information but are also embedded in a spatial context, the perceptual world. Each object we focus on is seen against the background of other meaningful objects, called the phenomenal background, which is a field of more vaguely represented objects. The object we focus on is necessarily seen as spatially related to the other objects. Visual consciousness provides us with a spatial "map" of our surroundings where the locations of different objects relative to each other are simultaneously present.

This phenomenal background is lost in simultanagnosia. A patient suffering from this disorder sees only one object at a time. The scope of consciousness seems to be strictly limited to that single object. Everything else disappears from consciousness. Thus, the patient does not even know *where* the object is located, because the relations between the central object and other objects cannot be represented in consciousness, as there are no "other objects" there anymore! Visual awareness presents a single object hanging in a void – a kind of "tunnel vision" where the tunnel can only accommodate a single object at a time. The object, however, may be big or small – size is not crucial – and, instead, the boundaries of the object determine the boundaries of awareness.

Balint's syndrome is the name for a neurological disorder characterized by simultanagnosia and deficient feature binding of objects. Patients with this syndrome can recognize the single object they can see but the binding of the single object to a coherent whole is sometimes compromised. Thus, if there is a red ball and a yellow box in front of the patient, the patient may report that he sees a yellow ball but nothing else, or that he sees a ball that sometimes seems red and sometimes yellow. Thus, the colours of different objects are not consistently bound together with the object shape and location where they actually belong. Instead, the visual representation of the object may include incorrect and unstable combinations of form and colour. It is as if the brain did not know which shape and which colour "really" belong together, and thus it switches the possible combinations in search of the right way to bind the objects together.

To see only a single, unstable object at any one time, not even knowing where the object is located in space, makes it difficult to navigate in the environment. Therefore, patients with simultanagnosia feel unsure and helpless when they try to find their way around. They are not much better off than patients with apperceptive or associative agnosia when it comes to visually guided behaviour. The patient suffering from Balint's syndrome may seem almost as helpless as if blind. Yet, they are not blind – they have not lost visual qualities or visual acuity. They have lost the ability to put the visual world together as a global, coherent representation of multiple visual objects laid out in egocentric space.

4.5 Neglect: Loss of phenomenal space

The objects we see occupy space. They are located in the overall, three-dimensional, globally unified perceptual space that seems to surround us seamlessly in every direction. Yet, somewhere hidden under the surface of spatial consciousness there must be invisible neural seams that keep the space together as one, unified, global whole. The space that seems so unified in our everyday experience is put together by several mechanisms of spatial representation and attention. When some of these mechanisms collapse, as seems to be the case in the neurological disorder called unilateral spatial neglect, parts of perceptual space seem to disappear from consciousness without leaving a trace behind. The damage in the brain is typically localized in the right posterior parietal lobe (Figure 4.1).

The left and right sides of perceptual space and perceived objects, although normally integrated wholes, can be dissociated from each other so that only one side of perceptual space is preserved. Usually it is the right side of space and objects that can still be seen by neglect patients, whereas they are totally unaware of things in the left perceptual field. Furthermore, they seem to be constitutionally unaware that such a space even exists, or that it *ever* existed or even that such a thing *should* exist. Thus, neglect patients usually do not notice that anything is wrong or that anything is missing from their perceptual space. For them, their world seems as complete as ever. But for outsiders it is only too obvious that the patient cannot become aware of the things in the left side of space.

Localization of damage in neglect

Figure 4.1 Localization of damage in neglect

The right posterior parietal lobe is the typical site of damage in most patients suffering from neglect

The loss of perceptual space is manifested in the patient's everyday behaviours. A neglect patient may eat his or her food only from the right side of the plate, because that is all she or he can see. The patient's outward appearance may be oddly one-sided. He may shave only the right side of his face, or she may comb or apply make-up only on the right side. In the mirror, they do not see the left side of their face. If asked to copy a picture of a flower or a clock by drawing it with a pencil on paper, the patient produces half-flowers or half-clocks, with all the details on the left side in the original picture (petals, numbers, clock-arms) either missing or unnaturally crowded on the right side of the drawing, with nothing on the left (see Figure 4.2). When reading a book, the patient may complain that the text does not make sense, as he or she can see only the words on the right side of the page. The lines are cut in half when reading, and the text becomes disconnected between lines.

Neuropsychological tests that reveal neglect

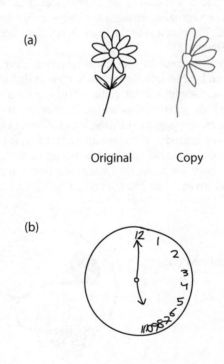

(a)

Original   Copy

(b)

Clock-face drawn from memory

Figure 4.2 Neuropsychological tests that reveal neglect

Asked to draw a copy of a flower, a neglect patient leaves out the details on the left, thus producing only a half-flower. Asked to draw a clock-face, the patient will try to fit all the numbers and clock-hands into the right side of the clock. These tests dramatically reveal that neglect patients have lost the awareness of the left side of perceptual space

All of this behavioural evidence suggests that neglect patients must experience a curious half-world but without realizing it themselves. The simulated world in their consciousness is only partial, but the missing part has not left any empty space behind it – the space itself has disappeared – so it is impossible for the patient to see that quite a bit is missing.

Neglect shows that phenomenal space is essential for consciousness. If there is no phenomenal space, there can be no phenomenal objects in that space either. Thus, not only is the space missing, but all the objects that should have been in that space are gone. Neglect may affect also the ability to imagine the left side of objects or scenes. When patients have been asked to draw or describe from memory a specific scene (say, a city square they know well in their hometown), they only draw or describe the buildings that would be on the right side of their imagined vantage point. If they switch the vantage point they will draw different buildings, but again only the ones on the right from the vantage point. They seem to have the knowledge about the whole space still in their memory, but in their mental images only the space on the right side can be reconstructed.

The paradoxical loss of space in neglect demonstrates that, normally, the world in visual consciousness is a world of coherent meaningful objects that are located in a perceptual space. The object representations and the space representations must be integrated with each other for a unified visual consciousness of the surrounding world to come about.

4.6 Akinetopsia: Loss of visual animation

The visual world is not only a world of meaningful objects in space, but an *animated* world where changes constantly happen. A perceptual world where nothing moves in relation to other things, a world that has come to a standstill, would look wholly unnatural. The stream of visual consciousness flows as the perceptual objects in it move and as the observer's body moves about. Birds and bees fly by, leaves are carried by the wind, people walk by, cars come and go and we ourselves move most of the time. In visual consciousness, perceptual objects smoothly change their location with respect to each other and the perceiver. While they are moving, they retain their coherency. The colour and the shape of the object – say, a black raven flying across the sky – stick together even when moving. The motion of the object is not separated from its other features. The whole package of phenomenal visual information changes its location along a trajectory, without leaving any parts or features behind.

Visual motion, as revealed in subjective experience, thus seems to be a further, dynamic feature of its own, added to the packages of information that constitute perceptual objects. Again, there is a neurological disorder that selectively disables the mechanisms that generate the experience of visual motion in consciousness. The damage in this case is located in a visual cortical area activated by moving stimuli, known as V5 or MT. It lies in the middle temporal lobe (in monkeys) and at the junction of the temporal and occipital lobes in humans. The perceptual deficit resulting from damage to this area is known as akinetopsia: a/kinet/opsia (no/motion/vision). The simulated visual world in consciousness comes to a standstill; the movie-in-the-brain becomes a sequence of frozen snapshots.

Patients suffering from pure akinetopsia are rare, but there are a few clear cases reported in the literature. The most famous of them was reported in a neurological journal in 1983. Case L.M. was a female patient in her early forties who, after sustaining brain damage, claimed that she no longer saw movement. She could see objects at different locations perfectly well, and she was sure that the objects never moved, but instead they appeared to be jumping from one position to the next so that there was nothing in between (Heywood & Zihl, 1999):

> The visual disorder complained of by the patient was a loss of movement vision in all three dimensions. She had difficulty, for example, in pouring tea or coffee into a cup because the fluid appeared to be frozen, like a glacier. In addition, she could not stop pouring at the right time since she was unable to perceive the movement in the cup (or a pot) when the fluid rose ... In a room where more than two people were walking she felt very insecure and unwell, and usually left the room immediately, because "people were suddenly here or there but I have not seen them moving" ... She could not cross the street because of her inability to judge the speed of a car, but she could identify the car itself without difficulty. "When I'm looking at the car first, it seems far away. But then, when I want to cross the road, suddenly the car is very near." She gradually learned to "estimate" the distance of moving vehicles by means of the sound becoming louder.
>
> (Zihl, von Cramon, & Mai, 1983, p. 315)

The visual world of an akinetopsic patient resembles a sequence of still photographs that suddenly change. Each frame in itself gives no indication of motion. Normally, when we see objects in motion we automatically predict their trajectory so that we immediately get an understanding of where the objects are heading and where they will be after the next few seconds. Without seeing visual motion, this is impossible. The akinetopsic patient can, however, still conceive of the motion of objects through other senses, such as audition or touch. Auditory stimuli give cues of the location and motion of objects. Unfortunately not all objects emit any sounds to be heard while they move. But some do, such as cars on the street.

In this respect achromatopsia and akinetopsia are different. Colour experiences are purely visual – the chromatic colours of objects cannot be perceived through any other senses such as audition or touch. Motion, by contrast, is a feature of the dynamic spatial location of objects that may be perceived through other sensory modalities as well as vision. In fact, when it comes to audiovisual objects, the patient with akinetopsia should get conflicting information through vision and audition. While the visual information represents the object as standing still (or suddenly appearing in a different place), the auditory information indicates that the object is moving along a continuous trajectory.

Chapter summary

The above cases described in the neurological literature show that the normal unified visual consciousness – the visual world simulation in the brain – is based on a number of mechanisms that may break down independently of each other. Colour, coherent shape, motion or the meaningfulness of visual objects may disappear while all the rest remains. The space in which perceptual objects are normally located may just vanish into thin air, leaving behind only a half-space (neglect) or an unstable centre of consciousness without any surrounding spatial context (Balint's syndrome).

Visual consciousness is an immensely rich field of experience where visual objects appear coherent and spatially well organized within an overall spatial context. To bring together in an organized manner such spatial unity with such variability of content must be an enormously complex achievement of the brain. Any theory of consciousness should be able to explain both the unity and the rich variability of consciousness, as well as the patterns of disunified consciousness that follow after brain injury. The neuropsychological data reviewed in this chapter are thus an important source of evidence for the science of consciousness as well as a challenge for any theory – and even for any philosophy – of consciousness.

Further reading

D'Esposito, M. (Ed.) (2003). *Neurological foundations of cognitive neuroscience*. Cambridge, MA: MIT Press.

Driver, J., & Vuilleumier, P. (2001). Perceptual awareness and its loss in unilateral neglect and extinction. *Cognition, 79*, 39–88.

Farah, M. J. (1990). *Visual agnosia*. Cambridge, MA: MIT Press.

Farah, M. J. (1994). Visual perception and visual awareness after brain damage: A tutorial overview. In C. Umiltà & M. Moscovitch (Eds.), *Attention and performance XV: Conscious and nonconscious information processing* (pp. 37–76). Cambridge, MA: MIT Press.

Farah, M. J., & Feinberg, T. E. (Eds.) (2000). *Patient-based approaches to cognitive neuroscience*. Cambridge, MA: MIT Press.

Feinberg, T. E. (2001). *Altered egos: How the brain creates the self*. New York: Oxford University Press.

Gazzaniga, M. S., Ivry, R. B., & Mangun, G. R. (2008). *Cognitive neuroscience: The biology of the mind* (3rd ed.). New York: Norton.

Heywood, C. A., & Zihl, J. (1999). Motion blindness. In G. W. Humphreys (Ed.), *Case studies in the neuropsychology of vision* (pp. 1–16). Hove: Psychology Press.

Hodges, J. R. (2003). Semantic dementia: A disorder of semantic memory. In M. D'Esposito (Ed.), *Neurological foundations of cognitive neuroscience* (pp. 67–87). Cambridge, MA: MIT Press.

Humphreys, G. W. (Ed.) (1999). *Case studies in the neuropsychology of vision*. Hove: Psychology Press.

Rapp, B. (Ed.) (2001). *The handbook of cognitive neuropsychology*. Philadelphia, PA: Psychology Press.

Revonsuo, A. (2006). *Inner presence*. Cambridge, MA: MIT Press.

Sacks, O. (1985). *The man who mistook his wife for a hat*. London: Picador.

Sacks, O. (1995). *An anthropologist on Mars*. London: Picador.

Zihl, J., von Cramon, D., & Mai, N. (1983). Selective disturbance of movement vision after bilateral brain damage. *Brain, 106*, 313–340.

Brief discussion questions

Look at the visual objects around you. When you look at an object (say, a table, a candle, a car, a bird, etc.), try to see the unified perceptual object in your consciousness as a complex product of the mechanisms of binding in your brain. Then consider two questions:

1   How many different perceptual features did the brain have to bind together to create the perceptual object right now in your consciousness?
2   How would the same physical object look to you in your perceptual conscious-ness if you suffered from any of the disorders mentioned in this chapter? Try to imagine seeing the object from the subjective perspective of achromatopsia, visual agnosia (apperceptive and associative), semantic dementia, akinetopsia, simultanagnosia, Balint's syndrome and neglect. Write down a short description of what you would see in each case.

Chapter 5

Neuropsychological dissociations of visual consciousness from behaviour

Introduction: What is a neuropsychological dissociation?

When damage to the brain has consequences for the functions of the mind, neuro-psychologists try to get an accurate picture of what mental functions have been compromised and what still works normally, in the same way as before the damage. In other words, neuropsychologists are interested in the *patterns* of performance. By the "pattern of performance" they refer to the *combination of preserved and damaged cognitive functions*. As every brain lesion is unique and each brain anatomically somewhat different, the patterns of performance found after a certain type of brain damage cannot be exactly predicted by just looking at the patient's brain scans and localizing the damage there. Although the anatomical localization of the damage usually gives good grounds to expect certain types of cognitive deficits, a variety of neuropsychological tests or experiments must be administered to figure out what the patient still can do without difficulty and what kinds of tasks have become difficult or perhaps altogether impossible.

The patterns of performance are divided into three different types. First, the pattern called *association* means that, typically, after a lesion in a certain part of the brain, the fate of certain cognitive capacities (or the performance of certain neuropsychological tasks) tends to be shared; they are in this sense "associated". The ability to recognize visual objects and the ability to recognize faces is a case in point. After damage to the visual areas in the occipitotemporal cortex, especially in the right hemisphere, it is likely that the patient will have difficulty in recognizing common objects or pictures of objects, and also difficulty in recognizing the faces of familiar people. Conversely, if the brain damage is located elsewhere, say, in the prefrontal areas of the left hemisphere, it is likely that the patient has no difficulty in recognizing either visual objects or familiar faces. Thus, the fate of these two deficits goes hand in hand: either *both tend to be preserved* or *both tend to be damaged*.

The association of various types of deficits is commonly found, which is no surprise. If different functions are localized in the brain in different places, then the larger the damaged area is, the more likely it is that several different cognitive functions have been damaged by the same brain lesion. In particular, if two cognitive functions use neural circuitry that is anatomically located just next to each other, it is highly probable that a lesion anywhere in that general area will damage both functions rather than neatly destroy only one of them, leaving the other intact. Brain lesions do not respect anatomical or functional borderlines in the brain, thus their effects usually are not confined to a single cognitive function.

But there may be another equally plausible explanation for why two cognitive functions are associated with each other. Perhaps the two functions are, from the perspective of the cognitive architecture in the brain, not two different functions at all but just *varieties of a single function* using the very same neural circuitry. Consider visual object recognition again. There are lots of different kinds of objects in the world: coloured and black-and-white objects, tiny and huge objects, inanimate objects, animals, faces, and so on. Now, is there a single perceptual master system in the brain that handles *all* these different types of objects when we see them or are there many smaller, independent systems that are specialized in recognizing only certain types of objects? Perhaps there could be different systems for recognizing tiny and huge objects, round and square objects, or faces and other types of objects? Is this at least conceivable? How could we ever find out?

To figure out the answers to questions concerning the number and the type of different, specialized cognitive systems in the brain, we have to pay particular attention not to associations of deficits but to *dissociations between preserved and damaged functions*. Associations leave it open whether two cognitive functions are taken care of by the very same system (and therefore are not genuinely two separate functions at all, but simply variations of a single function) or whether the two functions just happen to reside in the same neighbourhood in the brain and thus become wiped out together whenever an indiscriminate blow to that neighbourhood occurs. Dissociations, by contrast, reveal that the two functions really are different from each other, cognitively and anatomically.

Dissociation can be defined as the situation where *one cognitive function is preserved* and *the other one is damaged*. Thus, in the case of face recognition and object recognition, dissociation would be shown by a patient who is still able to recognize all other objects without difficulty but miserably fails in recognizing faces. Such a finding would be called a *single* dissociation between object recognition and face recognition, and it has in fact been observed: Object recognition can be preserved in a patient who has lost the ability to recognize faces. By contrast, no dissociations have been found between the recognition of round and square objects. Thus, they are all taken care of by the same object recognition system.

Even if face recognition and object recognition show the single dissociation described above (objects are recognized but faces are not), the possibility remains that face recognition is just a *particularly difficult type* of object recognition. Thus, if the object recognition system has suffered a blow, but not a fatal one, it may still be able to take care of the recognition of ordinary "easy" objects but cracks when faced with a more difficult task, that of recognizing a complex object such as a face!

To rule out this possibility, a special kind of dissociation must be observed – a *double dissociation* (see Figure 5.1), which refers to *two single dissociations that go in opposite directions in (at least) two different patients*. In the first patient we have the single dissociation discussed above: objects are recognized but faces are not. In the second patient we observe the opposite pattern: faces are recognized but objects are not. A double dissociation is theoretically the most interesting pattern of performance, because *only a double dissociation shows that two cognitive functions are truly independent functions and must use anatomically different neural circuitry*, even if localized near each other (when many patients have first shown the association of the deficits, we already know that the neural mechanisms must be close to each other).

The branch of neuropsychology that is particularly interested in the patterns of deficits is called cognitive neuropsychology. Cognitive neuropsychologists whose primary interest is to explain the cognitive deficits of neuropsychological patients and to build a cognitive model of the mind that can be used in those explanations are hunting for double dissociations. Whenever they find one, they are confident that the accurate cognitive model of the mind must include two separate systems for the two doubly dissociated functions, rather than treating them as varieties of a single function. Theoretical progress in cognitive neuropsychology thus largely depends on finding double dissociations in the patterns of performance of neuropsychological patients.

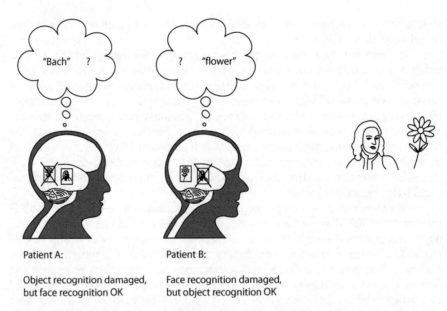

Patient A:

Object recognition damaged,
but face recognition OK

Patient B:

Face recognition damaged,
but object recognition OK

Figure 5.1 Double dissociation between object recognition and face recognition

To establish that two cognitive functions are doubly dissociable, at least two patients with exactly opposite deficits have to be found. Patient A can recognize familiar faces but not objects. Patient B, conversely, can recognize objects but not familiar faces. Double dissociation shows that the two tasks, object recognition and face recognition, are functionally and neuroanatomically distinct and independent of each other

5.1 Dissociations and consciousness

What does all this have to do with consciousness? To their own (and everyone else's) surprise, in the 1980s and early 1990s, cognitive neuropsychologists observed for the first time very peculiar dissociations that were not really dissociations between two different cognitive functions but *between the conscious experience* related to a cognitive function and the purely *nonconscious information processing* related to the very same function. These findings created unrest among cognitive neuropsychologists, as their cognitive theories did not really have a place for consciousness, but the research findings more or less forced them to theorize about consciousness. At that time, consciousness was not openly discussed in cognitive psychology and therefore the neuropsychologists did not quite know what to make of these findings. Yet, philosophers became immediately interested in these fascinating empirical data. The growing interaction between neuropsychologists and philosophers was in fact one of the first signs of the emergence of the multidisciplinary science of consciousness in the early 1990s.

The peculiar dissociations between consciousness and behaviour, or between the conscious and nonconscious processing of the very same information, became one of the most important lines of empirical research in the science of consciousness at its early stages. At first, cognitive neuropsychologists used terms that hid the fact that consciousness or subjective experience is involved. They talked about dissociation between the *explicit* and the *implicit* processing of information, or explicit and implicit perception, or explicit and implicit memory. Also the terms *covert recognition* and *overt recognition* were used in connection with face recognition. Nonetheless, the empirical facts showed that after brain damage it is possible for a patient to lose the subjective experience normally caused by a certain type of stimulus, but still the results of objective measurements may show that information about the stimulus is represented and processed by the patient's brain, somewhere outside consciousness.

Even more surprisingly, the nonconscious information may still guide some aspects of the patient's behaviour, even if the patient is completely unaware of the information or its influence on his or her behaviour: The patient can accurately point towards or pick up a visual stimulus without seeing it! This ability is almost eerie. At first sight it seems supernatural; there must be some sort of extrasensory perception going on! The real explanation is not supernatural, but still quite exciting: *There are zombies inside our heads!* The neural systems that process information and guide behaviour without and outside conscious experience are called "zombie systems". They are like zombies in the sense that they possess no consciousness and behave in an intelligent manner. But of course they do not look like the proto-typical voodoo zombie or the philosopher's zombies. Zombie systems in the brain are nonconscious processing mechanisms that guide behaviour. It has been suggested that perhaps many animal brains (like those of lizards and frogs) only contain such zombie systems to guide their behaviour (like catching flies with their tongue, which strikes as fast as lightning and accurately shoots at a fly in midflight). If that is true, then the whole animal must be a zombie (devoid of phenomenal consciousness). This impression is strengthened by the fact that frogs only perceive, catch and eat flies that are in motion, and would starve to death while sitting in the middle of a pile of dead flies! Clearly, the frog brain's concept of "food" is a moving dot in the air that must be met by the tongue. It is quite plausibe that such a rigid (even stupid) function might be handled without consciousness.

In dissociations of consciousness where the zombie systems are revealed, subjective conscious experience of the information is lost, but a nonconscious form of the same information remains intact. This is the core of the neuropsychological dissociations between consciousness and behaviour, or between explicit (conscious) and implicit (nonconscious) cognition. We will next take a look at some of the most famous cases of this phenomenon.

Blindsight

In the dissociation called blindsight, the neural damage is located in the primary visual cortex or area V1 (see Figure 5.2). The information from the eyes (or retina) comes through the optic nerve via the thalamus to the visual cortex, arriving first at V1 before being channelled to further visual areas in the cortex. The entire visual field is represented like an organized map on V1. In blindsight, V1 has been (partially) destroyed by a lesion. Thus, the part of V1 that is gone takes away the corresponding part of the visual field map. The larger the destroyed area of V1, the larger becomes

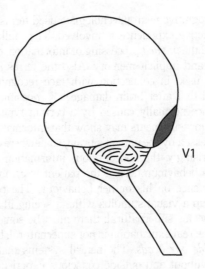

V1

Figure 5.2 V1 and blindsight

The primary visual cortex or area V1 is located at the back of the brain; its tip is visible on the cortical surface but most of it is not exposed as it lies folded in the space between the hemispheres. Blindsight patients have this area partly damaged, leading to cortical blindness in the corresponding part of the visual field, but preserved ability to process the unseen stimuli outside of consciousness (see text for details)

the missing area in the map. If the entire V1 in one hemisphere is destroyed, then blindness covers one half of the visual world (the other half is taken care of by the intact hemisphere's V1). In visual perception, the damaged area of V1 shows itself as a blind region in the visual field, that is, stimuli located in that part of the visual field are simply not seen. The subject has no idea, no conscious experience, of anything in the blind field. This is where the "blind" in blindsight is derived from.

But what about the "sight" in blindsight? This was the real surprise. In laboratory experiments, subjects with V1 damage were shown visual stimuli. In a typical experiment, points of light were briefly lit at different locations in front of the patient when the patient was looking straight ahead, without moving his head or eyes. The task of the patient would be just to report whenever he saw the light. As expected, the patients had no difficulty in seeing the stimuli in the intact parts of the visual field, but they could not see the stimuli located in the damaged part. Still, the experimenters encouraged the patients to just guess whether there was a light or not. The procedure is formally called "*forced-choice task*", which means that the subject must choose every time between two alternatives, such as "light" and "no light". There is no alternative for "I don't know", which the patients would have chosen every time if allowed. Sometimes the task required the patients to point with their finger to where the light might have been.

Anyway, the patients felt that the task was silly, because they really could not see the stimuli and were just guessing. It turned out, however, that their guesses were incredibly accurate, much more so than anybody would manage to get by truly blind guessing! Somehow, the responses ("light" or "no light") that the patients gave must have been guided by the unseen visual information – the zombie in the brain! That information never entered consciousness but, still, it must have been there and must have coded the presence or the location of the unseen stimulus and pushed the patient to respond in one way rather than another. The patients themselves were as thoroughly amazed about the results as were the neuropsychologists.

In further experiments, the nature of the unseen visual information was further explored (see Weiskrantz, 1997). It was found that the unseen information coded only relatively basic aspects of the stimulus, such as its presence (vs. absence), location, direction of movement and simple form (X vs. O, for example). It did not code such things as the identity or meaning of the stimulus. Thus, the blindsighted zombie system in the brain "knows" whether a stimulus is presented or not, whether it is moving or not and in what direction and whether the stimulus is round or square, but it has no clue whether the stimulus is an animal or an object, for example. Such higher type of information as semantic content or meaning, so characteristic of the conscious representation of visual objects, does not seem to be included in the nonconscious form of information that guides blindsight.

Implicit visually guided action

A patient known as D.F. in the neuropsychological literature is the most famous case of implicit visually guided action (see Goodale & Milner, 2005). She was the victim of carbon monoxide poisoning, which damaged her visual cortex severely. However, the main damage was not in V1 as in blindsight, but in a later area called LO or the lateral occipital cortex. The LO area is activated in the normal brain when coherent objects or shapes are shown, as opposed to scrambled objects or totally disorganized visual stimuli. Thus, the LO area most likely is necessary for putting together the coherent shape of objects. Damage to this area does not lead to blindness but to visual form agnosia, the inability to see visual objects as coherent wholes. D.F. was suffering from severe visual form agnosia. She could not name or describe objects shown to her. If asked to copy pictures or line drawings of objects, her drawings did not resemble the original models at all (but when she was asked to draw an object from memory, she could produce recognizable copies, showing that her internal visual memory images were preserved). She was not able to explain what her visual world looked like because it was not simply a blurred version of our normal visual world, like a near-sighted person sees the world without glasses. She was certainly not blind. On the contrary, D.F. could see elementary visual features such as colours and she could see fine visual details, but somehow those details were not bound together in stable coherent forms and shapes. Her condition was similar to visual agnosia described in the previous chapter.

The nonconscious visual information about objects that D.F. still possessed was manifested in tasks where D.F. was required to do something with the objects, to physically interact with them. In one task, objects of different sizes and shapes were placed before D.F. First, her conscious visual perception was examined by asking her to describe and recognize the objects before her very eyes. She was utterly unable to do this. Thus, D.F. had no idea of the shape, size or identity of the objects that there are in front of her eyes. Next, she was simply asked to try to pick up whatever objects there were in front of her. Her behaviour was recorded on videotape for closer analysis. Although she did not see what objects there were and did not know their size or shape or even exact location, amazingly enough her hand seemed to know all this! Her reaching and grasping behaviour was flawless. Her arm reached out in the correct direction, her hand opened and her fingers moved according to the shape and size of the object, to form an optimal grip. Somehow, nonconscious visual information from her eyes was guiding her reaching behaviour. A similar result was obtained in another task, which simulated posting a letter into a mailbox. There was a box with a narrow hole. The orientation of the hole (vertical, horizontal or anything in between) could be manipulated. When D.F. was shown the box and asked to describe the orientation of the hole, she was unable to do it. She could not consciously perceive the hole and thus had no idea of its orientation. However, when she was given a piece of paper that was supposed to be a letter and she was told that the box is a mailbox and she is supposed to put the letter into the mailbox, then again her performance was remarkably accurate. Her hand and arm seemed to know the orientation of the hole, as she invariably reached towards the hole with the letter oriented so that it perfectly fitted the orientation of the hole, and thus the letter was posted without difficulty.

The explanation offered for the performance of D.F. was that there are two major processing pathways for visual information in the cortex (see Figure 5.3). One of them, the *ventral visual stream*, is specialized in producing visual representations of coherent objects for consciousness. The damaged area, LO, is along this pathway. However, the second pathway, the *dorsal visual stream*, was intact in D.F.'s brain. This pathway is specialized into providing information concerning where the visual objects are located and how to interact with them. This information, as case D.F. made all too clear, is nonconscious. It guides our behaviour towards objects but it does

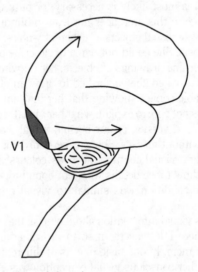

Figure 5.3 Ventral stream and dorsal stream

The two main pathways of visual processing that travel from the primary visual cortex to the temporal cortex (ventral stream) and the posterior parietal cortex (dorsal stream)

not generate any subjective experience or conscious representations of those objects. The dorsal stream is a zombie system in the brain!

This interpretation was further confirmed by showing that there can be a double dissociation between the ventral and the dorsal stream functions. Thus, a patient with a damaged dorsal stream but an intact ventral stream showed the exact opposite pattern to D.F. This patient could see, recognize and describe the visual objects before her perfectly well. But when asked to pick an object up, her hands and arms were groping randomly, like in the dark. They had no idea of the exact location, size or shape of the objects, and therefore grasping them could only be managed by hitting them by chance when waving the hands around. This patient's visual consciousness was not blind to the objects, but her actions seemed to be. This condition is known in neuropsychology as *optic ataxia*. In optic ataxia, the dorsal stream zombie has dropped dead (although in the horror genre, zombies are the *un*dead that cannot be killed by any means whatsoever!). Visual consciousness is intact, but left to its own devices, and in the absence of help from the visuomotor zombie it is unable to guide behaviour.

Implicit face recognition in prosopagnosia

We see hundreds of human faces every day and we immediately recognize them as familiar or not. Seeing and recognizing a face happens so quickly and effortlessly that it is hard to appreciate how complex an achievement it is for our brain. The complexities of face recognition are only revealed when something goes wrong with the face recognition systems in the brain.

What *could* happen then? Well, you might see people's faces as totally empty plates, or you might see them as Picasso-like paintings, as messy collections of eyes, noses, ears, lips. Or you might see them as normal faces but have no idea as to *whose* faces they are. Everyone has started to look like a stranger. What is going on?

Prosopagnosia is a deficit of face perception or recognition. There are different types of prosopagnosia. The first type is a deficit of basic face *perception*. When looking at a face, the patient reports not seeing a face, but only the parts of the face (eyes, lips, nose) in some kind of disorganized or unstable configuration. Some patients also say that faces look like empty oval plates with no detail at all. Because these patients cannot see the faces as faces, they obviously cannot recognize a person by looking at the person's face. The second type of prosopagnosia is a pure deficit of *recognition* rather than perception. The patients can see faces perfectly well and they can also describe the face that they see in terms of age, sex, attractiveness, and so on. Their only problem is that all the faces they see look like the faces of complete strangers. When they look at the faces (or the pictures of faces) of celebrities, friends, relatives or family members, the faces ring no bells for them. The patients have no idea whose faces they are looking at. They do not get any feeling of familiarity – the faces do not feel or look to them as if they have seen them many times before. The patients have not simply forgotten about the people they know. In fact, they can still recognize people normally from other cues, such as voice or clothing or style of walking. When talking on the telephone with familiar people, they have no problems in recognizing the person with whom they are talking. When dealing with the voice only, they feel that the person they are talking to is familiar to them and they can immediately tell who the person is.

Neuropsychologists have tried to understand what is going on in these cases by postulating a multistage model for the recognition of faces (Ellis & Young, 1988). When we see a face, the first stage of processing the face-specific information is called *structural encoding* (see Figure 5.4). It refers to the process where the coherent visual image of the face is put together. The result is that we see a face as a whole rather than just the various parts of a face jumping around incoherently. Obviously, for the first type of prosopagnosia it is exactly this stage that has been damaged. The brain no longer can put together coherent visual representations of faces.

The next stage in the face processing model uses *face recognition units*. Their function is to take the image of the seen face, constructed by the immediately earlier

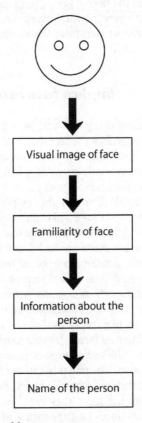

Figure 5.4 Cognitive model of face processing

According to this cognitive model of the different stages of information processing in face recognition, the brain first produces the visual image of the face, then this image is matched against all faces previously seen and stored in memory, to determine whether we are looking at a familiar face or not. If the face is familiar, then the brain fetches all the information we have about the person in our long-term memory files about that person. Finally, the name of the person is fetched from a different storage unit that combines faces with names

stage of structural encoding, and rapidly match this image with all the images of faces ever seen before. As a result, either a close enough match is found, or it is not found. If a match is found, the system indicates this result by producing a *feeling of familiarity* in consciousness. The subject experiences emotional familiarity that conveys "Yes, I have seen this face before; it is the face of someone I know". The stage of processing dealing with the feeling of familiarity has become deficient in the prosopagnosic patient for whom all faces look unfamiliar.

In addition to the first stage of structural encoding and the second stage of face-recognition units and feeling of familiarity, the cognitive model of face recognition includes two further stages: *person identity nodes* carry the information we have about the persons we know and this information can also be accessed via other routes such as hearing the voice or the name of the person; and the *names* of the persons we know are stored in a different place than all the other information.

Our everyday experience confirms that these stages of processing exist and that sometimes some of them do not work so well even in healthy brains. We sometimes see somebody on the street and get a strong feeling of familiarity; we are sure that we have seen that person before. Yet, we cannot recall who the person is, where we have met him or in fact anything else other than the fact, established by the feeling of familiarity, that we know him from somewhere. Thus, in this case our person identity nodes refuse to cooperate, and do not find or deliver the information they have about this person. Even more commonly it happens that we meet somebody on the street, get the feeling of familiarity, recall where we have met the person before but have no idea of the name of the person even though we know that we should remember his name. In this case, all the other stages work well apart from the name generation stage.

The prosopagnosic patients who can see faces but not recognize them as familiar seem to have nonconscious knowledge about the familiarity of the faces – their brain seems to house a face-recognition zombie! The first studies revealing this surprising and mysterious ability were conducted by measuring changes in the patients' electrical skin conductance – the same measurement that is used in lie detection. The patients were shown pictures of familiar and unfamiliar faces. They felt that all of the faces were unfamiliar and answered accordingly; yet, the skin conductance response was clearly different for familiar than unfamiliar faces. Skin conductance is related to emotional arousal, and familiar faces induce more of it than unfamiliar ones in normal people. Somehow the knowledge about the familiarity of the faces was available for the proposagnosic patients' emotional arousal systems, but not to consciousness. Further experiments showed that the familiarity of faces influenced the reactions of the patients in many other ways too: they had faster reaction times, different eye movement patterns and dissimilar EEG responses to familiar than to unfamiliar faces. All the evidence indicated that these patients (or at least many of them, if not all) still had somewhere in their brain the information about the familiarity of faces, and this information was activated when they saw a familiar face. The only problem was that the information about familiarity never reached consciousness. They still experienced all the familiar faces as totally unfamiliar, and consequently treated familiar people as strangers unless they used some other means than faces in the recognition. The information about familiarity and recognition could only be expressed through indirect routes, not in their conscious, deliberate behaviour. Their brains (or the zombies in their brains) seemed to know more about the familiarity of faces than did their conscious minds.

Implicit recognition of words and objects in neglect

A patient with neglect loses awareness of the left side of perceptual space and thereby is not aware of the existence of any objects in that space. But after the curious findings concerning blindsight and other nonconscious information in other neuro-psychological patients, the question arose whether neglect patients do know, at some nonconscious level in their brain, about the left side of space and its contents. After all, the damage in neglect is in the right posterior parietal lobe, not in the visual cortex. Thus, all the areas in the visual cortex and along the ventral visual stream should be intact and should continue processing visual information normally. These systems have the capacity to produce the representations of objects that normally enter consciousness. Do they go about their business also in neglect patients, producing high-level, detailed representations of objects that just cannot enter consciousness?

To study this, neglect patients were given stimuli that had something on the right side (which they could see and react to or verbally report) and something else on the left side (which they could neither see nor report). The idea was to check whether what is on the left, unseen side somehow affects their responses nonetheless. In one study, the neglect patient was shown two pictures that were identical on the right side but a slightly different picture on the left side. For example, in one of two pictures of a house there were bright red flames emerging from the left side of the house (see Figure 5.5). This is known as the famous "Burning House" experiment (Marshall & Halligan, 1988). The patient was asked first what she saw in the two pictures and whether she saw any difference between the pictures. She said she saw exactly the same house in both pictures; there was no difference between them. She never noticed the flames on the left. Then she was asked to select the house in which she herself would prefer to live. The patient thought this was a silly task as the houses looked just the same, but when pushed she chose one of the houses anyway. It turned out, as you might guess by now, that most of the time (80%) across several trials she chose the house without the flames. At some nonconscious level, her brain had detected that there was something wrong with one of the houses and therefore preferred the other one.

In other types of studies two words, or a picture and a word, were flashed in the right and left perceptual fields. The neglect patients could only see and report the right-sided stimulus, but still their reaction times were influenced also by the left-sided stimulus. If the right- and left-sided stimulus were strongly related through meaning (such as cloud – rain), then their reaction times to the seen stimulus were faster than if the two stimuli were totally unrelated (such as cloud – cheese). The meaning of the left-sided stimulus had been processed by the neglect patient's brain and it interacted with the meaning of the right-sided stimulus, but all this happened out-side of consciousness. The same results appeared also if pictures of objects, both pictures and words in combination, were used as stimuli (for a review, see Làdavas, Berti, & Farnè, 2000).

In neglect, the left-sided perceptual world is missing from consciousness but not from the brain. It is still processed and represented by the brain to a rather high level

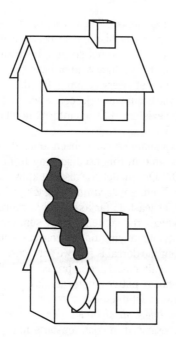

Figure 5.5 The Burning House experiment

A neglect patient sees these two houses as identical, because the crucial difference is on the left, neglected side. Implicit knowledge of the neglected information shows itself if the patient is asked to choose in which house he or she would prefer to live. Then the patients choose the intact house, although without being able to explain why it is better than the other one

that can extract the meaningful relations of the stimulus to other stimuli. This seems to be a higher level of processing than in blindsight where the nonconscious information codes quite primitive or low-level stimulus features, not their meaning.

5.2 Theories of the conscious/nonconscious dissociations

Blindsight in cortical blindness, nonconscious visually guided action in visual agnosia, nonconscious face recognition in prosopagnosia and nonconscious perception of objects in neglect are perhaps the clearest examples of the dissociation between conscious and nonconscious information in the brain. They are by no means the only cases of conscious/nonconscious dissociation: there are many more reported in the neuropsychological literature. Implicit memory in amnesia refers to the findings that people who have severe memory problems, and cannot remember anything for more than a minute, learn to implicitly remember things they have done: they just cannot remember *that* they have learned anything or *what* they have learned. But their skills get better and their reaction times faster if they practice, say, playing a computer game every day. They cannot remember that they have ever used the computer before, no matter how many times they have played with it.

Implicit processing of language has been detected in some aphasic patients who cannot understand words or sentences. Their reaction times or their EEG responses, however, reveal that their brain can distinguish between meaningful words or sentences and nonsense, although they do not seem to have any conscious access to the meaning of the words and sentences they read or hear.

Thus, the evidence is just overwhelming for the existence of nonconscious information processing in the brain when the corresponding information cannot enter consciousness. How can the existence of such information be explained? What does it tell us about consciousness?

Several different explanations have been offered to understand how consciousness could be dissociated in this peculiar way from nonconscious processing (Köhler & Moscovitch, 1997). One model (the distinct knowledge model; see Figure 5.6) suggests that in the brain there are *separate pathways for processing conscious and nonconscious information*, at least as far as vision is concerned. The ventral visual stream in the cortex produces the contents for visual consciousness, whereas the dorsal stream guides behaviour relying on nonconscious information. If the ventral stream alone is damaged but the dorsal is not, we get a case with visual consciousness wiped out (agnosia) but visually based action preserved. If the damage goes the other way around, we get the opposite pattern (optic ataxia).

Another explanatory model (the disconnection model; see Figure 5.7) suggests that in the brain there is *one central and unified consciousness system*, and that all information that is experienced in consciousness must reach this system. If the connections between, say, the face processing mechanisms and the consciousness system are cut, face processing may still continue to happen at a nonconscious level but the results of the processing never enter consciousness. The results can only influence behaviour indirectly, bypassing consciousness.

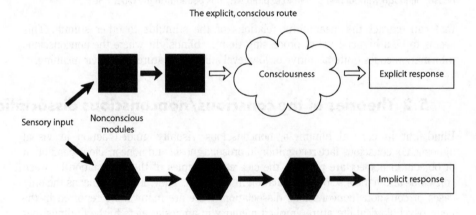

Figure 5.6 Distinct knowledge model of conscious/nonconscious dissociations

This model suggests that in the brain there are separate pathways for processing conscious and nonconscious information. The dissociation between the ventral visual stream (visual consciousness of objects) and the dorsal visual stream (nonconscious visuomotor functions) is in harmony with this model

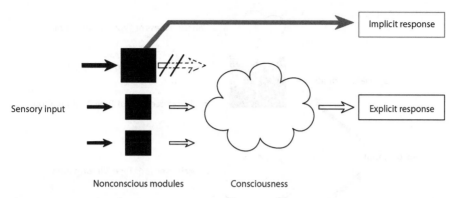

Sensory input

Nonconscious modules   Consciousness

Implicit response

Explicit response

Figure 5.7 Disconnection model

This type of model suggests that in the brain there is one central and unified consciousness system, and that all the different types of information that are experienced in consciousness must reach this system after they have first been processed in some specialized module. If the connections between one module (say, face recognition) and the consciousness system are cut, the implicit processing of that type of information may still continue, but the results of the processing never enter consciousness. The results can only be seen in implicit responses that influence behaviour indirectly, bypassing consciousness

A third explanatory model (the degraded representation model; see Figure 5.8) suggests that *each processing module generates its own type of conscious content*: the face processing module produces conscious face representations, the object processing module produces consciously seen objects, and so on. But the conscious representations are the ultimate product of the modules and require maximal activation levels in the module. If the module is damaged, it may be unable to reach a high enough activation level and therefore it cannot produce the conscious representations anymore. It only manages to produce nonconscious representations and send them along instead. There is no single system for consciousness where all the conscious representations should be sent; each specific content takes care of its own type of conscious representation.

Now each of the explanatory models seems to work in at least some cases, but none of them seems to work perfectly in every case. In implicit visually guided action, the separate pathways for conscious and nonconscious processing seem like a plausible explanation. In prosopagnosia, the activation level of the processing module does not seem to reach a level that would produce the conscious feeling of familiarity. In neglect, it seems that visual representations are being produced but they cannot reach the spatial consciousness system that places all conscious contents into the single unified perceptual space. In fact, some neglect patients see details or objects that are in fact in the left space as placed into the right side of space instead, as if the representations for consciousness would be there but the appropriate space not, therefore the conscious representations have to be forced into whatever space there is available, even if it is the "wrong" space.

So far, it is thus unclear which model or models are on the right track; perhaps all of them are to some extent applicable in different cases. However, what these

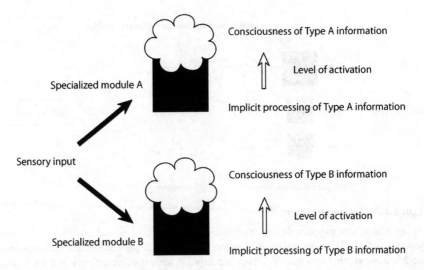

Consciousness of Type A information

Level of activation

Specialized module A

Implicit processing of Type A information

Sensory input

Consciousness of Type B information

Level of activation

Specialized module B

Implicit processing of Type B information

Figure 5.8 Degraded representation model

This type of model suggests that each processing module generates its own type of conscious content all by itself. The conscious experiences of the information constitute a high-level product of the modules and require maximal activation levels in the module. If the module is damaged, it may be unable to reach a high enough activation level and therefore it cannot produce the conscious representations anymore. It only produces nonconscious representations and sends them along instead. According to this model, there is no single system for consciousness where all the conscious representations are produced; instead, each specific content takes care of its own type of conscious representation. This model comes close to Zeki's microconsciousness theory (see Chapter 11)

dissociations tell us about consciousness seems clearer. In all the above-mentioned cases, *the patients cannot really use the nonconscious information to any useful purpose in their deliberate behaviour or decision making.* They do not know directly about the existence of that information, thus they do not see or recognize the stimuli as far as they are concerned, and their behaviour in everyday situations is as helpless as that of a person who has neither the conscious nor the nonconscious information available!

Conversely, this reveals how crucially important the conscious information is for us. It appears that all conscious information is functionally unified in the sense that only the information that enters consciousness allows us to evaluate it, consider different courses of action, make decisions, form or retrieve memories, plan and carry out deliberate interactions, and so on. Our intelligent, flexible, integrated, deliberately planned behaviour is based on the information that enters consciousness. Nonconscious information guides many rapid, automatic aspects of behaviour incredibly well, but it cannot take over the qualitatively different functions of conscious information when the latter is missing. To function normally, we need both types of information.

The conscious type of information emerges as functionally indispensable for our successful behavioural interactions with the world. This confirms the intuition that we need consciousness to navigate in the world towards meaningful goals that are chosen based on the best evidence we have. The nonconscious information only adjusts our responses a bit to make them faster or more accurate, but they do not really even know what they are doing. They are more like complex reflexes (like the frog's tongue automatically launched towards the moving fly), whereas consciousness constitutes the meaningful subjective world in which we live. When a representation is missing from consciousness, the subjective world becomes impoverished and we cannot navigate in those parts of the world anymore that are not represented in consciousness.

A final word about how this relates to philosophical mind–body theories: It seems that if consciousness is carved off and the nonconscious zombies alone are left to guide our behaviour, then we do not fare particularly well in the world. Consciousness seems necessary for our ability to navigate in the world. This evidence goes against epiphenomenalism (which says that our conscious experience does not matter) and supports our intuitive idea that our conscious minds are needed to initiate and guide complex behaviour: nonconscious systems, the zombies inside our brains, are not up to the task.

Chapter summary

When we perceive and act upon what we see, the brain processes information about the same situation both at the conscious and nonconscious levels. After brain injury, the conscious information in the brain can be dissociated from the nonconscious information, so that only the latter remains. This leads to the curious situation where a patient denies (conscious) perception of the stimulus but still reacts to or manipulates the stimuli as if something inside him – a zombie system – perceives the stimulus accurately. The most famous dissociations of this type are blindsight (loss of conscious vision, coupled with ability to guess many visual features of objects), implicit visually guided action (loss of object vision, yet ability to manipulate objects by using visual information), implicit face recognition (loss of the feeling of familiarity of faces, yet preserved differential automatic reactions to familiar vs. unfamiliar faces) and implicit perception in neglect (loss of objects in the left perceptual space, yet information from those objects affects behaviour).

Three different theories try to explain how the conscious information could be damaged while the nonconscious remains. First, both conscious and unconscious information is always routed along different pathways, and the conscious pathway is damaged. Second, there is a single unified consciousness system where all conscious information is normally sent, but now the connection between it and a specific module (e.g. face perception) has been cut, so the face information remains nonconscious. Third, the conscious type of information is more complex to produce so that after the damage only the nonconscious type can be produced by the module specialized for a particular content (e.g. faces). The dissociations show that conscious information has unique powers in the brain to guide our behaviour in an integrated and flexible manner that nonconscious information can never do – the patients for whom only nonconscious information remains cannot use the information for anything that would help them manage better (except perhaps to satisfy the curiosity of nosy scientists and neuropsychologists!). Thus, conscious experience does not seem epiphenomenal or useless to us at all; by contrast, the brain navigates in the environment mostly by relying on the world simulation in consciousness. When some information is lost from the internal world model in consciousness, the brain loses its functional awareness of the environment.

Further reading

Ellis, A. W., & Young, A. W. (1988). *Human cognitive neuropsychology*. Hove, UK: Psychology Press.

Goodale, M. A., & Milner, A. D. (1992). Separate visual pathways for perception and action. *Trends in Neurosciences, 15*, 20–25.

Goodale, M. A., & Milner, A. D. (2005). *Sight unseen: An exploration of conscious and unconscious vision*. New York: Oxford University Press.

Karnath, H. O., & Hartje, W. (1987). Residual information processing in the neglected visual half-field. *Journal of Neurology, 234*, 180–184.

Köhler, S., & Moscovitch, M. (1997). Unconscious visual processing in neuropsychological syndromes: A survey of the literature and evaluation of models of consciousness. In M. D. Rugg (Ed.), *Cognitive neuroscience* (pp. 305–373). Cambridge, MA: MIT Press.

Làdavas, E., Berti, A., & Farnè, A. (2000). Dissociation between conscious and nonconscious processing in neglect. In Y. Rossetti & A. Revonsuo (Eds.), *Beyond dissociation: Interaction between dissociated implicit and explicit processing* (pp. 175–193). Amsterdam: John Benjamins.

Marshall, J. C., & Halligan, P. W. (1988). Blindsight and insight in visuo-spatial neglect. *Nature, 336*, 766–767.

McGlinchey-Berroth, R., Milberg, W. P., Verfaellie, M., Alexander, M., & Kilduff, P. T. (1993). Semantic processing in the neglected visual field: Evidence from a lexical decision task. *Cognitive Neuropsychology, 10*, 79–108.

Milner, A. D., & Goodale, M. A. (1995). *The visual brain in action*. Oxford: Oxford University Press.

Pöppel, E., Held, R., & Frost, D. (1973). Residual visual function after brain wounds involving the central visual pathways in man. *Nature, 243*, 295–296.

Renault, B., Signoret, J. L., Debruille, B., Breton, F., & Bolger, F. (1989). Brain potentials reveal covert facial recognition in prosopagnosia. *Neuropsychologia, 27*, 905–912.

Revonsuo, A. (2006). *Inner presence: Consciousness as a biological phenomenon*. Cambridge, MA: MIT Press.

Revonsuo, A., & Laine, M. (1996). Semantic processing without conscious understanding in a case of global aphasia: Evidence from auditory event-related brain potentials. *Cortex, 32*, 29–48.

Rossetti, Y. (1998). Implicit short-lived representations of space in brain damaged and healthy subjects. *Consciousness and Cognition, 7*, 520–558.

Rossetti, Y., & Revonsuo, A. (Eds.) (2000). *Beyond dissociation: Interaction between dissociated implicit and explicit processing*. Amsterdam: John Benjamins.

Schacter, D. L., McAndrews, M. P., & Moscovitch, M. (1988). Access to consciousness: Dissociations between implicit and explicit knowledge in neuropsychological syndromes. In L. Weiskrantz (Ed.), *Thought without language* (pp. 242–278). Oxford: Oxford University Press.

Tranel, D., & Damasio, A. R. (1985). Knowledge without awareness: An autonomic index of facial recognition by prosopagnosics. *Science, 228*, 1453–1454.

Tranel, D., & Damasio, A. R. (1988). Non-conscious face recognition in patients with face agnosia. *Behavioural Brain Research, 30*, 235–49.

Volpe, B. T., Ledoux, J. E., & Gazzaniga, M. S. (1979). Information processing of visual stimuli in an extinguished field. *Nature, 282*, 722–724.

Weiskrantz, L. (1992). Introduction: Dissociated issues. In A. D. Milner & M. D. Rugg (Eds.), *The neuropsychology of consciousness* (pp. 1–10). New York: Academic Press.

Weiskrantz, L. (1997). *Consciousness lost and found*. Oxford: Oxford University Press.

Young, A. W. (1994). Neuropsychology of awareness. In A. Revonsuo & M. Kamppinen (Eds.), *Consciousness in philosophy and cognitive neuroscience* (pp. 173–203). Hillsdale, NJ: Lawrence Erlbaum Associates.

Young, A. W., & De Haan, E. H. F. (1990). Impairments of visual awareness. *Mind and Language, 5*, 29–48.

Young, A. W., & Ellis, H. D. (2000). Overt and covert face recognition. In Y. Rossetti & A. Revonsuo (Eds.), *Beyond dissociation* (pp. 195–219). Amsterdam: John Benjamins.

Brief discussion questions

1   When they were first discovered, the dissociations described in this chapter were surprising, even baffling, for scientists because there was no theory to explain them. Consider the following alternative explanations for dissociations such as blindsight, visually guided zombie systems and implicit face recognition:

    (i)   The patients are intentionally lying. They really can see or recognize perfectly normally, but the brain damage forces them to lie about this.

    (ii)   The patients are not lying, but the patient's brain does consciously perceive all the information at some level. There is no nonconscious zombie system, but there are two different consciousness systems, and the one that speaks cannot simply perceive the information guiding the responses, but another conscious system can. (This explanation is similar to the split-brain phenomenon explored in the next chapter.)

    What is wrong (if anything) with these explanations?

2   Try to think about situations in which your zombie systems largely guide your behaviour (e.g. very fast visuomotor reactions to rapidly approaching stimuli). Can you recognize actions during which such zombie systems are operating also in your brain?

Chapter 6

Neuropsychological disorders of self-awareness

Introduction

In the previous two chapters we explored neuropsychological deficits that directly affect phenomenal consciousness, the most fundamental form of consciousness. In Chapter 4 we learned about deficits that wipe out or distort particular features of visual consciousness and in Chapter 5 we learned about deficits that also wipe out aspects of visual consciousness but at the same time they preserve nonconscious visual processing that is able to guide responses to stimuli, revealing zombie systems in the brain.

In the present chapter we move from deficits of phenomenal consciousness to deficits in higher forms of consciousness: reflective consciousness and self-awareness. Thus, these deficits are more about how a person *thinks about* his or her phenomenal experiences, or how a person *interprets* them in relation to his or her own self, or how they affect the sense of a continuous self. Some of the deficits force the patient to form bizarre interpretations and far-fetched beliefs about his or her experiences and about him- or herself, twisting the patient's subjective psychological world into shapes difficult to imagine.

6.1 Amnesia

Sometimes in the morning when you wake up it takes a couple of seconds to become aware of who you are, where you are and what you are supposed to start doing. Imagine that one morning as you wake up you cannot come up with *any* answers to these questions (not even after two cups of strong coffee): you have lost your autobiographical memory and your ability to mentally travel in time. As you look around in bewilderment, you wonder where you are and, indeed, *who* you are. You look into the mirror and see a face that is vaguely familiar but looks much older than it should. You have no idea what is going to happen today or what you are supposed to do. You take a paper and a pencil and write down: *"It seems to me that I just woke up from a dreamless sleep. I cannot remember what happened before, but right now I am vividly conscious, I have just come to my senses for the very first time. I will now try to figure out what is going on"*. You search around the house, and after a couple of minutes you notice a notebook with some writing in it. The handwriting seems familiar, but you cannot remember ever writing this. It says, *"It seems to me that I just woke up from a dreamless sleep ..."*. *"What rubbish is this"*, you wonder, *"I have never written anything like this."* You take the pen, cross out the lines, and write, *"I cannot remember what has happened before, but right now I have just come to my senses from what seems like a long period of unconsciousness. Now for the first time I am really conscious ..."*. Then your doctor marches in, but you do not recognize him, and he explains to you that you have lost your memory and are suffering from dense amnesia.

Amnesia typically involves damage to a part of the brain called the hippocampus, located deep inside the temporal lobes of the brain. Damage to the hippocampus can be caused by head injury, Alzheimer's disease, alcoholism or carbon monoxide poisoning for example. Patients suffering from amnesia have either lost access to the existing memories that tell about the past or are unable to formulate any new memories about the experiences they are having right now, or both.

Imagine that you were involved in a traffic accident 1 year ago where you got a blow to your head, which caused amnesia. Let us say that, due to the damage, you cannot remember anything from 5 years before the accident. That type of loss of memory is called *retrograde* amnesia: loss of *old* memories that existed *before* the accident but were destroyed or became irretrievable after the accident. Let us further suppose that you have not been able to form any *new* memories after the accident. That type of memory loss is called *anterograde* amnesia, which in this case would encompass the year that has gone since the accident. Thus, the memory disorder would have left a blank of altogether 6 years of your life in your autobiographical memory.

Amnesic patients who cannot form new memories are doomed to live in a permanent present moment. They have lost the awareness of self as a temporally continuous being who has travelled a long road from the past to the here and now, to this very moment of present conscious experience, and who will be heading towards the future. Without any images about the moments that have passed minutes, hours or days ago, they have no awareness of the past where they came from. Some amnesic patients have described it as similar to waking up from a dream that quickly and totally escapes from memory – only knowing that one has dreamt vividly just a moment ago, but not having any idea what was going on in the dream. Furthermore, this feeling of waking up to a new reality happens again and again, all the time, not allowing the patient to reach a sense of subjective continuity. The amnesic patient does have the strong sense that *something* happened just a moment ago, but they cannot grasp what it was any longer. The past slips through their fingers and disappears into thin air. The only world that exists for them consists of the events and thoughts right now in consciousness.

One famous case suffering from global amnesia in fact did try to overcome the sense of discontinuity by keeping a diary. But this, it turned out, did not help him at all. Line after line he wrote in his diary: *"Now I am really conscious for the very first time"*. He crossed out the earlier entries when writing a new one, because he could not remember ever having written them, thus they seemed totally alien to him. At one point he wrote: *"All other claims to be awake are rubbish"* (Kapur, 1997, p. 4).

Amnesia is often described as a disorder of memory, but in fact it is at least as much a deficit of self-awareness. One substantial feature of self-awareness is the ability to mentally travel in time. When engaged in mental time travel to the past, we retrieve memory images and by relying on them we construct a story about the past events we have personally witnessed. When we travel to the future in our plans and dreams, we can literally see ourselves in other times and places where we hope to be some day. Mental time travel thus helps to create the sense of our personal temporal continuity – our life as a trajectory through time. It allows us to experience where we are coming from in the past (autobiographical memory) and where we are heading towards in the future (prospective memory).

Mental time travel to either the personal past or the personal future seems to be impossible for amnesic patients. When asked what they see in the future for themselves, or what they expect tomorrow will be like, they just draw a total blank. They have no idea, no conception of the future. They have lost the sense of self as a temporally continuous subject with a past and a future. Hence, they have lost a large part of their own self, or at least much information that used to be a part of their self-representation.

Self-awareness is altered in amnesia in a number of different ways. An amnesic patient only knows about his own personal past up to the point where the amnesia starts. Thus, it may be that a 50-year old person only remembers his life up to the time when he was 20. Furthermore, as an amnesic person does not directly realize or remember that he has lost a long stretch of time from memory, he feels and believes that he is the much younger person that he used to be long ago. There are stories of patients who take a look into the mirror and cannot believe their eyes because their own idea of what they should look like is several decades behind the reality. Also, an amnesic patient may wonder every day why other people look so much older than he remembers them or why the city has suddenly changed so much, old buildings have disappeared and new ones built overnight! (For well-documented patient cases, see Sacks, 1985.)

6.2 Split-brain

Split-brain is not a neurological disease, but the result of an intentional surgical lesion where the major neural connections between the left and right cerebral hemispheres have been cut (the major connection is called the *corpus callosum*, and sometimes also the smaller *anterior commissure* is cut). These operations were conducted as a last resort, especially in the 1960s, for patients who were suffering from severe epilepsy. When the connections between the hemispheres are cut, epileptic seizures starting from one hemisphere can no longer spread to the other hemisphere. Unfortunately, neither can any information be sent directly from one hemisphere to the other: The hemispheres are functionally isolated from each other. This raised the question: What happens to the consciousness of the patient? Is the conscious mind also split in two? After recovery from the operation, the patients were asked how they felt and their spontaneous behaviour was observed, but nothing out of the ordinary could be seen. The patients reported feeling all right, and did not complain that their mind felt split in any way.

However, sometimes the patients' spontaneous behaviour revealed that something unusual had happened to their mind. In some patients, sometimes the left and the right hand would act in conflict with each other, with one buttoning a shirt and the other unbuttoning it at the same time. Mark (1996) describes one patient who was asked by her doctor: *"Does your left hand feel numb?"*. The patient was confused about this question, answering both yes and no, switching the answer all the time back and forth. When shown the words "Yes" and "No" on two different pieces of paper, one hand pointed to "Yes" and the other to "No", and she seemed to be fighting with herself to come to a definite answer. Finally, the left hand forced aside the right and covered the word "Yes"! There definitely seemed to be two minds at play within this patient. The right hand/left hemisphere system was strongly of the opinion that the left hand indeed does feel numb, whereas the left hand/right hemisphere system had perfectly normal sensations in the left hand and strongly denied any numbness in it.

Laboratory experiments have confirmed that splitting the brain really does functionally isolate the hemispheres from each other. This was studied by briefly flashing a picture in only one visual field, the left or the right. When you stare at a dot in the middle of a screen, 30 cm in front of your nose, then the left and right visual fields are to the left and right of the fixation point, the dot. (Note that the visual fields are *not* the same thing as what the left and the right *eye* see; both eyes represent a part of both visual fields; see Figure 6.1a.) If certain arrangements (such as brief stimulus durations, 0.25 s at most) are made to prevent eye and head movements during stimulus presentation, then the information from the visual field only goes to the opposite (or contralateral) side of the brain; thus the left hemisphere "sees" the right visual field and the right hemisphere "sees" the left field.

Because speech is (in most people) exclusively controlled by the left hemisphere of the brain, questioning the patient verbally about what he has seen only produces a report about the stimuli that were shown in the right visual field. The speaking hemisphere has no idea whether something had been shown also to the right hemisphere (the left field). However, the patient's left hand, controlled by the right hemisphere, can point to what it had seen if given alternative pictures, for example. Thus, if shown a rabbit and a flower, the patient (or his left hemisphere) would *say* he saw a flower and *nothing else*, whereas his left hand (controlled by the right hemisphere) would point to a rabbit, not to a flower. It appears as if there is one person (or consciousness) who saw one thing and another who has seen another thing! But there is no-one who has seen *both* the rabbit *and* the flower! (Figure 6.1b).

From the outsider's point of view the mind of a split-brain patient is divided into two, but from the patient's point of view (or from the speaking, left hemisphere's point of view) everything seems and feels normal, with no split anywhere. In fact, the patient's left (speaking) hemisphere is eager to deny or explain away any evidence that hints to there being another subject involved in controlling a part of the behaviour. In tasks like the above, if the patient is asked why his left hand pointed to the bird, the patient's speaking, left hemisphere never explains that it must be because he has a split brain and that a part of his brain is not anymore under his (the speaker's) control, so it was that part that made the choice to point to the bird and he has nothing to do with it.

On the contrary, the left hemisphere will cook up a story about why he supposedly chose to point to the stimulus. In one famous experiment, the left hemisphere saw a picture of a chicken head and the right hemisphere saw a picture of a snowy winter scene (a snowman in front of a house) (Gazzaniga & LeDoux, 1978). The patient was asked to point to other pictures that go together with what he had seen. The right hand pointed to a chicken leg, the left hand to a snow shovel. When asked "What did you see?" the left (speaking) hemisphere answered that "I saw a claw and I picked the chicken, and you have to clean out the chicken shed with a shovel" (Gazzaniga & LeDoux, 1978, p. 148). Thus, the left hemisphere, the speaking subject, had no idea of the picture seen by the right hemisphere, which was the actual cause of choosing the shovel. In some rare cases, the right hemisphere also has been able to express itself verbally, but not by speaking out loud; instead it does this by arranging blocks of letters with the left hand, and spelling words in that way. Experiments with such patients revealed that the right hemisphere knows its name (or the name it shares with the left hemisphere and with the whole person) and it knows what it likes and dislikes. The right hemisphere answers some questions differently from the left hemisphere, as if it had a mind or self of its own (Gazzaniga, LeDoux, & Wilson, 1977).

The interpretation of the split-brain phenomenon has caused much controversy.

Some suggest that the patients really do have two minds or two separate streams of consciousness, created by the operation. Some have even argued that we *all* have two separate minds *all of the time* and that the operation does not *create* them; it only allows them to manifest themselves independently! Others, however, would be ready to grant the status of a conscious mind only to the left (speaking) hemisphere.

The most reasonable interpretation seems to be to say that when only phenomenal consciousness is concerned there are two independent streams of subjective

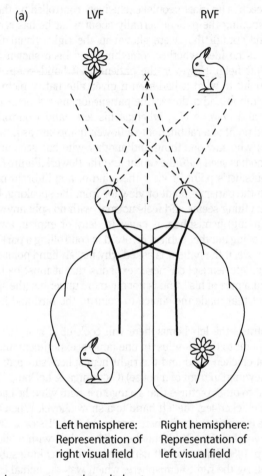

(a) LVF RVF

Left hemisphere: Right hemisphere:
Representation of Representation of
right visual field left visual field

Figure 6.1 Visual perception in the split-brain

(a) If the split-brain patient looks into the centre (X) and two images are briefly flashed, one (the rabbit) in the right visual field (RVF) and the other (the flower) in the left visual field (LVF), the following happens: Both the right and the left eye receive visual information from both of the pictures, but in the brain information from the RVF can only go to the left hempisphere visual cortex and information from the LVF can only go to the right hemisphere. (b, see opposite) In the split-brain patient the hemispheres cannot communicate with each other, so the information about each picture also remains only within one hemisphere

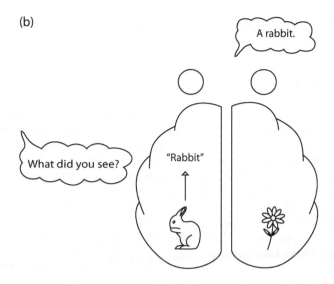

experience going on in the two hemispheres, but most of the time they overlap so much that there is no conflict. The conflicts arise only in laboratory experiments. Thus, the two phenomenal consciousnesses in the split-brain patient's two separated hemispheres are like two mirror sites in the internet; most of the time they are updated with the same information almost simultaneously, because when the patients move freely and look around, the same information falls at some point both into the left and the right visual fields and consequently the same overall picture ends up in both the right and the left hemisphere. But only the left hemisphere has a fully developed capacity for language, reflective consciousness and self-awareness. Thus, the left hemisphere attempts to explain away the discrepancies that arise from the independent behaviour of the right hemisphere in the laboratory experiments.

One of the leading split-brain researchers, Michael Gazzaniga, has suggested that the left hemisphere houses a special system for constructing narrative explanations for the person's behaviour. This is called "the left-hemisphere interpreter". Its job is to cook up a story – any story at all – that takes into account all the direct perceptual evidence available for the left hemisphere. The story explains why the person behaved as he did, even if a part of the real cause of behaviour is not known to the interpreter (such as the behaviour of the left hand in a split-brain patient). Some kind of plausible-sounding story must be concocted, nonetheless, to preserve the autonomy and the coherent self-image of the left-hemisphere-based self-awareness.

So, is the conscious mind of a split-brain patient *really* split into two? Well, I would say Yes! – and No! (It seems that my hemispheres will not agree about this.)

All right, *both* alternatives are in fact true, because each one is true about a different type of consciousness. Phenomenal consciousness is truly split: a slightly different version of it exists in each hemisphere independently, isolated from each other. By contrast, reflective consciousness and self-awareness are not split, as they are normally based on left hemisphere mechanisms, and therefore may continue their usual business as if nothing has happened; only sometimes they need to explain away some peculiar behaviours that the left hand engages in, not really knowing the real reasons for the behaviours but always eager to fabricate a story.

6.3 Anosognosia

Imagine that you break your leg but you do not take any notice of it: you just walk around as if everything is all right; or if you simply cannot walk and have to sit or lie down, you are still oblivious to the fact that you have a broken leg. If someone asks you why you do not get up, you say you are tired, or something like that. Anyway, you do not seem to be aware that you have a broken leg. If asked directly about it, you will deny that there is anything wrong with your leg.

Our imaginary case seems absurd. How could anyone have a broken leg and not know about it? Even though such cases perhaps do not exist in reality, neuro-psychological patients show at least an equally surprising and puzzling unawareness of the deficits they have. *Anosognosia* refers to *unawareness of deficit*. The term comes from *a* (un- or without), *noso* (disease or illness) and *gnosia* (knowledge) and literally means "lack of knowledge of the existence of disease" (Feinberg, 2001; Hirstein, 2005). It implies that there is something clearly wrong with your health, such as a part of your body is paralysed or you are blind; everybody else notices your problem immediately, and you yourself surely have abundant evidence of your own deficit and by all means *should* know about it.

It is difficult to understand how the affected person himself or herself could fail to notice his own paralysis or blindness (these two are the most common forms of anosognosia), yet an anosognosic patient does not report any knowledge or awareness of the deficit. But the issue is more complicated than simple lack of knowledge of or attention to the deficit. In fact, the patient cannot be convinced of their deficit even when it is explicitly pointed out to them. The patient seems to be under a delusion that cannot be removed by rational argument or factual evidence and thus he or she will resort to denial or confabulation to explain away any evidence that points towards the deficit.

If the deficit causes physical or behavioural difficulties, the patient attributes such things to tiredness, lack of motivation or anything else but the real cause. In other respects the anosognosic patient is perfectly lucid. The patient knows where he or she is, what day it is and other facts that a normal person is supposed to know. There is no general confusion or intellectual decline, severe dementia or memory problem that could explain the curious denial of deficit.

Thus, anosognosia is a specific deficit of self-awareness. The internal representation of the self should incorporate information about the undeniable deficit one has, but for some reason that information cannot be integrated to it. The self-model stubbornly indicates that there is no deficit, in the face of overwhelming contrary evidence.

Perhaps the most striking type of anosognosia, called *Anton's syndrome* (named after a 19th-century neurologist who discovered the phenomenon), is connected with cortical blindness. Some patients whose primary visual cortex has been destroyed and who are objectively blind to external stimuli do not seem to be aware of their own blindness. They say there is nothing wrong with their vision, and they may describe visual scenery that they seem to confabulate or make up. They may complain that the room is dark or that they do not see clearly because of some external circumstance, but it never seems to cross their mind that they have a problem with their own vision. It remains unclear what the subjective visual experience of these patients is like, or even whether they have any. One possibility is that they experience vague internally generated visual imagery that matches their expectations of what should be out there, and they take this to be normal vision even if it appears a bit murky and indistinct.

Neglect patients are often unaware of the fact that they miss the left half of perceptual space. They cannot directly experience that anything is missing from their subjective experience. When told about their deficit, they act as if they do not understand what is supposed to be missing. They do not understand the concept of "leftness", therefore they cannot formulate any conception as to *what* exactly it is that is supposed to be missing. It is as if you were suddenly being told that, as is obvious to everyone around you, you cannot see the sixth dimension and you do not even seem to be aware of your inability to see it. But how could you ever become aware of missing it if you have no idea what the sixth dimension is supposed to look like in the first place? Probably you would just shrug your shoulders, go on as ever and not worry too much about missing the sixth dimension; you are just fine as you are. Sometimes you wonder where things disappear from your view, and other people say they are in the sixth dimension, look there; but you do not know what they are talking about. This is how neglect patients feel when being told that the things they cannot see are on the left, look there!

Anosognosia typically appears in connection with damage to the right hemisphere, associated with neglect and left-sided paralysis or weakness of the extremities. The patients may be unaware not only of suffering from neglect, but also of the fact that their left arm or leg is dysfunctional. They may be unable to stand up, walk or lift their arm, but when asked about their physical abilities they say there is nothing wrong. Unawareness of paralysis comes rather close to our imaginary example of being unaware of a broken leg. The difference is that, unlike with a broken leg, in neglect and left-sided paralysis something has gone wrong in the brain, something that normally updates our self-representation so that we know fully well whether we are healthy or sick, or intact or crippled.

6.4 Somatoparaphrenia (asomatognosia)

To be unaware of a deficit such as paralysis in one's own body sounds weird enough, but sometimes things get even weirder than that. Sometimes the patient is unaware of – or even explicitly denies – the *ownership of a body part* such as a leg or a hand. "Asomatognosia" literally means "lack of recognition of the body" (Feinberg, 2001), and somatoparaphrenia is another name for the same deficit. Perhaps the most famous case of this kind was reported by the famous neurologist Oliver Sacks (1985) as "the man who fell out of bed". Sacks had been called by the nurses to see a patient who kept falling out of his hospital bed in the middle of the night. The man, sitting on the floor, explained that he had found somebody's severed leg in his bed and decided to throw the disgusting thing out, but somehow his own body had followed, and he was now inexplicably attached to this alien piece of meat. Sacks found it hard to believe that a man does not recognize his own leg, but that actually seemed to be the case. He asked the man where his *own* left leg is, if the one attached to his body is not his, but the patient could not answer; he became pale and exclaimed in desperation that it has disappeared without a trace; it is nowhere to be found!

In somatoparaphrenia, there is no experience of ownership of a body part; the patient seems to have lost the conscious feeling of being "inside" the body part as well as the ability to move or control it. The limb is felt to be not a part of one's own bodily self at all, but something alien. Thus, some patients go to bizarre extremes when trying to explain who the body part belongs to, if it is not their own. Some patients who are otherwise lucid and intelligent resort to farfetched, incredible explanations, such as saying that the arm attached to their body is not their own but belongs to somebody else, even to somebody who is not present at all, like their spouse or their child. Or the arm might be attributed to the doctor, while at the same time realizing that in that case the doctor must have three hands! For the patient, even such utterly bizarre accounts are more satisfactory than the real explanation: it is his or her own hand, but the internal experience of it has been lost because of brain damage and paralysis.

The case of one patient was decribed by her neurologists in the following manner:

> She denied that the affected limbs were hers and said that "yours" or anothers were in bed with her. When she was shown that they were attached to her and that the arm in question merged with her shoulder and that it must be hers, she said: "But my eyes and my feelings don't agree, and I must believe my feelings. I know they look like mine, but I can feel they are not, and I can't believe my eyes."
>
> (Feinberg, 2001, p. 11)

Delusions are defined as strong irrational beliefs that are held with conviction in the face of obvious contrary evidence and violation of common sense. Thus, somatoparaphrenia involves not only a distorted body image and self-awareness, but also delusional beliefs that are invoked to explain away the weird experience of seeing a body part attached to one's own body but failing to feel or recognize that body part as one's own. The explanations arrived at go against the facts that any outsider can immediately see, but the patient still clings to them; thus, they can be considered delusional.

A related disorder is called the *mirror sign delusion*, in which patients cannot recognize their own self anymore when they are looking at themselves in the mirror. Instead, they create the delusional belief that it is some other person in there that they see. Thus, they cannot recognize the visual appearance of their own body in the mirror, although otherwise they have no recognition problems (Spangenberg Postal, 2005). As mirror-self recognition is an important sign of self-awareness, and constitutes the most widespread test of self-awareness in humans and animals, this disorder seems to strike at the heart of self-awareness.

By the way, how do *you* relate to your own bodily self in the mirror? I assume you at least recognize yourself in your mirror image, but do you like what you see in the mirror when you look at yourself, and do you feel at home inside your own body? There are some people who absolutely do not, and one reason for that seems to be a distorted bodily self-awareness. In these cases there is no brain damage involved, however. The most common of such disorders is the eating disorder *anorexia nervosa*. The patients, when looking at their own bodies in the mirror, see them very differently from how others see them: fat and ugly, even if in reality they are not. In *body dysmorphic disorder*, the patients become obsessed with some particular (imagined) flaw in their outlook, such as a nose that is too big, hair that is too thin or emerging wrinkles, and see them as totally devastating (Phillips, 2005). They can spend hours just examining these (mostly imagined or at least greatly exaggerated) flaws in the mirror, and in extreme cases they refuse to meet other people and repeatedly engage in plastic surgery that never manages to remove the problem for good. Also these patients really do see their bodies, especially faces, differently from how others see them. Self-critical attitudes and low emotional self-worth contribute to these disorders, resulting in an altered self-awareness. Thus, it is not only the visual information that determines what we see – it is also what we strongly believe and feel we should be seeing, and the lens of belief and emotion can severely distort the information on its way to consciousness and self-awareness.

6.5 Cognitive neuropsychiatry and deficits of belief systems

Our belief systems – the formulation of coherent interpretations of reality and testing their credibility against the facts – may also become deficient after brain injury. While cognitive neuro*psychology* is concerned with deficits to perceptual, attentional and memory functions, cognitive neuro*psychiatry* focuses on the delusional beliefs and implausible interpretations that patients adopt to make sense of their experiences or to explain the effects of the deficits. Anosognosia and somatoparaphrenia are on the borderline of cognitive neuropsychology and neuropsychiatry because the patients seem to be unable to incorporate pieces of obvious evidence about themselves into their belief systems, and instead they formulate delusional interpretations that either deny or grossly misinterpret the facts. There are a few other equally surprising – and fascinating – neuropsychiatric disorders where subjective experiences and beliefs become oddly distorted. Next, we will look at some connected with disorders of face recognition.

Capgras delusion

In the 1950s sci-fi novel and horror movie *Invasion of the Body Snatchers* (Finney, 1976), people in a small town turn to the local doctor, complaining that their close ones have changed internally into mentally empty zombies but they still look and behave the same as ever. The good doctor joins one of them, Wilma, to see for himself if anything is wrong, but he cannot notice any difference in Wilma's uncle and aunt who she claims have drastically changed. The doctor asks her how she knows that something has changed; how exactly is the uncle different? Wilma admits that there is not any difference that one could actually see. She explains that her uncle still looks, sounds, acts and remembers exactly as the original uncle did, externally, but there is something different internally, emotionally. He is talking by rote when he remembers the past; the special look in his eyes that revealed he remembered the wonderful quality of those days has gone. Now there is only the pretence of emotion. The words, the gestures, the tones of voice and everything else are there, but not the feeling. It is definitely not the same person, she concludes.

In the story, Wilma turns out to be right and the real explanation for the imperceptible changes is the invasion of aliens from space who take over human bodies and minds. Of course, in science fiction anything can happen. But this seems to be the case in neuropsychiatry too: There is a syndrome called "Capgras delusion" whose symptoms are exactly like those that Wilma was suffering from. The patients complain that close family members are not the same anymore, but have been taken away and switched to doubles or robots that look exactly the same but are not really the same at all; they only pretend to be the same. At an intellectual level, the patient might admit that the "double"-theory sounds rather outlandish or unlikely, but no rational argument will make any difference to the delusion.

One patient, a teenage boy, exclaimed after a motorcycle accident causing a head injury that his parents had been switched (Ramachandran & Blakeslee, 1998). The parents were naturally shocked, but nothing they said could change the boy's mind; he firmly believed that the current parents were fakes and the real ones had been taken away. At one point the desperate father tried to play along with the same game: One day he declared to his son that, yes, he had been right about the conspiracy all along but now he, his real father, had returned and the fake one had been sent back to China. Unfortunately this trick did not help for long. After a while the boy returned to his delusion and said that the impostor was back.

Sometimes the delusion may be momentarily reversed. This typically happens when the patient is speaking on the phone with the people believed to be switched. On the phone the patient believes that he or she is speaking with the "real" people. Why this only happens during phone conversations gives away an important clue to the cause of the disorder. The explanation is that, on the phone, recognition of the person is based on the voice alone and not on the face.

Indeed, the neuropsychological explanation for the Capgras delusion refers to deficits in the emotional processing of faces. Recognition of one's closest family members normally involves strong emotional components. Due to brain injury, there is a disconnection between the emotional and the cognitive components of face recognition. Thus, seeing the face of a family member causes a direct conflict between emotion and cognition: The cognitive channel tells that this person sure *looks* like my father, while the emotional channel remains blank and tells that this person sure does not *feel* like anyone I know, and surely not like anyone as close as a family member. To interpret the contrary experiences and to resolve the conflict between them, a delusional belief system emerges, according to which the original (emotionally significant) persons have been taken away and replaced by outwardly identical but inwardly different (emotionally insignificant) strangers. It may also be that the ability to test the likelihood of one's own beliefs has suffered from the brain injury, making it difficult to reject the highly improbable interpretations of reality.

Fregoli delusion

In the Fregoli delusion there is a converse pattern. The patient believes that a particular person, usually someone emotionally significant, is following him or her all the time but in disguise. One patient complained that an old boyfriend of hers was following and stalking her (Marshall & Halligan, 1996). She saw him dressed as an old man, as a girl and as the driver of a car passing by. The man was supposed to be capable of disguising himself as almost anyone and, furthermore, of miraculous, immediate switches of disguise.

The neuropsychological explanation for this disorder is the overactivation of the representation of a particular person in the face recognition system. Thus, when the patient sees the face of almost any stranger, the face recognition system always lights up the representation of one and the same person, creating the strong impression of emotional familiarity and consequently cognitive recognition, despite the mismatch between the external features of the perceived face and the actual face of the "recognized" person. Hidden somewhere under the deceivingly variable disguises, the patient firmly perceives the very same person lurking. To interpret this strong experience of recognition, a delusional belief system emerges: perhaps the person that I strongly feel is hidden under the disguise *really is* following me all the time. If this theory holds, then the person must be able to switch disguise almost magically. As in Capgras delusion, in Fregoli delusion the patient cannot critically evaluate the credibility and coherency of his or her own beliefs.

These cases show that a cognitive-neuropsychological approach can be effectively applied to explain the weird distortions of a patient's subjective world in a wide range of deficits of perception, memory and other cognitive functions, as well as deficits of belief systems. In all of these cases, some particular components of the information-processing systems that produce subjective perceptual experiences and beliefs have become deficient, changing the patient's subjective world in peculiar ways. To understand such deficits, we have to figure out which components have become deficient or dissociated from the rest.

The left-hemisphere interpreter and the right-hemisphere devil's advocate

One attempt to explain the strong, persistent delusions that occur in connection with brain injury refers to the different roles of the right and the left hemispheres in our belief systems (Ramachandran & Blakeslee, 1998). In the left hemisphere, there is a system called "the left-hemisphere interpreter". Its job is to construct an internally coherent narrative of all the experiences and behaviours of the person. This system does not care so much about the credibility of the story it concocts, and it typically presents the self in a good light, biasing the facts a bit to keep up a coherent, positive self-image and high self-esteem. The right hemisphere, by contrast, houses a system called "the devil's advocate". Its job is to critically examine and question the narratives produced by the left-hemisphere interpreter. It can question even the most cherished core beliefs and thereby express thoughts and ideas that may be threatening for the self, but based on reality. Now, if the right hemisphere suffers damage so that the devil's advocate is incapacitated or disconnected, the left-hemisphere interpreter is left to its own devices. It produces or confabulates interpretations of everything within the sphere of its own experience, and there is no-one there to challenge the interpretations it offers.

In the split-brain patient we see the interpreter at work when the left hemisphere explains away the actions guided by the right hemisphere (see above). In anosognosia, somatoparaphrenia and neuropsychiatric delusions, we see belief systems that keep up an intact (but outdated and incorrect) image of the self and attribute the strange experiences to incredible events in the world: surely there is nothing wrong with *me*; somebody else's dead leg has been attached to my body; my family members have been switched and replaced by identical zombies; somebody is following me under a thousand disguises. The damaged or disconnected devil's advocate system is unable to challenge these belief systems and therefore they are nearly impossible to question or overthrow. Supporting evidence for this idea has come from experiments where anosognosia and somatoparaphrenia were momentarily removed when the right hemisphere received extra activation through cold-water stimulation in the ear channel. For a while, the patients fully admitted their deficits and recognized their paralysed body parts, but after the stimulation faded away they returned to their delusional belief systems and forgot all about the reversal (Ramachandran & Blakeslee, 1998).

Chapter summary

The world we see around us is a virtual reality of phenomenal consciousness constructed by the brain. Our *self* is in the centre of that world simulation – and the self also seems to be a *model* or a *simulation* construed by the brain. Our *current self-experience* tells us what we are like right now and our *self-representation in memory* tells us where we have been before. We become aware of our own self when we combine our current self-experience (such as our body image as it is felt or our own mirror image as seen) with the autobiographical self in long-term memory. *Self-awareness* involves the idea of a continuous sentient being who has had experiences in the past, has them right now in the present and who will have more in the future. *Amnesia* wipes out much of the autobiographical self, so that current experiences can no longer be connected with an enduring self. Amnesic patients live each moment disconnected from the past and the future. If they are aware of a self at all, it is a self of the distant past, constructed from the remaining available information in autobiographical memory – a badly outdated representation of the self.

In *split-brain* patients, the cerebral hemispheres are functionally isolated from each other. This condition reveals that our self-representation is heavily based on the narratives and explanations about ourselves produced by the left hemisphere, which constantly reflects upon and interprets the experiences available to it. In *anosognosia* (unawareness of deficit), the brain *refuses to update the self-representation* appropriately, to include information about specific deficiencies, such as the perceptual and motor disabilities caused by a stroke. Despite conspicuous symptoms, the patient seems incapable of representing him- or herself as having any such symptoms. In *somatoparaphrenia*, the patient *denies ownership of a limb* whose neural wiring has been affected by brain damage, although the limb is still normally attached to the rest of his or her body. In spite of the direct perceptual evidence of ownership, the patient feels that it is an alien body part and therefore it must belong to someone else. The patient can make up rather creative stories as to whose limb it is, if not her own, and how somebody else's body part has ended up attached to her body. The patient is not aware or worried that the explanations are not only implausible, but outrageous and physically impossible. These stories fulfil the definition of *psychiatric delusions: utterly implausible beliefs and convictions that are stubbornly held and strongly defended despite obvious evidence to the contrary*. Brain damage can thus also affect our *belief systems*. When this happens, we explain away our altered experiences by attributing the alterations to the external world rather than to ourselves or our medical condition. This happens in *Capgras delusion* and *Fregoli delusion*. In the former, familiar faces do not elicit emotional reactions in the patient and thus the patient believes that familiar people have been switched to identical doubles. In the latter, almost all faces elicit a strong, specific emotional recognition, which leads to the belief that a particular emotionally significant person keeps following the patient in a million different disguises. In fact, many psychiatric disorders, such as schizophrenia, include a variety of altered conscious experiences coupled with weird beliefs about the causes of those experiences – the patient may believe that he is being spied upon, that others are reading his mind from a distance or that many, even most, other people are involved in a conspiracy against the patient and persecute him in various ways.

All in all, the brain's simulation of a world involves not only sensory qualities and coherent objects around us, but also a self-image, bodily awareness, self-awareness and an interpretation (a web of beliefs) about what is going on and who we are. This subjective psychological reality – the world as constructed by the brain – is where we live our personal lives. When something goes wrong and the simulated world changes, we easily confuse our subjective world with the objective external world and believe that we are the same as ever but that the real world out there must have changed. The conscious brain is blind to many of its own deficits. To the science of consciousness, these deficits reveal that we – and our personal realities – owe our existence to an intact brain. In other words, tiny damage to specific parts of the brain may forever alter my subjective psychological reality or irreversibly erase the self-representation I have come to believe is "me".

Further reading

Bermúdez, J. L. (2009). Self: Body awareness and self-awareness. In W. P. Banks (Ed.), *Encyclopedia of consciousness* (Vol. 2, pp. 289–300). San Diego, CA: Academic Press.

Feinberg, T. E. (2001). *Altered egos: How the brain creates the self*. New York: Oxford University Press.

Feinberg, T. E., & Keenan, J. P. (Eds.) (2005). *The lost self*. New York: Oxford University Press.

Finney, J. (1976). *Invasion of the body snatchers*. London: Sphere.

Gazzaniga, M. S., & LeDoux, J. E. (1976). *The integrated mind*. New York: Plenum Press.

Hirstein, W. (2005). *Brain fiction*. Cambridge, MA: MIT Press.

Kapur, N. (1997). *Injured brains of medical minds: Views from within*. Oxford: Oxford University Press.

Mark, V. (1996). Conflicting communicative behaviour in a split brain patient: Support for dual consciousness. In S. R. Hameroff, A. W. Kaszniak, & A. C. Scott (Eds.), *Toward a science of consciousness* (pp. 189–196). Cambridge, MA: MIT Press.

Marshall, J. C., & Halligan, P. W. (1996). *Method in madness: Case studies in cognitive neuropsychiatry*. Hove: Psychology Press.

Phillips, K. A. (2005). *The broken mirror: Understanding and treating body dysmorphic disorder*. New York: Oxford University Press.

Ramachandran, V. S., & Blakeslee, S. (1998). *Phantoms in the brain*. New York: William Morrow.

Sacks, O. (1985). *The man who mistook his wife for a hat*. London: Picador.

Spence, S. A. (2009). Psychopathology and consciousness. In W. P. Banks (Ed.), *Encyclopedia of consciousness* (Vol. 2, pp. 245–271). San Diego, CA: Academic Press.

Brief discussion questions

1   How many minds does a split-brain patient have? Is the consciousness that you have right now a left-hemisphere consciousness, a right-hemisphere consciousness or the synthesis of both? If your own brain was split by cutting the corpus callosum, would you still be the same after the operation?

2   The deficits of self-awareness vividly illustrate how difficult it is to take the perspective of another mind. Can you imagine what it is like, from the first-person's point of view, to be an amnesic patient, a split-brain patient or a patient suffering from somatoparaphrenia, body dysmorphic delusion, Capgras delusion or Fregoli delusion? Or are they unimaginable as subjective experiences?

3   Some people have distorted self-awareness: their strong beliefs about themselves distort the visual information they see (e.g. in the mirror). Do you see yourself as you are or do your beliefs distort your self-image, at least to some extent? Look at yourself and write down on a piece of paper the most conspicuous features of your outlook. Then give the piece of paper to another student and ask if he or she agrees or not. Discuss which of the features that you see in yourself are purely based on direct perceptual information and which are based more on your prior beliefs about yourself. Discuss also whether the beliefs distort what you are seeing.

4   Do you recognize internal dialogues where you argue with yourself in the manner that corresponds to the left-hemisphere interpreter and the right-hemisphere devil's advocate? One point of view defends the status quo and explains away all problems and evidence of potential problems; the other is critical, revolutionary and demands that changes need to be made in your life. What are the topics about which you have these internal dialogues?

Central domains of consciousness science

II. Neural correlates of consciousness (NCC)

Introduction: What is a "neural correlate of consciousness" (NCC)?

The goal of cognitive neuroscience is to find out the underlying neural correlates and biological mechanisms of mental phenomena. To collect the empirical evidence that reveals them, cognitive neuroscience makes use of methods that measure different aspects of brain activity. The measurements are conducted at the same time as a subject is engaged in mental tasks, thus reflecting the brain activities that underlie the mental events. The methods of cognitive neuroscience (EEG, MEG, fMRI, PET and TMS) can be employed in a similar manner to find out about the neural mechanisms of consciousness. Consequently, the search for the neural correlates of consciousness has become the new, hot area of research where cognitive neuroscience overlaps with consciousness science.

When something (anything) happens in your subjective mental life – a burst of emotion, a feeling of pain, a visual sensation of colour – something invariably also happens in the brain. There cannot be, it seems, phenomenal events taking place in your conscious life not accompanied by any corresponding neural events in your brain. To capture this interconnection between the mind and the brain, philosophers talk about a *supervenience* relation that links conscious events and brain events: *For each and every conscious event, there is a corresponding brain event.* This is the *principle of covariance* between consciousness and brain. Note, however, that it only works in one direction – the converse statement is *not* true, that for each and every brain event there would be a corresponding conscious event. Changes in nonconscious brain events are possible without any changes in conscious events, whereas changes in conscious events are not possible without any changes in brain events.

Furthermore, the supervenience relation includes also the assumption that the conscious events *owe their existence* somehow to the brain events and thus could not float free of them. This is the principle of the *ontological dependency* of consciousness on the brain. There can be no consciousness if there is no brain, but there can of course be a brain without any consciousness.

Cognitive neuroscientists obviously take something like the supervenience relation for granted in their work. Following the principle of ontological dependency, they assume that consciousness without a brain is not possible, whereas a brain without consciousness is possible. If consciousness could exist independently of the brain, some sort of Cartesian dualism would have to be true. But as we have no undisputed evidence of conscious events floating about free of brain events, we have to conclude that conscious events supervene on brain events.

Note, however, that the supervenience relation by no means *explains why* consciousness and the brain are interlocked in this peculiar way. Incidentally, covariance coupled with ontological dependency is consistent with reductive and emergent materialism. Hence, one possible explanation for why the supervenience relation holds is that either reductive or emergent materialism is true – but that, of course, is an open philosophical question.

The supervenience relation lays the foundation for the neuroscientific research programme on consciousness. Based on the covariance principle, cognitive neuroscientists take it for granted that each and every subjective conscious phenomenon in the mind must invariably *correlate* with some objective neural phenomena in the brain. Thus, it makes sense to try to find out with objective measurements absolutely everything we can about the objective neuroanatomical and neurophysiological details of the union between consciousness and the brain.

What exactly does it mean to say that two different types of events *correlate* with each other? When two events correlate, they tend to occur hand in hand. If one of them appears or disappears, or changes in quality or quantity, then so does the other one, at about the same time. This opens up the possibility of finding out, by using objective measurements of brain activity, which neural events exactly correlate with each different type of conscious event. That would seem to be the first reasonable step towards an empirically based theory of the relationship between consciousness and the brain. Consequently, the search for the neural correlates of consciousness has become the major approach to the study of consciousness in neuroscience.

The long-term goal of this research is to figure out which neural events exactly correlate with each different state and content of consciousness. In the long run, this research should reveal what is *the minimally sufficient neural system or activity that invariably co-occurs together with a conscious experience of a specific kind*. This is the standard definition of the concept of "the neural correlate of consciousness" (a.k.a. the NCC) (Koch, 2004).

To reach the goal of finding the NCC requires that we can describe both the level of conscious events and the level of brain events with a detailed vocabulary or map, and then try to connect the two levels. First, a taxonomy or detailed classification of different states and contents of consciousness is needed at the level of consciousness, so that we can study the correlates of each type of conscious phenomenon separately. Second, we need to devise experiments where the neural correlates of each type of consciousness can be measured independently of other types. This research programme is already well under way in cognitive neuroscience.

Chapter 7

Methods and design of NCC experiments

Introduction: How to design NCC experiments

The basic principle behind NCC experiments is very simple. If you want to figure out the neural correlates of a conscious state or content "C", you must design an experiment where there are two different conditions. One of them is called the *control* (or *baseline*) condition. In this condition, the conscious state or content "C" is totally *absent* from the subject's mind. Thus, this condition serves as the *neutral baseline* against which the other condition is contrasted. The other condition is called the *experimental* condition, during which the specified conscious state or content "C" is vividly *present* in the subject's mind. Ideally, everything else is equal or kept constant between the two conditions: only the presence and absence of "C" varies in the subject's conscious mind.

The above design establishes the required, controlled variation at the level of conscious phenomena. To obtain information about simultaneous brain events, the subject's brain activity must be measured in one way or another. We can roughly divide the most common measurements into *functional brain imaging* methods and *electromagnetic brain sensing* methods.

7.1 Functional brain imaging methods: fMRI and PET

Functional brain imaging methods include *functional magnetic resonance imaging* (fMRI) and *positron emission tomography* (PET). Both have been frequently utilized in NCC experiments, but nowadays fMRI is more commonly used because it is cheaper and easier to use. In fMRI, the subject lies in a tube in a strong static magnetic field and the brain is bombarded by brief sequences of high-frequency (radiofrequency) electromagnetic pulses. The magnetic field and the pulses as such are harmless to the brain, but the combination of the magnetic field and the pulses influences the sub-atomic particles (i.e. protons) in the nuclei of hydrogen atoms in the brain so that they send back or "echo" the pulses. This echo can be detected from outside the subject's head. It contains signals that reflect the exact location and the magnetic properties of the different biological tissues and structures within the brain. Ordinary or structural MRI gives a high-resolution, three-dimensional anatomical picture of the brain; fMRI in addition reflects changes in the amount of fresh, oxygenated blood flowing in the brain. This is called the BOLD signal (i.e. "Blood Oxygen Level Dependent" signal). As the fresh blood is rapidly directed to brain areas where neurons increase their activity, the image indirectly reflects where in the brain the neurons increase their neuroelectrical activity. Thus, in an NCC experiment with fMRI, if we compare the *difference* of brain activity between the experimental and the control condition we can see where in the brain the neurons became more active as a function of the conscious phenomenon.

The minimum time-window that an imaging method summarizes in a single image is called its *temporal resolution*. It takes a few seconds for the blood flow to react to increased local neural activity; thus, at best fMRI reflects the changes in brain activity with a delay of about 5–10 s. The first changes in the fMRI signal appear after a couple of seconds from the start of stimulation, but the maximum of the fMRI response is reached after about 10 s from the start of stimulation.

This means that fMRI has a relatively *low temporal resolution*. A lot of mental processing and neural activity takes place in the first couple of seconds from stimulation, but fMRI is too slow to accurately see what is going on. By contrast, the *spatial resolution* of fMRI is relatively high. Spatial resolution is the minimum size of an image element (called "pixel" or "voxel") where the image summarizes an area as differing from the surrounding regions in terms of the amount of signals received (interpreted as "brain activity"). The spatial resolution of fMRI images is about 2–3 mm^2.

In PET, positron-emitting radioactive isotopes are attached to some carefully chosen types of molecules (e.g. radioactive oxygen is attached to the water molecule H_2O, resulting in radioactive water) and then delivered to the subject's bloodstream. From there the radioactive tracer molecules quickly travel everywhere in the body, including the brain. The radioactive isotopes are unstable and decay at a known rate, emitting positrons in this process. In the brain the positrons collide with electrons and both particles consequently annihilate and turn into energy in the form of two gamma rays that travel directly out from the brain in exactly opposite directions. The PET device is a ring of gamma ray detectors surrounding the subject's head. It thus detects the gamma rays that originated inside the brain and calculates backwards from them where in the brain the molecules were located when they decayed. Depending on what kind of molecule was used (water, glucose, dopamine analogue, etc.), its distribution inside the brain reflects a very specific aspect of brain activity or metabolism (e.g. blood flow, glucose metabolism or neurotransmitter binding). In most NCC studies using PET, blood flow has been measured by using radioactive water as the tracer. In that case, the result reflects a similar aspect of brain activity as fMRI: the blood flows more to areas where neurons are electrically and metabolically more active. PET is even slower than fMRI and at best a single image can only show the summary of changes that happened during 30–60 s. The spatial resolution is at best a few millimetres, which is usually a bit lower than in fMRI.

7.2 Electromagnetic brain sensing with EEG and MEG

Electroencephalography (EEG) and magnetoencephalography (MEG) are electromagnetic brain-sensing methods. They pick up signals that originate directly from the electrical activity of neurons. Neural firing generates dipolar electrical circuits inside the brain. A dipole is an electrical source with two poles, a negative and a positive. Inside the neuron, the current flows from the dendrites to the soma of the cell (this is called the postsynaptic potential) and further from the soma along the axon (called the action potential). These intracellular currents cannot be detected from the outside of the brain, but fortunately there are also return or volume currents outside the cells that complete the electrical circuit. The return currents thus flow outside the neurons, backwards towards the opposite electrical pole. They flow freely in the brain and spread unpredictably through the tissues in the brain, because the return currents follow the irregular paths determined by *least electrical resistance* inside the brain.

Some of the return currents also reach the skull and go through it to the scalp.

By placing EEG electrodes on the scalp it is possible to detect these tiny electrical currents as "brain waves". The changes in the electrical potential of the waves can be measured very accurately in the temporal domain, in a timescale of milliseconds (thus, the temporal resolution of EEG is one thousandth of a second). Unfortunately it is extremely difficult to localize accurately where in the brain the neurons are whose activity contributed to the measured waves, because the currents typically travel a long and unpredictable path through the brain before they meet the electrodes at the scalp, and during their journey currents that originate from many different sources and places interact, summate with each other or cancel each other out, or otherwise get so entangled together that the original sources cannot be decoded from the signal any more. Only an educated guess can be made, called the *source localization model*, by computing the most likely site of origin for the electrical sources that brought about the measured EEG pattern on the scalp. In terms of neuroanatomical localization, the spatial resolution of EEG is measured in square centimetres rather than in millimetres, which means that EEG has a very poor spatial resolution compared to fMRI or PET.

Unlike EEG, MEG measures the *magnetic* fields created by the electrically active neurons. The neuromagnetic field is generated by the very same electrical activity as the neuroelectrical fields detected by EEG, but the neuromagnetic fields behave very differently, which makes their measurement in some ways easier but in others more difficult than EEG. The good news is that the neuromagnetic fields spread directly out from their source of origin and they are not dampened or distorted by the brain or the skull. Thus, their exact place of origin can be figured out much better than in EEG. The bad news is that the neuromagnetic signals are so weak to begin with that only very few of them ever reach outside the brain. Thus, all the detected MEG signals necessarily reflect only the activities of cortical areas very close to the surface of the brain and the skull. Furthermore, the neuromagnetic fields are directed in only one direction, perpendicular to the electrically active neurons. Only neurons that are oriented so that their neuromagnetic field is directed towards the skull manage to create a measurable magnetic field outside the skull. The rest of the neuromagnetic fields stay inside the brain, undetectable by the MEG sensors outside of it. Consequently, MEG is blind to some neural activities that EEG can pick up. But, for the cortical signals that MEG can pick up, the temporal resolution is as good as in EEG (milliseconds) and the spatial resolution is a few millimetres.

An NCC experiment with EEG or MEG can tell us how long it takes for sensory-perceptual stimulus information to reach consciousness, because we can track the changes very accurately in time: We can measure up to a thousand contiguous data points within 1 s! Thus, we should be able to see that at some point, in the condition where the information becomes conscious and the experience is present, the electromagnetic response in the brain starts to differ from the baseline condition where the information never reaches consciousness. That is the critical point in time when the neural activity of the NCC steps in; all the activity before that point reflects processing outside consciousness. Furthermore, as the signals picked up by EEG and MEG are very complex, containing many different frequencies of electromagnetic energy, it may be possible to figure out what *kind* of electromagnetic energy is involved in the neurophysiological activity of the NCC. The sites on the scalp where the responses are recorded also roughly reflect the localization of the underlying brain areas where the activity probably was generated, but accurate localization of the response in terms of brain anatomy is difficult, especially with EEG.

Chapter summary

To summarize briefly the prototypical NCC experiment: During the experiment, the subject is exposed several times to two different conditions, "C present" (a specified state or content of consciousness is experienced by the subject) and "C absent" (the same state or content is not experienced by the subject), with everything else remaining the same between these two conditions. The subject's brain activity is simultaneously monitored by fMRI, PET, EEG or MEG. The functional brain imaging methods PET and fMRI reflect what happens in the brain metabolism or blood flow, and they can accurately locate these changes in terms of brain anatomy but not in time. The electromagnetic brain-sensing methods EEG and MEG reflect the neural, bioelectrical signalling in the brain, and can accurately locate changes in these signals in time but cannot very accurately locate their origin in brain anatomy. All of these methods have been used to find the NCC. An NCC experiment should always target some specific state or content of consciousness, to give information about only one very specific aspect of consciousness at a time. In the following two chapters we will briefly outline some typical experiments and their results, without going into the (rather complicated) details.

Further reading

Chalmers, D. J. (2000). What is a neural correlate of consciousness? In T. Metzinger (Ed.), *Neural correlates of consciousness* (pp. 17–39). Cambridge, MA: MIT Press.

Koch, C. (2004). *The quest for consciousness: A neurobiological approach.* Englewood Cliffs, NJ: Roberts & Company.

Revonsuo, A. (2001). Can functional brain imaging discover consciousness in the brain? *Journal of Consciousness Studies, 8,* 3–23.

Brief discussion questions

1   Does the supervenience principle really hold between consciousness and the brain? Give examples of:

(i)   a human brain without any consciousness;
(ii) an activity in the human brain without any corresponding conscious experience.

The following, by contrast, should be impossible to demonstrate – do you agree?

(i)   a (human) consciousness (or any type of consciousness) without a brain;
(ii) an event in consciousness (a subjective experience in the subjective psychological reality) without any corresponding neural events in the brain.

2   Design an experiment where you study the neural correlates of consciousness:

     (i)   what is the control condition like?

     (ii)   what is the experimental condition like?

     (iii)   which brain imaging measurements would you use and what would they show as results in this experiment?

Chapter 8

Studies on the neural basis of consciousness as a state

Introduction: Consciousness as a state

First, let us consider what would be an ideal experiment on the neural correlates of consciousness as a state. In Chapter 3, we defined the state of being conscious as *the background state of the brain or mind whose presence enables all types of subjective experiences in general and whose absence (the unconscious state) totally prevents any types of subjective experiences.* An experiment where the conscious state can be turned on or off in a controlled manner would constitute an ideal experiment to see what it is in the brain that "lights up" consciousness.

8.1 Anaesthesia

One way to induce controlled variation between the conscious and the unconscious state is to use *anaesthetic agents* to wipe consciousness out. Objectively, the effects of anaesthetic agents are such that the anaesthetized person first becomes extremely drowsy (like being heavily drunk) and then becomes unresponsive to any command or even to any painful stimulus. (Incidentally, the behavioural definition of "unconsciousness" in anaesthesiology is roughly "unresponsiveness or failure to move in response to command, and amnesia for the events", rather than our definition as "the total absence of subjective experiences".) The anaesthetized person's EEG signals also become slower, similar to the EEG of deep sleep, also called slow-wave sleep. In extremely deep anaesthesia, the EEG signal may disappear altogether (flat EEG, just a straight line without any waves).

Objectively, anaesthesia involves unresponsiveness to external stimulation. Subjectively, anaesthesia typically (though not always) leads to the total absence of phenomenal consciousness. During anaesthesia, there are no experiences going on and even the sense of time disappears, so that waking up after hours of anaesthesia may feel for the anaesthetized subject as if no time has passed. Rare exceptions to the unconsciousness are *anaesthesia awareness* – externally generated experiences (sensations, perceptions) reflecting what is really happening in the operation room – and *anaesthesia dreaming* – internally generated, hallucinatory or dream-like experiences that do not reflect what is really going on. These two types of subjective experiences are sometimes reported after awakening from the anaesthesia. But even if nothing is reported, there may have been experiences going on that were immediately forgotten. Sometimes patients are able to communicate during the anaesthesia by moving their arms (this is called the isolated forearm technique) and yet afterwards they deny any memory of awareness during anaesthesia. Some patients have been able to do this even though the EEG measurement reflecting the depth of the anaesthesia ("bispectral index") indicates that their brain is in the unconscious state. It may be that the EEG in this case is not sensitive enough to the neural processes underlying consciousness (Alkire, Hudetz, & Tononi, 2008).

By carefully regulating the concentration of the anaesthetic agent in the subject's brain it is possible to slowly extinguish consciousness or to slowly let consciousness re-emerge. Thus, the question is: What happens in the brain when consciousness goes away (or reappears) due to anaesthetic agents? This has been studied by using PET methodology. The results from several studies (using different anaesthetic agents) converge, in that when consciousness goes away there is a *decrease in the activity of the thalamus* (Alkire & Miller, 2006). The thalamus is a structure in the centre of the brain through which sensory information travels to the cortex. The thalamus has extremely dense and complex connectivity with the cortex, consisting of bidirectional loops. Thus, the thalamus and the cortex send information between each other, back and forth, in complex patterns. Some of the projections are very local: A specific part of the cortex or thalamus connects to a specific part of the other. Other connections are diffuse and global, so that a part of the thalamus may have widespread connections to places all over the cortex. The decrease in the activity of the thalamus, caused by the anaesthetic agents, probably precludes neuroelectrical activities in the thalamocortical loops, especially those that happen at the higher frequencies of EEG (beta and gamma bands).

The cortical areas that seem most critical for consciousness, and that engage in interaction with the thalamus when consciousness emerges, are located in the posterior cortex: the lateral temporo-parieto-occipital junction and the mesial-parietal cortex (Alkire, Hudetz, & Tononi, 2008). High-frequency neuroelectrical activity in the connections between these cortical areas and the thalamus seems to be necessary for the conscious state, perhaps because they integrate the different contents of consciousness into one unified whole (Alkire, Hudetz, & Tononi, 2008).

8.2 Epileptic seizures and deep sleep

Further evidence for the necessity of high-frequency electrical activity between the cortex and the thalamus comes from studies on epileptic seizures and deep dreamless sleep (NREM sleep stages 3 and 4). In both cases, all or most of the contents of consciousness are wiped out temporarily. In epileptic absence seizures this happens dramatically and suddenly, so that the patient just stops, even in the middle of a sentence, and stares into emptiness for a few seconds. After the seizure he may continue from where he was cut off. During the seizure, consciousness seems to be disabled and blank. At the same time, strong slow waves (3 Hz) can be seen in the EEG, which means that pathological slow-wave activity has suddenly seized the thalamocortical connections. This objective phenomenon in the EEG is accompanied at the subjective level by the absence of consciousness.

Although there are many different types of epileptic seizures, it may be that all the seizures that severely impair consciousness or wipe it out altogether involve slow-frequency EEG waves in the cortex, an EEG pattern similar to that seen in anaesthesia, natural deep sleep or coma. Complete loss of consciousness occurs when the abnormal activity takes over large networks between the cortex and subcortical regions (Cavanna & Monaco, 2009; Yu & Blumenfeld, 2009).

A similar EEG pattern of strong-amplitude, slow-frequency waves (delta waves, 0.5–3 Hz) can be seen in the deepest stages of sleep (NREM stages 3 and 4). These stages are usually dreamless. If any conscious experiences are reported after awakening from these stages, they are usually minimal, static and very simple in content.

Metaphorically speaking, when the phenomenal lights are "on", then thalamo-cortical (or subcortical-cortical) bidirectional neural loops display a mixture of high frequencies of complex bioelectrical activity; when the lights are "off", then those loops are seized by slow, big waves implying highly synchronized and less complex or less differentiated thalamocortical activity.

8.3 Locked-in syndrome

If intact thalamocortical activities are all that is required for enabling consciousness as a state, we may ask if it would be possible for someone to be internally conscious but to be totally "locked in", inside the brain, that is, without any ability to communicate with the outside world. In fact, such a condition exists in the neurological literature and is aptly termed the "locked-in syndrome". The patient with this unfortunate condition is totally immobile and does not respond to any stimuli. At most, eye movements or blinks can be used to communicate with the outside world. Yet, there is nothing whatsoever wrong with the patient's consciousness. The locked-in syndrome is not a deficit of consciousness at all, only a deficit of motor output. In PET images reflecting the levels of cerebral metabolism, locked-in patients show perfectly normal levels of brain metabolism and the metabolical activity is cortically distributed in a similar way as in healthy controls, with strongest levels of activity in the medial posterior cortex (Laureys, Owen, & Schiff, 2004). (Incidentally, these are the same cortical areas that are deactivated by anaesthetic agents!) The patient is merely outwardly unresponsive, not without conscious phenomenal experiences or reflective thoughts.

8.4 Vegetative state and other global disorders of consciousness

Global disorders of consciousness are states where brain injury or disease causes a state of deep unconsciousness (defined in clinical medicine as "unresponsiveness to stimuli"). Brain death, coma, vegetative state and minimally conscious state represent the different degrees of severity of global disorders of consciousness.

Functional brain images of cerebral metabolism in brain-dead patients show a picture that looks like an empty skull. Because no metabolical activity is detected – the brain tissue is dead – the inside of the skull is uniformly black in the images (Laureys, Owen, & Schiff, 2004)!

Patients in the *vegetative state* suffer from severe brain damage due to cardiac arrest, stroke or accidents or blows to the head, and are at first comatose but not suffering from brain death. When they emerge from coma and enter the vegetative state, they start to show spontaneous eye opening and closure (a kind of "wakefulness" and "sleep"), but nevertheless do not respond to any external stimuli. PET images of cerebral metabolism in the vegetative state show abnormally low levels of metabolical activity in the brain (Laureys, Owen, & Schiff, 2004).

The horrifying possibility of consciousness being trapped inside a nonresponsive body, like in the locked-in syndrome, has led to further questions concerning supposedly "unconscious" patients who also are outwardly unresponsive. Could some of them be internally conscious all the same? Recent experiments have shown that at least some vegetative patients may also be internally conscious, and thus in fact have been misdiagnosed as vegetative.

In one experiment, vegetative patients were requested to carry out simple mental imagery tasks, such as playing tennis or walking around the house. Surprisingly, the fMRI images of some patients' brains showed activity indistinguishable from that of healthy control subjects doing the same task! They seemed to be able to formulate mental images intentionally – a type of subjective conscious experiences – according to the instructions given to them, although they could not otherwise communicate with the researchers in any way (Owen et al., 2006). This experiment provides us with strong evidence to the effect that the state of consciousness (and thereby some particular contents as well) can exist even in persons who never respond to any external stimuli – who seem to be totally nonconscious.

When patients begin to emerge from the vegetative state, they enter a fluctuating state somewhere in between consciousness and unconsciousness. Thus, the patients sometimes are able to react meaningfully to stimuli or they respond to attempts to communicate with them, but this ability is not consistent and their responses are not coherent. This state has been named "the minimally conscious state". In PET images of the minimally conscious state, cerebral metabolism is higher than in the vegetative state but still lower than in the normal brain (Laureys, Owen, & Schiff, 2004).

8.5 Inverse zombies

In consciousness studies, the problem of detecting anaesthesia awareness, vegetative consciousness and other similar cases has recently received increasing attention. A new concept has been launched to describe conscious beings who possess all of the behavioural features and (lack of) responses of a nonconscious creature: *inverse zombies* (Mashour & LaRock, 2008). These are the reverse of the typical philosophical zombies (who externally seem conscious but internally are nonconscious): Inverse zombies are *externally nonconscious*, yet *internally conscious*. All patients who show the external signs of unconsciousness are at least potentially inverse zombies. To show empirically whether they are or not, we would need a brain imaging device that detects the presence (and absence) of phenomenal consciousness or qualia in the brain.

Chapter summary

The neural correlates of consciousness as a state can be explored by studying the effects of anaesthesia, epileptic seizures, deep sleep and global disorders of consciousness. The results show that the thalamus, thalamocortical connections, cortical-subcortical networks and posterior cortical areas may be critical for consciousness as a state. Furthermore, in the conscious state the large-scale neural networks in these areas engage in high-frequency electrical activities. When such activities in these networks are prevented by strong low-frequency waves, consciousness is lost.

When we study so-called "unconscious" subjects and design NCC experiments to find the NCC of consciousness as a state, we have to be careful to distinguish true unconsciousness (absence of phenomenal consciousness) from inverse zombiehood (absence of external responsiveness, but presence of inner phenomenal consciousness). Some totally unresponsive patients are not necessarily without phenomenal consciousness.

Further reading

Cavanna, A. E., & Monaco, F. (2009). Brain mechanisms of altered conscious states during epileptic seizures. *Nature Reviews Neurology, 5*, 267–276.

Laureys, S. (Ed.) (2006). *The boundaries of consciousness: Neurobiology and neuropathology (Progress in Brain Research)*. Amsterdam: Elsevier.

Laureys, S., & Tononi, G. (2008). *The neurology of consciousness: Cognitive neuroscience and neuropathology*. San Diego, CA: Academic Press.

Yu, L., & Blumenfeld, H. (2009). Theories of impaired consciousness in epilepsy. *Annals of the New York Academy of the Sciences, 1157*, 48–60.

Brief discussion question

If anaesthesia only makes people unresponsive (paralysed) and amnesic, is it in principle possible that many anaesthetized people are in fact "inverse zombies": conscious all the time, but when they wake up they have no memories about the experiences they had during anaesthesia? What difference does it make if we are truly unconscious or only paralysed and amnesic? How important would it be for you to know what happens to your consciousness if you were to be anaesthetized?

Chapter 9

Studies on the neural basis of visual consciousness

Introduction: Visual information and visual consciousness

In NCC studies, when particular contents of consciousness have been studied, visual consciousness is by far the most often studied modality. Thus, here we will take a look at some of the most revealing experiments on the neural correlates of visual consciousness.

Visual information travels from the eye to the brain via a nucleus in the thalamus (the lateral geniculate nucleus, LGN) and ends up at the primary visual cortex (V1), also known as the striate cortex. From there, it is channelled through a complex network of cortical areas that are specialized in processing different features of visual information. The two main pathways of processing are known as the *ventral visual pathway* (going from V1 to the extrastriate occipital cortex and then to the temporal lobe) and the *dorsal visual pathway* (going from V1 to the posterior parietal cortex) (see Figure 5.3). The ventral visual pathway contains areas that are concerned with such visual features as colour, shape and object type (e.g. face or animal or place). Thus, the ventral stream is supposed to put together the representation of coherent visual objects for object recognition. The dorsal visual pathway is concerned with the spatial location and motion of objects and it is thought to track objects in space, especially to guide our visuomotor interactions with objects.

The question is: Where in the visual cortex are the neural correlates of conscious visual perception? What happens in the brain when we subjectively see a visual object or feature, or when the visual information emerges into our consciousness in a coherent phenomenal form, clothed in beautiful, vivid visual qualia such as chromatic colours? To study this experimentally, we should design experiments where in one condition the visual information does *not* enter consciousness – there is no subjective seeing of the stimulus – and in the other condition the same visual information *does* enter consciousness and we have a subjective visual experience of the stimulus.

9.1 Binocular rivalry studies

To design experiments that separate the neural correlates of subjective visual experience from the activities directly caused by the visual stimulus, one especially fruitful approach is the phenomenon known as *binocular rivalry*. It can be induced by showing two different, visually incompatible stimuli at the same time, one to the left eye and the other to the right eye (see Figure 9.1). Normally our brain combines the information from the two eyes into one coherent three-dimensional image, but in this case such integration is impossible as the two representations do not match. Let us say that we show a picture of a rabbit to the left eye and a picture of a flower to the right eye. At first the brain tries to combine them, but when that does not work the two images start to compete with each other for access to consciousness. Thus, the subject first sees the flower and nothing else for a few seconds, and then the flower suddenly switches to the rabbit for another few seconds, only to switch back again. The spontaneous rivalry between the two eyes and the two stimuli then continues indefinitely. This phenomenon offers an ideal opportunity to study what happens in the brain when information emerges to

Left eye   Right eye

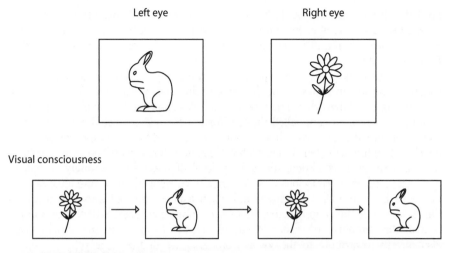

Visual consciousness

Figure 9.1 Binocular rivalry

The left eye "sees" only the rabbit all of the time and the right eye "sees" only the flower all of the time. In visual consciousness, however, the flower and the rabbit appear sequentially one after the other, with the content of consciousness changing spontaneously every few seconds

consciousness. During the experiment both stimuli are there in front of the subject's eyes all of the time – nothing whatsoever objectively changes in them. Therefore, we must ask the subject to report when the switch in consciousness happens, by pushing a key for example.

Binocular rivalry experiments have been conducted in both monkeys and humans (although, as you can imagine, it was a bit tricky to teach the monkeys to *report* what they were seeing!). In the monkey studies, single-cell activity in the visual cortex was recorded with invasive microelectrodes; they look like thin needles that are inserted into the visual cortex, and the tip of the needle picks up the electrical activity of the neurons close to it. Thus, it was possible to know exactly where in the brain the recorded activity was coming from, but the signal only reflected how one or a few neurons reacted to the change in subjective experience. First, the researchers recorded cells that were "interested" in the kinds of stimuli that were shown – the cells reacted to the presence or absence of the physical stimulus in a viewing condition without rivalry. Some cells specifically woke up for a face stimulus, and others for some other type of visual object, when shown alone.

When two pictures were shown simultaneously in a rivalrous situation, the results showed that in the primary visual cortex (V1) only a minority of the recorded cells (about 20%) correlated their activity with the change in the content of consciousness. When other areas along the ventral visual stream were recorded, the proportion of cells correlating with consciousness increased the further along the ventral stream the cells were. Thus, in the farthest recorded site in the temporal lobe, as many as 90% of the measured cells – those interested in that type of stimulus – also correlated their activity with the change in the content of consciousness: they were maximally active when their favourite stimulus was consciously seen, as opposed to merely present in front of the eyes and received by the brain but not currently in conscious-ness. The cells became silent during the time their favourite stimulus faded from conscious perception and the rivalling stimulus ruled in consciousness (Leopold & Logothetis, 1999).

Following these exciting experiments on monkeys, a similar experiment was conducted in human subjects but this time brain activity was recorded with fMRI. First, it was found that when a picture of a face was shown to the subject, a particular area in the ventral stream called the "fusiform face area" activated maximally, and when a picture of a house was shown, another area called the "parahippocampal place area" was highly activated. When both a face and a house were shown at the same time in a rivalrous condition, the activity level of these areas strongly correlated with the content of consciousness. When a face popped into consciousness the face area became highly activated, and when a house popped into consciousness the place area became highly activated, respectively. Thus, it seems that areas special-ized in the stimulus processing of specific types of objects in the human brain also directly contribute to the visual consciousness of the same type of objects (Kanwisher, 2001).

9.2 Visual hallucinations

Independent evidence to the same effect has been obtained from experiments where the presence or absence of a particular content in visual consciousness comes about spontaneously, without any stimuli at all. A neurological disorder called "Charles Bonnet syndrome" is characterized by spontaneous visual hallucinations of objects, faces, people or other visual features. The hallucinations may be as vivid and realistic as to be confused with reality. However, each patient usually sees idiosyncratic but always the same visions, so they can easily learn to recognize their own hallucinations and not confuse them with reality (ffychte et al., 1998).

The experiment recorded brain activity with fMRI. In the control condition the patient did not experience any hallucinations, but in the experimental condition the hallucinated contents were vividly present in visual consciousness. The results revealed that the hallucinations were correlated with activity in specific areas along the ventral visual stream.

In sum, the evidence from these (and many other) experiments points to the ventral visual stream as the seat of the content of visual consciousness – or at least as the seat of the neural correlates of such content. When this evidence is combined with the independent evidence from neuropsychological patients who have lost their ability to see visual objects (we reviewed this evidence in Chapter 4), we observe an assuring convergence that points to the same anatomical areas along the ventral visual stream as necessary for visual consciousness of particular contents.

The ventral visual stream is a complex set of cortical areas, so to say that activity somewhere along it correlates with visual consciousness does not imply ter-ribly accurate localization of the neural mechanisms of consciousness. So far it is still unclear where and when along the ventral stream information first enters conscious-ness. Most studies point to later areas in the temporal lobe as being most important for visual consciousness, but many studies also show that the activity in the primary visual area (V1), where the input information first arrives, can reflect the contents of visual consciousness rather than the physical stimulus (Rees, 2007).

The role of V1 in visual consciousness has been a controversial question, with some evidence indicating its involvement and other evidence showing that it is not necessary for visual consciousness. For example, people who have lost their V1 due to brain injury and are cortically blind can still experience visual dream images (Solms, 1997), showing that V1 is not absolutely necessary for visual experiences. Even if V1 contributes to visual awareness in some way, it does not do it all by itself. It probably interacts back and forth with several areas further along the ventral visual stream, and the contents emerge into consciousness only after such complex interactions. (For more on this idea, see "Recurrent processing theory" in Chapter 11.)

In many brain imaging studies of visual consciousness, brain areas other than just the ventral visual stream have been activated, particularly regions in the frontal and the parietal cortex. It is not clear whether these areas are truly necessary for visual consciousness or whether they are activated in visual tasks simply because such tasks also require higher cognitive functions, such as selective top-down attention and working memory. Frontal and parietal networks are, in any case, involved in spatial attention and spatial consciousness, because damage in these areas is associated with neglect of stimuli in one side of space (Rees, 2007).

The interpretation that frontal and parietal areas might not be necessary for visual consciousness after all has been strengthened by experiments showing that when selective top-down attention is not needed in a visual task these areas do not become activated, although the stimulus information enters visual consciousness (Eriksson, Larsson, & Nyberg, 2008). Other experiments have shown that the frontal areas are activated not only in correlation with visual consciousness but also in correlation with auditory consciousness (Eriksson, Larsson, Ahlström, & Nyberg, 2007). This is exactly what we should expect to find if the frontal areas have more to do with modality-independent attention, reflective consciousness and working memory rather than with modality-specific phenomenal consciousness.

The discrepancy between different results and interpretations concerning the NCC of visual consciousness is, however, far from solved. Some of the disagreements go deeper into theoretical and philosophical presuppositions about the nature of consciousness: Is there such a thing as pure phenomenal consciousness at all, or is all conscious experience necessarily in reflective consciousness, that is, is all conscious visual content dependent on selective attention, working memory and verbal reportability? We will return to these questions when we discuss different theories of consciousness, where this dispute re-emerges.

9.3 EEG and MEG experiments on visual consciousness

In EEG and MEG experiments we can track in time when the information from a visual stimulus enters consciousness. The EEG and MEG signals show, with the temporal scale of 1/1000 s, how the electromagnetic brain responses develop. By comparing the brain responses to seen stimuli (conscious) with similar stimuli that were not seen, the responses should show that at some point in time the brain starts to respond differently to the stimuli that enter visual consciousness compared with those that remain outside of it. When does that happen? When and where in the brain does a visual stimulus enter consciousness?

The basic idea of the EEG and MEG experiments on NCC is already familiar to us: to contrast the presence with the absence of consciousness. To make the same stimuli sometimes invisible and sometimes visible, they are often shown near the subjective perceptual threshold. This means that they are shown so briefly or they are so difficult to distinguish from the background that the typical subject sees them only sometimes and misses them at other times. Thus, with this experimental design it is possible to contrast seen and unseen stimuli when everything else is equal (or at least very close to equal).

In experiments of this kind, the stimuli are shown for tens or even hundreds of times for the same subject, because the EEG response to a single stimulus is so small in relation to all the other ongoing EEG activity that it is almost impossible to discern it at all. A normal ongoing EEG always contains all kinds of spontaneous electrophysiological activities of the brain that are not related to any external stimuli. The tiny EEG responses generated by the stimulus each time are *averaged to form an average response curve*, which cancels out all the EEG activity that had nothing in particular to do with the stimulus. The average response curve to a stimulus is called *an event-related potential* (ERP) because it shows only those electrical brain events that were specifically related to the event we are interested in, in this case the visual stimulus.

The event-related electrical responses show the first reliable difference to seen (conscious) and unseen (nonconscious) stimuli, starting around 150–200 ms from stimulus onset and typically peaking at 250–300 ms. In EEG studies, this response has been termed the "visual awareness negativity" (VAN) because it typically appears in the event-related brain potential curves as a negative-going waveform that only appears for stimuli that reach consciousness (Koivisto, Kainulainen, & Revonsuo, 2009; Wilenius & Revonsuo, 2007). It is strongest in the back of the head, in electrode sites over the occipital, temporal and posterior parietal lobes – in scalp areas directly above the visual cortex.

In a MEG study, a similar response to seen objects was localized in the right occipital lobe at around 250–300 ms from stimulus onset (Vanni, Revonsuo, Saarinen, & Hari, 1996). The neural activities that elicit VAN are believed to be the electrical brain correlates of phenomenal visual consciousness. If this interpretation is accurate, it takes about 0.2–0.3 s for the brain to process the stimulus information in the visual cortex before the information can enter consciousness.

This sounds quick enough, but in fact for the brain this is a rather slow response. Visual information enters the primary visual cortex already within the first 20–30 ms and is rapidly processed through all visual areas within the first 100 ms. This kind of processing is believed to be totally automatic and outside of consciousness, but it may still guide our rapid motor reactions to visual stimuli (it is the nonconscious visuomotor zombie in action again!). If you have ever returned a tennis serve or a badminton strike faster than lightning, although you never even saw the ball you hit, then your rapid but successful response was very likely handled by the nonconscious, fast processing sweep. Consciousness of the stimulus, by contrast, requires complex feedback processing between different cortical areas, and that takes time. Therefore, conscious perception and the action based on it are usually much slower than the 0.1 s required for the first fast responses. (For more on the differences between fast and slow processing of visual stimuli, see Lamme's theory in Chapter 11.)

The VAN response is usually followed in the EEG by another wave called "late positivity" (LP), which is a slow, broad wave around 400–600 ms from the stimulus. It is closely similar to the P3 family of EEG waves, which are believed to reflect attention and working memory. In the consciousness experiments, the late positive wave has been interpreted as a correlate of reflective consciousness: the attentive selection, classification, naming and reporting of the conscious visual percept (Koivisto, Kainulainen, & Revonsuo, 2009). Thus, the EEG studies also have revealed a pattern of responses that can be neatly interpreted in terms of the concepts of phenomenal consciousness (indicated by VAN) and reflective consciousness (indicated by LP). Furthermore, the late positivity has not been observed if the stimulus that reaches phenomenal consciousness and generates VAN does not require any special attention, any particular response or any other type of conscious reflection (Koivisto, Kainulainen, & Revonsuo, 2009).

9.4 Transcranial magnetic stimulation (TMS)

Recently, a new experimental method has been added to the cognitive neuroscientist's arsenal that complements the above-mentioned approaches. Transcranial magnetic stimulation (TMS) is not a brain imaging or sensing method at all, but rather a way to locally *intervene with* the normal functioning of the brain in a controlled manner. With TMS, brief magnetic pulses can be targeted at specified locations on the cortical surface. They cause an abnormal burst of neuroelectrical activity that prevents the normal activity for a short while. In TMS experiments we can observe the consequences of the interventions to behaviour and consciousness.

When the visual cortex has been stimulated with this device, many kinds of effects have been observed. With low magnetic pulse intensity (which creates only a tiny artificial burst of activity in the visual cortex), it is possible to actually *create* visual experiences by directly stimulating the cortex, visual areas V1 and V5 for example. When these areas are stimulated, people report seeing brief visual phenomena called *phosphenes* – flashes of light and brief visual patterns. Phosphenes come in various shapes and forms, and sometimes they are coloured or moving. By contrast, if the TMS pulse intensity is high, then the affected part of the visual cortex seems to go temporarily out of function. The area is temporarily blind to visual stimuli (creating a "scotoma" or blind part of the visual field) or at least there is lowered visibility of stimuli in the corresponding part of the visual field.

Results from TMS studies have shown that different visual areas are in interaction when visual phenomenology is generated. For example, when moving phosphenes are generated, both V1 and V5 must be engaged. If V1 is disturbed with a TMS pulse at the same time as V5 is stimulated to generate moving phosphenes, the subject does not see the phosphenes at all. Thus, V1 and V5 appear to be in reciprocal interaction when visual phenomenology in motion is created (Silvanto, Cowey, Lavie, & Walsh, 2005).

TMS is crucially important to establish *where* the neural mechanisms of visual consciousness are located. It has one advantage over the other methods we have mentioned: With TMS we can find out not only what areas are *correlated* with consciousness, but also which ones of the correlating areas are actually doing something worthwhile that is *necessary* for visual consciousness. All the other methods are purely correlative, in that they show that the consciousness of a stimulus and the activity of an area tend to co-occur. But such a correlation does not tell us *what* the area is doing. With TMS we can stop the area from doing its task, and then check how missing the area's contribution changes consciousness. The changes between knocking the area out versus leaving it intact reveal, at least indirectly, how the normally functioning area contributes to consciousness. In that sense, TMS experiments are closer to brief, small lesions or temporary neuropsychological deficits than to functional brain imaging maps.

Chapter summary

Overall, the functional brain imaging studies and the electromagnetic brain sensing studies deliver converging evidence concerning the neural correlates of visual consciousness. When visual information enters phenomenal consciousness, the cortical areas along the ventral visual stream become activated. The activity spreads quickly forward, but to reach visual consciousness a complex feedforward–feedback interaction between different cortical areas is required. Thus, it takes some time for the information to enter consciousness – at least around two-tenths of a second – and this is reflected in the timescale at which the first reliable electrical responses to consciousness typically emerge. Immediately after the information has first entered phenomenal consciousness it will be channelled to reflective consciousness, especially if the information is needed to accomplish a current task or goal or decision. The stage of reflective consciousness is correlated with activation of frontoparietal brain areas known to be important for attention and working memory. An EEG waveform ("late positivity") also known to correlate with these cognitive mechanisms indicates that the visual information has reached reflective consciousness.

This view of the neural correlates of visual consciousness is further supported by the evidence from neuropsychological patients who have damage in the ventral visual stream. If the ventral areas not only *correlate* with but are truly *necessary* for visual consciousness of objects, then destruction of those areas should lead to deficits of visual consciousness where objects or their features cannot be seen. This is exactly what happens: Damage to area V4 leads to achromatopsia or disappearance of phenomenal colours from visual consciousness, damage to lateral occipital cortex leads to an inability to consciously perceive coherent visual objects (although nonconscious visually guided actions towards the objects are still possible), and so on. (For more details, see the earlier section on Neuropsychology of consciousness, Chapters 4–6.) Similar effects can furthermore be temporarily created in normal healthy subjects by TMS stimulation of the intact visual cortex.

Research on the neural correlates of consciousness continues and new results appear almost daily in the leading scientific publications in cognitive neuroscience. Thus, there is no doubt that the experimental approach of NCC research will lead us ever closer to the neural mechanisms of consciousness. Whether or not all that empirical data will deliver a final solution to the philosophical problems about the relationship between consciousness and the brain remains to be seen. So far, no such revolutionary findings or theories have been published that could even begin to cross the Explanatory Gap. Even if we figure out where, when and what kind of neural activity is involved in visual experience, will we understand *how* the neural activity *results in* or *produces* the subjective visual phenomenology?

Further reading

Kanwisher, N. (2001). Neural events and perceptual awareness. *Cognition, 79,* 89–113.

Koch, C. (2004). *The quest for consciousness: A neurobiological approach.* Englewood Cliffs, NJ: Roberts & Company.

Koivisto, M., Kainulainen, P., & Revonsuo, A. (2009). The relationship between awareness and attention: Evidence from ERP responses. *Neuropsychologia, 47,* 2891–2899.

Rees, G. (2007). Neural correlates of the contents of visual awareness in humans. *Philosophical Transactions of the Royal Society of London, Series B, 36,* 877–886.

Revonsuo, A. (2006). *Inner presence: Consciousness as a biological phenomenon.* Cambridge, MA: MIT Press.

Silvanto, J., Cowey, A., Lavie, N., & Walsh, V. (2005). Striate cortex (V1) activity gates awareness of motion. *Nature Neuroscience, 8,* 143.

Brief discussion questions

1   The best imaginable NCC experiment. Try to imagine what kind of experiment would really reveal the neural correlates of consciousness in the clearest manner. What would the subject's task be? What measurement methods would you use? Would the results help to solve the Explanatory Gap?

2   If phenomenal consciousness and reflective consciousness happen almost simultaneously in the mind when we see a stimulus, is it really possible to measure separately the NCC for phenomenal consciousness and the NCC for reflective consciousness? What kind of experiment should we run if we wanted to study the NCC for pure phenomenal consciousness?

Part two

Central domains of consciousness science

III. Theories of consciousness

Introduction: What is a theory of consciousness?

A science that deals with consciousness requires a theory of consciousness that explains what consciousness is and how it hangs together with the rest of the world. In this section we briefly introduce some of the most influential theories of consciousness that have been put forward in the science of consciousness. The theories are divided into two types: philosophical (Chapter 10) and empirical (Chapter 11). The former are "philosophical" because, put forward by philosophers rather than scientists, they offer general metaphysical solutions to the problem of consciousness rather than detailed empirical accounts. They radically disagree with each other about the fundamental nature of consciousness and its place in the world. They can be seen as attempts to find the metaphysical starting points or background commitments for the empirical science of consciousness. In Chapter 11 we review modern empirical theories of consciousness, especially theories about the neural basis of consciousness. They do not explicitly tackle the metaphysical questions concerning the ultimate nature of consciousness. Rather, they make more detailed attempts to link specific conscious phenomena to specific cognitive and neural mechanisms in the brain. Although they, too, disagree with each other quite strongly in some places, at least a few core issues can be found where several theories begin to meet with each other. Such convergence between different theories will pave the way towards the future where the ultimate goal is a single, unified theory of consciousness.

A theory is something that is supposed to do explanatory work, and "explanation" is something that is supposed to make us understand what is really going on. Theories help us to understand what kind of phenomena there are in the world, what they are composed of, how different phenomena interact to produce causal effects and, in general, how the world works. The atomic theory of matter tells us what kind of elementary units all physical matter consists of, the cell theory in biology tells us what the microscopic elements of biological tissues and organisms are like and the evolutionary theory explains the process through which all the different kinds of organisms on this planet have been brought about.

A theory of consciousness is supposed to describe and explain consciousness: tell us what consciousness is and how it relates to other things in the world, in particular the brain. To *describe* consciousness means to define it, to introduce concepts that convey the essential features of consciousness clearly and systematically, to give paradigm examples of the phenomenon and to differentiate it from other phenomena with which it may be easily confused. To *explain* consciousness is to connect it with other phenomena by outlining the mechanisms and principles that underlie it or are responsible for bringing it about, and by showing what kind of causal roles consciousness plays in the brain and in guiding our behaviour.

A full explanation thus leads to a deep understanding of the *nature*, the *constitution*, the *origins* and the *function* of a phenomenon. An ideal theory of consciousness will deliver an explanation that makes us understand consciousness for what it is and defines its place in nature. And as consciousness is basically what *we* are – after all, it constitutes our subjective, personal existence in this world – a theory of consciousness will necessarily also tell us what *our* place is in the universe: drops of eternal nonphysical soul-stuff, or fragile, temporary bioelectrical field patterns in the brain; or perhaps we have been mistaken all along and consciousness will turn out to be something totally different from our everyday intuitions and our traditional explanations. A complete theory of consciousness should also explain or predict in detail what happens to consciousness under exceptional circumstances, such as different types of brain injury or during dreaming, anaesthesia, out-of-body experiences and near-death experiences. The existence and the features of such experiences should follow naturally and logically from the final Grand Unified Theory of Consciousness. I am sure we would all be very curious to see such a theory!

There is no lack of theories of consciousness in the recent literature, but unfortunately none of them quite seems to qualify as the Grand Unified Theory. The diversity and multiplicity of theories of consciousness is both a strength and a weakness. It is a strength in the sense that different theories explore different potential approaches to explaining consciousness, thus we are more likely to find the most fruitful approaches that yield the most credible explanations. But it is also a weakness, because the theories are so diverse that it is not even clear whether they all talk about the *same* thing when they use the word "consciousness". Moreover, most theories concentrate on explaining only a few selected aspects of conscious experience. It remains unclear whether they apply to other phenomena too or to consciousness as a whole at the general level.

In any case, the final goal in the science of consciousness surely is not to have a million different theories of consciousness, incompatible with and ignorant of each other, but rather to have a single, Grand Unified Theory of Consciousness that describes and explains all types of conscious phenomena across the board, once and for all. At this early stage we do not yet even know what the right direction is in which to look for the unified theory of consciousness. Philosophers have searched for explanations of consciousness far and wide; first, let us see what they suggest might be the right way to go.

Chapter 10

Philosophical theories of consciousness

10.1 Review of current philosophical theories of consciousness

Multiple drafts theory (Dennett)

Daniel Dennett is one of the most influential philosophers of our time. Throughout his career, starting in the late 1960s, he has developed a view of consciousness that is in harmony with his wider commitments concerning the nature of the mind. To understand Dennett's theory of consciousness it is necessary to understand his philosophical background assumptions. First, he believes that all science is made from the objective, third-person's point of view. The science of consciousness is no exception to this rule. Thus, the science of consciousness cannot be based on a methodology that would heavily rely on introspection or on the subjective first-person perspective. Subjective impressions and intuitions on what consciousness is like have no authority in the science of consciousness. By contrast, it must be based on objective observations and collections of public data about the physical and intentional behaviours of other people, especially their verbal behaviours. The consciousness scientist thus should look at other people's consciousness as it is revealed from the outside perspective rather than turn inside into one's own experiences and introspections to find the truth about consciousness.

Dennett is committed to cognitive science, the science that sees the mind primarily as an information-processing system, and therefore he conceptualizes consciousness as a special variety of information processing. According to Dennett's definition, consciousness is that part of the information processing going on in the mind that the person *has access to* ("access-consciousness"). Well, what could that possibly mean? For a person to have access to some information is for the person to be able to *express* the information through voluntary behaviour, especially *verbal behaviour*. This leads to the methodology for studying consciousness that Dennett calls *"heterophenomenology"* (as opposed to "autophenomenology" or observing one's own conscious experiences through introspection). The consciousness scientist's primary task is to collect the verbal reports that the subject expresses – reports that describe what the subject experiences, revealing "what it is like" for him. Such objective verbal data constitute "narratives" that describe the contents of experience. All the consciousness scientist can ever know about consciousness is thus contained in masses of verbal and other behavioural data collected from other people.

The Dennettian consciousness researcher should resist the temptation to treat the verbal reports – the narratives – as referring to an internal phenomenology, a subjective, qualitative world where all the reported experiences originally really took place or were actually presented for an internal subject to view and enjoy them. Our everyday conception of consciousness easily invites such a naive interpretation, fears Dennett. He calls this intuitive but wrongheaded theory "the Cartesian theatre" in the brain: a mythical place where all the experiences and the qualia are presented for the mythical "subject", a little person inside the brain who is the audience of the Cartesian theatre.

Dennett emphasizes that behind the narratives we produce there is *no internal subject or self*, there is *no internal phenomenal world* or centre of consciousness in the brain and there are no qualia. He tries to overthrow our deep-seated everyday views of consciousness as a unified seat of subjective experience somewhere inside the brain, a place where it all comes together in a theatre of consciousness and is presented for the subject (the Cartesian theatre). Although from our first-person's point of view we may mistakenly come to believe that the contents of consciousness are presented to us as a unified phenomenal world, in fact no such world *really – objectively, physically –* exists anywhere in the brain. And what does not exist objectively or physically *does not exist at all* – at least if we ask Dennett.

According to Dennett, there is no objective evidence in neuroanatomy and neurophysiology for such a mythical place in the brain. Furthermore, he believes that the Cartesian theatre also leads to the philosophical paradox known as the *homunculus* problem (homunculus = little man). If there is an internal, mythical subject in the brain to whom the qualia are presented, then the internal subject must in turn somehow perceive or become aware of the internal presentations. Thus, it should have a tiny consciousness of its own inside *its* head, with another presentation and audience, and so on, in an endless regression of smaller and smaller homunculi where the true explanation for consciousness is never found.

Therefore, Dennett rejects the Cartesian theatre. For objective, third-person science, no such thing exists. The data – the narratives – describing subjective experience should not be taken literally, but rather as works of elaborate fiction that the various subsystems and modules of the brain (such as the left-hemisphere interpreter) tend to produce. When the fiction is fabricated by the brain, the verbal output systems use whatever information they have access to in the brain. The resulting narratives are not necessarily internally coherent or perfectly continuous through time, because at different times different pieces of information in the brain gain access to the output systems and become reportable. In Dennett's theory, consciousness is identified with the objective physical information that is expressed in observable voluntary behaviour and speech – consciousness is in fact constructed into a somewhat coherent narrative only at the output stage. What we call our "self" is not any internal entity, it is only the *fictional* subject, the main character of the narrative or, in Dennett's terminology, *the centre of narrative gravity.*

The different streams of information in the brain that gain access to output systems are the "multiple drafts" referred to in the name of the theory. The streams of information in the brain compete with each other for access to output systems – or for *fame in the brain*, as Dennett metaphorically expresses it – and the ones that happen to gain access are what constitutes consciousness. Consciousness consists of those information contents in the brain that win the competition for access, achieve momentary "fame" or "political influence" in the brain and thus drive and control behaviour (Dennett, 2005).

Philosophically, Dennett is some sort of functionalist (although it is difficult to say exactly what kind of functionalism his theory is committed to, and he himself is explicitly vague about this). Thus, to describe and explain consciousness, a standard cognitive science approach is sufficient, according to Dennett. Explaining consciousness only requires a description of how certain types of information come to win the competition for access and how the selected information then drives external behaviour. To explain human consciousness is not in principle any different from explaining how a complex robot's external behaviour is controlled by certain types of carefully selected information.

Dennett's theory has been heavily criticized because it seems to redefine "consciousness" in such a way that the term comes to mean something very different from what we originally set out to explain. Dennett's famous 1991 book is titled *"Consciousness explained"*, but many felt it should have been called *"Consciousness explained away"*. What most people wanted to find an explanation for is phenomenal consciousness, qualia and subjectivity, but Dennett dismissed them as mere illusions. He redefined consciousness as information that has access to output systems and went on to explain that. Thus, Dennett provided an explanation for a functional notion of (access) consciousness but no explanation for phenomenal consciousness, because according to him no such thing exists – it is just a die-hard Cartesian myth.

As a philosophical position, Dennett's theory includes ingredients from eliminative materialism, behaviourism and functionalism. Echoes of behaviourism's rejection of consciousness can be heard in Dennett's arguments when he dismisses qualia and phenomenal consciousness on the basis that their existence cannot be objectively verified from the third person's point of view. Dennett's strategy of argumentation here is also closely related to those used by eliminativists, as Dennett tries to show that our ordinary, everyday or folk-psychological idea of consciousness is mistaken. However, Dennett does not propose that we should totally eliminate the concept of consciousness from science. We should eliminate only the notions of "qualia" and "phenomenal consciousness". The "real" consciousness that is left after the elimination is actually something quite different from what we first thought consciousness to be. It is a complex, parallel information-processing system that simulates a serial machine, and thus creates the impression of a single "subject" or "self" that expresses itself through speech and is in control of voluntary behaviours.

Although widely discussed in the philosophical literature, Dennett's idea of consciousness has not been widely accepted by other philosophers. As an empirical theory, Dennett's position comes close to the global workspace theory (to be discussed in Chapter 11) and other theories that identify consciousness with widespread cognitive access rather than with the purely phenomenal qualities. This approach thus does have its supporters among empirical consciousness researchers and to some extent Dennett has joined forces with them. Dennett's theory of the self as "the centre of narrative gravity" is more plausible than his theory of consciousness. Data from both normal subjects and neuropsychological patients show that the self is like a theory or a story that our brain tells to itself, and the story is rather changeable and not very well in accordance with the objective facts.

The main problem with Dennett's theory is the bland view of the nature of the mind. Dennett leaves out, eliminates or ignores exactly those aspects of consciousness that are most puzzling and most in need of an explanation. Furthermore, he seems to promote a view of us humans as nothing more than complex information-processing zombies with no phenomenal, qualitative subjectivity. Few people find such a view of conscious beings inviting or acceptable, because it seems to deny the only fact about which we have certain knowledge in this world: that my own phenomenal, qualitative, inner experiences exist and that they are very different from and exist independent of the external verbal behaviours that can be externally observed. Sure, the knowledge we all possess about our own qualia is not objective, third-person knowledge, but no science of consciousness that denies the fundamental first-person facts of subjective experience is ever going to get off the ground. Unless behaviouristic functionalism makes an unexpected, forceful comeback into the study of the mind, Dennett's approach is unlikely to become the basis for the future Grand Unified Theory of Consciousness.

Sensorimotor theory (O'Regan and Noë)

Alva Noë is a philosopher who at one time was Dennett's disciple, whereas Kevin O'Regan is an experimental scientist with a somewhat behaviouristic inclination. Not surprisingly, the sensorimotor theory thus shares much the same ground with Dennett's approach, especially in its denial or elimination of phenomenal consciousness and qualia. And, like Dennett, this theory replaces the notion of consciousness as inner phenomenal experience with another notion: consciousness as embodied sensorimotor interaction with the world. Consciousness is defined by this theory as *ways of acting* or as *something we do*, rather than an internal phenomenal experience or an internal representation of the world (O'Regan & Noë, 2001). Noë has recently formulated this position in the following manner:

> I advance this truly astonishing hypothesis: To understand consciousness in humans and animals, we must look not inward, into the recesses of our insides; rather, we need to look to the ways in which each of us, as a whole animal, carries on the processes of living in and with and in response to the world around us . . . You are not your brain . . . Meaningful thought arises only for the whole animal dynamically engaged with its environment . . . And indeed the same is true for the quality of our conscious episodes . . . The taste of licorice is not something that happens in our brains.
>
> (Noë, 2009, pp. 7–8)

Because consciousness resides in our behavioural interactions with the world rather than in our brain, the theory postulates that consciousness does not derive from brain activity at all. Consequently, there is no need to explain how brain activity causes or constitutes consciousness, because it does not. Furthermore, O'Regan and Noë believe that the theory gets rid of the Hard Problem for good by simply denying phenomenality:

> [T]he concept of phenomenal consciousness must be (and can be) rejected, and so there is no longer any puzzle about how to explain that . . . [O]ther aspects of consciousness can indeed be explained according to our view . . .
>
> Although we reject accounts of phenomenal consciousness as a property of subpersonal states, we do not deny that there are experiences and that there are facts about what experiences are like. But these . . . are not facts about a person's qualia . . . They pertain, rather, to the person's . . . active engagement with the world he . . . inhabits.
>
> (O'Regan & Noë, 2001, pp. 963–965)

If consciousness is neither phenomenal nor in the brain, the problem of how the brain, or any other physical process, can give rise to phenomenality can be forgotten as a misguided question:

> An important advantage of this view is that it allows us to escape from the problem of having to explain how brain activity could give rise to experience. We escape from the problem because we propose that experience does *not* derive from brain activity.
>
> (O'Regan & Noë, 2001, p. 968)

The sensorimotor theory has been regarded as rather behaviouristic in spirit, perhaps even more so than Dennett's theory. Be that as it may, it is clear that both theories eliminate rather than explain phenomenal consciousness. After the elimination of phenomenality, they misleadingly use the concepts "consciousness" and "experience" to refer to something else, something objective and physical, such as behaviour, organism–environment interaction or information processing.

An obvious counter-argument to the sensorimotor theory points out that there are conscious phenomenal experiences, such as nocturnal dreams, in the total absence of any sensorimotor interactions with the world. Indeed, empirically incontestable data from dream research show that vivid dream experiences with an active and embodied dream-self regularly occur during REM sleep at the same time as our bodies and brains are completely incapable of engaging in any sensorimotor interactions with the surrounding physical world. This poses a serious challenge for the sensorimotor theory of consciousness (as well as for the highly similar neurophenomenological theory of consciousness; see below) (e.g. Revonsuo, 2001, 2006).

One way to deal with dreaming is to deny, as Dennett has done in his earlier work, that dreams are real conscious experiences at all. This line of argument is taken by Noë (2009) too; according to him, dream experiences and perceptual experiences are completely distinct types of experience, no matter how similar they may subjectively feel. Thus, *real* experiences cannot exist in the absence of sensorimotor interaction, only *dream* experiences can. The argument appears to be circular, ending up in the same background assumption that the sensorimotor theory originally started with. Dream experiences cannot be counted as real experiences, no matter how real they feel, because the background assumptions of the theory have already ruled out the possibility that real experiences could happen without sensorimotor interaction.

But in fact, as far as the best empirical evidence we have is concerned, dreams *do* feel as real as perceptual experiences. As to their subjective qualities – as to what conscious experiences are made of – dreams and wakeful experiences are made of the same ingredients and thus constitute the same phenomenon, consciousness, in dreaming and wakefulness. Experiments have been conducted in the sleep laboratory where dreamers, immediately after awakening, report the perceptual qualities of their dreams and also match them with the visual qualities of different photographs. According to the results, the dream world really does look like the perceptual world. At least that was the conclusion the researchers reached:

> [I]t must be recognized that dreams only very rarely have the dark, murky, confused qualities that are frequently attributed to them in myths and movies. From what subjects have conveyed to us by their matches of photographs to

dream images, the dream is most frequently a highly organized, coherent perceptual production that is usually not drastically different from the way we see the outside world while we are awake.

(Rechtschaffen & Buchignani, 1992, p. 155)

Thus, the results of dream research pose strong empirical evidence against the sensorimotor theory. Yet, the sensorimotor theory, or something along the same lines, has gained high popularity in some corners of consciousness research, such as machine consciousness and cognitive robotics. This is understandable, because if the sensorimotor theory turns out to be the correct philosophical take on consciousness, then there will be no deep metaphysical reasons against building all sorts of conscious machines and robots as long as such mechanical systems can be programmed to interact smoothly with their environment in sufficiently rich and flexible ways.

If you accept the sensorimotor definition of consciousness, then a machine that can engage in flexible sensorimotor interactions with its environment is conscious by definition. If you do not accept the sensorimotor definition, you will most likely suspect that, instead of machine consciousness, the engineers have only managed to build a computerized mechanical zombie that manages to imitate superficially the external behaviour and the nonconscious sensorimotor information processing of a human being.

We can only hope that one fine day the ingenious machine consciousness engineers will build a phenomenally conscious robot that just quietly hangs around, all the while enjoying wonderful subjective qualities in a rich internal phenomenology, resembling vivid dream experiences! Such a fellow would be a truly amazing conscious machine! But if the sensorimotor theory is true, this kind of a conscious machine is a contradiction in terms: no sensorimotor interaction with the environment implies no consciousness.

Biological naturalism (Searle)

The American philosopher John Searle fervently opposes the above types of eliminative or behaviouristic theories where consciousness is redefined as something else, something objective or behavioural, and is thus flatly denied and dismissed. John Searle is a philosopher who started his career in the philosophy of language in the 1960s. He became widely known as an ardent critic of artificial intelligence and cognitive science with his famous "Chinese Room argument" in the 1980s. He argued then that the computer metaphor of the mind is mistaken: Digital computers and human minds are fundamentally different because computers cannot even in principle understand any of the symbols they process, whereas for human minds understanding the meaning (semantics) of natural language is a part of the biological nature of our minds. Computers may externally mimic human behaviours – a computer can be programmed to print out the words "Of course I understand what you say!" – but such external outputs by no means guarantee that the internal processes producing them are genuinely mental. By contrast, when a human speaker utters the same words we know that he understands what they mean.

In the early 1990s Searle turned his attention to the problem of consciousness.

In his widely known book *The rediscovery of the mind* (1992), Searle formulated a view of consciousness called "biological naturalism". According to this view, consciousness is a biological phenomenon, a higher level feature of brain activity. All conscious phenomena are emergent properties of neuronal systems. Consciousness is entirely caused by neurobiological processes and is realized in brain structures. However, conscious phenomena have the unique feature of subjectivity or first-person ontology, which is irreducible to any objective neurophysiological phenomenon. Thus, consciousness cannot be reduced to just objective brain activity.

Although Searle's theory of consciousness is basically philosophical rather than empirical, he sees the role of the empirical sciences as absolutely crucial in solving the problem of consciousness. Once the basic philosophical issues are clarified, neuroscientists should take the lead in this project; philosophers had just better quickly get out of the way! Thus, Searle's task is merely to clarify the basic philosophical issues at the outset so that empirical scientists can more easily avoid making elementary philosophical mistakes in their work.

For Searle, "consciousness" is much the same thing as what we have called "phenomenal consciousness": the inner first-person experience of our own existence constituted by subjective, qualitative states. In contrast to Dennett, Searle holds that "qualia" and "consciousness" are not two different things, but boil down to one and the same thing (whereas Dennett denies qualia and redefines consciousness in other terms). As it is difficult to precisely define "consciousness", Searle prefers to point to unambiguous cases of it. His favourite example is to say that consciousness consists of those states of sentience or awareness that begin when we wake up in the morning from dreamless sleep and go on until we go to sleep or die or otherwise become unconscious. This sounds as if he would identify "consciousness" with "wakefulness", but he does admit that dreams involve some sort of consciousness as well, though of a different kind than wakefulness.

According to Searle, the phenomenon to be explained by a theory of consciousness is *unified, qualitative subjectivity*. Consciousness is unified or holistic in the sense that every content of consciousness is embedded into a holistic field where each separate content, say, the feeling of pain in the foot, the sight of red colour in the traffic lights, the smell of smoke, the sound of a church bell, is related to each other to form one momentarily unified experience. Searle opposes what he calls *building-block theories* of consciousness, which assume that the qualitative experiences are first produced somehow in isolation from each other in the brain, and only then are related or integrated with each other, as if consciousness would be gradually built up from small bits and pieces of isolated qualities. On the contrary, conscious events can only emerge inside the unified field where they are automatically related with every other currently existing subjective quality within the same person's consciousness; no isolated qualia first exist on their own. Therefore, to seek for an explanation of consciousness is to seek for the neural mechanism of the unified field of consciousness. Searle has named his theory *the unified field theory of consciousness*.

Although Searle himself does not refer to the history of consciousness studies in this context, it is obvious that his unified field theory comes very close to the holistic theories advocated by Gestalt psychologists, originally proposed in the late 1920s. Likewise, the building-block theories he criticizes are reminiscent of Titchener's atomistic approach to explaining consciousness in the early 1900s, also known as structuralism, and at the time criticized by Gestalt psychologists. Incidentally, in modern consciousness research, there is at least one obvious building-block theory: Semir Zeki's microconsciousness theory, to be presented in Chapter 11.

Unlike Dennett, Searle takes phenomenal consciousness seriously as the most important thing that requires an explanation (rather than an elimination). Searle insists that we know as a fact that brain processes *cause* conscious states; what we do not know or understand yet are the details of how this happens. In opposition to Searle we could point out that all we know for a fact is that conscious phenomena exist and they closely *correlate* with neural activities in the brain. But correlation is an extremely weak relationship that tells us nothing about the nature of the things that correlate – even an immaterial soul could correlate its states with brain activities. Furthermore, causal relationships between brain processes and conscious phenomena are very difficult to establish objectively, because the conscious phenomena themselves cannot be observed, measured or detected objectively.

Another weakness of Searle's position is that his idea of causation is unconventional because he regards the hierarchical micro–macro relationship between lower level and higher level features of a system as a causal relationship. Thus, according to this line of thought, millions of microscopic water molecules "cause" the macroscopic, observable round shape of a water drop. But usually causation is defined as a relationship that involves entities interacting across a stretch of time. We can say that a water drop that hit me from above *caused* a dark wet spot on my shirt, because this involves a sequence of interacting events and objects where the drop falls on my shirt and is absorbed by the fabric. But considering the relationship between the shape of the drop and the molecules, it would be more natural to say that the molecules *constitute* the shape rather than that they cause it. Micro–macro relationships are constitutive rather than causal.

Searle's biological naturalism frames the brain–consciousness problem in a useful manner but does not solve it for good. Searle fails to provide any decisive evidence for the fact that brain activities actually do cause consciousness rather than just correlate with it. He also fails to tell us in what way we could empirically figure out how the brain exactly causes consciousness – and until such details become available, the problem of consciousness remains unsolved.

Naturalistic dualism (Chalmers)

David Chalmers is an Australian philosopher who started up his professional career in the study of consciousness in the early 1990s when the new wave of interest in this subject was just about to emerge. He played a central role in getting the field organized, initiating or actively participating in the professional organization dedicated to the study of consciousness (*Association for the Scientific Study of Consciousness*, ASSC) and organizing some of the first and largest conferences ever that exclusively focused on the problem of consciousness, in Tucson, Arizona. Chalmers's theory of consciousness was published in his book *The conscious mind* (1996).

Chalmers became famous also for coining the term the "Hard Problem". He argued that science could conceivably solve many of the "easy" problems of consciousness, such as the neural and cognitive correlates of conscious phenomena, but it seems impossible to solve the Hard Problem: the problem of explaining how *any* physical system could ever have or produce *any* experiential, qualitative states at all.

Chalmers believes that the Hard Problem cannot be solved by reductive or mechanistic explanation. Subjective experience or qualia are features that cannot be explained by referring to an underlying physical phenomenon or mechanism. Thus, they have to be taken as *fundamental* features of the universe – features like mass, spin, gravity, the speed of light or the relationship between mass and energy. Fundamental features cannot be explained any further; they do not seem to be based on anything even more fundamental – they themselves constitute the fundamental bottom level of the world. Everything else must be explained by referring to the fundamental entities and laws, but there, further reductive explanation comes to an end.

A theory of consciousness should thus be more like a theory in fundamental physics than like a theory in the biological sciences. A theory of consciousness cannot tell us what consciousness is or how or why it exists, but it should nevertheless tell us how consciousness is connected to other phenomena in the world, for instance our brain. Consequently, *psychophysical laws* form a central part of a theory of consciousness. They are the fundamental laws of nature that describe how phenomenal experience correlates with or depends on physical features. Chalmers outlines a few principles that are candidates for being psychophysical laws. One of these is the *principle of structural coherence* between subjective experience (phenomenology) and cognitive function (the information processing and representation going on in awareness). The cognitive information processing in awareness is the objective physical counterpart of phenomenal consciousness. Any information that is experienced in phenomenal consciousness is also cognitively represented in the brain.

Phenomenal experience itself, however, is not a part of the physical world at all – that is why Chalmers' theory represents dualism. Also, experience is not a logically necessary part of information processing, but could conceivably be detached from it. A thought experiment that he presents to defend the idea that the phenomenal is not a necessary part of the physical describes a world that is physically in every way identical to ours, but in that world no-one is conscious; everyone is a neurobiological zombie. Yet, our counterparts in that world have physically, biologically and cognitively identical brains with us – it is just that the fundamental psychophysical laws of nature do not hold in that world as they do in ours. Chalmers claims that this zombie-world thought experiment is not logically incoherent or inconceivable, therefore consciousness is not a part of the physical. We can imagine all of the objective physical, biological, cognitive and behavioural ingredients of the world without any of the phenomenal ingredients.

Unfortunately, when the phenomenal is detached from the physical in this way, it becomes causally impotent in the physical world. Thus, in Chalmers' theory, phenomenal consciousness has no causal powers over physical phenomena: the theory implies epiphenomenalism.

The theory also implies (or at least plays with) the ideas of panpsychism and double-aspect theory. Chalmers finds the idea inviting that phenomenality exists, at least in some extremely simple form, in all information-bearing events in the universe. Information, thus, is necessarily coupled with consciousness; it has a double aspect, being both physical and phenomenal. This, he suggests, is the most fundamental psychophysical principle. Phenomenal properties are the internal aspect of information.

In the human brain, information becomes organized in more complex ways than in perhaps any other system. From (some of) this information processing and functional organization emerges human consciousness. One empirical theory, called information integration theory (developed by Giulio Tononi; see Chapter 11), includes a similar idea, namely that consciousness consists of complex but unified information in the brain (although that theory is not explicitly committed to dualism, epiphenomenalism or panpsychism).

In addition to epiphenomenalism, another uncomfortable consequence of the coupling between phenomenality and information is that very simple physical systems, such as electrons, thermostats and pocket calculators, must also have some sort of simple consciousness. As with all panpsychist theories, Chalmers' theory sees consciousness everywhere around us. It is a comforting idea, as Fechner already has argued, to see the world inhabited by countless centres of consciousness. Unfortunately it is an empirically untestable idea, a mere figment of wild imagination, at least until somebody produces the consciousness detector that objectively senses all the invisible centres of consciousness that supposedly hang around everywhere all the time.

Chalmers himself has described his theory as a combination of functionalism and property dualism, or as *naturalistic dualism*. Although a variety of dualism, it does not postulate an immaterial soul or anything like that; it only postulates that consciousness is a fundamental but nonphysical feature of the universe, coupled to the physical through fundamental psychophysical laws. Thus, it is a variety of dualism that may be much easier to incorporate into the modern scientific view of the world than Descartes' interactionist theory. Still, the problems of Chalmers' theory are conspicuous. Phenomenal consciousness is rendered causally ineffective and thus cannot make any difference in the physical world. We, as subjects, are mere powerless puppets: worthless spectators under the illusion of being able to make a difference in the world. Furthermore, subjective experience is distributed widely in the universe: it is to be found in every physical system carrying information. Anywhere you look around, there are physical systems carrying information and thereby having conscious experiences. All in all, this is a world-view that may be too hard to swallow for anyone who opposes the more bizarre implications of epiphenomenalism and panpsychism.

Higher order theories (HOTs) of consciousness

Higher order theories (HOTs) include a set of approaches presented by several different philosophers recently, each defending his own idiosyncratic version of HOT. The best-known HOT theorists include the philosophers David Rosenthal and Peter Carruthers (e.g. Carruthers, 2007). All HOTs do have a common core, and it is the common core rather than all the varieties that we will mostly focus on here.

A HOT holds that conscious mental states are to be explained not by referring to their physical or neural correlates, but by referring to relations between mental representations that are not conscious. Thus, conscious mental states arise out of representational mental states that are not conscious. But what are "representational mental states"? The traditional definition of mental states in philosophy refers to *intentionality* as the mark of the mental: States that have *intentional content about things outside of themselves*, or *aboutness*, or *directedness*, or they *represent* something in the external world, are mental states. This is also the standard idea in the cognitive science account of the mind: that it consists of representational states. But not all representational mental states are conscious states – our minds also include representations and information about external stimuli outside consciousness. Such states are unconscious mental states.

Consciousness arises out of the relation between a lower order state and a higher order state, such as a higher order thought *about* the lower order state. For example, the pure sensation of pain is a lower order state. It becomes conscious only if there is a higher order thought about it (the thought "I am in pain"). Otherwise, it remains an unconscious state.

The higher order thinking that does the trick in these theories seems to be closely related to what we have called "reflective consciousness". Thus, one way to formulate the idea of HOTs, using terminology more familiar to us, would be to say that according to HOTs the contents of phenomenal consciousness are unconscious unless and until they are taken as objects of top-down attentional mechanisms and reflective consciousness, which select, name, conceptualize and introspectively report them. The contents of consciousness in HOTs thus are identical to the contents of a cognitive form of consciousness (reflective consciousness or access consciousness): mental contents that are conceptualized and can be verbally expressed.

One serious problem with HOTs is that they deny consciousness from all such creatures who have no capacity to formulate higher order thoughts (or that have no reflective consciousness). Therefore, infants and animals are nonconscious zombies, because they do not have what it takes to lift a mental state to consciousness. What, then, is going on in the minds of such creatures? According to some versions of HOT, infants and animals can have *nonconscious* pains, colour sensations, smells, etc., but such states of course do not *feel* like anything, they have no phenomenality, because they are not conscious. According to other versions, infants and animals do not have any kinds of pains, colour sensations or smells at all, not even nonconscious ones. I am afraid that neither of these alternatives sounds particularly assuring.

In some versions of HOT, the higher order state is taken to be more like a perceptual state than a thought-like state. Thus, the lower order states have to be *perceived* by the higher order state (higher order perception, or HOP). Consciousness is the internal perception of what is going on in one's own mind. (Incidentally, Sigmund Freud held a similar idea of consciousness as an internal perceptual mechanism.) Furthermore, some versions of HOT do not require that the lower order states have to be *actually* thought about or *actually* perceived to become conscious – it is sufficient that they are *potentially* perceived or thought about (i.e. that they are *in principle accessible* to higher order states, though not necessarily accessed right now). Formulated in our terminology, consciousness would consist of those contents in primary phenomenal consciousness that are potentially accessible to reflective consciousness. That would leave some room for conscious events also outside the current scope of attention, in the periphery of consciousness. Still, in the final analysis, conscious states would derive their existence from reflective consciousness: from the thoughts and concepts that are (potentially) applied to the contents of phenomenal consciousness.

Creatures without such capacities would be devoid of consciousness. Also, the contents of phenomenal consciousness that cannot be taken as objects of thoughts and cannot be reported (e.g. dream images that leave no clear memory traces, unattended stimuli that fade before attention is targeted at them) do not count as conscious states at all. But this does not sound quite right either. Whether or not we, when waking up, are able to remember and report a dream cannot determine, through backward causation in time, whether the dream involved phenomenal experiences to us when it took place!

Although HOTs have become immensely popular among philosophers of the mind and they have generated a virtual industry that produces different versions of HOTs (nearly every philosopher of consciousness seems to have developed his or her own pet version of HOT), these theories have not had any major impact on the empirical study of consciousness. The basis of the theories is perhaps too deeply embedded in philosophical notions and definitions, whereas the connection of these theories to the neural and cognitive mechanisms that empirical scientists deal with remains unclear. It is also not easy to determine whether these theories are empirically testable. In spirit, these theories do closely resemble empirical access-consciousness theories (to be discussed in Chapter 11) that equate the contents of consciousness with the contents of attention, working memory and reportable content. In both cases, pure phenomenal consciousness is denied and reflective consciousness is taken as the basic form of consciousness. As we will see in connection with the empirical theories, the problem is to determine which neural activities and information contents are coupled with subjective experience and which are not – are they also the ones that happen before global cognitive access, reflection and working memory, or only the ones that happen after such higher order cognitive functions are engaged?

Externalist representationalism (Tye, Dretske)

The core assumption in representationalist theories is that all conscious states are representational states, that is, states that carry information about external (or intentional) objects or states of affair. Contents of consciousness necessarily refer to "outside" of themselves. This is easiest to understand in the case of perception: Our conscious visual experience represents the visible objects and events out there in the world around us. Clearly, our perceptual experience carries information and intentional content about external states of affairs. Traditionally, in the philosophy of the mind, intentional content has been regarded as only one feature of our mental states. Conscious mental states additionally have phenomenal content that provides the subjective "feel" of those states. Simple sensory experiences such as pain have been thought to be purely phenomenal without any representational content at all. But representationalist theories try to show that all kinds of conscious states are in fact representational states, and that their phenomenal content can be reduced to or fully explained by their representational content (see the theories presented by Dretske, 1995; and Tye, 1995).

This is a clever move, because while it seems hopeless to explain the phenomenality of conscious states, the case for explaining intentional or representational properties is not all that discouraging. Consequently, if phenomenality is nothing over and above representation, then phenomenality can be explained as well. The phenomenal is reduced to the representational – a strategy similar to reductive materialism that reduces the phenomenal to the neurophysiological. How, then, does the representationalist deal with phenomenality? The idea is that conscious states in the brain are representations like words printed in a book. The words "blue sky" printed on a page represent things in the world without resembling those things in any way. The ink that makes up the word "blue" is not blue, and the pattern of letters that the ink constitutes only refers to blueness. The objects or contents of the representation "blue sky" are physical things or processes in the external physical world. Thus, the real, qualitative blueness resides in the scattered sunlight in the atmosphere: it is a physical process. Now, when we have a conscious experience of the blue sky, there is nothing blue in our brain, just like there is nothing blue in the word "blue" printed here; there are only neural activities in the brain that represent the presence of blueness out there in the world.

The representationalist should be able to tell us in more detail what *kind* of representation is involved in feelings of pain, sensations of colour, smell or itch. It is by no means obvious that qualitative experiences are representations at all, and it is even less obvious that they are nothing over and above being representations.

The representationalist argues that when we turn our attention towards sensory experiences we find only representational features, nothing over and above. If we have a pain in the back, in our conscious experience we only discover features of *an event going on in our back*. We do not get any hold of experiential features in our minds that would be separate from what is going on *out there*; the experience has no purely intrinsic phenomenal features at all. Thus, all of its features are representational. The form of such a purely sensory representation is, however, different from the form of our typical cognitive representations (such as words). The representation of pain is *nonconceptual* – we have no exact words or concepts to describe its nature. It is also nonpropositional: The representational content cannot be carried by sentence-like symbolic representations, but rather by map-like pictorial or spatial representations. The pain representation, for example, must be encoded in a topographic map of the body. The vehicles of such representations in the brain could be neural activation patterns in a neural network that represents the body.

Representations consist of, first, the *vehicle* of representation – the neural system in the brain that carries and expresses the information (or the ink on the page). Second, it consists of the *content* of the representation: the painful event in the back or the external event the representation is about and which was the external source of signals that activated the representation. Thus, the *vehicles* of representation are *inside* the head, but the *contents* of representations are *outside* the head.

Now, if phenomenal content is nothing over and above representational content, then it follows that also phenomenal content – the subjective qualitative "feels", the phenomenal character of experience – is outside the brain. All the colours we see are real physical properties of light-reflecting physical objects. If we see external visual stimuli that are located very far away – say, the red giant star Betelgeuze in the constellation of Orion, or the galaxy of Andromeda in the clear starry night-sky – the contents of our consciousness become outrageously distant from our own physical location. In the case of the visual experience of the constellations in the starry sky, the contents of the stargazer's visual consciousness, along with all the qualia involved, must be literally all over the Milky Way galaxy, light-years away!

But how on earth does our brain manage to project them over there with a mere glance at the right direction – are the qualia travelling backwards in space and time, along the causal pathway to the stars, faster than light? We often see stars that are many hundreds or thousands of light-years away, which means that we see into the stars' distant past when we are looking at them. Recently, the red giant star Betelgeuze has shown signs of becoming a supernova, which means it will explode and be destroyed. Unfortunately, we cannot get any data concerning the star's current state; we only see what was going on about 600 years ago, because the star is 600 light-years from Earth. It may not be there anymore – perhaps it exploded 300 years ago – yet we still see the bright red star in the night-sky. How could the qualia I see now here on Earth, when I look at the star, be really located on a faraway star that no longer even exists?

Another problem arises when we consider experiences that have no direct causal links to any external stimuli. During dreaming, we experience sensations and percepts that may be radically unlike those we have ever experienced during wakefulness. And even if they are similar to wakeful experiences, where are their contents supposed to be located? Externalist representationalists cannot say that the phenomenal contents are in the brain – they explicitly deny that our phenomenal experiences could reside there. They even regard the search for the neural mechanisms of the contents of consciousness a futile project, because if their philosophical view is correct the contents simply cannot be found in the brain, nor can any mechanisms that would somehow resemble or be similar to the contents reside inside our heads.

The representational vehicles that are in the brain in no way resemble the representational contents that are outside the brain. Thus, my visual experience of a yellow banana can be represented by a population of neurons firing in my visual cortex, but nothing in their neural activity resembles the visual experience I have (the yellowness, the oblong shape) – only the external physical banana itself does. The intrinsic features of the neural activity as such, if isolated from its causal connections to physical bananas, include nothing intrinsic that explains *why* it is the representational vehicle of bananas and, say, not apples or blueberries. Only the external relations (causal and intentional) to *real* bananas out there make a particular neural firing the representational vehicle of bananas. To count as the representational vehicle of bananas, a group of neurons in the brain must become selectively activated by input from real physical bananas. Conversely, any neural activity that occurs if and only if there are bananas around sending signals to sensory organs is a representation of bananas.

To summarize, the representationalist approach takes phenomenal consciousness seriously and does not eliminate it. But by treating phenomenality as identical to representational content, it ends up throwing the contents of phenomenal consciousness out from the mind of the subject, into the external physical world. Qualia turn out to be mind-independent physical properties of physical objects out there. Our brains are aware of qualia by representing them with neural activation patterns. Thus, there is very little – in fact, nothing at all – we could find out about the qualitative features of conscious experience by studying the brain.

Unfortunately (for the representationalist), empirical neuroscientists do not seem to fully embrace or understand the implications of representationalism because they still continue the search for the secrets of phenomenal consciousness by probing the brain with NCC experiments – a misguided research programme for the serious representationalist.

Furthermore, the idea that colours and other phenomenal features are physical properties outside the brain seems to directly contradict what the physical sciences say is really out there. After all, if we know anything about physical objects and electromagnetic radiation, we know that they do not have *any* qualitative colours that resemble what we see. And if we know anything at all about the causal order of perception, we know that it runs from external physical stimuli to sense organs to brain activities. Only at the last stage, in the brain, are any qualitative colour experiences generated – how could they then be transported back out from the brain to be superimposed on the physical objects that originally sent the physical signals to our sense organs? When I perceive the starry sky, light from the stars strikes at my retina and excites my visual cortex; how is the redness of Betelgeuse transported instantaneously from my tiny brain to a giant star light-years away? How could the phenomenal contents *be* out there, for me to see across the galactic voids of time and space? Representationalism leaves us no less puzzled about consciousness than we were at the onset.

Neurophenomenology (Varela, Lutz, Thompson, Noë)

The neurophenomenological approach to consciousness is based, not surprisingly, on the school of thought in philosophy called phenomenology, founded by Frantz Brentano (1838–1917) and his student Edmund Husserl (1859–1938), contemporaries of Wundt and other classical introspectionists. Philosophical phenomenology, however, rejected introspection as an appropriate method to study the mind. Brentano's psychology was empirical in the minimal sense that it was based on subjective experience, but it was far removed from the experimental approach of Wundt. Instead, Brentano and Husserl believed that experience must be explored purely from the philosophical first-person perspective and in particular through a logical analysis of the structure of experience. Husserl in fact rejected the natural sciences altogether, considering their approach philosophically naive. Hence, phenomenology distanced itself from scientific psychology and became a purely philosophical enterprise.

Francisco Varela (1946–2001), who was a neuroscientist keenly interested in phenomenology, coined the term "neurophenomenology" in the 1990s. Varela's purpose was not to preserve Husserlian philosophical orthodoxy (there is an army of philosophers already involved in that line of business) but to use phenomenology as a source of inspiration for the neuroscience of consciousness, because in his opinion this school of philosophy has reached deep insights into the nature and structure of experience. At one point Varela admitted that perhaps the very notion of "neurophenomenology" might make Husserl turn in his grave (Varela, 1999, p. 273)!

Husserl regarded intentionality as the unique mark of the mental. In this philosophical context, the notion "intentional" refers to aboutness or the directedness of mental states at something beyond themselves. A further idea in phenomenology is that all mental states, including consciousness, have a particular structure: Mental states contain a mental act that is directed to its object. This is the bipolar *act–object* structure of consciousness. In any instance of conscious experience, an act (of awareness) must reach outside of itself to some (so-called intentional) objects. This famous phenomenological idea of the fundamental structure of consciousness forms also the basis of neurophenomenology.

Long before introducing neurophenomenology, Varela had launched the popular idea of "embodied cognition", the idea that the mind does not reside on an abstract mental level (of computation or pure cognition) but is necessarily embodied in a biological, moving, acting body. Embodiment is a crucial feature of our consciousness too, in that we subjectively experience being very intimately connected to ourselves – we experience being embodied and active in the world, rather than isolated Cartesian minds that consist of pure thought. The intimate relation of experience and bodily self goes to the very bottom level of consciousness. In neurophenomenology, the most fundamental form of consciousness is called (following the phenomenological tradition) "pre-reflective self-consciousness": the experiences I go through are *mine*; there is an *I* who goes through the experiences; thus, the experiences necessarily refer to a person, a self, me – the experiences are self-referential; and the self they refer to is an embodied self. Pre-reflective self-consciousness thus involves, at least tacitly, a reference to *bodily* self-awareness – a pre-reflective experience of *bodily subjectivity* or experiential embodiment. Bodily experience is built deeply into consciousness from the very beginning; there can be no consciousness without this primitive form of self-awareness (Gallagher & Zahavi, 2008; Lutz & Thompson, 2003).

Here, neurophenomenology borrows from another famous representative of phenomenology, Maurice Merleau-Ponty (1908–1961), who emphasized the embodied nature of intentionality. A conscious subject already presupposes a bodily existence situated in an environment, or a pre-reflective embodied intentionality. The commitment to embodiment at every level of consciousness leads to the enactive view of consciousness, according to which consciousness is not located in the brain but instead resides in the bodily interactions between the organism and the world. This view is also closely related to the sensorimotor theory by O'Regan and Noë, already mentioned above. Both theories eventually lead to the rejection of both the standard neuroscientific research programme on consciousness and the search for the NCC in the brain (the neural mechanism that constitutes the necessary and sufficient ground for conscious experience):

> [T]he processes crucial for consciousness cut across the brain–body–world divisions, rather than being limited to neural events in the head . . .
> [C]onsciousness depends crucially on the manner in which brain dynamics are embedded in the somatic and environmental context of the animal's life, and therefore there may be no such thing as a minimal internal neural correlate whose intrinsic properties are sufficient to produce conscious experience.
> (Thompson & Varela, 2001, pp. 422 and 425)

The "embodied consciousness" approach is not too clear about where exactly consciousness is supposed to be located. Only the hazy idea of some kind of complex, mutually embedded systems of brain, body and environment is offered, which sounds at best imprecise but at worst utterly confusing. Neurophenomenologists (following traditional phenomenology) hold the puzzling idea that brain, body and environment cannot be said to be internally or externally located with respect to one another (Thompson & Varela, 2001). It remains a complete mystery how this deliberate obscurity about the spatial location of not only consciousness but also the whole brain, the body and the environment in relation to each other could ever turn to an explanatory theory of consciousness.

But perhaps an explanatory theory of consciousness is not even the goal of neurophenomenology – at least traditional phenomenology rejects the whole framework of science as naive and chooses to operate outside of it. Perhaps neuroph-enomenology also chooses to operate outside the empirical science of consciousness, instead settling for shooting critical arguments at the naive neuroscientists who try in vain to find and explain consciousness within the philosophically inadequate framework of natural science.

Be that as it may, the embodied consciousness theory seems to confuse the internal spatial relations and locations *within* phenomenal consciousness with those of the external physical counterparts of the phenomenal contents. Noë and Thompson (2004) argue that a visual experience presents how things are *in relation to oneself* and in relation to one's potential movements in the surrounding world. This statement clearly illustrates that they believe (apparently following Merleau-Ponty) some kind of bodily self-awareness to penetrate consciousness at every level. Consequently, they believe that no neural system inside the brain could be the bearer of this sort of representational content – only a whole perceiver as an intentional agent could. From this they derive the conclusion that consciousness simply cannot be located in the brain.

What the embodied consciousness theorists probably have failed to appreciate is the fact that the bodily self, in relation to which the other contents of consciousness are presented in subjective experience, is *not the physical organism* as such but only the phenomenal body image within consciousness. The embodied consciousness approach confuses the physical, biological organism with the phenomenal body image. The latter is constructed inside the brain, whereas the former is (mostly) outside the brain. The embodiment we directly feel in our experiences is the embodiment based on the phenomenal body image. We can never directly feel the physical organism that forms our own biological body, just like we can never directly experience distant physical objects; instead, our brain constructs a conscious percept from the available stimulus information, and then we treat this percept as if it was the distant physical object itself. The relationship between our experience of phenomenal embodiment and our physical organism of flesh and bones can only be indirect, as the many cases of bodily illusions and hallucinatons (phantom limbs, somatoparaphrenia, dreams) so vividly illustrate. As we already discussed above in our critique of the sensorimotor theory, the empirical data from dream research have established that *some* system strictly confined to the brain in fact *does* present experiences where perceptual objects are related to oneself in exactly the same manner as in conscious visual perception!

These problems with dream experience aside, at least neurophenomenology favours the use of a first-person approach to the empirical study of consciousness. Subjects highly trained in first-person methods should be used in the science of consciousness, somewhat like the trained introspectionists in Wundt's and Titchener's laboratories. Training makes all the difference – in this, Varela agrees with the introspectionists:

To do good accounts of what you experience is not a trivial affair. In fact, if you do that with normal subjects – if you bring them to the lab and ask them about emotions, you ask What are you experiencing – most people go blank. It is not given to man to be experts of their own experience; the fact of having an experience is not a qualification to be an expert reporter on it, just as much as walking in the garden does not make you a gardener, or a botanist. You need to have a very substantial amount of training.

(Varela, in Blackmore, 2006, p. 225)

But the first-person methods that Varela has in mind are totally different from classical introspectionism: "[W]e need to introduce new first person methodologies way beyond those we have at the moment, and that means a sociological revolution in science" (Varela, in Blackmore, 2006, p. 225).

The new first-person methodologies should not be derived from the classical introspectionists or even from current psychological science, but rather from Eastern and Buddhist contemplative practises, suggests Varela. In those traditions, people have been trained for thousands of years to observe their own consciousness from the first-person perspective in a manner that surpasses anything that psychological science has achieved in the West.

The neurophenomenological research programme thus involves the unlikely marriage (or perhaps shotgun wedding) of a number of disparate approaches that seem to originate from entirely different planets: Husserl's heavily conceptual philosophy from the early 1900s, sometimes bordering on the obscure and the anti-scientific; Merleau-Ponty's embodied and enactive view of the mind; modern neuroscience and brain imaging; and the ancient Buddhist practise of meditation, contemplation and calm observation of one's own conscious states. From this extremely mixed bag, a broad – and in some respects bewildering – philosophical approach to mind, cognition and consciousness has emerged.

Despite its theoretical murkiness, the neurophenomenological approach has contributed to the empirical science of consciousness by suggesting new and important lines of reasearch in consciousness science, focusing on such topics as bodily awareness and agency, and on the altered states of consciousness that only experienced meditators and Buddhist monks are capable of reaching.

Reflexive monism (Velmans)

The mind (or the brain) produces the qualitative features of our experiences. However, we experience the qualities not as spatially located in the mind or the brain, but out there in the world: pains and tickles located in parts of our bodies, colours located in distal external objects. How do they get out there? There must be some sort of *projection* going on that transmits the qualities from their original source (mind/brain) to where they are experienced (in the external objects of the world). The results of sensory processing somehow get projected back out of the brain to be superimposed on the external world.

Max Velmans, a professor of psychology from London, England, has developed a theory of consciousnes along these lines. To figure out the location of consciousness is his first goal: "In order to learn *what* something is, it is useful in the initial instance to know *where* it is, so that one can point to it . . . But where does one point, when one is pointing at consciousness?" (Velmans, 1996, p. 183). Velmans argues that, in order to decide where consciousness is, one has to attend to its actual phenomenology. Thus, if you stick a pin in your finger, you experience the pain in your finger: "The pain one experiences is in the finger. If one had to point at it one should point at where the pin went in" (p. 184). In his view, experiences are where we experience them to be, and there is no other or second experience of pain in the brain or anywhere else. Velmans agrees that there is information about the pain in the finger encoded in a mental model realized by a brain state, but the mental model is not identical with the experience.

A puzzle for this view, as Velmans admits, is the question: If the neural causes and correlates of pain are in the brain, *how does the resulting experience get to be in the finger?* Velmans says that a psychological process of "perceptual projection" takes place and results in conscious experience. The experience is "projected" in the sense that, from the perspective of the subject, it is located in the phenomenal space beyond the brain rather than in the region of its neural causes or correlates. However, this projection should not be understood as a mechanism that actually broadcasts something somewhere.

The central notion of his theory, "perceptual projection", remains obscure: it refers not to a physical but to a *psychological* process, he explains, and yet says that "psychological processes may, in part, *be* physical processes" (Velmans, 1996, p. 194). The muddled boundaries between the physical and the psychological in this theory derive from the underlying idea that, in fact, the physical, third-person perspective to the world and the psychological, first-person perspective are intimately joined and cannot be separated. Velmans treats the first- and the third-person views as complementary:

> I would say that in a rough way the situation is not unlike the sort of thing that occurs in quantum mechanics, where you find that if you try to give a complete description of something like an electron, the way the electron is described very much depends on the observational arrangements: in certain kinds of observational arrangements the electron simply looks like a wave, and in other observational arrangements the electron simply looks like a particle. I think that there's a direct analogy with what's going on with conscious experiences and their neural correlates in the brain.
>
> (Velmans, in Blackmore, 2006, p. 240)

The name of Velmans' theory, reflexive monism, derives from the idea that perhaps all of the physical world forms a kind of double existence: a subjective and an objective perspective entangled into one. In human consciousness, the subjective perspective has evolved to such a high level that the first-person consciousness can experience and think about the entire objective physical universe, while at the same time being one with (a tiny part of) the physical universe. Thus, in human consciousness the physical universe reflects upon itself, through its double-aspect nature. In us, the universe has become reflexively conscious of itself!

The location of consciousness, however, presents a nagging problem for this theory too. Velmans denies that there is *any* sense in which the sphere of phenomenal experience is actually located *in* the brain. According to him only the proximal causes and direct correlates of conscious phenomenology are in the brain, but the subjective effects – consciousness *itself* – are not. He says that "one can safely conclude . . . that although a neural encoding of the world is within the brain, the phenomenal world is outside the brain (Velmans, 2003, p. 429).

But is it not possible to cause sensations by directly stimulating the brain? Does that not show that the sensations happen there? Velmans (2009, p. 162) denies that the brain stimulation studies would show any such thing: "[S]cience has found *no* evidence of tactile sensations in the brain. Direct microelectrode stimulation of soma-tosensory cortex causes tactile sensations that are *subjectively located in different regions of the body*. That is exactly what the reflexive model describes."

Velmans (2009) rejects the view that the phenomenal world is literally inside the brain, because that would lead to the conclusion that the real world (including the real physical skull inside which the brain is located) must be somewhere beyond the boundaries of the world we experience. This is, for him, too much. Yet, as we will see below, the virtual reality theories of consciousness are prepared to swallow the radical conclusions that follow from the internal location of consciousness.

Velmans fails to tell us *where* in the world as described by physics the sphere of phenomenal experience is located, if it is *not* located in the brain. Reflexive monism leaves us flabbergasted with the question. The next theory, however, bites the bullet and locates *all* experiences firmly and literally inside the brain.

Virtual reality theory (Metzinger, Lehar)

Most of the philosophical theories of consciousness struggle hard with the paradox of the location of consciousness: Our experiences *seem* to happen in a *real* world, a spatially extended physical world beyond our bodies. The visual qualities we see are located distally, not *in here* but *over there*, on the surfaces of external objects. Our bodies seem to be in the centre of this world, and interacting directly with the physical objects of the world. One thing is for sure: Our experiences do not *seem* to happen somewhere, or indeed *anywhere*, inside our brains!

Many of the above-mentioned theories take the seeming externalization of consciousness at face value: Somehow consciousness, or its qualitative contents, must literally reside *out there* where they *seem* to be located, and not *in here*, inside our brains. This position is in harmony with our naive realist conception of the world. But maybe the science of consciousness will show that our naive idea is simply based on an exceptionally compelling illusion, just like the idea that the Sun "rises" up, "moves" across the sky above the stable earth we stand on and then "sets". It seems indubitably to be so, yet we know for a fact that in this case we *are* deceived by our perception.

Some theories try to reveal an even grander illusion, the one relating to the location of our own consciousness. It is called the *out-of-the-brain illusion*, or the *being-in-a-world* illusion (Revonsuo, 1995, 2006). Although it seems to us that we definitely are not located somewhere inside our brains but inside the familiar physical world of real objects, what is really going on is a massive conjuring trick in our brain.

If we all are constantly under the *out-of-the-brain illusion*, however, the shocking truth is that in our experiences we are not in *any* direct contact with the external physical world, but only with an internal phenomenal world: There is a virtual reality inside the brain!

In the Preface to his book *The world in your head*, Steve Lehar (2003), a consciousness researcher developing the Gestalt psychological approach further in his theory, describes how the grand illusion suddenly dissolved when he tried to figure out how a perceived visual object can be both the original source of physical stimulation out there in the physical world and also the final phenomenal percept that appears to be out there in the corresponding place:

> I knew that without my cortex I could see nothing at all, and that therefore in some sense this image of the world around me was itself somehow produced by my cortex, but while in my cortex, it was at the same time also out in the world around me. It seemed that the world around me had a dual character, it was both the real world, and a perceptual world, and that the two appeared to be some-how superimposed. There was a curious paradox wrapped up in this idea of perception that I just could not seem to get straight, for how could the world of perception escape the confines of my head to appear in the world around me? Then one day it hit me all of a sudden like a lightning bolt, in the form of a vivid mental image. Suddenly I could see in my mind's eye that the world I saw around me, including the picture of myself sitting in my chair, was merely an image generated inside my head, and therefore it could not be out in the world. In other words, out beyond the walls and floor and ceiling of the room I saw around me was the inner surface of my true physical skull, and beyond that skull was an immensely remote external world, of which this world that was in my experience was merely a miniature virtual-reality replica. For what I could now see was that the brain is capable of generating vivid three-dimensional images of a fully spatial world, like the one I see around me right now. I came running into school the day after my great introspective discovery, only to find that nobody knew what the hell I was talking about. The idea of an enormous world out there above the dome of the sky, they said, was just plain absurd.
>
> (Lehar, 2003, Preface)

Although this insight was totally mind-blowing for Lehar (and unacceptably absurd for his colleagues), the idea of a world in your head is actually an old one in both philosophy and psychology, held in some form by Immanuel Kant, Bertrand Russell and the Gestalt psychologists. In philosophy, this theory of consciousness would be classified as an *internalist* theory of consciousness and as based on an *indirect theory of perception*: When we perceive the world, what we are directly in touch with in our experience are not the external physical objects themselves, but only their phenomenal representatives or images generated in the brain's virtual reality of consciousness.

Thomas Metzinger is a German philosopher who has developed a philosophical theory of consciousness based on the idea of a virtual reality inside the brain: "I claim that phenomenal first-person experience and the emergence of a conscious self are complex forms of virtual reality" (Metzinger, 2009, p. 106).

Metzinger's self-model theory of subjectivity goes roughly like this: The conscious brain drills a phenomenal tunnel through physical reality. The flow of phenomenal experience inside the phenomenal tunnel in the brain is an extremely selective and narrow reflection of the actual physical reality surrounding the brain. Our senses can only take in a tiny part of the physical information bombarding us, and our brain can only represent phenomenally a fraction of it. Still, phenomenal experience generates a unified world-simulation in the tunnel. Furthermore, it places an inner image of ourselves, the phenomenal self-model, in the centre of the simulation:

> By placing the self-model within the world-model, a center is created. That center is what we experience as ourselves, the Ego. It is the origin of what philosophers call the first-person perspective ... We live our lives in the Ego Tunnel.
>
> (Metzinger, 2009, p. 7)

Normally, we do not have the slightest idea that we live inside our brain's ego tunnel, because we seem to live in a world and not inside a brain, and certainly not inside any kind of "tunnel". Our carefree ignorance of our true condition is, however, all part of the plot. As Metzinger says (2009, p. 10): "The robust experience of not being in a tunnel, of being directly and immediately in touch with external reality, is one of the most remarkable features of human consciousness".

Why do we never experience being in the brain's ego tunnel? One part of the explanation is the nature of the phenomenal representations: they are *transparent*. The transparency of a representation means that the representation looks exactly like the thing it represents (or, at least, exactly like the physical thing itself is *believed* to look). Thus, we confuse the phenomenal representations (virtual objects in the brain) with the real physical objects somewhere outside the brain. In fact, we have never seen the real physical objects as they are in themselves: if we could, they would be totally colourless clouds of elementary physical particles and fields that reflect electromagnetic energy for our senses to pick up. We have only seen their phenomenal images – but those images are transparent to us, and we look right through them, as we would look through a window, and believe we see the things themselves, not just images generated by our own brain. Furthermore, it gets even worse: Our own self is just one of the phenomenal images generated by the brain and placed into the centre of the simulation. Of course, we take the special phenomenal image that houses our bodily feels, our visual body image and our thoughts to be our real self: an enduring subject of experiences. How mistaken can we poor creatures get?

> The brain is like a total flight simulator, a self-modelling aeroplane that, rather than being flown by a pilot, generates a complex internal image of itself within its own internal flight simulator. The image is transparent and thus cannot be recognized as an image by the system ... The "pilot" is born into a virtual reality with no opportunity to discover this fact. The pilot is the Ego. The total flight simulator generates an Ego Tunnel but is completely lost in it.
>
> (Metzinger, 2009, p. 108)

The other part of the explanation (for why we do not realize we are in the brain's ego tunnel) is evolutionary. For the survival of the conscious animal, it was only necessary to equip its brain with a world-simulator navigation system that informs it where and when dangers or opportunities appear and then guides its behaviour appropriately, either away from or towards them. Thus, we need not know that, when detecting a bear in the woods, what we are *really* seeing is only a phenomenal bear image that is inserted into the brain's phenomenal navigation system along with our self-model, coupled with the emotional experience of fear and with the overwhelming motivation to get the hell out of there. No, we see the bear as a very real, dangerous living creature out there and feel the corresponding fear that motivates us to perform immediate avoidance behaviours. There is no reason for our brain to inform us that we were in fact reacting to a phenomenal *model* of a bear – such information would needlessly consume time and resources. It is better to keep us in the dark about all the neural (and phenomenal) machinery working behind the scenes of our seemingly direct perception.

The virtual reality approach to consciousness has no difficulty in dealing with hallucinations, dreams and other internally generated altered states of consciousness. In fact, such dissociations between the physical world and the phenomenal world constitute the most decisive empirical evidence showing that there *must* be an internal phenomenal world independent of the external stimulus world, because in some cases the phenomenal world becomes totally dissociated from external stimulation (Revonsuo, 2006).

The difficulty with this theory is its intuitive implausibility: it goes so radically against our naive perception of ourselves and the world that many find it just far too incredible a view. Are we supposed to believe that we are not real humans at all, but only neurosimulations or phenomenal avatars trapped somewhere inside our brains, forever alone in a virtual reality dreamworld? If that is true, then all the objects and people we ever see or touch are but phenomenal images – other avatars – inside our own brain, even if somewhere far behind the images there may be some real but alien physical stimulus object. Whenever we are asleep and dreaming, we are absolutely alone and isolated in our own brainworld, even if we seem to be present in a world and interact with other people in our dreams. The dream avatars are just like the perceptual avatars we see during wakefulness; the only difference is that behind the origins of the dream avatars there is no external human agent directly driving the avatar, only the neural simulation machinery of our own brain that is programmed to produce avatars also during sleep.

Well, it seems we will have to choose between two absolutely incredible alternatives: consciousness somehow escapes from the brain and gets miraculously projected out, or it is superimposed upon the real physical world (as in Velmans' theory), thus bringing us into direct contact with the real external objects and other people. The former view is incredible because we know of nothing short of a supernatural phenomenon that could really escape the brain when we are perceptually conscious of our real environments through the incoming sensory information. Phenomenal experience simply has no physical escape routes (at least none that science knows anything about) to get out from the brain.

Thus, consciousness *must* reside somewhere inside the confines of the brain. Look around and explore your phenomenal experiences (either during wakefulness or during dreaming): What you see directly cannot be the physical world as such, but it must be the insides of your own brain! Incredible! Insane? But could it be true, nevertheless?

Chapter summary

The theories of consciousness developed by current philosophers are, to put it mildly, a *very* mixed bag. They reflect the wide (or should I say wild) variety of philosophical world-views that battle with each other in current philosophy of mind. We have explored some of the leading philosophical theories of consciousness: Dennett's multiple drafts model, O'Regan and Noë's sensorimotor theory, Searle's biological naturalism, Chalmers' naturalistic dualism and panpsychism, higher order thought (HOT) theories, externalist representationalism, Varela's neurophenomenology, Velmans' reflexive monism and, finally, the virtual reality theories of Metzinger and Lehar.

Considering the strengths and the weaknesses of these theories, it seems obvious that the philosophical problems of consciousness remain far from solved. The strength of the behaviouristic or eliminative approaches (multiple drafts model; sensorimotor theory) is that they get rid of the Hard Problem, but their weakness is that they deny the existence of phenomenal consciousness and qualia – the very data they are supposed to explain! To deny phenomenal consciousness equals denying your own subjective existence – a very bad move for a theory of consciousness, obviously. The strength of the externalist approaches (externalist representationalism; neurophenomenology; reflexive monism) is that they need not explain how qualia arise from brain processes or where in the brain the contents of phenomenal consciousness are, because they say that the contents of consciousness are not in the brain but in the world out there. Their weakness is that the qualitative contents of consciousness cannot be found anywhere in the external world, nor is there any physical mechanism that could project the phenomenal qualia we experience from the perceptual mechanisms in our brains back to be superimposed on the external stimulus objects. Thus, it remains a complete mystery how the phenomenal properties of the world we experience are generated, where they are located and how they get there. The strength of the virtual reality theories (Metzinger, Lehar) is that they can explain both stimulus-generated and stimulus-independent, purely internal experience by the same mechanism, the virtual reality in the brain. Their weakness is that they have to face the Explanatory Gap (how do neural firings create phenomenality) and, moreover, the incredulous stares of all those people who refuse to believe that we are not biological organisms directly present in a physical world; we are merely phenomenal neurosimulations – the brain's avatars of the biological organism – embedded in a simulated world inside the brain but forever under the unbreakable spell of the out-of-the-brain illusion. Somewhere out there, far below our feet and high above and beyond the dome of the sky, is the real brain, the real skull and the impenetrably dark, purely physical world in which the giant biological organism that we confuse ourselves with roams. Our phenomenal world is merely the minuscule neurophenomenal navigator system that guides this giant organism through the dark physical world; we ourselves, always located in the centre of the simulated world, are but a virtual pilot of the navigator system. Thus, the virtual reality view is not an easy one to swallow, either, because it implies that we are living under a massive illusion of proportions equalling *The Matrix* – an inconvenient truth if anything is!

The different philosophical approaches do not agree even minimally about the nature of consciousness or where it is located (inside or outside the brain). Unlike in empirical science, in philosophy we should not even expect the various approaches to finally converge on a generally accepted and shared view. It is the philosophers' job to explore and defend radically dissimilar world-views, to figure out how far each metaphysical line of thought can take us if we consistently follow it. Sometimes they take us rather far from the empirical reality, or at least from what is empirically plausible or testable. However, it is useful also for empirical scientists to be aware of the different philosophical alternatives, because every empirical theory also necessarily involves some sort of implicit philosophical commitments. In the history of psychology, introspectionists, Gestalt psychologists and behaviourists not only differed in their empirical approach to consciousness, but also, and perhaps first and foremost, in their philosophical ideas about what science is, what the mind is and which methods are scientific. The overall empirical approach that a scientist takes to consciousness is guided by his prior philosophical commitments or intuitions about the nature of science and the nature of consciousness, whether he is aware of such commitments or not. Knowing about the different philosophical alternatives makes it easier to understand and back up with good arguments the fundamental metaphysical views that one wishes to advocate, or to reject the ones that seem empirically implausible (or outright crazy), and then connect the favoured philosophical approach with a more detailed empirical approach to consciousness consistent with it.

Next, we will turn to the theories that are empirically based – but probably not philosophically altogether innocent either.

Further reading

Blackmore, S. J. (2006). *Conversations on consciousness*. New York: Oxford University Press.
Chalmers, D. J. (1996). *The conscious mind*. Oxford: Oxford University Press.
Dennett, D. C. (1991). *Consciousness explained*. Boston: Little, Brown.
Dennett, D. C. (2005). *Sweet dreams: Philosophical obstacles to a science of consciousness*. Cambridge, MA: MIT Press.
Dretske, F. (1995). *Naturalizing the mind*. Cambridge, MA: MIT Press.
Gallagher, S., & Zahavi, D. (2008). *The phenomenological mind*. London: Routledge.
Lehar, S. (2003). *The world in your head*. Mahwah, NJ: Lawrence Erlbaum Associates, Inc.
Metzinger, T. (2003). *Being no one: The self-model theory of subjectivity*. Cambridge, MA: MIT Press.
Metzinger, T. (2009). *The ego tunnel*. New York: Basic Books.
Noë, A. (2009). *Out of our heads*. New York: Hill & Wang.
O'Regan, J. K., & Noë, A. (2001). A sensorimotor account of vision and visual consciousness. *Behavioural and Brain Sciences, 24*, 939–1031.
Revonsuo, A. (2006). *Inner presence: Consciousness as a biological phenomenon*. Cambridge, MA: MIT Press.
Searle, J. R. (1992). *The rediscovery of the mind*. Cambridge, MA: MIT Press.
Searle, J. R. (1997). *The mystery of consciousness*. New York: The New York Review Books.
Searle, J. R. (2000). Consciousness. *Annual Review of Neuroscience, 23*, 557–578.
Tye, M. (1995). *Ten problems of consciousness: A representational theory of the phenomenal mind*. Cambridge, MA: MIT Press.
Velmans, M. (2009). *Understanding consciousness* (2nd ed.). Hove: Routledge.
Velmans, M., & Schneider, S. (Eds.) (2007). *The Blackwell companion to consciousness*. Oxford: Blackwell.

Brief discussion questions

1   Do any of these philosophical theories of consciousness really manage to solve the Hard Problem, the Explanatory Gap or the What-it-is-like-to-be problem?
2   Compare the modern theories of consciousness with the traditional philosophical mind–body theories presented in Chapter 1. Is it possible to classify each of the modern theories into some of the traditional categories?
3   Which philosophical theory of consciousness seems the most plausible one for you? What are its strengths and weaknesses?

Chapter 11

Empirical theories of consciousness

11.1 Review of current empirical theories of consciousness

Global workspace theory (Baars)

Bernard Baars is a cognitive psychologist who has played a decisive role in modern consciousness studies. His groundbreaking book *A cognitive theory of consciousness* was published as early as 1988, at a time when empirical theories of consciousness were few and far between. Baars is also the co-founder of the leading peer-reviewed academic journal in the science of consciousness, *Consciousness and Cognition*, which was launched in 1991.

Global workspace theory (GWT) is grounded in the standard cognitive science view of the mind that was very popular in the 1980s when the theory was first developed. According to the cognitive view, our mind is an information-processing system that can be divided into two different types of processing architectures. The first consists of many separate cognitive modules that analyse sensory input, and the second consists of a more unified central system of higher cognition (see Figure 11.1).

A *module* is a processing mechanism that is specialized to handle only one specific type of information, say, the recognition of familiar faces or the recognition of spoken words. Only the appropriate type of information can be taken as input by the module. When that type of information is available, the module processes it rapidly, automatically, alone or in isolation from other modules, and without any voluntary effort or any conscious experience involved. The module produces output that can become available to consciousness, say, the information that the face is familiar, or an interpretation of what the word means. The phrase "modularity of the mind" (Fodor, 1983) refers to the idea that all sensory-perceptual information is first analysed by the appropriate modules and that our mind contains hundreds of such processing mechanisms, each specialized to only one single type of information, one single type of function.

Traditional cognitive theory has concentrated on describing the modular structure of the mind but has been silent about consciousness. GWT attempts to describe how the information first processed by the modules eventually enters the central unifying system of consciousness. The global workspace is the cognitive architecture into which the modules send their outputs. Each module attempts to send "messages" into this vast network that allows the modular outputs to interact with each other, although the modules themselves are isolated from each other. Thus, the modular outputs can be treated as "messages" sent into the network. There they start to compete with each other for "global access", that is, for a dominating position in the network. The winner of this competition gets its message "globally broadcast" and the message thereby forms the momentary contents of consciousness. Messages that win the competition must have some minimum duration of at least 50–250 ms – messages broadcast for a shorter duration do not have the time to spread across the whole workspace and therefore fade before they become conscious. Messages that win the competition must furthermore be internally consistent and informative – internally inconsistent messages cancel themselves out, and uninformative, totally predictable messages do not have any news for the system and thus fade quickly. The global workspace is, according to Baars, a *publicity organ* in a system of

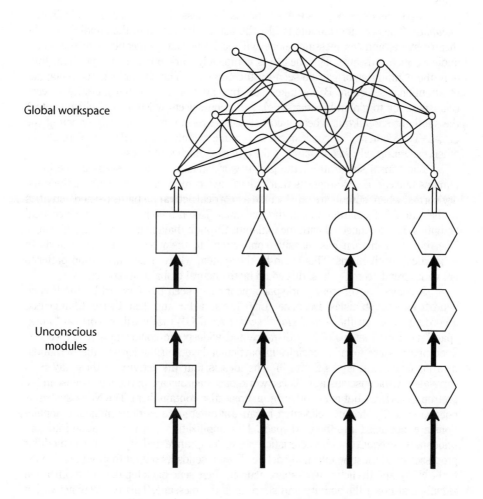

Global workspace

Unconscious
modules

Sensory input

Figure 11.1 Global workspace

In the theory presented by Baars, consciousness resembles a wide network of connections between specialized, nonconscious processing modules that compete for access to the global workspace. The message that wins the competition and spreads across the whole workspace forms the current content of consciousness

specialists, the informational web where any information can potentially be related with any other information. But it is not an executive system that makes decisions and plans.

Baars has described his theory of consciousness also with the help of a *theatre metaphor*. The winning module is like the actor who gets into the spotlight on the theatre stage, and his message alone will be broadcast momentarily to the whole audience in the theatre. The theatre is completely dark outside the spotlight, thus only the winning actor can be seen by the audience. The spotlight is the metaphor of attentional selection. Baars takes selective attention to be the gateway to consciousness (or to global broadcasting). Attention selects where or on which content the spotlight should fall, whereas consciousness results from the *illumination* of the target. The contents of consciousness become widely accessible and verbally or otherwise reportable: *Reportability* is the *criterion* of consciousness.

The neural substrate of the global workspace of consciousness in the brain remains unclear. Baars suggests that at least two components are required: the sensory cortex, where stimuli are represented as cortical activation patterns; and activities in the reticular formation and in the thalamus. Taken together, the sensory cortical activities can be connected with the thalamus through thalamocortical feedback loops. The thalamus in turn has massive connections to the whole cortex as well as to subcortical mechanisms. This could be the system where neural activation patterns get widespread access – thus, this could be the neural global workspace.

A somewhat different workspace theory has been put forward by the French neuroscientists Stanislas Dehaene, Lionel Naccache and Jean-Pierre Changeaux, according to which the *neural global workspace* (NGW) is based on cortical "workspace" neurons that make long-distance and widespread connections in the cortex. Such neurons are found especially in particular layers of the cortex (the pyramidal neurons of cortical layers 2 and 3). The idea is that the activity in those layers is correlated with consciousness. These workspace neurons are particularly dense in the prefrontal cortices, but many other brain areas also contain them. The NGW system is not anatomically sharply delineated, because at different times different neural populations are mobilized into the workspace. The mobilization – or participation into consciousness – requires a characteristic type of long-range activity. First, the modular processor itself must be internally active. Then it sends its output (bottom-up signals) to the NGW, and the active workspace neurons there send back top-down amplification signals that boost the activity and strengthen the message. This two-way activation results in a self-amplifying, self-sustaining loop of neuronal activity that delivers its contents into the stream of consciousness. Unlike the original model proposed by Baars himself, this purely cortical workspace model does not give any decisive role to thalamocortical loops of activity. The proposed neural circuitry in the NGW links consciousness closely to top-down attention and working memory – perhaps so closely that consciousness becomes nearly identical with attention and working memory.

Neurobiological theory (Crick and Koch)

Only a couple of years after the GWT by Baars was first published in 1988, another influential theory of consciousness was proposed by Francis Crick and Christof Koch in 1990. They subsequently developed their approach to consciousness in a series of papers, until the death of Francis Crick in 2004. Whereas Baars' approach is almost purely "cognitive", Crick and Koch approached consciousness from the perspective of neuroscience and argued in their landmark paper "Towards a neurobiological theory of consciousness" (1990) that the time was ripe for neuroscience to take consciousness seriously. Thanks to this well-timed manifesto by two highly respected, hard-nosed neuroscientists, consciousness quickly became an acceptable topic of enquiry also in the neurosciences.

Their message was taken seriously, not least because of the reputation of Francis Crick as one of the most influential scientists of the 20th century. In 1953 he had figured out, together with James Watson, the double helix structure of DNA – they discovered the "secret of life" – and were awarded the Nobel prize for this work in 1962. In the 1980s Crick turned more and more towards cognitive neuroscience, publishing articles on the neural mechanisms of REM sleep and the thalamic mechanisms of attention, for example. Then, in the late 1980s he joined forces with the young neuroscientist Christof Koch, and the rest is history in the study of consciousness.

Crick and Koch outlined a broad approach or research programme for the study of consciousness rather than a detailed theory. According to them, we should not try to define consciousness precisely at this stage, because it is impossible, and we should not worry about explaining qualia as the first thing in neuroscience; we can leave such things for later. What neuroscientists can and ought to do, urged Crick and Koch, is concentrate on finding the neural correlates of consciousness, defined as *the smallest set of brain mechanisms and events sufficient for some specific phenomenal state*. Ultimately, however, if consciousness can be explained at all, it will be explained in neuronal terms.

The sensory cortex contains what Crick and Koch call *essential nodes*. They are neural populations that express one particular aspect of sensory perception, say, the colour of a perceived object. Thus, essential nodes are the necessary neural basis for qualia. Still, a node cannot produce qualia all by itself, even if its neurons were firing like crazy. The node must be connected to a wider network, called a *coalition* of neurons. The coalition is the collection of a number of essential nodes in a distributed network. Only when the coalition becomes active as a whole, probably by synchronizing the activity of all its member neurons, has the perceptual representation thus formed the potential to become a content of consciousness.

However, the coalition needs to have neural projections from the sensory areas in the back of the brain (where the nodes are located) to the attentional areas in the front of the brain, and receive appropriate feedback from there. Only this kind of *top-down feedback* can raise the activity level of the coalition above a critical threshold for a sufficiently long duration to become a winning coalition. Top-down attention can thus be seen as a mechanism that biases the competition and helps one coalition to synchronize itself internally and thus win the competition for access to consciousness. This proposed feedback-loop mechanism for consciousness closely resembles the neural workspace theory presented above.

In the first version of their theory, Crick and Koch proposed the famous 40 Hz hypothesis of how the neural coalitions that emerge to consciousness are generated:

> In 1990, Francis and I asserted that synchronized 40-Hz oscillations within the subset of neurons that correspond to an attended object is a signature of the

NCC. In other words, the content of consciousness can be identified, at that moment, with the set of forebrain neurons firing in a phase-locked manner with a 20 to 30 millisecond periodicity.

(Koch, 2004, p. 45)

The 40 Hz hypothesis (also known as the gamma-band hypothesis) generated widespread enthusiasm and interest because it was the first concrete, empirically testable idea of the neural mechanism of consciousness. Evidence supporting the idea turned up (Engel & Singer, 2001), but it also became clear that the hypothesis was too simple as such. Obviously, sometimes there can be 40 Hz synchronization without consciousness (showing that it is not sufficient for the NCC) and sometimes there is consciousness without 40 Hz synchronization (showing that it is not necessary either). Thus, later on Crick and Koch gave up the 40 Hz hypothesis:

Today, Francis and I no longer think that synchronized firing is a sufficient condition for the NCC . . . Once a coalition has established itself as a winner and you are conscious of the associated attributes, the coalition may be able to maintain itself without the assistance of synchrony . . . Thus, one might expect synchronized oscillations to occur in the early stages of perception, but not necessarily in later ones.

(Koch, 2004, p. 46)

Consciousness works in a *winner-takes-all* manner so that the winning coalition subsequently expresses the actual content of consciousness. The winning coalition recruits neural populations widely in the cortex, thalamus and other networks. In addition to the NCC itself, the winning coalition also activates a *context* or *background* or *penumbra* to the NCC. The background involves many such things, what others have called the "fringe" of consciousness, the "phenomenal background" or "peripheral awareness": associations, memories, expectations and future plans related to the content of the NCC, but not directly part of it. These contextual contents may be very close to the threshold or surface of consciousness, and a small proportion of them may momentarily become a part of the contents of consciousness. The penumbra helps to interpret the wider meaning of the experience by placing it into the appropriate context.

The function of consciousness is to *summarize the current state of the world in a compact representation* that is consequently used for the planning and execution of voluntary behaviour. Much of behavioural control, however, happens outside of consciousness and is taken care of by highly specialized and trained *zombie agents*. They can respond to external events rapidly, nonconsciously and in a stereotyped manner – they are reflex-like modules working at the output side of the brain.

The Crick and Koch framework is not very different from the ideas of Baars' GWT and the related NGW theory. Indeed, these ideas seem to converge quite well into an overall modern theory of the neural basis of consciousness. Still, Crick and Koch want to emphasize that, in their view, the microlevel activities at synapses and single neurons are crucial for understanding the specificity and the fine detail of phenomenal states. Thus, their approach is somewhat more microscopic in spirit than the more holistic approaches of others who emphasize global neural populations and activities instead of single neurons. At one point, Crick and Koch even suggested that there may be a subset of anatomically and physiologically special types of neurons that are the "consciousness neurons".

Crick and Koch admit that finding the NCC does not in itself solve the problem of consciousness. Yet, it would be a crucial step towards a solution, because then we could specify in detail the neurobiological and neuroelectrical circumstances under which very complex biological entities have subjective experiences. Perhaps this knowledge would be sufficient to make a genuine breakthrough in understanding also why and how the phenomenal, qualitative states themselves arise from the neural activities. In any case, without this knowledge we surely do not stand a chance.

The dynamic core (Tononi and Edelman) and the information integration theory (Tononi)

Here we meet another pair of scientists where a Nobel-prize winner (Gerald Edelman) is coupled with a young neuroscientist (Giulio Tononi) to solve the problem of consciousness. Edelman had published books about consciousness already before he started collaborating with Tononi (*The remembered present: A biological theory of consciousness*, 1989) but the dynamic core theory is a collaborative effort with Tononi, published in *A universe of consciousness* (2000).

The dynamic core theory is based on Edelman's earlier theory (called neural Darwinism) that describes the brain as a Darwinian system in which some groups of neurons are selected over others during brain development, partly based on experience and behaviour. The final step is the formation of re-entrant or reciprocal connections between distant neural populations, allowing their activities to become spatiotemporally coordinated. The massive re-entrant, reciprocal connections between the thalamus and the cortex are the seat of the mechanisms of consciousness. The spatiotemporal coordination of activity binds the different perceptual elements into coherent objects and further into a global scene, thus solving the binding problem of the unity of consciousness.

The dynamic core is a holistic functional cluster of neural activity in the thalamocortical system, a cluster composed of neuronal groups that strongly interact with each other. This activity cannot be identified with particular types of neurons or localized neural populations that would be necessary and sufficient for it. Rather, different neural populations participate in the dynamic core at different times, and it is the holistic, integrated *activity* that correlates with consciousness rather than the participating neurons as anatomical units.

Recently, Tononi (2009) has developed these ideas further in his *information integration theory of consciousness*. The starting point in his new theory is the insight that consciousness is both highly integrated and highly differentiated. High integration means that consciousness always appears as a globally unified field of experience; high differentiation means that consciousness has a rich variety of specific contents and an uncountable number of states that differ in their contents.

Phenomenal consciousness as an overall state is identified with *integrated* information: *Any physical system will have subjective phenomenal experience to the extent that it is capable of integrating information.* Phenomenality is conceived as a fundamental informational quantity of a system that can be precisely expressed as a numerical value. What counts for the emergence of consciousness is *how much integrated information is generated by the system*, not (like in GWT) how widely the information is distributed in the system.

The level of consciousness of a system is related to the repertoire of different states that the system could display. Clearly, phenomenal consciousness is an immensely rich system in terms of information content: just think about all the different phenomenal experiences that a person could potentially have – all the possible combinations of different qualia. Metaphorically, having an experience is like throwing a die with trillions of faces: only one out of the trillions of possibilities comes up at any one time. Thus, whichever experience one has, it is enormously informative because we *could* have had trillions of other experiences instead; the state that was realized ruled out countless others. One traditional definition of information is "reduction of uncertainty" (of the state of affairs). Thus, the higher the number of different states a system could have, the more any single state reduces the uncertainty about the state of the system and thus the more information it carries. Furthermore, experiences are internally unified – we have only a single phenomenal field or stream of subjective life at any one time, thus all the information in consciousness is integrated into a single holistic state.

Roughly, the *level* of consciousness or the *quantity* of consciousness generated by the system is directly proportional to the *degree of information integration* in the system, and the *quality* of consciousness is determined by the *internal informational relationships* within the system. These relationships can be described within a multidimensional qualia space. Different experiences are different shapes in the qualia space. Pure, primitive qualia – Titchener's fundamental elements of consciousness – are primitive shapes in the qualia space that cannot be further decomposed to simpler subshapes.

If consciousness is nothing over and above (a high degree of) integrated information, then it becomes possible in principle to separate phenomenal conscious experience from higher level cognitive functions such as language, self-awareness and verbal reports. If it were possible to measure the degree of information integration in infants or animals, we would be able to infer whether they are phenomenally conscious or not. The objective qualia-detector or consciousness-monitor could thus be designed on this principle: to detect the degree of informational integration of a system and give the output readings in terms of the presence versus absence (or the graded level) of consciousness. Perhaps also the complexity of the contents of phenomenal consciousness could be objectively revealed through measurement.

The identification of consciousness with the level of information integration leads to the ontological separation of phenomenal consciousness from its biological basis, in the same sense as the computer metaphor of cognitive science (or functionalism) separated mind (software) from brain (hardware). Any physical system capable of integrating information would have some degree of phenomenal consciousness, even if it is not made of neurons or any biological components whatsoever. Thus, this theory, if correct, would open the door for engineers to build machine consciousness out of nonorganic components as far as the components produce and integrate information.

Treating information as the key ingredient of consciousness also relates this theory metaphysically with the proto-panpsychism proposed by David Chalmers (see the section on naturalistic dualism in Chapter 10), according to which all information possesses elementary, primitive forms of consciousness, and when integrated into complex wholes in the way that occurs in the brain the phenomenal consciousness as we know it comes about. Neither of these theories explains why information (of any kind) should be accompanied by any phenomenal experiences at all. Thus, they cannot get rid of the Hard Problem or the Explanatory Gap.

One danger with Tononi's theory is that consciousness becomes identified with information integration by theoretical conjecture alone, and consequently this objective feature of a system is self-evidently taken as its consciousness without ever questioning the original theoretical assumption. Instead of uncritically embracing the identification, we should come up with critical empirical tests. What kind of experiment could potentially falsify the assumed connection between integrated information and consciousness? We should look for informationally unintegrated systems that nevertheless are phenomenally conscious and for informationally integrated systems that are mere nonconscious zombies. If no plausible candidates for such systems can be found, the information integration theory will fare well.

Both the dynamic core and the information integration theory regard the thalamocortical system as the most important neural mechanism of consciousness, because it has the re-entrant structure that can integrate information from a wide variety of sources from both cortex and thalamus, thus generating or binding together one holistic scene. The contents of phenomenal consciousness are both highly differentiated by the rich variability of specific features and highly integrated by being bound into one coherent experience of a single sensory-perceptual world. At least this theory thus preserves our intuitive ideas about phenomenal consciousness as a unified internal world of rich subjective experience.

Thalamocortical binding theory (Llinás)

Rather similar in spirit to the dynamic core is the theory presented by Rodolfo Llinás in a number of papers during the 1990s and in his book *I of the vortex* (2001). Information integration and binding play a central role in this theory too and, like above, the neural mechanism for consciousness and binding is the thalamocortical system. Llinás, however, gives us a more detailed account of the neuroanatomical and neurophysiological features of the thalamocortical system that are, in his view, responsible for generating consciousness and binding it together.

One theoretically relevant feature of thalamocortical connectivity is its bidirectionality. Thalamic nuclei receive reciprocal pathways from the same cortical areas that they project to. In fact, the number of corticothalamic fibres is significantly greater than the number of thalamocortical axons. These reciprocal thalamocortical connections create bidirectional neuronal loops between the thalamus and the cortex. Hence, the distributed neural representations of simultaneous perceptual features or events could be related to each other within the thalamocortical system so as to bind input from different sensory modalities into a single perceptual event. Therefore, the thalamocortical system is a plausible candidate for playing a role in the binding or integration of multiple distributed representations to a coherent perceptual world.

The theory presented by Llinás is based on two facts: (1) there are abundant reciprocal thalamocortical connections that establish large-scale reverberating activity between the thalamus and cortex; (2) some cortical and thalamic neurons are capable of generating intrinsic 40 Hz oscillations. This leads to the view that the thalamo-cortical network can generate global oscillatory states on its own, even in the absence of sensory input. When we perceive an external stimulus, the intrinsic activity of the thalamocortical network is modulated by sensory input, which thereby becomes incorporated into the functional state of the brain. When we hallucinate or dream, the intrinsic activity runs free on its own, without being modulated by external stimuli.

Llinás proposes that cells in one part of the thalamus (the reticular thalamic nucleus) could be responsible for the synchronization of the 40 Hz oscillations in distant thalamic and cortical territories. This mechanism involves two thalamocortical resonant loops: the specific thalamocortical loop and the nonspecific thalamocortical loop. The reticular nucleus of the thalamus is in interaction with both of these loops and could thus synchronize the activity in both of them.

This model of thalamocortical interaction can be directly related to two different types of binding or unity in conscious experience. The specific thalamocortical loop is assumed to be responsible for the binding of distributed sensory fragments into single coherent objects of awareness. The nonspecific thalamocortical loop is assumed to provide the overall context or functional conscious state where the individual objects of awareness are related to each other within one globally coherent representation (the consciousness of *myself located within one unified perceptual world*). Consistent with this model, lesions of specific thalamic nuclei abolish modality-specific contents of consciousness, whereas lesions of nonspecific thalamus (especially the intralaminar nuclei) abolish the global background state of consciousness, resulting in coma. Thus, the interaction of these two thalamocortical loops through synchronous neural activity around 40 Hz is hypothesized to take care of the binding of perceptual content into a single coherent experience.

As in Tononi's theory, information integration seems to be the key to generating consciousness. Llinás (2001, p. 126) goes so far as to express the intimate relationship between binding and consciousness by paraphrasing Descartes: "It binds, therefore I am!" – where "it" here refers to the thalamocortical system!

Recurrent processing theory (Lamme)

Victor Lamme is a Dutch cognitive neuroscientist who has studied the neural basis of visual processing in monkeys and humans. Thus, he bases his theory of consciousness on what is known about the neural processes underlying conscious visual perception. What is crucial for consciousness according to Lamme (2000) is the speed and the direction of processing in the visual cortex. The speed of processing can be measured as the time of arrival to a cortical area of the first signals from a visual stimulus. The different cortical areas processing visual stimuli can be ordered into a temporal hierarchy or a series of levels according to how long it takes for them to become activated by the stimulus. The signal rapidly proceeds in steps of 10 ms from area to area through feedforward connections. It takes only 100–150 ms for the activation from the stimulus to have travelled through all visual areas and reached the motor areas in the frontal cortex. This first, fast wave of visual processing is called the feedforward sweep (see Figure 11.2.). Although the brain in some sense "knows" about the stimulus when the fast feedforward sweep has brought the message, this knowledge or representation of the stimulus happens outside of consciousness and thus the stimulus cannot be verbally reported yet. However, rapid, unconscious, reflex-like actions can be guided by this information.

After the feedforward sweep all the visual areas remain active. Two types of neural connections now come into play. Within each visual area, neurons start to interact through horizontal connections. Between different visual areas, higher and lower areas (or later and earlier areas in the feedforward temporal hierarchy) also start to interact through feedback connections. This type of interaction is called *recurrent* (or re-entrant or resonant) processing. The different areas exchange and integrate information through recurrent processing, binding together the different features of perceptual objects, such as shape, colour and motion. When the recurrent processing reaches the parietal and frontal cortex, the content of perception becomes reportable and voluntary actions can be directed at the stimulus. However, Lamme (2003, 2004) is careful to distinguish between reportability and consciousness. He identifies consciousness with recurrent processing as such, regardless of whether the processing has or does not have access to language or voluntary behaviour. In his view, it is entirely conceivable to have recurrent processing (and the associated subjective phenomenal experience) going on in isolation from verbal reports, so that the person would deny seeing the stimulus even though there would be an isolated perceptual experience in her brain, caused by the stimulus. Language and voluntary motor behaviour are not necessary for phenomenal experience. By taking this stance, Lamme

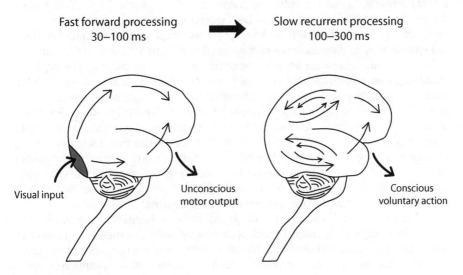

Figure 11.2 Lamme's model

According to Lamme's model of visual consciousness, visual information is first processed rapidly but nonconsciously through fast feedforward pathways in 30–100 ms from stimulus onset. Then it is processed "backward" and more slowly through recurrent connections, and in this process the information becomes conscious at around 100–300 ms from stimulus onset

defends the idea that pure phenomenal consciousness need not be reportable at all. He joins forces with the philosopher Ned Block (2007), who also has defended pure phenomenal consciousness as distinct from reportability.

Others have denied the possibility of unreportable experiences existing in an isolated manner in our brains – the opponents of Lamme's and Block's pure phenomenal consciousness argue that there is only access consciousness – conscious experience necessarily has access to voluntary behaviour, language and verbal reportability. The information that exists before access is not conscious or phenomenal information, it is merely *preconscious* or potentially conscious information, information that is *visible* but *not seen* (Dehaene, Changeux, Naccache, Sackur, & Sergent, 2006). Lamme disagrees, because he does not deem it plausible that access to language or working memory would as such be able to add the crucial feature of phenomenality to the processing of the information; by contrast, the phenomenality must be there to begin with when the information reaches the language areas and the output systems. As different types of information and different types of qualia have the same kind of access to the same higher systems, the only source for the multiple, radically different kinds of qualia must come from their separate, specialized neural sources rather than from the common system that they all access.

One advantage of identifying consciousness with recurrent processing and separating consciousness from access to output and behaviour is that now consciousness can be regarded as independent from other higher cognitive functions. It is different from language, from episodic memory and from attention. This point is elaborated in Lamme's theory in detail, because in many other theories there has been a tendency to identify reportability and attention with consciousness. Lamme (2003, 2004) argues that attention and consciousness can be dissociated from each other in both ways: there can be attention to stimuli without consciousness of the same stimuli and there can equally well be consciousness of the stimulus without attention to the stimulus. He identifies attention with what he calls the "depth" of processing. The *depth* of processing that a stimulus reaches is the *amount of attention* that is allocated to the stimulus. Shallow processing means the stimulus goes unattended, whereas deep processing means the stimulus is attended and selected. The shallow–deep distinction is independent of the feedforward–recurrent distinction, thus attention and consciousness are independent of each other. It follows from this that a stimulus can be phenomenally seen even in the absence of attention (shallow recurrent processing) and that a stimulus can be attended even when it is not seen (deep feedforward processing). However, typically when we consciously perceive a stimulus it is both attended and conscious, involving deep recurrent processing.

Lamme's theory is an attempt to get rid of the problems that the subjectivity of consciousness and its coupling with reportability bring to experimental research. If recurrent processing is identified with phenomenal consciousness, then phenomenal consciousness becomes an objectively measurable phenomenon. Lamme repeatedly emphasizes that this solution would finally get rid of the philosophical disagreements and turn the debate into a scientific one where evidence from behavioural and neural observations can solve under what circumstances consciousness is present and when it is absent.

This may be true, but only at a high price that comes close to what we know from the problems of reductive materialism as a metaphysical theory of consciousness (see Chapter 1). Even if we were prepared to identify consciousness with recurrent processing, this move would hardly resolve the most difficult questions: Are we leaving subjectivity and qualia out? "Recurrent processing" does not seem to involve either. *Why* and *how* does a certain type of recurrent processing produce certain types of phenomenal qualia? Why does *any* recurrent processing bring about *any* qualia at all? It is hard to see in what way recurrent processing could be so special as to generate qualia. And anyway, the qualia themselves, their presence, absence or qualitative nature, cannot be resolved by the mere declaration that recurrent processing just *is* all there is to qualia, end of discussion! Obviously, we can describe all the neurophysiological features of recurrent processing without mentioning qualia at all. No measurement of recurrent processing shows us in any objective manner whether or not there are qualia involved. Thus, unless qualia become objectively detectable as intrinsic higher level features or causal products of recurrent processing, phenomenal consciousness will remain as elusive as ever for objective measurements, even if we were to accept Lamme's proposal.

Lamme's theory is not radically different from Tononi's information integration theory or Llinás's binding theory: all these theories see the role of the integration of information through multidirectional processing as crucial for consciousness. Lamme's theory, however, describes how this happens at the *cortical* level in visual processing whereas the dynamic core theory and the binding theory place much greater weight on the *thalamocortical* system. Lamme's theory favours a neural reduction of consciousness (consciousness is identified with a specific type of neural activity), whereas Tononi advocates a cognitive or informational reduction of consciousness. Hence, they run the risk of inheriting some of the insurmountable problems of reductive materialism and functionalism as philosophical theories of consciousness.

Microconsciousness theory (Zeki)

Whereas several theories identify consciousness with information integration or binding, or at least argue that binding is necessary for consciousness – that information must be first perceptually coherent and form a holistic representation before it becomes conscious – Semir Zeki (2003; Zeki & Bartels, 1999) argues the opposite. In his theory, consciousness is generated already at a stage where only the elementary features of perception – the isolated qualia if you like – are first processed.

As is well known both from neuropsychological patient cases and from brain imaging experiments, the different elementary features of visual consciousness, especially colour and motion, are processed at anatomically distinct cortical areas (known as V4 and V5). The corresponding phenomenal features can be lost independently of each other through localized brain damage (as happens in achromatopsia and akinetopsia – see Chapter 4 on neuropsychology).

Zeki takes this evidence as showing that the elementary phenomenal experiences themselves, colour and motion, must be *generated in* those localized anatomical regions (V4 and V5) in an isolated manner before they are ever bound together into more complex representations of unified coloured objects in motion. Thus, each cortical region that is specialized in generating a specific type of qualitative experience is a consciousness of its own, or a microconsciousness! To generate its own typical microconsciousness, the specialized cortical area must be in a heightened level of activity and cross a critical activation threshold, but it need not know what other areas are doing or integrate its output with anyone else. If the activity in the area fails to reach the critical threshold, then the information is processed at an unconscious level only.

Microconsciousness theory implies that consciousness is fundamentally disunified and that its neural correlates are distributed over the sensory cortex. There is no single unified neural mechanism of consciousness anywhere to be found, therefore to search for such a thing is based on a mistaken background assumption about the nature of consciousness. When we are presented with a complex visual stimulus, such as a colourful bird flying by, the microconsciousnesses corresponding to the location, shape, colour and motion of the stimulus emerge independently of each other in distinct cortical sites. Furthermore, some of the phenomenal features emerge earlier than others, because the wiring in the brain allows faster processing of some features than others. Thus, first appears location-consciousness, then shape-consciousness, then colour-consciousness and finally motion-consciousness. All of this temporal asynchrony happens within the first half-second, so we do not ever really notice it in our reflective consciousness and introspection. At longer time-scales, the attributes of the object are bound together to form a *macroconsciousness*: a phenomenal unified experience of a coloured moving object, such as the bird. How and where this happens is not specified in Zeki's theory.

Above the level of macroconsciousness there is a third level, which is the highest level of consciousness, called *the unified consciousness*. It contains the entire unified perceptual world and the self as a perceiving entity within one globally unified representation. Zeki is a bit unclear about what precisely he includes in the unified consciousness: Is it simply one unified perceptual representation where all the different phenomenal contents exist in register or does it also involve higher order reflective consciousness and self-awareness? We could easily imagine that animals and children have a global unified perceptual representation without being self-aware. Zeki says that consciousness of oneself as the perceiving person amounts to being aware of being aware, which requires communication and language. His "unified consciousness" thus seems to go beyond mere *perceptual* unity: it seems to be a higher level cognitive achievement, unique to humans.

Consciousness as the feeling of what happens (Damasio)

Antonio Damasio is a neurologist who has published many groundbreaking studies on neurological patient cases who have had surprising deficits in reasoning, emotion, memory and consciousness. As to theoretical issues, he is best known for his somatic marker theory of decision making, according to which reason and rational decision making is guided by bodily-emotional signals; thus, emotion is necessary for reason. Patients with frontal-lobe lesions have lost the emotional signals and are therefore unable to make rational decisions in real-life situations. He popularized the somatic marker theory in his book *Descartes' error* (Damasio, 1994).

Damasio's theory of consciousness was first published in his book *The feeling of what happens* (1999). This theory, unlike the theories we reviewed above, emphasizes the role of *"body and emotions in the making of consciousness"*; in fact this is the subtitle of the book.

The theory introduces a number of (somewhat idiosyncratic) concepts that are used to describe how consciousness relates to the brain. First, there are *nonconscious neural patterns* that consist, for example, of the neural activities in the sensory cortices when they are activated by incoming stimulus information. The neural patterns can be seen, measured and detected objectively from the third-person perspective. The first problem of consciousness, according to Damasio, is this: How are the neural patterns turned into *explicit mental patterns* or *"images"*. The fundamental components of images are *qualia*, says Damasio. Thus, the first problem of consciousness is to explain the relationship between qualia and neurobiology, and Damasio believes that eventually qualia can be neurobiologically explained. But this is as much as he says about the first problem.

So far, Damasio's framing of the problem makes sense, but when we proceed to the higher levels of consciousness his account gets a bit murky. Although images are composed of qualia, images can be conscious or nonconscious, says Damasio. Thus, it seems he accepts the controversial idea that qualia can exist in a form that need not be conscious! This goes against the way qualia are defined in this book (see Chapter 3) but sounds similar to the HOTs (in Chapter 10).

If simple qualia can exist without being conscious, then when does consciousness come into play? Consciousness is the *unified* mental pattern that *brings together the object and the self*. He speaks, metaphorically, of the "movie-in-the-brain": the qualitative mental patterns or sequences of dynamic images as such. But this is not yet consciousness. There must also be the *sense that there is an owner or an apparent observer for the movie within the movie*. The presence of the self in the movie is based on an image as well, but not a *perceptual* image, rather a *feeling*. To be precise, *the feeling of something-happening-in-your presence*. This special feeling is the ongoing image or mental pattern that represents how the organism *relates* to perceptual objects outside the biological organism. Inside the brain, the interplay of the organism with its environment is captured in the phenomenal movie by inserting into it a self-image that feels the presence of object images and constantly interacts with them, being constantly changed in its interrelation to them in the process producing consciousness.

So far, Damasio's theory sounds like a combination of neurophenomenology, emphasizing the role of the self in embodied interaction with the environment, and virtual reality theories, because the embodied interaction happens within the brain between an image of the organism and the images of objects.

The simplest kind of consciousness for Damasio is *core consciousness*. It represents the here-and-now, online relations between the *core self* and the objects (object images) present now for the core self. *Extended consciousness*, by contrast, operates across autobiographical history and presents the temporally continuous autobiographical self and its relations to past and future objects. In this book, we have previously called this ability "mental time travel", which requires self-awareness.

Core consciousness is stable across the lifetime of an organism and it requires no working memory, no long-term memory, no language or reasoning. We share it with animals. Extended consciousness is virtually identical to the notion that we have previously called "self-awareness" in this book.

The neural mechanisms of consciousness are threefold: (1) the neural patterns that create the images of the organism (the self); (2) the neural patterns that create the images of objects; and (3) the neural patterns that create the image of the relationship between the two. "Understanding the biology of consciousness becomes the matter of discovering how the brain can map *both* the two players *and* the relationship they hold" (Damasio, 1999, p. 20).

The internal maps of objects change and are updated constantly, whereas the internal map for the organism (body and self) is very stable. We become conscious when the relationship between the two internal brain maps changes and produces a specific kind of knowledge, the *knowledge that the organism's own state has been changed by an object*. Organisms *without* core consciousness (that are nonconscious biological zombies) can also make images of sight and sound, etc., in their brain but they cannot come to *know* that they did. This statement is again a bit puzzling, because it implies that nonconscious organisms have qualia that are not known or felt in any way.

Core consciousness depends on brain structures that are phylogenetically old, such as the brainstem, which takes care of the most basic vital functions of the organism, and the somatosensory and the cingulate cortices, which map the organism's body and emotions. The early sensory cortices provide the images of objects. The neural patterns underlying core consciousness engage a large-scale network that combines the images for the self and the images of objects.

Damasio's theory combines features from many other theories and it is not easy to say where exactly the theory stands philosophically. One thing is clear: Damasio denies atomism; his view of consciousness is holistic. Consciousness does not emerge in the form of isolated qualia, it emerges only at the level of the complex dynamic world with a self. His theory, however, contains the puzzling idea that qualia (the images or mental patterns as such) can exist in a nonconscious form and also in nonconscious organisms. The nonconscious images only become conscious when they are integrated into a higher level image, where they are related to the image of the organism in an act of knowing. This suggests that Damasio's theory is closely related to the HOTs (see Chapter 10). A higher representational relationship (between the images of self and object) constitutes the crucial "act of knowing" and thereby makes consciousness. The act of knowing sounds a lot like "a mental act" in a HOT where a higher order representation takes a lower order object. Then, again, in some respects Damasio's core consciousness is different from the HOTs' notion of consciousness. Core consciousness seems very simple in content and completely independent of the typical features of reflective consciousness, such as language and conceptual or propositional thought, whereas consciousness in HOTs seems to be much closer to reflective consciousness than to phenomenal consciousness.

Damasio's theory has been criticized for not tackling the Hard Problem of explaining qualia. He openly admits this shortcoming, but at the same time seems to suggest that maybe consciousness does not emerge at the level of qualia at all, but only at the higher level of self and images:

> I am open to the criticism that I am *just* addressing the problem of so-called self consciousness and neglecting the remainder of the problem, namely the qualia problem. If "self-consciousness" is taken to mean "consciousness with a sense of self" then all human consciousness is necessarily covered by the term, there is just no other kind of consciousness as far as I can see.
>
> (Damasio, 1999, p. 19)

At this point, Damasio seems to be close to neurophenomenology and the idea of "pre-reflective self-consciousness" – a primitive self-awareness – as the most fundamental form of consciousness. But is all human consciousness necessarily coupled with a sense of self? If the sense of self implies the sense that there is an owner or an apparent observer for the movie within the movie, then one type of dream experience may pose a problem for the theory. Approximately 10% of dreams contain no dream-self, that is, no character that would be the apparent observer of the dream. The dream image (the movie in the brain during sleep) in these cases is experienced from a selfless, third-person point of view, or a camera-eye perspective. Are these dreams conscious experiences without a sense of self? Are they experiences of a form that should not exist if Damasio's theory is correct? Damasio does not tell us, because he does not consider evidence from dream research in the context of his theory.

The great contribution that Damasio delivers to theories of consciousness is his emphasis on the role of emotions and the body (or at least images of the body). Consciousness is embodied and owned by a self and created by emotionally based feelings. Its core resides under the cortex, in neuroanatomical structures that we share with other animals. Many of the other theories of consciousness reviewed above are more narrowly focusing on only visual or perceptual consciousness – the perceptual object images – neglecting emotions and the body. The main problem with Damasio's theory is the use of idiosyncratic concepts and obscure ideas that mix together philosophical ideas from many different sources. In some sense his theory is in accordance with emergent materialism and Searle's biological naturalism, but in other ways he seems to mix phenomenal consciousness, reflective consciousness and self-awareness together into a combination that sounds like a neurophenomenological HOT of consciousness.

11.2 Analysis: Major issues of disagreement in theories of consciousness

There are three major issues that divide the theories of consciousness. These issues have to do with the fundamental background assumptions adopted in the theories: the philosophical, metaphysical views of what consciousness is and what its place in nature is supposed to be.

The location of consciousness: Externalism vs. internalism

Where is consciousness to be found? The empirical theories we have looked at are committed to internalism. According to these theories, consciousness and qualia are features of brain activity and therefore literally located within the brain. Thus, when we have visual experiences we are directly in touch with a neural reality inside the brain, an internal simulation of the world, although it looks to us as if we would see the outside world and its physical objects directly. The key to finding out where the conscious reality is in the brain is to explore the neural correlates and mechanisms of consciousness in the brain through neuroscientific methods.

By contrast, according to some of the philosophical theories (in particular the sensorimotor theory and the representationalist theory), consciousness does not derive from brain activity at all and, consequently, the contents of consciousness cannot be located in the brain. Thus, the search for the neural correlates of consciousness is a misguided research programme. These ideas follow from philosophical externalism: the view that mind and consciousness (and especially their mental, experiential contents) are not contained in the head or the brain, but are in some sense in the world outside the head. When we open our eyes we see the real world out there, not the insides of our brain.

The mainstream empirical theories in cognitive neuroscience all seem to accept internalism, at least implicitly, and therefore in cognitive neuroscience the search for the neural correlates of consciousness is believed to be an important step towards an explanation of consciousness.

The fundamental nature of consciousness: Phenomenology vs. cognition

What is the relationship between consciousness and cognitive functions? Is consciousness something independent of cognition, especially of "higher" cognitive functions such as attention, thinking, working memory, voluntary action, verbal reporting, or is it dependent on them or perhaps identical to them?

Some theories view consciousness as pure phenomenology – pure experiential subjective qualia – that is independent of cognitive functions. For these theories, the fundamental form of consciousness is pure phenomenal consciousness. It exists in the form of qualitative subjectivity that emerges out of a special type of neural activity in brain regions that have no necessary connection to higher cognition. Thus, phenomenality emerges also in states and in creatures that lack higher cognitive functions and verbal reportability. The criterion of phenomenality is the underlying neural mechanism or activity, such as recurrent processing, that integrates information.

Other theories view consciousness as a cognitive function or at least as necessarily dependent on such functions. For them, the fundamental form of consciousness is reflective consciousness or access consciousness, which can be defined by its functional (rather than phenomenal) features. For these theories, the criterion of consciousness is access to output mechanisms and verbal reportability. The neural mechanism of consciousness is some sort of global workspace with wide cognitive and behavioural access. Information becomes conscious or enters the workspace only through top-down frontoparietal attentional selection or by higher order thought shining on lower order posterior sensory states.

This disagreement is currently the most serious dividing line that separates different theories of consciousness from each other and also colours the interpretation of empirical results on the neural correlates of consciousness. Thus, whether a neural phenomenon that has been detected to correlate with conscious perception will be interpreted as a correlate of the actual *subjective experience* involved in perception depends largely on who interprets the results and on what background theory of consciousness it is based. For one theorist, an activity pattern in the early visual cortex is interpreted as a sign of visual phenomenal consciousness going on, whereas for another theorist it is at most a nonconscious or preconscious visual processing that happens in the dark until touched by higher cognition. Without an objective consciousness detector, this (basically philosophical) disagreement seems impossible to resolve through any conventional behavioural tests or neurophysiological measurements.

The fundamental form of phenomenal consciousness: Atomism vs. holism

The third disagreement concerns an old issue that has resurfaced in modern consciousness studies. In the history of consciousness studies, this battle was fought between structuralism and Gestalt psychology. Now similar positions have been adopted by modern theorists. The microconsciousness theory by Zeki represents an atomistic view in the spirit of structuralism: Consciousness is basically a collection of simple qualia, each one brought about independently of and in isolation from each other in the brain, and only later bound together to unified percepts. The opposite pole is represented most clearly by the unified field theory (Searle), the dynamic core theory (Tononi and Edelman), the information integration theory (Tononi) and Damasio's theory of consciousness. They all suggest that consciousness is basically a unified, holistic phenomenon. Individual qualia are mere modulations of the unified field: ripples on the surface of a global, integrated experiential sphere. Unity and integration are necessary prerequisites for consciousness; nothing phenomenally subjective can exist all by itself outside the unified field.

The stance we take on this issue will also have crucial consequences in the search for the neural mechanisms of consciousness in the brain. Are we looking for multiple microconsciousnesses distributed all over the cortex or a single unified bioelectrical sphere within the thalamocortical networks?

Conclusions

The search for the neural correlates of consciousness is going to look quite different depending on whose theory we take as the starting point of our exploration. Are we looking for a bunch of widely distributed microconsciousnesses from different cortical modules? When the activity level in the V4 colour module reaches a certain level, colour phenomenology is supposed to be generated. Is it subsequently transported elsewhere to be bound together with shape, location and motion, or should we look for recurrent processing between different cortical areas? Maybe the phenomenal features come into being only at this stage where unified perceptual representations are bound together, even if in isolation from language and verbal reports. The third alternative is to look for a single, unified consciousness system, such as the dynamic core in the thalamocortical system: Perhaps phenomenology is not generated before the results of cortical processing reach such a global unified system or perhaps consciousness is the global unified field that is modulated by stimuli (or modular outputs)? Or maybe access to verbal reports and higher cognitive reflection is necessary, in which case we should look for cortical working memory and language systems as necessary for consciousness.

As long as we do not have a clear and shared understanding of what consciousness is – is it a unified whole or a collection of phenomenal pieces, is it located bit by bit in the cortical modules or in a unified manner within the thalamocortical system, is it necessarily tied to selective attention and verbal reportability or not? – we will not have a clear and shared understanding of how and where to search for the neural mechanisms of consciousness either. Although some headway has been made, there is a lot further to be made before we are anywhere close to a Grand Unified Theory of Consciousness.

Chapter summary

We have explored the leading empirical theories of consciousness: Baars' global workspace theory, Crick and Koch's neurobiological framework, Tononi and Edelman's dynamic core theory, Tononi's information integration theory, Llinás' thalamocortical theory, Lamme's recurrent processing theory, Zeki's microconsciousness theory and Damasio's the "feeling of what happens" theory. These empirical theories, unlike the philosophical theories of Chapter 10, at least agree that consciousness is inside the head in some sense, but still they disagree about the basic form of consciousness, the neural mechanisms of consciousness and the relation between higher cognition and consciousness.

Further reading

Baars, B. J. (1988). *A cognitive theory of consciousness*. New York: Cambridge University Press.
Baars, B. J. (1997). *In the theater of consciousness: The workspace of the mind*. New York: Oxford University Press.
Baars, B. J. (1998). Metaphors of consciousness and attention in the brain. *Trends in Neurosciences, 21*, 58–62.
Block, N. (2007). Consciousness, accessibility, and the mesh between psychology and neuroscience. *Behavioral and Brain Sciences, 30*, 481–499.
Crick, F., & Koch, C. (1990). Towards a neurobiological theory of consciousness. *Seminars in the Neurosciences, 2*, 273–304.
Crick, F., & Koch, C. (1998). Consciousness and neuroscience. *Cerebral Cortex, 8*, 97–107.
Crick, F., & Koch, C. (2003). A framework for consciousness. *Nature Neuroscience, 6*, 119–126.
Damasio, A. R. (1994). *Descartes' error*. New York: Putnam.
Damasio, A. R. (1999). *The feeling of what happens*. New York: Harcourt Brace.
Dehaene, S., Changeux, J. P., Naccache, L., Sackur, J., & Sergent, C. (2006). Conscious, preconscious, and subliminal processing: A testable taxonomy. *Trends in Cognitive Science, 10*, 204–211.

Dehaene, S., & Naccache, L. (2001). Towards a cognitive neuroscience of consciousness: Basic evidence and a workspace framework. *Cognition, 79,* 1–37.

Edelman, G. M. (1989). *The remembered present: A biological theory of consciousness.* New York: Basic Books.

Edelman, G. M., & Tononi, G. (2000). *A universe of consciousness.* New York: Basic Books.

Fodor, J. A. (1983). *The modularity of the mind.* Cambridge, MA: MIT Press.

Kouider, S. (2009). Neurobiological theories of consciousness. In W. B. Banks (Ed.), *Encyclopedia of consciousness* (Vol. 2, pp. 87–100). San Diego, CA: Academic Press.

Lamme, V. A. (2000). Neural mechanisms of visual awareness: A linking proposition. *Brain and Mind, 1,* 385–406.

Lamme, V. A. (2003). Why visual awareness and attention are different. *Trends in Cognitive Sciences, 7,* 12–18.

Lamme V. A. (2004). Separate neural definitions of visual consciousness and visual attention; a case for phenomenal awareness. *Neural Networks, 17,* 861–872.

Lamme, V. A., & Roelfsema, P. R. (2000). The distinct modes of vision offered by feedforward and recurrent processing. *Trends in Neurosciences, 23,* 571–579.

Llinás, R. (2001). *I of the vortex: From neurons to self.* Cambridge, MA: MIT Press.

Llinás, R. R., & Paré, D. (1991). Of dreaming and wakefulness. *Neuroscience, 44,* 521–535.

Llinás, R. R., Ribary, U., Contreras, D., & Pedroarena, C. (1998). The neuronal basis for consciousness. *Philosophical Transactions of the Royal Society of London, Series B, 353,* 1841–1849.

Tononi, G. (2009). An integrated information theory of consciousness. In. W. B. Banks (Ed.), *Encyclopedia of Consciousness* (pp. 403–416). San Diego, CA: Academic Press.

Zeki, S. (2003). The disunity of consciousness. *Trends in Cognitive Sciences, 7,* 214–218.

Zeki, S., & Bartels, A. (1999). Towards a theory of visual consciousness. *Consciousness and Cognition, 8,* 225–259.

Brief discussion questions

1   What kind of theory do you regard as most plausible in terms of the three major issues of disagreement: holistic or atomistic theories; externalist or internalist theories; purely phenomenal or higher cognition theories?

2   Choose one of the philosophical theories at a time and try to find an empirical theory that would work well in combination with the philosophical theory. What are the best combinations that you can identify? What are the least workable combinations?

3   Do you believe we will one day have a Grand Unified Theory of Consciousness? What do you imagine that theory will look like?

Central domains of consciousness science

IV. Altered states of consciousness

Chapter 12

What is an "altered state of consciousness" (ASC)?

Introduction

The stream of our subjective experiences flows steadily on, following the course of its river-bed, with the sensations, perceptions, emotions and thoughts merging with each other as they gradually flow by in ever-changing patterns and tapestries. Although the patterns of subjective experience are enormously variable, they still seem to remain within certain bounds, at least most of the time. Sometimes the stream of experience seems to take altogether unusual forms, creating patterns not normally enabled. The stream of consciousness sometimes runs through rapids, ravines or waterfalls, sometimes it enters perfectly still and calm waters, sometimes the waters are muddy and at other times crystal clear. The unusual varieties of experience are called "altered states of consciousness".

12.1 How to define "altered state of consciousness"

The notion of "altered state of consciousness" (ASC) presupposes that there is some defineable *normal* or *baseline* state of consciousness (NSC) that is temporarily transformed into an altered state but will return back to the baseline state sooner or later. To a first approximation, *an ASC is a temporary, reversible state of consciousness that significantly differs from the baseline state and typically lasts from a few minutes to at most a few hours*. Permanent, irreversible changes in conscious experience, such as neuropsychological deficits caused by brain injury, are usually not counted as ASCs. To have a terrible nightmare, to be heavily drunk, to sleepwalk around the house, to enjoy a "runner's high" during a marathon competition or to have an "out-of-body" experience is to be in a paradigmatic altered state of consciousness.

One way to define the concept of ASC more precisely is to say that in an ASC the *overall pattern* of subjective experience is significantly different from the baseline NSC. The idea behind this definition is that the change that has happened in consciousness is *global* in nature and therefore affects several different dimensions of experience, cognition or behaviour. The dimensions of experience where the changes may take place include, for example, attention (in meditation, attention becomes super-focused), perception (a sleepwalker may see things in the bedroom that are not really there), mental imagery (hypnosis may make mental images extremely vivid), inner speech (in meditation or a flow experience, inner speech may disappear), memory processes (during dreaming or hypnosis we often cannot remember the facts of our waking life), thought processes (during dreaming we accept totally illogical or uncritical thoughts), meaningfulness of experience (in a runner's high, the runner may feel mystical oneness with the surrounding nature), time experience (during meditation or in a flow experience, an hour may pass in what feels like 5 min), emotional feelings and expressions (when drunk, both aggression and affection are felt and expressed more strongly than otherwise), self-control (when drunk, indecent behaviour becomes more likely), suggestibility (in hypnosis, suggestions given by the hypnotist become a reality for the hypnotized), body image (in an out-of-body experience, the subject sees one body but feels and identifies with another one, a more ethereal body where the self is located floating in the air) and personal identity (in a dream, the dreamer may appear as another person than in real life).

However, in some ASCs the contents or overall patterns of experience are not much different from the NSC. Sometimes we have extremely realistic dreams that depict places, people or events that seem identical with our real waking life. Our thought processes may also be similar to what they are in the normal state. A special type of dream that closely simulates waking experience is called *false awakening*. During this experience, we seem to wake up, get out of bed, start to do our morning routines, perhaps worrying about being late for work or school, only to suddenly wake up again in our beds and to find out that in fact we never *did* get out of bed after all, we only dreamt about it!

Thus, the definition of ASC as an "overall altered pattern of experience" may not be able to demarcate all kinds of ASCs from the NSC in a reliable manner, because in some ASCs the content of experience may closely simulate normal waking life even though it is a hallucination.

Perhaps a better definition could be reached by adding a further condition: The subject having the ASC must *feel* or *recognize* that his or her experience is remarkably different from the normal state. This definition adds the requirement that an ASC must be *recognized at the level of reflective consciousness* by the subject having it. When we are drunk, we are aware of the fact that we have been drinking and that our minds are not working normally. But, clearly, this kind of reflective awareness of our own state is not true about many other ASCs during the time they take place. For example, during dream experiences we are usually oblivious to the fact that we are dreaming, and it is extremely difficult to arrive at the conclusion that "this is a dream" while we continue to dream. Conversely, sometimes in the NSC we may mistakenly believe we are in an altered state, if something utterly unexpected or shocking suddenly happens so that we have difficulty in believing what we see before our very eyes, but might for a moment think that we must be dreaming.

If we allow that the recognition of the ASC as an ASC may take place *after* the altered state itself is already gone, then we will be able to correctly classify most ASCs (such as dream experiences) as ASCs.

One of the leading researchers of ASCs since the 1960s, Charles T. Tart, offers a definition that is consistent with the above ideas:

> An "altered" state is then a qualitative, as well as perhaps a quantitative, alteration in the overall pattern of mental functioning relative to some state of consciousness chosen as the baseline (usually ordinary consciousness), such that the experiencer feels her consciousness is qualitatively (and often radically) different from the way it functions in the baseline state.
>
> (Tart, 2000, p. 257)

A third potential definition of ASCs says that the core of all ASCs is *not* the change in the overall patterns of experience (which may or may not happen) or in our ability to recognize this change (which also may or may not be the case), but rather the fact that *while in an ASC, the content of our experience relates differently to the real world than in the NSC* (Revonsuo, Kallio, & Sikka, 2009). According to this definition, the causal or representational relation between contents of experience and their typical sources breaks down in such a way that contents of experience in consciousness tend to carry *false* information about the world or ourselves. The contents of experience, in other words, in some way *misrepresent* external reality or the self: We hallucinate, we are under delusions.

This definition applies to all cases where the ASC is characterized by hallucinations or delusions. Hallucinations by definition involve perceptual experiences that do not correspond to the real stimulus environment. Delusions refer to strongly held beliefs, judgements and persistently deficient reasoning that is illogical or contrary to obvious objective evidence. Thus, hallucinations distort the contents of phenomenal or perceptual consciousness whereas delusions impair the higher level thought processes at the level of reflective consciousness. However, this definition should be refined so that not every kind of trivial perceptual illusion, misperception or false belief counts as an ASC. One way to refine it is to say that an ASC is a *globally misrepresentational state* – a state where there is an overall tendency for the brain to produce hallucinations and delusions. This clearly happens in dreaming, psychotic episodes, hypnosis and mystical experiences, whereas perceptual illusions, misperceptions or isolated hallucinations would not count as ASCs (Revonsuo, Kallio, & Sikka, 2009).

Chapter summary

To define "altered state of consciousness" is almost as difficult as it is to define "consciousness" itself. There are many different definitions of ASC, and all of them agree about the following two issues: In an ASC, something in the way consciousness functions or what it contains (or both) has been altered, relative to a baseline state that is considered the standard or normal state of consciousness.

We have explored three different ways to define ASC more precisely: by using altered patterns of experience as the criterion; by using the feeling or recognition of an alteration as the criterion; or by using the altered informational or representational relation between consciousness and the world as the criterion. All of the above definitions have their strengths and their weaknesses.

Perhaps the most workable definition of an ASC could be arrived at by combining all of the above ideas: An ASC is any *temporary, reversible* state of consciousness in which the *relationship* between the *patterns of experience* and *their typical, appropriate causes has been changed* so that patterns of experience tend to occur without their appropriate causes (positive hallucinations), or some patterns of experience do not occur despite the presence of their appropriate causes (negative hallucinations), or both. The hallucinations are often coupled with delusional beliefs, so that the person is in a globally misrepresentational state (perceiving and believing things that are not really there). Furthermore, either the subject or outside observers should be able to *recognize* either during the ASC or after it that an ASC is or was occurring: that the experiences and beliefs were not equally accurate as in the normal waking state.

There are many different kinds of ASCs, induced by a variety of different causes. Perhaps the most typical ASCs are the following: dreaming and other sleep-related altered states, hypnosis, drug states, psychotic episodes, meditative states, mystical experiences and out-of-body experiences. We will take a closer look at some of these states in the chapters that follow.

Further reading

Farthing, W. G. (1992). *The psychology of consciousness*. New York: Prentice-Hall.

Revonsuo, A. (2009). Altered and exceptional states of consciousness. In W. P. Banks (Ed.), *Encyclopedia of consciousness* (Vol. 1, pp. 9–21). San Diego, CA: Academic Press.

Revonsuo, A., Kallio, S., & Sikka, P. (2009). What is an altered state of consciousness? *Philosophical Psychology, 22*, 187–204.

Tart, C. T. (Ed.) (1990). *Altered states of consciousness*. New York: Harper Collins.

Tart, C. T. (2000). Investigating altered states on their own terms. In M. Velmans (Ed.), *Investigating phenomenal consciousness* (pp. 255–278). Amsterdam: John Benjamins.

Vaitl, D., Birbaumer, N., Gruzelier, J., Jamieson, G. A., Kotchoubey, B., Kübler, A., et al. (2005). Psychobiology of altered states of consciousness. *Psychological Bulletin, 131*, 98–127.

Brief discussion questions

1   What is the "normal" state of consciousness? How would you define it?
2   How much time and how often do you spend in some kind of altered state of consciousness (following the definitions of ASC given in this chapter)? What are the most common types of altered states in your life?

Chapter 13

Dreaming and sleep

Introduction: A brief history of dreaming and consciousness

The ancient conceptions of dreaming were, like the first ideas of consciousness in general, thoroughly dualistic. According to traditional beliefs, during sleep the body enters a death-like state, whereas the soul escapes from the body and enters a spirit world. There it meets with the spirits of dead ancestors or perhaps the messengers of gods, and may get warnings or symbolically coded messages from them. The dream messages may be interpreted by prophets and oracles to see into the future, or to understand what the spirits and the gods want.

If this ancient dualistic account of dreaming were true, what we think of as an altered state of consciousness during sleep would in fact be the adventures of our disembodied soul in another, nonphysical realm!

It is quite understandable why people all over the world have come up with a dualistic theory of dreaming where the soul enters another reality. Dreaming as a subjective experience feels like *being in a world* – the world of the dream is presented to the dreamer in much the same way as the waking world is. The world in the dream, obviously, is not the waking world; thus, it must be some sort of alternative reality. The dreamer in the dreamworld, presumably, has not taken his physical body with him into the dreamworld; thus, it must be the dreamer as a spiritual being only who has entered the dreamworld. A rather plausible story when you do not know anything about the science of consciousness, I suppose!

The first scientific dream studies started in the latter half of the 19th century, around the same time as introspectionism ruled in psychology. In that era, dreaming was defined as a succession of mental images that the dreamer perceives as real, and the study of dreams focused on the subjective appearance and experience of dreams, not on the meaning or the function of dreams. The introspective dream report was considered as a valid testimony of what had been experienced during dreaming (Schwartz, 2000).

A student of William James, Mary Calkins, who later became the first woman President of the American Psychological Association, conducted the first statistical studies on dreams in 1893. She calculated the frequency of occurrence of the various sensory modalities in dreams and came up with similar figures to those of modern dream researchers (Schwartz, 2000).

In spite of this promising kickoff, the kind of scientific dream research that takes consciousness seriously soon collapsed with the rise of Freud's psychoanalysis and Watson's behaviourism. According to Freud, the experienced (or manifest) dream is not the *real* dream; it is merely a disguised and distorted *symbolic representation* of the real (or latent) dream. The manifest dream must be interpreted by a psychoanalyst, who alone has the abilities to decipher what the true (but totally unconscious) dream was all about. Thus, the focus turned away from the actual phenomenology of dreams to the psychoanalytic fabrications consisting of obscure and absurd dream symbolism, turning the dream into something the dreamer could not recognize anymore as his or her own experience at all. The science of dreaming was thereby replaced by the art of dream interpretation. In the 20th century dream interpretation became a fad as popular as phrenology had been in the 19th century. In terms of low scientific validity but widespread cultural popularity, psychoanalytic dream interpretation for the 20th-century culture was what phrenological personality analysis had been in the 19th century.

After the era of introspectionism, academic psychology as a science also became hostile towards scientific dream research, because dreaming is a subjective phenomenon of consciousness. Dream research has little to do with objective physical stimuli and measurable behaviour but everything to do with subjective experience and introspective reports, thus dreaming was doomed to become a phenomenon thrown out from the scope of the behaviouristic approach to psychology.

In philosophy, two behaviouristically inspired theories of dreaming were put forward. The first one was presented by Norman Malcolm in 1959, in the tradition of Ludwig Wittgenstein's philosophy and Gilbert Ryle's logical behaviourism. Malcolm argued that the only evidence we have of dreaming is the impression of having dreamt when we wake up. From this impression we jump to the conclusion that the remembered events must have occurred during our sleep. But this commonsense interpretation, says Malcolm, makes no sense. To say that a sleeping person who shows no overt behaviours at the time is having experiences or mental states of any kind is just unintelligible and cannot be verified in any imaginable objective means. The concept "dreaming" really refers to the *impressions* and the *reports* of *having* dreamt, which occur immediately after awakening from sleep, not during sleep. The concept of dreaming does not and cannot refer to experiences (or any other mental events) during sleep.

In 1976, in a paper called "Are dreams experiences?", Daniel Dennett returned to Malcolm's argument and presented his own sceptical hypothesis concerning the nature of dreams. Dennett (1976) considers the following possibility as an alternative explanation of dreams (or, rather, as an explanation of dream-reporting behaviour): There may be a library of undreamed dreams somewhere in the brain. When the dreamer wakes up, one of the dream cassettes that has an ending consistent with the events at the time of waking up (say, hearing the alarm clock ring and merge with the dream events) is fetched and fed into memory. Consequently, the contents of this dream cassette will be recalled as a false memory of experiences supposedly happening during sleep. There are no conscious experiences really going on during sleep, merely the unconscious insertion of a dream recollection into memory. Dennett's cassette-theory of dreams thus suggests that, for all we know, dreams *could* be false memories, unconsciously composed during REM sleep and unconsciously implanted to short-term memory just before awakening.

Malcolm's and Dennett's theories of dreaming show beautifully how a behaviouristic approach to subjective experience gets rid of first-person consciousness by objectifying it into something directly observable from the third-person point of view. The reality of the subjective dream experience is denied, and replaced by dream-reporting behaviour whose causal explanation is not allowed to refer to any subjective experiences going on during sleep, only to unconsciously produced false memories.

The behaviouristic interpretation of dreaming did not strike empirical dream researchers as convincing, and was ignored by them. Still, the methodological point, that subjective dream experiences cannot be objectively verified in empirical dream research, continues to be valid. Research has not been able to pinpoint any absolutely reliable neurophysiological sign that would reveal with 100% accuracy whether or not a sleeping person is dreaming at any particular moment. The subjective content of the dream is obviously even further beyond objective measurments. Also, retrospective

237

reports of dreams are never totally reliable, because they depend on our fragile memories of dreams. In fact, some dream researchers hold that dreaming happens throughout the night and dreamless sleep does not exist at all. It is only that our memory for the dreams we have had sometimes fails, and subsequently we will be under the impression that we did not dream at all. This *amnesia theory of dreaming* is the exact reverse of Malcolm's and Dennett's false-memory theories.

These discussions concerning the reality of dream experiences reveal once again the difficulties that follow from the problem of other minds and from the inability to detect or measure consciousness objectively. In principle, at least, it is possible to defend the behaviouristic view that we *never* have any subjective experiences during sleep (we only falsely remember having had them), or the opposite amnesia theory that we *always* have ongoing subjective experiences when we sleep (we just sometimes cannot remember them)! As neither one of these theories presents any convincing arguments or evidence as to why our memory systems should work in such peculiar ways, it does not strike me as unfair to reject both of them.

The dream researcher David Foulkes (1985) considered the philosophical discussions but did not let them interfere with the empirical studies of dreams:

> What dreams are really like is impossible to say in any ultimate sense, because by the time I remember mine or you tell me yours, they're gone and it is impossible to match the recollection or report with the original dream. Philosophers love to descend into mental morasses such as this, and they generally return with the message that we can't be sure there are any such things as mental experiences at all, or that we can't be sure about anything at all ... Along with common sense, I'm assuming that there are such things as dream experiences.
>
> (Foulkes, 1985, p. 33)

In the 1950s, empirical dream research made a sudden comeback on two different fronts: the study of dream content and the study of the neurophysiological mechanisms of dreaming. The psychiatrist Calvin Hall started to publish new descriptive statistics on the phenomenological contents of large samples of home-reported dreams. In 1966, this work was summarized in a famous book called *The content analysis of dreams* (Hall & Van de Castle, 1966), a landmark study that described the phenomenology of hundreds of dreams in a systematic manner. The Hall and Van de Castle method of content analysis has become the most widely used way of comparing the phenomenological content of dreams across different populations and samples (see Domhoff, 1996). In this way the line of research originally started by Mary Calkins in 1893 was finally resurrected and the dark ages of psychoanalysis and behaviourism were gradually left behind.

In sleep laboratory studies, REM sleep and its close connection to dreaming was discovered in 1953 by Aserinsky and Kleitman. The discovery of the physiological correlates of dreaming led to great hopes for a reductive explanation of dreaming: If dreaming can be identified with REM sleep, then by studying the physiological and neural mechanisms of REM sleep we should be able to explain dreaming. This line of neurophysiological theorizing reached its peak in the activation-synthesis theory of dreaming by Hobson and McCarley in 1977.

The role of subjective dream experience in the activation-synthesis theory was, however, rather weak. The main focus of the theory was in the neurophysiology of REM sleep, and dreaming was seen only as a byproduct of the neurophysiological events during REM sleep. The patterns of physiological activation in REM produce internally generated stimuli for the brain, whereas external sensory stimuli and motor output are blocked. The brain attempts to synthesize a series of images that would match the unpredictable patterns of internally generated activity, using memory as the source of the images. Dreaming has no purpose, function or meaning; it is only the brain's attempt to make sense of the peculiar internal stimulation it receives in REM sleep. Our state of mind during dreaming resembles psychosis or delirium, because we are under hallucinations, delusions and bizarre thoughts and percepts. Thus, compared to waking consciousness, dream consciousness is seen in this theory as a disorganized and deficient form of consciousness.

However, another theoretical approach to dreaming had developed almost simultaneously within psychology, and it was based on the purely cognitive view of the mind. In the spirit of classical cognitive science, the representatives of this approach (e.g. David Foulkes, 1985) argued that dreaming is a cognitive phenomenon that should be explained at the purely mental level of information processing. It cannot be reduced to or explained by neurophysiology. Clearly, in its opposition to neurophysiological theories of dreaming, this approach was philosophically based on the underlying functionalism that dominated psychology and cognitive science in those days.

The cognitive approach paid more attention to dreaming as a significant form of consciousness in itself and argued against the view that dreams are incoherent, disorganized and full of bizarre elements. By contrast, Foulkes (1985) regarded dreams as "credible world analogs", an organized form of consciousness that simulates what life is like in a nearly perfect manner. Dreams are coherently organized experiences, in the sense that what we experience at any given moment in a dream makes sense to us: the dream situation is comprehensible. Furthermore, across time, the dream evolves around a continuous narrative or story not so very different from the episodes of waking experience.

The cognitive-psychological view of dreaming was based on the phenomenology of dreams as described in both home-reported dreams and laboratory-reported dreams. It criticized the activation-synthesis view of dreaming as being based more on our stereotypical and biased memories of dreams than on the representative samples of dreams collected for research purposes.

Thus, in the 1980s, dreaming was again taken seriously as a form of consciousness or subjective mental experience. Dream experience was again studied systematically by looking at detailed introspective dream reports. Dreaming was to be explained by either the underlying cognitive or neural mechanisms, or both in combination. With the advent of cognitive neuroscience and consciousness studies in the 1990s, dreaming became a natural part of the mainstream research in these fields.

This is a fortunate development for modern consciousness research, because sleep- and dream-related ASCs are the most commonly occurring altered states in normal adults and hence are a most valuable source of evidence about consciousness. We sleep about 8 h per day or one-third of all the available time. It is sometimes mistakenly stated that when we are asleep we are not conscious at all, but most of the time that we spend sleeping we are in fact in some kind of altered state of consciousness rather than totally unconscious. Next we will take a look at the rich variety of ASCs that occur during sleep.

13.1 Hypnagogic and hypnopompic hallucinations

"Hypnagogia" is the brief transitional state from wakefulness to sleep (literally, "leading to sleep"). The internally generated images in this state are called hypnagogic hallucinations. By contrast, hypnopompic hallucinations (literally, "leading out of sleep") occur in the transitional state from sleep back to wakefulness. The content of the hallucinations is quite similar in both stages. According to one explanation of these ASCs, the mechanisms of REM sleep that normally produce dream images are activated when the brain is just about to lose or gain the state of wakefulness. The result is an ASC that combines some features of wakefulness with some features of dreaming. During these hallucinations some degree of perceptual or bodily awareness remains, but other aspects of experience consist of hallucinatory images. Most typical are visual hallucinations of various kinds: simple geometric forms, objects, faces or entire landscapes. Also auditory phenomena are common: noises, sounds, music or human voices. Other sensory modalities may also be involved, such as bodily feelings of various kinds or tactile sensations. These two ASCs reflect consciousness at the borderline between an externally modulated perceptual world and an internally generated dreamworld.

13.2 Sleep paralysis

Have you ever had the experience of waking up, being sure that there is someone evil watching you in the bedroom; perhaps you even can see a menacing figure standing in the shadows in the corner. You try to scream or stand up, but you notice that you cannot move or make a sound: you are paralysed and helpless!

An ASC that often takes place in the hypnagogic or hypnopompic state is called sleep paralysis. It is a mixture of wakefulness and REM sleep-related muscular atonia: the subject feels awake, but cannot move any part of his or her body. This may be accompanied by the belief that one is having a heart attack or dying, because breathing seems difficult and something heavy seems to be pressing against the subject's chest. Sometimes this is perceived to be an evil character (a.k.a. "the old hag") that is sitting on the chest. Sleep paralysis is often associated with the sense of an evil presence or the strong feeling that there is another person, or being, present somewhere close by, observing the subject and having some sort of evil intentions towards him or her.

Thus, sleep paralysis may be a frightening experience emotionally, not only because it is shocking to find out that you cannot move a finger, but also because you see or believe that some malevolent creatures are hanging around in your bedroom, about to do something terrible to you. It has been speculated that the true origin of many so-called "paranormal" experiences (ghosts, apparitions, UFO abductions) is to be found in the combination of sleep paralysis and hypnagogic hallucinations in subjects who do not know that the experience did not depict what was really going on in the bedroom, it was only a harmless ASC. The "paranormal" experiences typically happen during the night when the subject is lying in bed in a dark room and likely to be intermittently in a transitional state between sleep and wakefulness. As the experiential content of these ASCs can be intense, realistic and extremely frightening, the subject who has never even heard about sleep paralysis or hypnagogic hallucinations may easily interpret the experiences as representing real but "supernatural" events.

13.3 Sleep mentation vs. dreaming

During sleep, subjective experiences of some kind occur most of the time. About 85% of REM sleep awakenings and about 25–50% of NREM awakenings lead to reports of subjective experience, establishing the abundance of phenomenal consciousness during sleep. The subjective experiences during sleep can be roughly divided into two categories: *sleep mentation* and *dreaming*. The difference between these two is in the *complexity* of experience. Typical sleep mentation consists of a single image that occurs in a single sensory modality and remains static or repeats itself in the same form. An image of a visual object, a word or sentence or sound heard repetitively or a thought that runs through the mind again and again are common types of sleep mentation.

By contrast, dreaming involves complex, organized and animated imagery in multiple sensory modalities that shows progression and change through time. Thus, dreams depict a sensory-perceptual world with objects and characters, and simulated events that take place in such a world. A dream is, in essence, a *simulated world* (see Figure 13.1).

Most people report that they remember their dreams at least sometimes, but a few (about 5%) say they do not remember any dreams at all. In one study, 1000 people in Switzerland were asked the question "How often do you dream?". The results showed that 37% of people remembered dreaming either every night or frequently. A further 33% reported dreaming every now and then and 24% answered that they dream only rarely. Only 6% of the study group responded "never" (Borbély, 1984, quoted in Strauch & Meier, 1996). The results suggest that about 95% of people have personal experiences of dreaming. However, most of the remaining 5% will also start to remember their dreams if only woken up directly from REM sleep, which shows that it is not a problem of not dreaming but a problem of not recalling dreams. Only much fewer than 1% of people *never* remember *any* dreams, no matter what.

13.4 The contents of dreaming

According to questionnaire studies conducted all over the world, the most universal theme in our dreams is that of being chased or pursued. Note that "universal" does not mean that all people dream about this all of the time, but rather that this theme has occurred at least sometime in almost all dreamers all over the world. It has been reported by approximately 80% of dreamers in different countries and in cross-cultural studies. Incidentally, being chased or attacked is also the most common

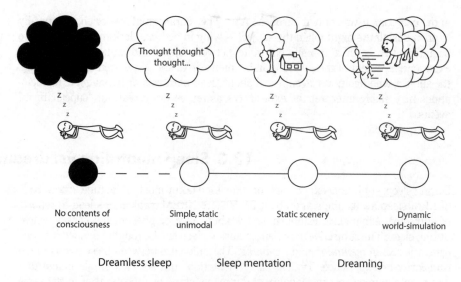

Figure 13.1 The continuum of consciousness in sleep

During sleep, consciousness may be totally absent (dreamless sleep), or it may contain simple, repetitive thoughts or images (sleep mentation), or static scenery (borderline between sleep mentation and dreaming), or multimodal, animated, dynamic world-simulation where the dreamer is involved as a central character (genuine dreaming)

earliest remembered dream in children, and the most common theme in recurrent dreams in both children and adults. Recurrent dreams are dreams that occur in an almost identical form again and again for months or years.

Other themes that many people have in their dreams include being physically attacked or being frozen with fright, as if falling from high places or being on the verge of falling. Being trapped and not able to get out, being lost or drowning are also universally dreamed about.

As the examples from universal and recurrent dreams suggest, negative themes seem more common than positive ones. Flying is one of the leading positive themes. Many people have dreamt that they fly in their dreams – not in an aeroplane, but just like Superman, their bodies soaring through the air.

The above results are mostly based on what people spontaneously happen to remember about their dream themes when questioned or interviewed about their dreams. Dream content can be studied much more accurately and in more detail by collecting introspective verbal reports describing the content of dreams in great detail. Preferably the dream experiences are reported immediately after awakening from a dream, either orally to a tape or in writing to a dream diary. In this kind of research, all the limitations of introspective reporting should be carefully taken into account to minimize their distorting effects on the data (see Chapter 3 for more on descriptive introspection). The dream reports can be subsequently analysed with a method called *content analysis* (Domhoff, 1996; Hall & Van de Castle, 1966), with which it is possible to quantify the occurrence of different contents of consciousness (objects, persons, places, emotions, etc.) in dreams, and to report how much of each type of content usually occurs in dreams. The quantified dream contents can then be used to calculate statistics or compare the dreams of different groups with each other quantitatively, just like any other scientific data.

Systematic research on the content of dreams has shown that all of our sensory modalities are involved in dreams. Visual experiences are the most common, and practically all dreams include them. The visual qualities of dream experiences were explored in an ingenious experiment by Rechtschaffen and Buchignani (1992). They had a selection of more than 100 photographs in which the visual features (e.g. chromaticity, saturation, illumination) varied from normal to light or dark, clear or unclear, and so on. Immediately after awakening the subject in the sleep laboratory, he or she selected the photograph that most accurately matched the visual quality of the dream. The most often picked photographs had visual qualities that closely resembled the way we perceive the world while we are awake – dream visions most of the time are as clear and vivid as visual perception.

Most dreams are seen in colour (approximately 50–70%). Still, some people dream more in black and white than others; some only dream in colour. According to one hypothesis, people who have been exposed to black-and-white visual media in their childhood have more dreams in greyscale (Murzyn, 2008). Auditory experiences occur in most dreams, very commonly in the form of spoken language that the dreamer hears, but music and other kinds of sounds and noises sometimes occur too. Musicians hear music more often in their dreams – sometimes pieces they have never heard in reality (Uga, Lemut, Zampi, Zilli, & Salzarulo, 2006)! Bodily and tactile experiences are found in some dream reports but smell and taste experiences in only about one dream report in a hundred. Pain experiences are even less common, but sometimes they do occur in an intense and realistic form. The dream pain seems to be often caused by the dream events (such as putting hot coals on your palm or stabbing a knife into your dream body), not by any external, physical pain stimulus.

Most dreams have a central character or a *dream-self*, who is a representation of the dreamer in the dream (Revonsuo, 2005). The dream-self usually feels and seems to be the same person we are in our waking lives: it is me myself, personally present there in the dreamworld! Even so, in some respects I am not quite the same, or at least I do not have at my disposal all the mental powers and cognitive skills I have during wakefulness. In our adventures in the dreamworld, we suffer from memory lapses, confabulation and lack of insight into our own condition. The dream-self often has a limited access to his or her autobiographical memory – we suffer from transient amnesia – and is disoriented to time and place: In our dreams we usually have no idea what time or day it is and where exactly we are and how we got there, and what is going to happen tomorrow or in the future. While we may remember some facts concerning our lives correctly when dreaming, often we lose the ability to contemplate whether the events, persons, places or objects in our dreams are possible. For example, we can meet dead friends and relatives without the realization that they have, in fact, died years ago. We can also create false memories in our dreams and not be able to reflect on the peculiarity of the dream. For instance, we can confabulate characteristics for our known dream-persons that they do not have in reality, like a different home, hobby or profession. Sometimes we manage to create friends or relatives that we do not have in our waking reality, and we have no insight into the fact that these people do not exist in real life. In fact, we are often totally unable to reflect upon the credibility of any of our own beliefs in our dreams.

Most dreams also include other human (or animal) characters, and social inter-action and communication between dream characters is common. The dream-self is an active participant in the dream events in approximately four out of five dreams and an uninvolved observer only occasionally. The dream-self interacts with other dream characters and various social interactions take place in dreams. Interactions with other characters are more often aggressive than friendly. Almost half of our dreams include an aggressive component, and the dreamer is personally involved in most of these, more often being the victim than the aggressor. In general, negative emotions are more frequently experienced in dreams than positive emotions. In the classic Hall and Van de Castle (1966) study of home-reported dreams, of the over 700 emotions explicitly mentioned in the 1000 dream reports of college students, 80% were negative and only 20% positive. Later, Snyder (1970) and Strauch and Meier (1996) acquired similar results in REM dreams collected in the laboratory, indi-cating that two-thirds of emotions in dreams are negative. The most commonly reported negative emotions are fear and anger.

Some activities we often engage in in the real world are much less frequent in the dream world, such as reading, writing, typing, working with computers, calcula-ting and watching TV. It seems that dreams are not keen to simulate these cognitive activities, perhaps because they involve skills and habits that only relate to the modern world and not to the original biological features or environments of the human species. Although many technological devices certainly do find their way to our dreams, it appears that elevators, telephones, cars and other wonders of the modern world do not work very well in our dreams, and we often experience problems with them in the dreamworld.

Dreams often include bizarre contents and events that would be impossible or highly unlikely in the real world. One specific form of dream bizarreness, the *incongruity* of dream images, can be characterized in the following way: Incongruous dream elements are dream elements that either *have features that do not belong to corresponding elements in waking reality* or *appear in contexts in which the correspond-ing elements would not appear in waking reality*. Thus, seeing a blue banana, encountering a person with a distorted face, finding a normal banana growing in an apple-tree or bumping into the President of the United States in one's home would all be examples of incongruous elements in dreams.

The bizarre elements of dreams can be characterized in more detail with the help of the concept of binding. A blue banana is a good example of erroneous *feature binding*: The representation of "banana" in our semantic memory should primarily associate the colour yellow and to a lesser degree the colour green with bananas, but not the colour blue. And a banana growing in an apple-tree, or the President having a cup of coffee in my kitchen, are cases of erroneous *contextual binding*: Though the elements of such dream images are *internally* coherent, they do not fit together in the light of our semantic knowledge of the world. Another variety of dream bizarreness is the *discontinuity* of dream elements: for example, a banana may suddenly appear, disappear or be transformed into an apple in a manner not possible in the waking world. Discontinuity seems to be a case of *inaccurate binding across time*: Successive dream images do not always retain or update the phenomenal representations in a coherent way, which leads to the sudden and inexplicable changes of objects, persons and places in dreams.

The bizarreness of dream images, that is, the unusual combinations in binding different information sources together to produce coherent phenomenal representations, may shed light on the mechanisms involved in the construction of unified phenomenal objects and the unified phenomenal world that we normally enjoy in waking perception (Revonsuo, 2006).

Bizarre elements are easily found in dream reports (the following are excerpts from the dream diaries of university students that I have collected in my studies):

> I am with some friend at a department store. We are looking for lockers there, and the store suddenly turns into a swimming hall. In its own way, the place is also a hotel and at times a ship. Nevertheless, when we get out, there is no water nearby.

This dream is a vivid example of a bizarre dream feature called discontinuity: The identity of the place where the dreamer is keeps switching in a manner not possible in real life. Below, there is another dream reported, with many people in it, but there is something a bit odd with most of them:

> I entered a house with my father. I was walking around the house when I saw someone sitting by a table. I recognized this person; she was my grandmother *(she didn't look like my grandmother and in real life my grandmother is dead)*. I went to her and gave her a hug. Beside another table I saw my mother and gave her also a hug *(in real life my mother is dead)*. Further away there were people dancing. I was wondering if there were any other familiar people there. I thought that I could look for Jarkko, because he should be there also because he was also dead *(Jarkko is my classmate from years ago and in real life he is still alive)*. I found Jarkko, but his outlook was quite different from Jarkko's appearance in real life.

This dream displays lots of bizarre elements related to the people observed in the dream (Revonsuo & Tarkko, 2002). The identity and outlook of familiar persons in this dream are unclear or misrepresented, and the dreamer is very confused about who is alive and who is dead, although in real life we surely do remember such facts about the people close to us.

13.5 Why do we dream?

The most popular modern theories of dreaming include: the idea that dreaming has no function whatsoever – dreaming is only a useless side-effect of neuronal activations that take place in the dreaming brain for purely biological reasons (random activation theory); the idea that dreaming solves problems (problem-solving theory) or is like psychotherapy, trying to make us feel better about the negative things in our lives (mental health theory); and the idea that dreaming is a simulation of the world to let us practice certain things in a safe place, especially dangerous and threatening situations that are too risky to practice in the real world (threat simulation theory).

The random activation theory would have to show that dreams are purely random as to their content, but this does not seem to be the case; instead, dreams are organized sequences of conscious experience that mimic perception and action in the real world. Sometimes dreams present a complex storyline that evolves like a good action movie or adventure. Such complex, organized experiences could not be the products of just random activation of the brain.

The problem-solving theory would have to show that in our dreams we often actually find solutions to unsolved issues, but this does not seem to be the case either. Only very rarely does it happen that a dream comes up with a workable solution to a problem that we did not know how to solve. There are some well-known anecdotes about scientists coming up with new theoretical ideas in dreams, or composers hearing new music in their dreams, which seems to support the problem-solving theory. Even if the anecdotes are accurate, occasions of major problem solving in dreams happen so very rarely that it can hardly be considered as the function of dreaming.

The mental health theory would have to show that dreaming really helps to get rid of unpleasant memories and experiences, like real psychotherapy does. Dreams certainly *could* help us forget about our problems and difficulties; they *could* take us into pleasant, even ecstatic worlds of joy and happiness when the real world has become too frightening or overly depressing. Unfortunately that does not seem to be the case. Instead of comforting us, dreams much more often repeat or exaggerate our traumatic experiences and fears in nightmares and bad dreams. In harmony with this, also the results from sleep-related memory research have shown that, during sleep, emotionally negative memories are selectively *strengthened* by the brain rather than toned down! The theoretical idea that explains this observation says that sleep consolidates memories, especially those memories that are the most important for the person and his or her survival. Emotional memories are emotional just because they signify events that make a difference for us.

The threat simulation theory (Revonsuo, 2000) says that dreaming activates emotional memories and simulates threatening situations to give us training for future threats. Threat simulation was supposed to be especially valuable for our ancestors, who, during human evolution, lived in an environment full of threats to survival. Those ancestors with an efficient threat simulation system were more likely to survive the real threats, and thus dreaming got gradually selected for its function as a threat simulator. The evidence from dreams shows that they actually do contain many threatening events (chases, escapes, attacks, failures in risky or important tasks or repeated attempts to perform, accidents, being trapped or lost, falling, losing valuables), and that the threats are targeted at the dream-self and his or her close ones (Valli & Revonsuo, 2009). Furthermore, the number of threats, bad dreams and nightmares increase if a person lives in a threatening environment or is emotionally stressed. However, there is no direct evidence so far that dreaming about threatening events actually leads to better performance in a similar task during wakefulness.

13.6 Lucid dreaming

Reflective consciousness involves the ability to focus on some particular aspect of the content of consciousness and think about it, evaluate it or pass a judgement over it (see Chapter 3). During dreaming our ability to critically reflect upon the events we witness is diminished, but not completely wiped out. In a fair proportion of dreams we do wonder at least a little bit about some of the bizarre oddities we witness there. However, we are quick to dismiss and forget about them, even if they are things that we would be totally flabbergasted about in real life and surely would not immediately forget or take for granted. Although we do not realize that the overall dream event itself is impossible or improbable compared to waking life, we act and think in the situation (rather than about the situation) in the same way as we would if we were awake. We just accept the situation as a fact, and in our reflective consciousness we try to think ahead about what to do now that the gorilla *is* in the house where I seem to be living, although it does not look like my real home and although my dead grandfather is there with me. We fail to question the credibility of the scene as a whole.

Although difficult, we sometimes manage to question the credibility of dream events, so much so that we realize that this cannot really be happening! The defining feature of lucidity is the cognitive realization or reflective consciousness of the fact that "this is a dream". When this realization takes place, the dream changes from an ordinary one to a lucid dream, and lucidity lasts as long as the dreamer is aware of the fact that he or she is dreaming. Lucidity is like an awakening within the dream. It is to possess the revelatory knowledge that the whole world around me right now is unreal or hallucinatory and none of the objects or persons around me really exist, they are mere inventions of my dreaming mind. Once lucidity ensues, the dreamer can deliberately pay attention to features of the dreamworld, make deliberate plans of action and carry them out within the dream, or explicitly recall the facts of waking life from long-term memory. Lucid dreamers have experimented, for example, with flying in the dreamworld, walking through walls and even interviewing the dream-people they meet, asking them a few tricky questions to figure out how intelligent and logical they are!

Frederick van Eeden was an early dream researcher who experimented with lucid dreaming. When he was dreaming lucidly, he was totally aware of his condition and decided to perform various experiments, just out of curiosity, to see what would happen. Some of his experiments are perfect demonstrations of the differentiation of the phenomenal body image from the physical body:

> In the night of January 19–20 [1898], I dreamt that I was lying in the garden before the windows of my study and saw the eyes of my dog through the glass. I was lying on my chest and observing the dog very keenly. At the same time, however, I knew with perfect certainty that I was dreaming and lying on my back in my bed. And then I resolved to wake up slowly and carefully and observe how my sensation of lying on my chest would change into the sensation of lying on my back. And so I did, slowly and deliberately, and the transition – which I have since undergone many times – is most wonderful. It is like the feeling of slipping from one body into another, and there is distinctly a double recollection of the two bodies ... This observation of a double memory I have had many times since. It is so indubitable that it leads almost unavoidably to the conception of a dream-body ... In a lucid dream the sensation of having a body – having eyes, hands, a mouth that speaks, and so on – is perfectly distinct; yet I know at the same time that the physical body is sleeping

247

and has quite a different position. In waking up the two sensations blend together, so to speak.

(van Eeden, 1913/1990, pp. 181–182)

The ability to carry out deliberate and even preplanned actions during lucidity was the key to the groundbreaking laboratory studies in the 1980s in which it was shown that lucidity actually occurs during continuous REM sleep. Highly trained lucid dreamers are able to give preplanned eye-movement signals in the dream when lucid. The eye-movement recordings show that the objective signs of lucidity appear in the eye-movement recordings at the same time as the EEG shows uninterrupted REM sleep. No disruption of sleep nor any brief awakening is involved in lucidity. Before the objective measurements produced the unquestionable evidence, most sleep researchers had believed lucidity to happen during brief moments of wakefulness and thus not be a genuine phenomenon of sleep at all.

Although many people may have been briefly lucid during dreaming, for most people lucidity happens only very rarely, if ever. In dream samples, lucidity occurs on average only in a couple of dream reports out of a hundred. Only about 20% of people report having lucid dreams at least once per month. However, lucidity is a skill that can be learned and through training the probability of becoming lucid can be increased significantly. The training methods include, for example, asking yourself constantly during the day "Am I dreaming now?" and reminding yourself just before going to sleep that "Tonight when I am dreaming I will recognize that it is a dream". In general, writing down your dreams and paying much attention to what goes on in them will increase the likelihood of lucidity, because then you are more likely to recognize also during dreaming some things that you know only ever happen in your dreams, never in real life.

13.7 Bad dreams and nightmares

Lucid dreaming is typically a pleasant, even ecstatic experience. Unfortunately there are also extremely unpleasant dreams. Bad dreams are disturbing dreams that do not awaken the dreamer, whereas nightmares are disturbing dreams that wake the dreamer up. Nightmares are long, intense, vivid dreams that depict extremely frightening content, such as threats to the survival, security or self-esteem of the dreamer. When the dreamer is woken up by a nightmare, he or she becomes quickly aware of reality, remembers the dream that awoke him or her but may remain emotionally aroused or upset so that going back to sleep can be difficult, at least immediately. Nightmares and bad dreams are thus just a variety of dreaming, characterized by a strong negative emotional charge. On average, people report bad dreams and nightmares a couple of times per month, but some people have them almost every night. If nightmares are frequent and distressing, disturb normal sleep patterns and regularly lead to loss of sleep, the condition is diagnosed as a clinical sleep disorder.

Why do we have bad dreams and nightmares, and why are they so common? In fact in our dreams negative emotions and events in general tend to be much more common than positive ones. Lucidity – a highly enjoyable form of dreaming – is extremely rare compared to highly unpleasant forms of dreaming. According to the *threat simulation theory* our dreaming brain simulates threatening events to rehearse our survival skills and to make us more prepared to handle such adversities efficiently in real life. This function is supposed to be selected for during the evolution of our species, and also be present in other mammals. That is why many of our most potent nightmares depict rather primitive threats, such as chases and aggressive attacks by monsters, wild animals, or evil guys; or powerful natural forces such as storms, floods, or tidal waves.

13.8 Night terrors

Strongly negative emotional charge is common in some other sleep states as well. In a night terror attack the sleeping person suddenly screams loudly, gets up and looks terrified, but is not fully aware of reality and may be difficult to calm down or communicate with. Night terror is an ASC where some features of deep NREM sleep are mixed with wakefulness. Night terror does not involve genuine dreaming at all, but it may involve some kind of hypnopompic hallucinations, usually frightening imagery of malevolent beings or strangers in the bedroom, dangerous animals or monsters in the bed, such as spiders or snakes, or delusions about burglars or intruders in the house. Familiar people and surroundings may be misperceived as dangerous enemies, and violent escape or defence behaviours may be carried out. The episode dissolves either when the subject goes back to sleep or awakens fully. In any case, the subject may have only fragmentary recall of the event afterwards. Night terrors are more common in children, but they also occur in adults. If the sleeper tends to make dangerous escapes from the house, or punch and kick the nearby bedfellows, night terrors may require medical treatment by a sleep specialist. One patient, for example, once ran with full force against a closed window on the second floor, jumped right through it and landed on the ground in front of his house! Fortunately, the condition responds well to certain drugs and can be easily treated if needed.

13.9 Sleepwalking and nocturnal wandering

Sleepwalking and nocturnal wandering involve complex behaviours and locomotion in an altered state of consciousness where the subject is partially aware of or register-ing the environment (eyes are typically open) but unable to realize that he or she is asleep and pursuing goals that are unreal. Typical sleepwalking consists of routine behaviours such as opening and closing doors or windows, dressing or undressing, or walking around in the house as if checking that everything is all right. Nocturnal wandering involves prolonged episodes of sleepwalking where the subject may leave the house or even take the car and drive it for several minutes before waking up.

Night terrors, sleepwalking and nocturnal wandering are closely related ASCs where the deepest stages of NREM sleep are mixed with partial arousal and complex behaviours. They are all likely to occur early in the night when NREM sleep reaches its deepest stages. The subject usually does not remember the episodes at all or remembers them only very poorly. Although the subject is partially aware of the surroundings during the episode, the delusions and hallucinations as well as the lack of critical reflection may induce behaviours that are risky or may lead the subject to dangerous situations. If the subject can be calmed down and led back to bed, he or she immediately falls back to deep sleep. If awakened instead, the subject may be disoriented and confused.

However, it is only a myth that waking up the sleepwalker would be dangerous. The myth probably originates in the traditional folk-beliefs that the soul departs the body during sleep and returns at the time of awakening. According to this idea, it is the soulless body that is wandering around, and if suddenly awakened the soul may not find the body or have time to return to it, which, if true, would understandably lead to serious problems: the body would have become a mere soulless zombie!

13.10 REM sleep behaviour disorder and dreamwalking

NREM sleep allows complex behaviours to occur in the body if only sufficient motor activation takes place in the brain. REM sleep, by contrast, involves a "paralysing" mechanism in the brainstem that *actively stops all the motor commands from the cortex to the muscles*. In fact, muscle atonia or the loss of muscle tone (total relaxation or virtual paralysis of voluntary muscles) is one of the physiological hallmarks of REM sleep. But what happens if the paralysis mechanism malfunctions? During REM sleep and dreaming, the motor cortex is highly active. The bodily movements we only dream about doing actually generate patterns of activity in the motor cortex, identical with the patterns of activity that occur when we perform the same movements for real. Thus, unless the motor commands during REM sleep are rigorously extinguished before they reach the muscles, they will lead to potentially harmful motor activities.

The pathological condition where this happens is known as *REM sleep behaviour disorder*, or RBD. Patients suffering from this disorder have violent, action-filled nightmares and their bodies react to the dreamed behaviours as if they were for real. Thus, the patients move around in their beds, they throw punches or kick around, or jump out of bed and collide violently with the bedroom furniture. This condition is totally different from sleepwalking and should properly be called *"dreamwalking"* instead. The patients often injure themselves and sometimes their spouses as well. Most of the patients are elderly males, and they have an increased risk of developing Parkinson's disease later on. As a conscious experience for the subject, RBD is no different from other types of frequent, intense nightmares. The only exception is that while dreaming the patients suffer actual physical injuries to their bodies, such as bruises or even bone fractures. But phenomenologically, the RBD patient is simply in the midst of a frightening, life-threatening situation, does not realize it is a dream and thus tries to survive as best he can, by escape or defence. Suddenly he wakes up on the floor as he collides with objects of the real world. The patient does not know how he ended up there on the floor or how he got all the bruises and other injuries – if anything, he only remembers what was going on in the nightmare.

Chapter summary

The history of dream research parallels the history of consciousness science: A promising start during the introspectionist era, then the Dark Ages in the grips of behaviourism and psychoanalysis, followed by two strictly separate research programmes: the cognitive and the neurophysiological. Finally, the study of dream consciousness has recently become a natural part of modern consciousness science and cognitive neuroscience, where evidence from all sources, both subjective phenomenological and objective neural and behavioural, are combined into one.

Sleep and dreaming are a treasury of altered states of consciousness. During sleep, the brain internally generates patterns of experience. During dreaming these patterns simulate a whole world with colours, sensations, objects and people. Although the dream world also contains many bizarre features, we do not realize that it is a dream: our reflective consciousness and self-awareness are diminished. In lucid dreaming the realization that "this is a dream" does take place, but lucidity is a relatively rare phenomenon. The internal images may also become mixed with externally generated perception, as in hypnagogic and hypnopompic hallucinations, or they may guide external behaviour, as in sleepwalking and in REM sleep behaviour disorder or dreamwalking.

It is still unclear how and why the brain produces complex internal experiences during sleep. Functional brain imaging has shown that during dreaming visual (occipitotemporal), emotional (amygdala) and motor areas (frontal cortex) are active in the cortex, whereas the areas concerned with critical thinking and self-awareness (in the prefrontal cortex) are deactivated. The patterns of brain activation are exactly what we should expect, considering the typical content of dreams. The leading theories about the function of dreaming can be divided into four categories: (1) dreams have no function – they do nothing useful at all for us; (2) dreams solve problems for us; (3) dreams are our internal psychotherapists and they help us cope with difficulties and they make us feel better; (4) dreams were selected for during evolution to force us through training sessions, especially ones where potential dangers and threats are simulated, so that we will be better prepared to survive such events in wakefulness.

Further reading

Barrett, D., & McNamara, P. (Eds.) (2007). *The new science of dreaming* (Vols. 1–3). Westport, CT: Praeger.

Cheyne, J. A., Rueffer, S. D., & Newby-Clark, I. R. (1999). Hypnagogic and hypnopompic hallucinations during sleep paralysis: Neurological and cultural construction of the nightmare. *Consciousness and Cognition, 8*, 319–337.

Domhoff, G. W. (1996). *Finding meaning in dreams: A quantitative approach.* New York: Plenum Press.

Farthing, W. G. (1992). *The psychology of consciousness.* New York: Prentice-Hall.

Foulkes, D. (1985). *Dreaming: A cognitive-psychological analysis.* Hillsdale, NJ: Lawrence Erlbaum Associates, Inc.

Green, C., & McCreery, C. (1994). *Lucid dreaming: The paradox of consciousness during sleep.* London: Routledge.

Hall, C. S., & Van de Castle, R. L. (1966). *The content analysis of dreams.* New York: Appleton-Century-Crofts.

Hobson, J. A. (1988). *The dreaming brain.* New York: Basic Books.

Hobson, J. A. (1997) Dreaming as delirium: A mental status exam of our nightly madness. *Seminars in Neurology, 17*, 121–128.

Hobson, J. A. (2001). *The dream drugstore: Chemically altered states of consciousness*. Cambridge, MA: MIT Press.

LaBerge, S. (1985). *Lucid dreaming*. New York: Ballantine.

Mahowald, M. W., & Schenck, C. H. (1992). Dissociated states of wakefulness and sleep. *Neurology, 42*, 44–52.

Mavromatis, A. (1987). *Hypnagogia: The unique state of consciousness between wakefulness and sleep*. London: Routledge.

Rechtschaffen, A., & Buchignani, C. (1992) The visual appearance of dreams. In J. S. Antrobus & M. Bertini (Eds.), *The neuropsychology of sleep and dreaming* (pp. 143–155). Hillsdale, NJ: Lawrence Erlbaum Associates, Inc.

Revonsuo, A. (2000). The reinterpretation of dreams: An evolutionary hypothesis of the function of dreaming. *Behavioral and Brain Sciences, 23*, 877–901.

Revonsuo, A. (2005). The self in dreams. In T. E. Feinberg & J. P. Keenan (Eds.), *The lost self: Pathologies of the brain and mind* (pp. 206–219). New York: Oxford University Press.

Schwartz, S. (2000). A historical loop of one hundred years: Similarities between 19th century and contemporary dream research. *Dreaming, 10*, 55–66.

Strauch, I., & Meier, B. (1996). *In search of dreams: Results of experimental dream research*. New York: SUNY Press.

Uga, V., Lemut, M. C., Zampi, C., Zilli, I., & Salzarulo, P. (2006). Music in dreams. *Consciousness and Cognition, 15*, 351–357.

Valli, K., & Revonsuo, A. (2009). The threat simulation theory in light of recent empirical evidence: A review. *American Journal of Psychology, 122*, 17–38.

van Eeden, F. (1990). A study of dreams. Reprinted in C. T. Tart (Ed.), *Altered states of consciousness* (pp. 175–190). New York: HarperCollins. (Original work published 1913.)

Brief discussion questions

1   What are the earliest dreams you remember having as a child? What kind of dreams often recur in your dream life? Compare your own dreams with others in the classroom and with the results mentioned in the text.

2   Which theory of the function of dreaming is able to explain the evidence we have about dreaming, if any?

3   Do you think that ghosts, UFO abductions and other paranormal experiences that happen during the night, when people are in their beds, could actually be explained by altered states of consciousness, such as hypnagogic hallucinations and sleep paralysis, that are not recognized as such?

Chapter 14

Hypnosis

Introduction

Hypnosis is of great interest to consciousness science, because it involves – sometimes drastic – alterations in subjective experience. Thus, it is at least potentially an altered state of consciousness – but this question is exactly what hypnosis researchers fervently disagree about.

To make matters worse, the term "hypnosis" is full of controversy and definitional difficulties. Originally and literally, "hypnosis" refers to "sleep", but in the present context this is a misnomer: Whatever the state of hypnosis is, it is not a state of sleep. To add confusion to the terminology, the word "hypnosis" has another usage in anaesthesiology, where it refers to the loss of consciousness that occurs when anaesthesiologists put a patient into artificial drug-induced "sleep". But in the present context, hypnosis does not refer to sleep nor to anaesthesia.

A hypnotic situation includes two elements that should be clearly distinguished from each other (Barnier & Nash, 2008). First, there is "hypnosis-as-procedure", the event in which two people, the subject and the hypnotist, communicate about what is going to happen. The hypnotist tells the subject that he is going to suggest that changes in the ways the subject thinks and feels will happen and, if the subject is fine with that, then the hypnotist will proceed to give such suggestions. At that point we may say that the subject has been "hypnotized", at least in the minimal sense that the hypnosis-as-procedure has occurred. But this by no means guarantees that hypnosis in the second sense, called "hypnosis-as-product" or simply the *hypnotic state*, has or will occur. In addition, the subject must be motivated and willing to experience the suggested changes and should expect such changes to occur. A reluctant and unmotivated subject will not experience any alterations in consciousness. Furthermore, the subject must possess at least some degree of the somewhat mysterious characteristic called "hypnotizability".

Hypnotic alterations in consciousness thus require a willing, motivated and hypnotizable subject who first undergoes the hypnotic induction or hypnosis-as-procedure. A hypnotic alteration in consciousness is all about subjective experience – as Kihlström (2008, p. 32) says: "Subjective experience is at the heart of hypnosis". By this he means that it is not the external behaviour of the hypnotized subject that is interesting as such (that the subject behaviorally does or says peculiar things), but the fact that the behaviours are *driven by altered subjective experiences*! The subject reacts to conscious experiences that have been triggered by the hypnotic suggestions:

> It is not interesting that a hypnotized subject will lower his outstretched arm when told that it is becoming heavy. What is interesting is that the arm actually begins to *feel* heavy. It is the subject's conviction that the suggested event is really happening that distinguishes a genuine hypnotic experience from overt behavioural compliance.
>
> (Kihlström, 2008, p. 32)

What makes the alteration of subjective experience even more intriguing is that it happens without any voluntary effort. This distinguishes hypnotic experiences from ordinary mental imagery, where we effortfully and voluntarily try to make ourselves feel or see something in our imagination.

[A]nother element in the subjective experience of hypnosis is the experience of involuntariness in response to hypnotic suggestions. The outstretched arm does not just feel heavy: it appears to become heavier all by itself, without the subject deliberately constructing the image. The experience of involuntariness is part and parcel of subjective conviction: one cannot believe that one's arm has become light, being pulled up by helium balloons, if one is deliberately imagining that it is so, or voluntarily raising the limb.

(Kihlström, 2008, p. 33)

Clearly, something very interesting is going on here, something that falls exactly within the scope of the science of subjective experience. But what, and how can we explain it? We will return to that question, but let us first take a brief tour of the colourful history of hypnosis.

14.1 Brief history of hypnosis

Originally, hypnosis was called "mesmerism", referring to Franz Anton Mesmer (1734–1815), an Austrian medical doctor. When he treated his patients with magnets, he discovered a phenomenon that he started to call "animal magnetism". He noticed that when he touched his patients (most of whom were suffering from various mental or psychosomatic symptoms) in particular ways and patterns, the patients went into a peculiar state after which they felt significantly better. Mesmer first used real magnets with which he touched and caressed the patients in certain ways. He believed that the magnets acted as a balancing force against the imbalances in the body caused by the gravitational forces of the celestial bodies. Soon Mesmer discovered that the same effects could be achieved by simply using hands; no magnets were necessary. From this he concluded that there is a special form of magnetism in himself – animal magnetism – that acts in a manner similar to real magnets. Consequently, he developed and published his theory of animal magnetism and connected it, very speculatively, with Newtonian physics and astronomy – or what he understood of it.

Later Mesmer moved to Paris, where animal magnetism became very popular. He gave treatments to groups of people gathered in special rooms that were magnetized. To deliver an extra dose of magnetism to each patient separately, he walked among the patients, touched them, looked them in the eyes or pointed at them with his wand. As a result, many patients experienced an altered state of consciousness.

A commission led by Benjamin Franklin was set to investigate whether animal magnetism really exists and whether it is useful. In what we could now regard as the first controlled scientific experiments on hypnosis, the commission however found no objective evidence that animal magnetism, as a real physical force, exists. All the effects were due to ordinary touch, imagination and expectations of what should happen. (Animal magnetism, a force of nature believed to have effects on human bodies and minds, was thus eliminated from science, in the manner discussed in the context of eliminative materialism in Chapter 1.)

The early history of hypnotism set the stage for two entirely different, competing interpretations of what is going on during hypnosis. Although nobody anymore believes in Mesmer's animal magnetism, the explanation of hypnosis is still almost equally as controversial as it was in Mesmer's times. Now the controversy is about whether there is an ASC involved in hypnosis or not.

In our times, the popular image of hypnosis depicts it as an ASC where the hypnotist has some mysterious, extraordinary mental powers not unlike the special animal magnetism possessed by Mesmer. By using these powers, the hypnotist forces the hypnotized person to fall into a zombie-like state reminiscent of sleepwalking (or "somnambulism", an old term that was used to describe the hypnotic state in the 1800s). The hypnotized person has glazed eyes, his or her own will has been wiped out and she or he follows any and all commands given by the hypnotist, no matter how ridiculous.

If hypnosis is not animal magnetism or magical mental powers of the hypnotist over the hypnotized, then what is it? And, most importantly, does hypnosis involve an ASC? Modern hypnosis research may finally be able to give us an answer.

14.2 Hypnotic induction

Hypnosis occurs in a situation where a hypnotist gives first a hypnotic induction to a subject ("hypnosis-as-procedure"). Typically, the hypnotist tells the subject to intensely focus on something (such as the hypnotist's voice, his finger or a light), relax and let one's eyes close slowly, as the hypnotist counts from one to ten. After the induction to hypnosis, the hypnotist gives more specific suggestions about specific changes in experience for the subject.

The standard suggestions typically concern changes in how the subject feels his or her own body or actions (*ideomotor suggestion*):

> Stretch out your arms in front of you. Now imagine that in the left arm you hold tight the handle of a big, heavy bag full of stones, trying with all your strength to support the bag in the air, and in the right you hold the string of a huge helium balloon that pulls your arm strongly upwards. Your left arm feels terribly heavy and tired, the weight irresistibly pulling it downwards, whereas your right arm feels light as a feather, floating upwards all by itself.

As a result of this ideomotor suggestion, one arm is expected to move downwards, and the other upwards.

In a *challenge suggestion*, the subject is asked to try to do something quite easy that he or she will fail to do because of an earlier suggestion that prevents exactly that kind of action: "Close your eyes. Now, even if you try, you cannot open your eyes, the eyelids feel like glued together. Now try to open them."

The third type of suggestions are called *cognitive suggestions*. Changes in sensation, perception, memory or thinking are suggested to occur: "If you listen carefully, you will hear somebody playing 'Für Elise' with the piano in the next room" or "You cannot remember your own telephone number even if you try".

If the suggestions induce truly altered experiences for the subject (as opposed to mere compliance, faking or role-playing), the suggested experiences should come about effortlessly, involuntarily and with an almost delusional subjective conviction that the described events are really happening.

14.3 Hypnotic suggestibility

The standardized scales of hypnotic suggestibility go through a set of different types of suggestions (similar to the above three types) and, after the session, the subject evaluates whether he or she had the suggested experiences or not. The total score reveals the hypnotizability of the subject. Different people respond very differently to hypnotic inductions and suggestions. Some experience almost nothing at all (these people are called "low-hypnotizable"), no matter what the hypnotist tries, whereas others report that they really experienced all the things that the hypnotist suggested to them (the "high-hypnotizable"). Most people are somewhere in the middle of these two extremes.

14.4 Is hypnosis an ASC?

Among hypnosis researchers, there is a long-lasting controversy over whether hypnosis involves an ASC or is just a peculiar social situation where subjects behave according to their expectations and play along with the rules of the "game" (just like in any other social situation) but do not enter any kind of ASC in the process. The former views are called the "state" theories of hypnosis and the latter are called the "nonstate" theories of hypnosis.

This "state–nonstate" controversy has been difficult to resolve empirically as there have been no universally accepted definitions or measurable criteria for what would count as an ASC. What could be counted as a decisive sign or undeniable evidence that an ASC is present in a hypnotized person? The most obvious criterion is to hold the altered experiences themselves as the hallmarks of an ASC. Following this criterion alone, the conclusion that hypnosis reflects an altered state of consciousness seems unavoidable, because hypnosis alters both the subjective experience related to our awareness of the surrounding world (what is out there and what is not) and the voluntary control over ourselves, our actions, our thoughts, beliefs and memories. These can be called the *monitoring function* and the *controlling function* of consciousness, and hypnosis arguably alters both of them:

> Hypnotized subjects see things that are not there, and fail to see things that are there; they fail to remember things that they just experienced, and they remember things that didn't happen; they cannot control their bodily movements, and they execute post-hypnotic suggestions without knowing why they are doing so ... [T]he only way to deny that the phenomena of hypnosis reflect alterations in consciousness would be to deny that the phenomena themselves are genuine.
>
> (Kihlström, 2008, pp. 35–36)

One additional source of evidence that may be of help in settling the disagreement over the ASC of hypnosis comes from neuroscientific studies of hypnosis. Recently, functional brain imaging studies have shown that hypnotic hallucinations are correlated with changes in brain activity. For example, when the suggestion implies that a greyscale stimulus that is shown is actually coloured, the highly hypnotizable subjects report actually *seeing* the colours. Furthermore, at the same time, the

257

cortical areas in the brain involved with colour vision have been found to be highly active, as they would be if activated by a colourful stimulus (Kosslyn, Thompson, Costantini-Ferrando, Alpert, & Spiegel, 2000)! Thus, the subject's report seems to be confirmed as genuine by such objective evidence, and the colour experience seems to be "real" for the subject in the sense that the brain is activated in the same way as if by an actually coloured stimulus. However, similar changes were also observed when nonhypnotized control subjects simply imagined that the grey stimuli were coloured – thus, the changes were not unique to hypnosis nor objectively different from voluntary imagery.

But would the ability to hallucinate colours under hypnosis count as an ASC? This kind of hallucinatory state at least fulfils the definition of ASC that we outlined above: Temporarily, the relationship between the world and consciousness has changed so that consciousness represents something that is not there. And if the highly hypnotizable persons can hallucinate colour under hypnosis, who knows what *else* they would see or believe if given the corresponding suggestions! Surely the potential effects of hypnosis are not restricted to colour perception but are more widespread, perhaps so much so that hypnosis would fulfil the definition of a globally misrepresentational state: potentially, almost *anything* could be seen or believed in this state if the corresponding suggestions are issued.

Hypnotic suggestibility (the tendency to experience the suggested changes) is normally distributed in the population. Most people are moderately suggestible, responding to some relatively simple ideomotor suggestions, such as feeling one arm become heavier than the other one. A small proportion of people are not suggestible at all: they feel no changes whatsoever in experience, no matter what kind of suggestion they are given. An equally small proportion are highly suggestible and feel many kinds of changes in experience if such changes are suggested to them under hypnosis.

One possibility to solve the question "Does hypnosis involve an ASC?" is to say that the right answer is "both yes and no". Perhaps only a tiny proportion of highly hypnotizable subjects truly enter an ASC after getting the hypnotic induction. These extraordinarily hypnotizable people, also called "hypnotic virtuosos", do experience genuine and vivid hallucinations, amnesia and other drastic, completely involuntary changes in their conscious experience in response to hypnotic suggestions. They may also totally forget what happened during the hypnosis session or have an altered sense of time, thinking that they were under hypnosis only for a few minutes when in fact an hour has passed.

According to this idea, what happens in hypnosis for most people, especially the low and moderately hypnotizable ones, does not involve any ASC. Whatever they experience only involves ordinary mental imagery, coupled with strong expectations of what "should" happen when the hypnotist gives them a suggestion. They just play voluntarily along with the hypnotists' suggestions and with their own mental images. Only the rare hypnotic virtuoso enters an almost sleep-like or dream-like altered state of consciousness where the hallucinatory experiences, delusions and amnesia go clearly beyond what mere voluntary imagination could provide (Kallio & Revonsuo, 2003). If this view is on the right track, then we should find that only in hypnotic virtuosos is something quite extraordinary going on in the brain when they are hypnotized, and the hypnotic ASC should thus also show itself as an altered brain state. By contrast, in less hypnotizable people no altered brain state would be found. Some evidence already exists that backs up this idea, but much more is needed before we can treat it as an established fact.

14.5 What happens to consciousness under hypnosis?

Granted that something peculiar happens to at least some people in the hypnotic state, how could we theoretically describe and explain what is going on? Ideas that have been put forward to explain the alterations in consciousness observed in hypnosis have described the hypnotic state in terms of *divided consciousness* or in terms of *dissociation* of mental processes from consciousness (Hilgard, 1977; Woody & Bowers, 1994). Dissociation theories of hypnosis include the idea that the alterations in perceptual and sensory experience, voluntary action and memory take place because the relevant information becomes dissociated from consciousness and guides behaviour via routes that bypass consciousness. For example, the experience of involuntariness and automaticity with which hypnotic responding takes place is explained by a dissociation of the highest cognitive control system from conscious experience. For the hypnotized subject, his own body or memory seems out of control: he cannot move his limbs or open his eyes or remember his own name by will, no matter how hard he tries. Or his limbs seem to move by themselves or seem to be paralysed or stiff, directly realizing the suggested experiences.

According to the dissociation theories, at some deeper level bypassing consciousness, the subject is himself actively and voluntarily carrying out (or stopping himself from carrying out) all the suggested actions. In Hilgard's "neodissociation" theory of hypnosis (Hilgard, 1977), an entire dissociated subject separate from the hypnotized subject and called the "hidden observer" is postulated. This somewhat mysterious entity is supposed to be somehow aware of the real state of affairs all the time, and even able to communicate his awareness, in a manner resembling the hidden multiple personalities in psychiatric disorders. However, there is only very scarce and anecdotal evidence that any such intelligent but unconscious agent as the "hidden observer" would really exist and underlie hypnotic responding.

The dissociated control functions that cause loss of voluntary control would have to involve top-down attentional mechanisms and working memory. The neural mechanisms participating in voluntary selection and execution of goal-directed actions are located in the prefrontal cortices. Hence, the dissociated control theories of hypnosis have led to the neuropsychological hypothesis that the hypnotized subject's prefrontal cortex is inhibited and therefore their behaviour resembles that of neuropsychological patients whose frontal lobe has been damaged (Woody & Bowers, 1994). And, at least superficially, highly hypnotized subjects may resemble patients with frontal-lobe damage in that they show a general paucity of spontaneous self-generated behaviour and execution of self-generated plans and a weakening of voluntary control while in the hypnotic state. If left on their own, both hypnotized subjects and patients with frontal-lobe damage seem indifferent and blank, without internally driven motivation or initiative. Still, the evidence from neuropsychological tests and from neuroimaging of hypnotized subjects has given only meagre support for the theory of frontal inhibition as an explanation of hypnosis.

A closer parallel may be drawn between hypnosis and another type of neuropsychological disorder, namely the dissociations between conscious and non-conscious processing of information that we explored earlier (in Chapter 5). We learned that conscious and nonconscious information about the same stimulus or sensory modality or cognitive process may become dissociated after brain injury, so that the nonconscious form still drives behaviour whereas the conscious form has disappeared. In some of these neuropsychological cases, the nonconscious information was still able to drive quite complex behaviour, such as accurate reaching and picking up of objects. However, the subjects felt fully in control of their voluntary actions, even if the actions proved to be more accurate and successful than they would have predicted based on their poor perceptual abilities. No illusion or dissociation of voluntary control was associated with the neuropsychological cases, which makes them unlike the hypnotic dissociations. Nevertheless, Kihlström (2008) suggests that the conceptual framework of dissociations between "implicit" (non-conscious) and "explicit" (conscious) processes is the way to go also in the explanation of hypnosis, and may connect hypnotic phenomena with the mainstream theories of dissociation:

> Dissociations between explicit and implicit memory, and between explicit and implicit perception are not a unique signature of hypnosis: they are also observed elsewhere, in a wide variety of normal and pathological conditions. But they do appear to be the signature of the kind of alteration in consciousness that occurs within the domain of hypnosis.
>
> (Kihlström, 2008, p. 38)

Chapter summary

Hypnosis involves a hypnotic induction ("hypnosis-as-procedure"), followed by specific suggestions about changes in the experience of sensation, perception and action. Low-hypnotizable persons do not experience anything special, whereas the highly hypnotizable may experience everything that was suggested to them as real, thus experiencing the hypnotic state (or "hypnosis-as-product").

The question whether hypnosis involves an ASC remains controversial. The changes in experiences due to suggestion may be due to strong expectations, mental imagery and playing along with the hypnotist. Increasing evidence, however, shows that at least some highly suggestible persons do experience drastic changes in their perception, sensation and cognition due to hypnotic suggestions, and that such changes are accompanied by objective changes in brain activity. Such studies give relatively strong evidence that at least some people reach an ASC in hypnosis, although we still do not understand what kind of altered state this is in terms of altered cognitive processes or changes in brain function. The concept of dissociation seems, however, to be helpful when theoretically modelling the ASC of hypnosis. The dissociations characteristic of hypnosis may, to some extent, resemble dissociations seen in some neuropsychological patients, for example those whose frontal lobe functions are impaired or those who show dissociations between explicit and implicit processing of information.

Further reading

Barnier, A. J., & Nash, M. R. (2008). Introduction: A roadmap for explanation, a working definition. In M. Nash & A. Barnier (Eds.), *The Oxford handbook of hypnosis* (pp. 1–18). New York: Oxford University Press.

Heap, M., & Kirsh, I. (Eds.) (2006). *Hypnosis: Theory, research and application*. Aldershot, Hants: Ashgate.

Hilgard, E. R. (1977). *Divided consciousness: Multiple controls in human thought and action*. New York: John Wiley & Sons.

Kallio, S., & Revonsuo, A. (2003). Hypnotic phenomena and altered states of consciousness: A multilevel framework of description and explanation. *Contemporary Hypnosis, 20*, 111–164.

Kihlström, J. F. (2008). The domain of hypnosis, revisited. In M. Nash & A. Barnier (Eds.), *The Oxford handbook of hypnosis* (pp. 21–52). New York: Oxford University Press.

Kosslyn, S. M., Thompson, W. L., Costantini-Ferrando, M. F., Alpert, N. M., & Spiegel, D. (2000). Hypnotic visual illusion alters colour processing in the brain. *American Journal of Psychiatry, 157*, 1279–1284.

Nash, M., & Barnier, A. (2008). *The Oxford handbook of hypnosis*. New York: Oxford University Press.

Woody, E. Z., & Bowers, K. S. (1994). A frontal assault on dissociated control. In S. J. Lynn & J. W. Rhue (Eds.), *Dissociation: Clinical and theoretical perspectives* (pp. 52–79). London: Guilford Press.

Brief discussion questions

1   Have you ever been hypnotized? What did it feel like? Discuss in the classroom the experiences of those students who have been hypnotized on a previous occasion.

2   Try in pairs the simple suggestion of heavy arm (bag full of stones) / light arm (big helium balloon), described in the text above. The subject's eyes should be closed the whole time, and both arms should be outstretched and at the same level before the suggestion is given. When the suggestion has been given in full, measure the difference between the "heavy" and the "light" arm, and let the hypnotized subject give a report on what he or she experienced.

3   Do you think that the hypnotized person is in an ASC, or is he or she only play-acting and imagining it all? What kind of brain-imaging experiment might solve this question for good – what kind of changes should we find in the brain to settle the issue that hypnosis is or is not an ASC?

Higher states of consciousness

Introduction

Higher states of consciousness are ASCs that are considered deeply meaningful, satisfying and desirable, but also difficult to reach or maintain. They go beyond the normal baseline state of consciousness in the sense that in them subjective experience reaches extreme attentional, emotional or cognitive levels. In higher states of consciousness our mind literally gets into a "high"!

Higher *attentional* states come in two opposite forms, one involving total absorption with the object in the narrow focus of attention (one-pointedness of mind) and the other involving widening of the scope of attention to simultaneously cover the entire sensory-perceptual field (full awareness or mindfulness). Higher attentional states are often characterized by the absence of reflective thoughts, especially negative ones, and a deep inner peace or calmness of mind.

Higher *emotional* states typically involve strong positive feelings of well-being, contentment, loving-kindness, compassion, joy, elation or bliss. The quality of inner emotional experience is thus characterized by the presence of intense positive affect and the absence of negative affect; that is, pure happiness.

Higher *cognitive* states involve feelings of deep understanding, sudden revelation or insight into the nature of things, glimpses of higher knowledge about the order of the universe or feelings of being directly connected to or absorbed into the cosmos or with higher spiritual realms or beings, such as God. In these states, one seems to get in touch with deeply meaningful information about the nature of reality or have direct knowledge of it. However, it is unclear whether such information or knowledge is actually possessed or is only a *feeling* of deep insight without any actual informational content. In any case this knowledge is often impossible to express precisely in words and it is easily lost when one returns to the ordinary state and level of consciousness. Even when not lost but recalled, it may lose its original significance and seem a trivial platitude when reconsidered in the normal state of consciousness.

The attentional, emotional and cognitive elements of higher states of consciousness may appear separately or in various combinations in different ASCs. Next, we will review some paradigm examples of higher states.

15.1 Meditation

Meditation as such is not a higher or altered state of consciousness, but rather a set of various techniques and practices that aim at controlling and altering consciousness. Thus, meditation may lead to an altered or a higher state, and sometimes this is the explicit goal of meditation. There are far too many radically different meditation techniques and traditions to cover in this context, thus only some of the most central principles and techniques can be mentioned here.

In one way or another, different meditation techniques involve the deliberate control or manipulation of attention. In *concentrative* meditation, the scope of attention is kept narrow and highly selective. Only a particular content of consciousness (an object, a mental image, a word or a sentence, a repetitive action such as breathing) is fixed into the focus of attention for prolonged durations, whereas everything else (all the distractions) is driven out of consciousness. In *mindfulness* meditation, by contrast, the scope of attention is widened to encompass all available sensations, percepts, emotions, bodily feelings, etc., to be vividly aware of all of them in as much detail and intensity as possible.

In Buddhist and Yoga literature, the term *samadhi* refers to a higher state of meditative consciousness in which perfect concentration is reached and where the distinction between the object of meditation and the subject who meditates totally disappears. This state is characterized by mental one-pointedness and a merging together of the object and the subject. According to some traditions, the systematic practice of meditation to reach *samadhi* states can lead to progressively higher mystical states of consciousness, such as *nirvana* or enlightenment (to be discussed below).

Some forms of meditation combine the attentional and the emotional components of higher states and deliberately focus on diminishing negative emotions (such as hate, fear or pessimism) or strengthening positive emotions (such as loving-kindness or compassion). Thus, meditative practice may lead to higher states of consciousness with intense positive emotional experiences. There is evidence from recent brain imaging and EEG studies that Buddhist monks who have practiced this type of meditation for decades actually do reach a state of consciousness unreachable by beginners or laymen, evidenced by the strong changes in brain activity that correlate with their meditative state. More precisely, the monks showed increased high-frequency power or 40 Hz EEG activity. The level of this activity was higher also at baseline, but rose even higher during the meditation. The difference between the monks and the control group (beginners in meditation) with regard to the level of this activity was huge: the beginners had hardly detectable levels of 40 Hz activity, no matter how hard they tried to meditate (Lutz, Greischar, Rawlings, Ricard, & Davidson, 2004).

15.2 Optimal experience and flow

Optimal experience is a higher emotional (and attentional) state of consciousness that characterizes the best moments of our lives: moments during or after which we feel deep enjoyment, exhilaration or happiness and forget about everything else. Empirical studies have revealed that people reach this kind of "flow" state of mind when there is a certain kind of order in consciousness: our attention is firmly focused on reaching a meaningful, challenging goal, we are intrinsically motivated to reach the goal for its own sake and our skills and resources are just sufficient to reach the goal. When we struggle towards such goals, we momentarily forget about everything else, including the sense of time and our own selves; we become fully immersed in the actions necessary to reach the goal.

In some ways, intense flow experiences are similar to meditative *samadhi* states where self-awareness disappears and experience becomes one with the focus of attention. Indeed, as in meditation, the control of attention plays a crucial role also in reaching flow:

> William James . . . once wrote, "My experience is what I agree to attend to." This is a revolutionary thought. What you notice and what you pay attention to *is* your experience; it *is* your life. There's only so much attention that you have to

go around, so how and where you choose to invest it is critical. To enter the state of flow, attention needs to be directed fully to the task at hand . . . Your aim is to gain control over what you pay attention to – in a sense, to gain control over the contents of your consciousness moment by moment. Controlling your consciousness means controlling the quality of your experience.

(Lyubomirsky, 2007, p. 184)

To reach the flow state, the skills that we have and the challenges we are faced with have to be in balance. Too high levels of challenge in relation to skills lead to anxiety and fear of failure; too low levels of challenge lead to indifference and boredom.

The sources of flow are different for every person. For some, flow takes place during physical activities such as rock climbing, windsurfing, skiing or playing badminton. For others, painting, singing, playing an instrument or performing in front of an audience may do the trick. Flow activities need not be anything out of the ordinary, though; you may reach it also when playing with your dog or children, having an engaging conversation with an interesting person, dancing at a club or hiking in beautiful countryside.

Unless we pay careful attention to our own experience, we might not be reflectively aware of what brings us flow and what does not. Many people experience flow in their work, because at work they have to use all their skills to meet interesting challenges. Still, most people say they prefer doing something else, say, lying passively in front of the TV, although studies also show that this type of pastime typically produces very low levels of flow and little happiness; it is more likely to produce boredom or depression because there are no challenges or skills involved.

The flow state itself may, however, in some cases have negative consequences, because if it occurs in connection with addictive behaviours such as computer game playing, netsurfing, gambling, and so on, a person may lose sense of time and self and neglect everything else in life to get back to the addictive flow state. If one cannot exert any voluntary control over one's own behaviour and simply cannot stop or choose to do anything else, but is uncontrollably drawn to an activity again and again, we are dealing with an addictive rather than a healthy form of flow.

By engaging in the healthy, nonaddictive forms of flow, we can improve the quality of our conscious experience and thus the quality of our subjective lives. Flow leads us to be involved in life rather than isolated or alienated; we enjoy what we are doing (rather than find it boring or burdensome); we have an increased sense of control and self-efficacy. The most intense flow experiences, called "superflow", border on becoming mystical experiences of absolute trancendence (Luybomirsky, 2007) and may thus be among the most significant positive moments of our subjective lives.

15.3 Runner's high

A higher state of consciousness that sometimes occurs during endurance running is known as runner's high. It has to some extent similar phenomenological features to flow and *samadhi* experiences. This is understandable because, like some forms of meditation, endurance running is associated with highly regular, long-lasting rhythmic patterns of action and breathing. And, like typical flow-producing activities, it is challenging but not anxiety-arousing and involves physical activity where awareness and action can become merged together. In runner's high, reflective or analytical thoughts disappear and subjective experience becomes immersed in the here and now. Intense feelings of pure happiness, timelessness, unity with nature, inner harmony, boundless energy and floating may emerge. At the same time, there is reduced awareness of one's surroundings and reduced sensitivity to bodily discomfort or pain. A similar state may emerge also in connection with other types of endurance training.

15.4 Out-of-body experiences (OBEs)

One of the fundamental philosophical assumptions in cognitive neuroscience is the principle that the existence of consciousness depends on the activities of the brain. Conversely, there can be no conscious experiences floating free of the brain, taking place outside of the brain or happening in the absence of corresponding brain activity.

These are profound philosophical background assumptions, and if they are true, no convincing empirical evidence should ever be found that is in disagreement with them. Out-of-body experiences, however, at first glance *seem* to challenge these assumptions. The phenomenology of OBEs strongly suggests that consciousness can float free of the brain and the body. Does this mean that OBEs are evidence for a dualistic theory of consciousness after all? Or is cognitive neuroscience able to explain what OBEs are without giving up its thoroughly materialistic philosophy? Let us look at the latest evidence and theories of OBEs for an answer.

An OBE is an experience where a person's centre of conscious experience, the point from which the world is being observed by the subject, occupies a visual perspective or a seemingly spatial location outside the same subject's physical body. The thinking, acting and perceiving subject or self seems to have left its physical body behind and may see its body from the outside, usually from above (see Figure 15.1). The subject has the strong impression that the perceptual environment seen in this state is identical with the actual environment, not a dream or a mental image. The subject may feel that although the physical body has been left behind, he or she still possesses some kind of ghostly body. In the old parapsychological literature this "other" body is known as the astral body. In some cases the subject has no clear body image at all, but constitutes a vague cloud or only a formless point-of-view.

In neurology and psychiatry, the experience of seeing oneself from the outside, from the third-person's perspective, is called *autoscopy*. Here is one typical description of such an experience connected with migraine:

> This sensation came just before a violent headache attack and at no other time. Very often it came as I was serving breakfast. There would be my husband and children, just as usual, and in a flash they didn't seem to be quite the same. I felt as if I were standing on an inclined plane, looking down on them from the height of a few feet, watching myself serving breakfast. It was as if I were in another dimension, looking at myself and them. I was not afraid, just amazed. I

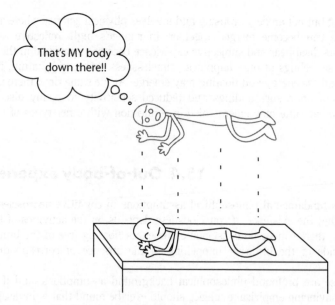

Figure 15.1 Out-of-body experience

In a typical OBE, the subject sees his or her own physical body lying on a bed, viewing it from a perspective floating somewhere above the bed

always knew that I was really with them. Yet, there was "I", and there was "me" – and in a moment I was one again.

(Lippman, 1953, p. 346, quoted in Blackmore, 1992, p. 160)

An autoscopic hallucination does not necessarily fulfil all of the defining features of an OBE, though. The OBE has been formally defined as the presence of the following three phenomenological features (Blanke & Dieguez, 2009):

1 Disembodiment, or the feeling of being outside of one's physical body.
2 Dislocated perspective, or the perceived location of the self at a distanced and elevated visuospatial perspective.
3 Autoscopy, or the experience of seeing one's own body from the elevated perspective.

It is difficult to estimate precisely how common OBEs are, because different studies have used different methods and definitions. A cautious estimation is that 5–10% of the general population have experienced an OBE (Blanke & Dieguez, 2009).

In most cases, OBEs occur when the person is lying down but apparently in the waking state rather than sleeping. OBEs may occur at any time and under any circumstances, however: during intense physical and mental activity, and sometimes in response to life-threatening situations as part of a more complex near-death experience (see below). An OBE is usually brief, lasting for a few seconds or minutes only.

OBEs often have features that are similar to other higher and mystical states of consciousness. The subject may have the impression of being able to see distant events or to travel at will to any place. A sense of freedom and control reminiscent of lucid dreaming may occur, as well as feelings of exhilaration or elation, resembling mystical experiences.

People typically interpret OBEs as evidence that something purely mental – a spirit or a soul – actually *does* leave the body during the experience. Some anecdotal evidence exists that supports this view, but it seems to be mostly indirect hearsay rather than well-documented empirical data. There is no solid objective evidence that anyone would ever really have been out of their physical bodies and brought back incontestable evidence about their spiritual voyages. Experiments where the OBE subject's task has been to retrieve some otherwise unaccessible information from the world (e.g. a number written on a piece of paper and placed out of ordinary sight) while out of the body have not produced any convincing results.

Cognitive and neuropsychological theories try to explain OBEs by referring to hallucinatory dissociations between visual perspective and body image. In recent studies, OBEs (and other similar distortions of body image in relation to visuospatial perspective) have been correlated with neurological pathology. OBE-like experiences have been reported by patients who have neurological abnormalities, in particular cortical areas and especially the temporoparietal junction (TPJ). There is converging evidence that shows this cortical area to be crucial for OBEs. People who have brain damage or abnormal electrical activity (due to a migraine attack or an epileptic seizure) in this area have reported OBEs. If this cortical area is directly stimulated by a tiny electrical current, OBE-like experiences can be induced in controlled experiments.

Thus, one perfectly natural neuroscientific explanation for OBEs, supported by all the evidence, is the temporary failure to bind the body image and the visuospatial representation of the world coherently together in the temporoparietal cortex. Interestingly, OBE-like experiences or bodily illusions have recently been induced also for healthy participants in the laboratory merely by giving them unusual and mismatching information about the location of their own body (Metzinger, 2009). These experiences are called virtual OBEs (VOBEs). The subject stands in front of a camera and wears a head-mounted display that shows a three-dimensional, real-time image of the same space but from the camera's point of view. Thus, the subject actually sees his own back in front of him, as if he himself were standing in front of himself! Next, tactile stimuli are added to this scenario, so that the experimenter strokes the subject's back with a stick, and the subject sees the stick stroking the virtual body in front of him in perfect synchrony while at the same time experiencing being touched in his back. In this condition, the subject often feels as though the virtual figure, seen in front of their real location, is their own body. Consequently, the centre of their experiencing self suddenly jumps into the virtual body! They thus identify themselves with the image of their own body, which is visually in front of them, but nevertheless they feel they are "in" that body. The OBE in this case is the feeling of seeing your body from the backside: The seeing self is located behind the back of the bodily self!

In terms of Metzinger's (2009) "self-model theory", an OBE is a state of consciousness where two self-models are active at the same time within the same subject's virtual reality. Only one of them is in the place where the centre of experience is felt to be located and which constitutes the origin of the first-person perspective; the other self-model is seen from an external perspective. It is recognized as "my own body", but not as the "me" as an experiencing subject.

These two self-models can be called "the bodily self" and "the seeing self". Normally, they are coherently superimposed on each other. The bodily self constitutes the spatial experience of me inhabiting my own body, of being inside it, my being filling the space of the body or being identical with this felt body. The seeing self is more like a camera eye or a visual perspective that forms the centre point of the visuospatial world we see around us. In OBEs and VOBEs these two (partial) self-models, both constructions of the brain, are enticed or perhaps forced to go separate ways – and thus a miracle happens and we experience being out of our bodies! But nothing leaves our physical bodies behind – it all happens in the virtual reality of consciousness inside the brain that now houses two different self-models at the same time. An OBE is not the immaterial soul flowing out from the material body; an OBE is, rather, neuroelectrical patterns of pure phenomenal information, flowing away from each other inside the brain:

> The bodily self is phenomenally represented as inhabiting a volume in space, whereas the seeing self is an extensionless point – namely, the center of projection for our visuospatial perspective, the geometrical origin of our perspectival visual model of reality. Normally this point of origin (behind the eyes, as if a little person were looking out of them as one looks out a window) is within the volume defined by the felt bodily self. Yet, as our experiment demonstrated, seeing and bodily self can be separated, and the fundamental sense of selfhood is found at the location of the visual body representation.
>
> (Metzinger, 2009, pp. 100–101)

The case for dualism seems closed when it comes to OBEs, because cognitive neuroscience coupled with monistic theories of consciousness seems to be able to give a satisfactory account of the evidence. OBEs do not seem to seriously challenge the materialist assumptions of cognitive neuroscience – saying that consciousness cannot flow free of the brain. OBEs turn out to be distortions of the phenomenal world and the phenomenal body image, all safely remaining within the brain, although creating, for a naive observer, the strong illusory impression of something leaving the physical body. Unless new and more challenging evidence turns up, OBEs pose no problems for science. Interestingly, that kind of more challenging evidence may in fact already be at hand, in connection with the next phenomenon of consciousness we are going to look at.

15.5 Near-death experiences (NDEs)

Near-death experiences provide an even tougher challenge for the basic materialistic assumptions of cognitive neuroscience. If materialism is correct, there should not be any conscious experiences ever floating free of the brain or in any way taking place outside of the brain or ever happening in the absence of corresponding brain activity. NDEs seem to seriously challenge all of these assumptions. Anyone willing to defend a dualistic theory of consciousness is probably clutching at the straws provided by NDEs.

NDEs occur when a person's life is physically threatened (e.g. by cardiac arrest or drowning, resulting in a lack of oxygen in the brain), when the person perceives that death is imminent even without or before any fatal physical damage (e.g. falling from a height) and sometimes in connection with nonlife-threatening events (e.g. general anaesthesia).

The most systematically documented cases involve patients who have suffered cardiac arrest and show all the signs of clinical death but who respond to cardio-pulmonary resuscitation (CPR) and recover back to life. Because at least some of the patients fulfil, for a while, the criteria of clinical death, it has been suggested that a more appropriate term to describe this phenomenon would be "temporary death experience" or TDE (Fenwick & Fenwick, 2008).

During cardiac arrest there is no cardiac output, no autonomous, independent breathing takes place and externally measurable brain activity, including reflexes such as the pupillary reflex to light, has disappeared. When the heart stops pumping blood, loss of consciousness happens in a few seconds and the brain's externally measurable EEG goes flat. In line with the physiological signs, the patient does not behaviourally respond to any stimuli but fulfils the criteria of being in deep coma or, as far as it can be externally evaluated, in a totally unconscious state.

All that we know from the neural correlates of consciousness, and every biological theory of consciousness we have, predicts that subjective experience is simply impossible in such a state. Without any blood pressure or blood flow into the brain there can be no supply of oxygen or glucose to the brain either. The neural activities of the brain, including those supporting any type of conscious experience, cannot go on in such a gravely pathological environment. Cerebral neurons will in fact start to suffer irreversible damage and cell death within only a few minutes, typically resulting in permanent brain damage even if the resuscitation efforts prove successful.

Let us take a closer look at one particular case study. One of the most famous NDE cases ever reported in the scientific literature (Smit, 2008; van Lommel, van Wees, Meyers, & Elfferich, 2001) was a 44-year-old man from The Netherlands who had been found unconscious in a meadow by passers-by. He was rushed into the hospital with no pulse, he was not breathing, he had no pupillary reflexes, he was ice cold (severely hypothermic), bluish in skin colour and seemed clinically dead. As it turned out, he had suffered a massive heart infarct. His resuscitation started immediately: artificial respiration, defibrillation and heart massage. Then he was intubated, but before that could be done a nurse removed dentures from the patient's mouth and placed them on a cart. During the first 15 min of resuscitation they could see no improvement and seemed to be losing the patient. Finally, after 1.5 h of resuscitation efforts the patient's heart rhythm and blood pressure had returned to such an extent that he was moved to the intensive care unit.

After more than a week, one of the nurses who was involved in the resuscitation of this patient met him for the first time after the incident in the patient's room in the hospital. The patient spontaneously recognized the nurse and said: "that nurse knows where my dentures are". The patient then described how his dentures had been removed during the resuscitation. He had perceived himself and the room from above but was able to describe it in detail. He had been very much afraid that the team would stop the CPR and that he would die (the team had been very negative about the chances of success). He was desperately trying to make it clear to the team that he was still alive, but did not succeed in this. He was deeply impressed by his experience and said that he is no longer afraid of death (Smit, 2008; van Lommel et al., 2001).

This case is particularly impressive because the medical status of the patient was extremely poor – he was, for all intents and purposes, clinically dead – and because his story included perceptual information about the events that were going on in the resuscitation room that he should have had no opportunity of getting through any normal routes of perception. Although this case has been controversial and questioned as being only anecdotal, its details have been recently checked and mostly confirmed (Smit, 2008).

The above case is a typical OBE in connection with an NDE. The OBE, however, is only one of the features of NDEs. NDEs typically involve further subjective events that sometimes lead to what can only be called a mystical experience.

The following case, also well documented in the scientific literature, shows a more advanced NDE. It was experienced by a 12-year-old boy who was undergoing surgery under general anaesthesia (Lopez, Forster, Annoni, Habre, & Iselin-Chaves, 2006, pp. 86–87):

> I was sleeping and suddenly I felt awake and had the impression that I was leaving my body through my head ... I could see from above my whole body lying on the back on the operating table ... and surrounded by many doctors ... I felt as being above my physical body ... and I was lying face down ... I was like a spirit ... without my own arms and legs ... and I was floating under the ceiling of the room. Initially, while feeling detached from my real body (which was lying on the operating table), I felt a little bit scared and weird, ... but then I had a sensation of lightness ... and I felt relaxed and comfortable ... I had the impression that everything was real ... I distinguished the operating room and the surgeons ... I then saw a dark tunnel in front of me ... and I felt attracted to it ... I passed through the tunnel very fast and at its end I saw ... a bright light ... that did not hurt my eyes. As I was passing through the tunnel ... I heard noises ... which sounded like when you are watching TV without a program ... then these noises became voices ... Suddenly I felt again attracted to my body ... in which I went again through my head. At this time point the experience was over and I was asleep.

The five core features of typical NDEs are, in the order in which they are usually experienced: (1) peacefulness and weightlessness; (2) an out-of-body experience (OBE); (3) a dark tunnel into which the subject is drawn and through which the subject feels he is moving; (4) seeing a brilliant light at the end of the tunnel; (5) entering the light or another world at the end of the tunnel. This last stage may be associated with meeting others (often dead relatives), seeing religious figures or a review of one's life. Also, at this stage, the experience becomes very difficult to describe, reminiscent of other mystical experiences.

The estimations of the incidence of NDE in people who have become near to death vary from 6% to 50%. This large variation reflects the differing definitions of NDE, the differing nature of the life-threatening situation in question and the different methods used to collect the data. A cautious number based on the best studies suggests an incidence of around 10% (Blanke & Dieguez, 2009).

Among the people who have experienced NDE, most have reported only the first stage of feeling peacefulness (about 60%). About 25% experience the tunnel and the light, and about 10–30% experience the life-review or a chronological sequence of instantaneous, vivid visual images representing past events from the person's life. About 40–50% of NDEs include encounters with other beings, either human characters (typically close relatives or friends who have deceased) or various "spiritual" beings or guides, or religious figures. About 20–50% of NDEs lead to some kind of mystical experience of "oneness" or to a visit in what appears as a supernatural "other world". The NDE usually ends abruptly and the subject's centre of experience is back inside the physical body, feeling the pains of the serious medical condition (Blanke & Dieguez, 2009).

The core content of NDEs is similar across cultures, times and different study populations. However, only few subjects have experienced all the typical features of NDE. Thus, Blanke and Dieguez (2009) suggest that there is no reason to assume that NDE is just *one*, single and unified, phenomenon as opposed to a group of loosely associated experiences due to interference with different brain functions and mechanisms. Personality or religious beliefs do not separate people who have had NDEs from those who have not, even though being equally close to death. According to some studies, women are more likely to have NDEs than men, and young patients more likely than older ones.

Explanations of NDE can be roughly divided into supernatural (dualistic) and natural (physiological, psychological and neurocognitive). According to the supernatural explanation, which can also be called the *afterlife hypothesis*, what happens in an NDE is that a nonmaterial soul or self is detached from the body and travels through the tunnel into another, spiritual, realm where it is met by deceased relatives and angelic or god-like beings radiating unconditional love. There, the person's life is reviewed like a film and some sort of self-judgement takes place, as well as a decision on whether to go back to Earthly life. After returning, the subjects themselves often feel profoundly transformed and regard the afterlife hypothesis as a self-evident explanation for their experience.

According to the naturalistic explanations, also called the *dying brain hypothesis*, changes in physiological processes and brain function can account for NDEs. First, the feeling of peacefulness, positive emotion and bliss could be brought about by increased endorphin release in the brain under stress. Endorphins are the brain's own morphine-like chemicals, which create the feeling of well-being and absence of pain at times of extreme stress. Endorphins may also trigger abnormal or seizure-like activity in the temporal lobe. Epileptic seizures and direct stimulation of the temporal lobe (or the temporoparietal junction) can induce a variety of anomalous experiences, such as OBEs, distortions of body image, realistic memory images and feelings of the sense of presence of some other conscious being. Anoxia (lack of oxygen) of the brain might lead to the release of cortical inhibition that is known to induce visual hallucinations in other conditions (e.g. drugs, neurological damage of visual pathways). Tunnels are one of the four most common types of visual forms typically experienced when visual hallucinations are induced by drugs, seizures or other causes.

In a recent review, Blanke and Dieguez (2009, p. 320) summarize the neurocognitive evidence that could explain NDEs in this way:

> We have reviewed evidence that suggests that some NDE phenomena can be linked to distinct brain mechanisms. This was shown for the OBE (damage to the right TPJ), tunnel vision and seeing of foveal lights (bilateral occipital damage including the optic radiation with macular sparing and/or foveal hallucinations), feelings of a presence and meeting of spirits (damage to left TPJ), as well as memory flashbacks, life review, and enhanced emotions (hippocampal and amygdala damage). All structures have been shown to be frequently damaged in those cardiac arrest patients that show excellent recovery and who are so far the best studied patient group with NDE phenomena.

It goes without saying that because the "afterlife hypothesis" implies a dualistic theory of consciousness, it is impossible to integrate it together with the current physicalistic world-view of science. The naturalistic explanations are able to account for many of the core features of NDEs, but only by using speculative and indirect evidence, leaving many open questions. There is no direct evidence that during NDEs the hypothesized physiological or neurocognitive mechanisms would actually be at work and would therefore correlate with specific aspects of the experience or cause them. Thus, we have no direct evidence during an NDE of increased endorphin levels, cerebral anoxia or seizure-like cortical activity in the occipital, parietal and temporal lobes. This is not to say that such things do not occur, only that it is extremely difficult to get direct measures of them while a person is having an NDE. Another feature that may be difficult to explain by referring to abnormal or pathological brain activity is the well-organized nature and relative universality or uniformity of NDEs. Other hallucinations induced by epileptic seizures in the temporal lobe, by drug states or by dream-like states show an enormous variability of experiential content both within and between subjects. Furthermore, the contents are often disorganized and full of bizarre features and a negative emotional tone. A relatively uniform and seemingly well-organized experience such as an NDE would seem to be based on a brain mechanism that is widely shared and activated in a roughly similar manner and order in different people, rather than by a variety of chaotic processes running wild in a brain under high metabolic stress, very low arousal (unawareness of and unresponsiveness to the external world) and burdened by pathological electrophysiological seizures.

To ever find out which theory might best explain NDEs, we simply need much more and much better data about NDEs: we need a cognitive neuroscience of NDE phenomena (Blanke & Dieguez, 2009). The brain activity of patients who are potentially undergoing an NDE should be measured with multichannel EEG. The possible brain damage caused by the life-threatening event should be explored with structural and functional brain imaging methods as soon as possible after recovery from the life-threatening situation. And the cognitive, emotional and behavioural changes in the NDE patients should be carefully charted and documented by applying standardized neurological and neuropsychological tests and examinations to the patients. Only this kind of empirical data-driven approach and converging evidence could help us to finally demystify NDEs.

Another approach is to try to experimentally induce NDE-like experiences in normal healthy subjects: for example, through hyperventilation techniques that cause temporary anoxia and fainting but are not dangerous, or through direct brain stimulation studies. If NDEs could be experimentally (and safely) induced in the laboratory, they could be studied in a similar systematic, controlled manner as OBEs already are being studied, and thus the underlying mechanisms would be revealed to scientific scrutiny.

On the other hand, it should also be conceivable, at least in principle, to come up with new data that may potentially *falsify* the dying brain hypothesis, or call the philosophical commitments of cognitive neuroscience to question. As Fenwick and Fenwick (2008) suggest, the most fundamental problem of the temporary death experience is its timing: When *exactly* does it occur and what is going on in the brain at that time, if anything?

> In our study the patients themselves felt that the experiences occurred during unconsciousness ... we have no idea how clear consciousness can be experienced during a period of clinical death with a flat EEG. This question is absolutely crucial because it is central to one of the biggest problems facing neuroscience: is consciousness entirely a product of brain function and is it confined to the brain? ... From the point of view of science, TDEs cannot occur during unconsciousness, and yet there is some tantalizing evidence that that is just when they do seem to occur.
>
> (Fenwick & Fenwick, 2008, pp. 209–210)

For the time being we have to admit that there are not enough data, and not the right kind of data, about NDE that would let us choose between the different theories and settle the issue for good. One scenario is that the cognitive neuroscience approach will show us that NDE phenomena are in fact caused by different neural systems breaking down, and in the process showing pathological neural activities that cause the characteristic experiential phenomena that tend to occur together in various combinations in NDEs. An alternative scenario is that we get objective confirmation of the total absence of brain electrical activities during the unconscious period, but incontestable confirmation of veridical perception or other subjective experiences going on during the very same time when there are no brain correlates of experience to be found. Needless to say, such findings would be revolutionary for both philosophy and science, and also a huge challenge to all the modern scientific theories of consciousness.

15.6 Mystical experiences

Mystical experiences are perhaps the "highest" of all the "higher" states of consciousness. They involve many similar features to some of the other higher states, but in an extreme form. Also the effects of mystical states on the subsequent life of the person are often deep and long-lasting. Such experiences, even if relatively brief, are vividly recalled for years and they may be regarded as among the most significant moments of life. In his classic study of religious experiences from 1902, William James considered mystical experiences as the root of all personal religious experience.

Mystical states are difficult to describe in words or communicate to other people. William James took this feature, ineffability, as one of the defining features of mystical states. Mystical states involve both emotional and cognitive components. Emotionally, mystical states are intensely positive, involving overwhelming feelings of peace, calmness, harmony, joy, love, elation, awe or bliss. Cognitively, mystical states seem to communicate highly significant information for the subject about the true nature of the world, revealing the underlying, hidden order of the universe and its guiding principles. Perceptually, mystical states may involve unusual visions or other forms of imagery, or seeing the ordinary perceptual world as unusually bright, clear, radiant and beautiful. Mystical experiences are characterized by a sense of heightened reality and significance, and the sense of time may be distorted. The experiences are usually brief, from a few seconds to 1 h at most, but their after-effects may last throughout life. They happen unexpectedly and suddenly and cannot be summoned by will, although certain practices (such as yoga or meditation) or drugs (hallucinogens) enhance the likelihood of their occurrence.

Cosmic consciousness is a term introduced by Canadian psychiatrist R. M. Bucke in the early 20th century to describe a paradigmatic mystical experience (quoted by William James in his classic work *The varieties of religious experience*, 1902):

> The prime characteristic of cosmic consciousness is a consciousness of the cosmos, that is, of the life and order of the universe. Along with the consciousness of the cosmos there occurs an intellectual enlightenment which alone would place the individual on a new plane of existence – would make him almost a member of a new species. To this is added a state of moral exaltation, an indescribable feeling of elevation, elation, and joyousness, and a quickening of the moral sense, which is fully as striking, and more important than is the enhanced intellectual power. With these come what may be called a sense of immortality, a consciousness of eternal life, not a conviction that he shall have this, but the consciousness that he has it already.
>
> (James, 1902, p. 389)

Cosmic consciousness entails a widening of consciousness to encompass the entire universe and its deeper working principles. Although such insights are experienced as being absolute truths by the subject of the experience, outsiders may remain doubtful, and rightfully so. The conviction of the subject and the felt authority of the experience are no guarantee that the insights gained during the mystical state of consciousness carry any truth or validity in the objective sense.

Bucke described his own, brief mystical experience that changed him profoundly:

> I had spent the evening in a great city, with two friends, reading and discussing poetry and philosophy. We parted at midnight. I had a long drive in a hansom to my lodging. My mind, deeply under the influence of the ideas, images, and emotions called up by the reading and talk, was calm and peaceful. I was in a state of quiet, almost passive enjoyment, not actually thinking, but letting ideas, images, and emotions flow of themselves, as it were, through my mind. All at once, without warning of any kind, I found myself wrapped in a flame-coloured cloud. For an instant I thought of fire, an immense conflagration somewhere

close by in that great city; the next, I knew that the fire was within myself. Directly afterward there came upon me a sense of exultation, of immense joyousness accompanied or immediately followed by an intellectual illumination impossible to describe. Among other things, I did not merely come to believe, but I saw that the universe is not composed of dead matter, but is, on the contrary, a living Presence; I became conscious in myself of eternal life. It was not a conviction that I would have eternal life, but a consciousness that I possessed eternal life then; I saw that all men are immortal; that the cosmic order is such that without any peradventure all things work together for the good of each and all; that the foundation principle of the world, of all the worlds, is what we call love, and that the happiness of each and all is in the long run absolutely certain. The vision lasted a few seconds and was gone; but the memory of it and the sense of the reality of what it taught has remained during the quarter of a century which has since elapsed. I knew that what the vision showed was true. I had attained to a point of view from which I saw that it must be true. That view, that conviction, I may say that consciousness, has never, even during periods of the deepest depression, been lost.

(James, 1902, pp. 390–391)

Interestingly, the vision revealed in Bucke's experience seems, philosophically, not very far from the panpsychist world-view of Fechner, who saw the world as composed of a hierarchy of consciousness at every level of being, the highest level being universal consciousness (see Chapter 1).

Bucke's experience is a strong spiritual awakening or enlightenment. *Enlightenment* is the ultimate form of mystical experience and, we could say, an ultimate or highest conceivable state of consciousness, usually associated with Eastern religions such as Buddhism. Enlightenment is an experience where one reaches, through meditative practice, complete and total understanding of the nature of reality and of the nature of oneself in relation to reality. In those traditions, the terms *bodhi* and *budh* refer to awakening, wisdom and brightness – hence "Buddha" literally means "the awakened one". Enlightenment thus is a mystical experience that awakens ordinary consciousness into seeing the true nature of reality and thereby transforms consciousness into a qualitatively different, higher form that transcends normal consciousness, perhaps in a somewhat similar manner as becoming lucid reveals the true nature of the dreamworld to the dreamer whose conscious state thereby transcends the ordinary dreaming mind.

According to Buddhist thought, enlightenment entails the cessation of all selfish desires and all clinging to material possessions, sensory pleasures, human relationships and other external, passing things. The true nature of everything is seen to consist of impermanence and emptiness; thus even one's own self is seen as a mere illusion. (This idea resembles some of the modern theories of consciousness, which argue that there is no self, only an illusion of a self; see Metzinger, 2003, 2009.) The meditative state *samadhi*, discussed above, involves the mystical union of subject and object, or disappearance of self, which is an important step towards full enlightenment. These revelatory insights and experiences are supposed to bring about an absolute emotional calmness, peace of mind, cessation of suffering and deep compassion and unconditional love for all the unenlightened conscious beings who continue to suffer in their unawakened ignorance. It is unclear, though, whether the state of enlightenment once achieved subsequently persists. If it is a persisting condition, then it would not fulfil our definition of ASC, which excludes permanent changes in experience.

Chapter summary

Higher states of consciousness consist of a variety of altered states that involve positive, desirable and insightful experiences that are felt to be personally deeply meaningful, sometimes leading to profound and long-lasting transformations of personal beliefs and experiences afterwards. Typical higher states include flow, meditation, out-of-body experiences and mystical experiences.

Altered and higher states of consciousness reveal the richness of the many different forms and varieties of our subjective existence. Any theory of consciousness should be able to explain not only the typical features and mechanisms of normal waking consciousness, such as sensory and perceptual experiences in response to physical stimuli, but also the experiential features and the underlying mechanisms of altered states. This may be a real challenge to the scientific study of consciousness because: many altered states are difficult or impossible to control experimentally; they are highly subjective in that their content is difficult to verify by outsiders; and sometimes their precise experiential nature is impossible to describe or communicate.

Nonetheless, there is growing evidence that dreaming, OBEs, hypnotic hallucinations, meditation and other exotic ASCs are real, measurable phenomena in the sense that they have specific, objectively detectable neural correlates and mechanisms in the brain. Many ASCs may in fact be related through shared underlying biological mechanisms. Dreaming, hypnosis, meditation and flow may all involve the relative inactivity or the functional disconnection of prefrontal brain areas. This might also account for some of their common phenomenological features, such as total absorption, lack of critical thinking, diminished inner speech and altered sense of time. Brain stimulation studies of the temporal lobe have furthermore established that OBEs, and perhaps even fully mystical experiences, can be triggered by simply stimulating the brain in the appropriate locations (near the temporoparietal junction). There is thus some hope that even the most mysterious of ASCs are not entirely beyond the reach of scientific experimentation, and that they are based on – or at least they correlate with – characteristic and localized activity patterns in the brain.

Further reading

Blackmore, S. J. (1992). *Beyond the body: An investigation of out-of-the-body experiences*. Chicago: Academy Chicago.

Blackmore, S. J. (1993). *Dying to live: Near death experiences*. Buffalo, NY: Prometheus Books.

Blanke, O., & Dieguez, S. (2009). Leaving body and life behind: Out-of-body and near-death experience. In S. Laureys & G. Tononi (Eds.), *The neurology of consciousness* (pp. 303–325). New York: Elsevier.

Bünning, S., & Blanke, O. (2005). The out-of body experience: Precipitating factors and neural correlates. *Progress in Brain Research, 150*, 331–350.

Farthing, W. G. (1992). *The psychology of consciousness*. New York: Prentice-Hall.

Fenwick, P., & Fenwick, E. (2008). *The art of dying*. London: Continuum.

Green, C., & McCreery, C. (1994). *Lucid dreaming: The paradox of consciousness during sleep*. London: Routledge.

Hobson, J. A. (2001). *The dream drugstore: Chemically altered states of consciousness*. Cambridge, MA: MIT Press.

James, W. (1902). *The varieties of religious experience*. New York: Longman, Green.

LaBerge, S. (1985). *Lucid dreaming*. New York: Ballantine.

Lippman, C. W. (1953). Hallucinations of physical duality in migraine. *Journal of Nervous and Mental Disease, 117*, 345–350.

Lopez, U., Forster, A., Annoni, J. M., Habre, W., & Iselin-Chaves, I. A. (2006). Near-death experience in a boy undergoing uneventful elective surgery under general anesthesia. *Pediatric Anesthesia, 16*, 85–88.

Lutz, A., Greischar, L. L., Rawlings, N. B., Ricard, M., & Davidson, R. J. (2004). Long-term meditators self-induce high-amplitude gamma synchrony during mental practice. *PNAS, 101*, 16369–16373.

Lyubomirsky, S. (2007). *The how of happiness*. New York: Penguin Press.

Metzinger, T. (2003). *Being no one: The self-model theory of subjectivity*. Cambridge, MA: MIT Press.

Metzinger, T. (2009). *The ego tunnel*. New York: Basic Books.

Revonsuo, A. (2009). Altered and exceptional states of consciousness. In W. P. Banks (Ed.), *Encyclopedia of consciousness* (Vol. 1, pp. 9–21). San Diego, CA: Academic Press.

Smit, R. H. (2008). Corroboration of the dentures anecdote involving veridical perception in a near-death experience. *Journal of Near-Death Studies, 27*, 47–61.

Tart, C. T. (Ed.) (1990). *Altered states of consciousness*. New York: Harper Collins.

van Lommel, P., van Wees, R., Meyers, V., & Elfferich, I. (2001). Near-death experience in survivors of cardiac arrest: A prospective study in the Netherlands. *Lancet, 358*, 2039–2045.

Brief discussion questions

1   Make a list of all ASCs you have ever experienced, and arrange them subsequently in the order from most common in your life to most rare in your life. Make another list where you order them from most positive to most negative. Compare the lists with other students and discuss whether you can find a name and a scientific explanation for all of your ASCs.

2   If dualism is true, how should ASCs and especially higher states be interpreted? If materialism is true, how can they be explained in that case?

3   Most of the theories of consciousness reviewed in the previous chapter are not specifically based on the evidence from ASCs. Do you think the theories can handle ASCs, or are ASCs a problem for them? Which theories might have the best chances of dealing with ASCs?

Epilogue

Reflections on the science of subjective experience

We are nearing the end of what I hope has been a fascinating and worthwhile expedition into consciousness and the science of subjective experience. We have probed the metaphysics of the mind–body relationship, explored the history of psychological science, defined the concepts of consciousness, examined the strange experiences of brain-damaged patients, discovered the neural correlates of consciousness with neuroimaging methods, tried to understand a bunch of theories of consciousness and, finally, arrived at altered states that appear to take us to other mind-worlds: the unshakable calmness of the meditative consciousness, the nocturnal brain simulation of the dreamworld, the gates of death in near-death experiences, the exhilarating happiness of flow and the profound insight and bliss of mystical, cosmic consciousness.

Our subjective inner life has been ignored in science (especially in psychological science) since the 1920s, but now we may witness the science of consciousness taking the place it deserves among the sciences of the mind. Although we have barely been able to scratch the surface of this fascinating new field in this book, I hope that the main message is loud and clear: Consciousness science is a genuine new branch of science with a broad philosophical basis, a long history of its own, a network of interrelated, clearly definable concepts that provide its conceptual foundations, solid empirical data about many empirically approachable phenomena and sophisticated research methodology from neuropsychology, neuroscience and experimental psychology, and evolving theories that try to put it all together into a coherent story and integrate it with an overall metaphysical account of our place in the universe. Consciousness is not just a single, irritating "problem" to be solved by some clever philosopher with a witty argument, nor does consciousness science consist of just the neuroimaging of the correlates of visual perception. No, consciousness science is an immensely broad field of studies at the intersection of philosophy, psychology and neuroscience, encompassing our subjective psychological reality from several different angles.

In this Epilogue, I will provide some reflections and speculations on the science of consciousness, in particular its future prospects and its potential implications for our world-view. So far in the book I have mostly attempted to remain silent about my own theories or favourite approaches (with less than perfect success, I know), but in the following I will openly reveal what I find the most plausible approaches to the explanation of consciousness and what seem the most promising and most exciting lines of research in the future. My own approach is presented and argued in detail in another book, *Inner presence* (Revonsuo, 2006); the more detailed arguments and data by which I defend my views can be found there.

Philosophical reflections

Have we found any answers to the most fundamental questions presented at the outset of the book? Do we now understand what consciousness is, how it is related to the brain and what happens to our subjective psychological reality during dreaming, in death or in mystical experiences?

Unfortunately (or perhaps fortunately) the science of consciousness does not (yet) provide us with final answers to any of these questions. The best we can do at this point is to narrow down the plausible alternatives a little bit. Of course, what is plausible to one may be implausible to another, so my suggestions here reflect my personal take – or hunch – with regard to these issues. No-one knows how things *really* are when it comes to consciousness, but maybe we can be pretty sure about how things most likely are *not*.

The least plausible world-views

In my personal ranking list of least plausible philosophical theories, eliminative materialism is at the top because it denies the existence of the only thing in the universe (and in our personal lives) about which we cannot be mistaken: our own inner subjective, qualitative existence – our own phenomenal consciousness. It is difficult to think of a more implausible move a theory could make.

Reductive materialism fares slightly better, but it, too, seems to deny our subjective, qualitative existence, or at least it does not give us a clue how consciousness could be just an ordinary brain process like any other: purely objective neurophysiology, nothing over and above that. Reductive materialism is responsible for *creating* the Explanatory Gap rather than for closing it! (My analysis on the Explanatory Gap and how to close it is presented in Revonsuo, 2006, Chapter 17.)

Epiphenomenalism and parallelism deny consciousness any causal role in the world. Therefore, they deny that we as subjects, our personal psychological realities, make any difference whatsoever, at least within the natural world. That view is not only intuitively unacceptable, but it also contradicts all the evidence we have from neuropsychological zombie systems. Patients who lose conscious information but retain similar nonconscious information are deeply incapacitated in their dealings and interactions with the world. Thus, the conscious, psychological reality does have a significant causal role in guiding our bodies – the biological organisms where consciousness is housed – through pathways across the physical world that keep us safe and sound. Nonconscious information processing in the brain can never do the same job: Phenomenal consciousness in the brain has unique and significant causal powers that are engaged when our bodies navigate through the physical world, and self-awareness is required when our future trajectories are planned or past ones are recalled. (For more on the causal powers of consciousness, see Revonsuo, 2006, Chapters 22–23.)

The externalist theories of consciousness must also be placed in the category of least plausible theories, because they cannot account for many types of data in a satisfactory manner. According to externalism, consciousness is not located within the brain, but is somehow in the whole body or in the interactions between the body and world, or in the distant objects out there. But in direct conflict with externalism, we know for a fact that consciousness exists in or at least is generated by the living human brain in a manner that does not directly require any contact with the external world outside the brain. When we are asleep, phenomenal consciousness can be either fully engaged (vivid dreaming or world-simulation) or totally absent (dreamless sleep). The crucial difference between these two states – the scientific explanation for the presence versus absence of the subjective psychological reality – will have to be primarily based on the different states of the brain in these two different conditions (Revonsuo, 2006).

At this point externalists usually point out that the conscious brain always needs an environment (blood supply, oxygen, glucose, the whole body) and always has a causal history (it must be the product of individual development and evolutionary history), and thus the brain alone cannot be the explanation of consciousness. Here lurks a confusion between different *dimensions* of explanation: downward-looking (constitutive) and backward-looking (historical, causal).

When we are interested (as we usually are in science) in the *immediate* causation and *constitution* of consciousness, or the absolutely decisive minimal differences in the physical world between the *presence* and the *absence* of consciousness, then we should figure out *what happens in the physical world just at the moment when consciousness is turned on* (or off). If we have two minimally different conditions where consciousness is totally present in one and totally absent in the other, but everything else is equal, then where in the physical world do the crucial changes happen and what kind of phenomena are they? As far as we can tell, the crucial physical differences happen in the brain and they consist of complex, large-scale neuroelectrical activity patterns. Thus, the directly underlying, constitutive phenomena for consciousness must happen in the brain and most likely are some sort of bioelectrical phenomena.

We know this for a fact because nothing else that has a direct effect on consciousness needs to change in the world between the presence and the absence of consciousness – especially in the paradigm case of dreamless sleep versus dreaming. Similar minimal contrasts between the presence and absence of consciousness can also be found in the loss and regaining of consciousness during anaesthesia, and in the unreportable conscious mental activity in the vegetative state versus a totally unconscious vegetative state. The minimally sufficient difference between a world with consciousness and one without it consists only of those differences inside the brain. Therefore, externalism is doomed (Revonsuo, 2006).

The (slightly) more plausible world-views

A useful way to think about the explanatory task of consciousness science is the multilevel model of explanation, a framework widely used in the biological sciences. The multilevel model of a phenomenon includes three types of explanation:

1   The *downward-looking explanation* specifies the *constitutive mechanisms* of the phenomenon at the lower levels of description – in the case of consciousness, the underlying neural mechanisms.

2   The *upward-looking explanation* specifies the role function of the phenomenon at the higher levels of organization – in the case of consciousness, it describes how conscious perceptions, intentions and emotions drive our externally observable behaviour, defining the role of consciousness in guiding our body through the physical world.

3   The *backward-looking explanation* includes the temporally preceding events that led to or causally affected the phenomenon (immediately, during individual development or during evolutionary history) (see Figure).

The explanation of consciousness, I propose, should take place in the context of multilevel explanation. Can we discover and fully describe the constitutive mechanisms, the aetiological pathways and the contextual role functions of consciousness (Revonsuo, 2006)?

Philosophically, the multilevel framework sees phenomenal consciousness as an emergent biological phenomenon, a higher level of biological organization that can only come about in the brain. I call this approach *biological realism*. As the name of my approach reveals, my view is closely similar to the "biological naturalism" presented by John Searle. In the context of biological realism I have defended the idea that the emergence of consciousness is *weak* emergence. I am optimistic about the prospects for science one day to be able to explain how consciousness emerges from brain activity, just as it is possible now to explain how life emerges from nonliving physical matter.

At this point, however, we are unable to imagine how the emergence happens. But in the future we will have new kinds of brain imaging methods that may actually "see" the phenomenal level in the brain more directly and thus function as objective consciousness detectors, solving the problem of other minds, and maybe even let us know what it is like to be a bat. The brain imaging method that will "see" consciousness in the brain is called the Dream Catcher, because with that method it should be possible to reconstruct the phenomenal contents of dreams objectively by just scanning the sleeping person's brain, without even asking the subject afterwards whether he or she recalls any dreams (Revonsuo, 2006). With the Dream Catcher method, the subjective contents of consciousness will become objective data just like any other brain scanning data!

Thus, weak emergent materialism is my first choice as the most plausible theory of the relationship between consciousness and the brain. How plausible is it, exactly? In one way it is extremely plausible because so far there are very few or no data that would directly contradict it. The supervenience relationship holds between consciousness and the brain, as far as we know from all our empirical data. Change something – anything at all – at the level of the contents of consciousness and the

The Multilevel Framework

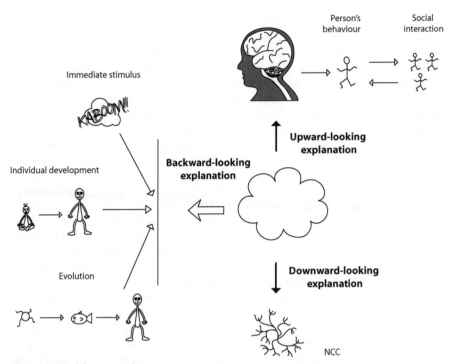

The multilevel framework

The explanation of a phenomenon requires multiple levels of description and three different directions of explanation. The phenomenon to be explained, in this case consciousness, is in the centre of the explanation. First, consciousness itself should be described at its own level, so that we know what the phenomenon is that we are trying to explain. Then we can start to explore the different directions of explanation. The downward-looking explanation describes the lower level neural mechanisms that directly underlie consciousness in the brain. The upward-looking explanation describes the higher level role that consciousness plays in the whole brain, the whole person and especially in guiding his or her behaviour. The backward-looking explanation moves backwards in time, tracing the causal chain of events that resulted in or causally modulated consciousness. This explanation can look to the immediate past when explaining how a preceding stimulus resulted in a conscious experience, or to the individual's past, describing how conscious experience emerged and changed during individual development from newborn baby to adult, or to the evolutionary past, describing how human consciousness emerged during human evolution or how any type of consciousness at all emerged during the evolutionary history of life on the planet Earth

phenomenal change in qualia is *necessarily* coupled with a physical change in the brain (the covariance principle). Dampen or wipe out the electrical activity of the brain and you wipe out the conscious state altogether: Consciousness does seem to be *ontologically dependent* on brain activity, and cannot exist without it.

The only data that might conceivably contradict the ontological dependence of consciousness on the brain come from OBEs and NDEs, but at least OBEs have turned out to be hallucinatory states of the brain rather than disembodied consciousnesses escaping from the brain. NDEs are the only potential anomaly that, if they really were what they appear to be, are inconsistent with any form of monistic materialism. But the evidence concerning NDEs is at best incomplete and at worst suspect. If the brain has a built-in capacity for mystical states of consciousness, as it seems to have, it may be that this capacity is activated in NDEs and the mystical experience is going on inside the dying brain, as the last goodbye to the phenomenal world before the lights go out for good. But if it turns out that the dying brain hypothesis cannot explain NDEs after all, then materialism may be in trouble.

The more worrying weakness of weak emergent materialism, however, is the toughness of the Hard Problem. Our imagination may fail us totally when we try to visualize how consciousness eventually will be explained as an emergent feature of brain activity. We already know quite a bit about the electrical brain activities that are connected with consciousness, but we have no idea how phenomenality is (or ever could be) generated by such activities. This weakness is only to be expected, because all major scientific breakthroughs are unimaginable before their time has come. To be able to *imagine* a scientific breakthrough (in detail) is more or less the same thing as *making* the breakthrough! The failure to imagine thus tells us very little about the problem or about the probability with which we might solve it.

Emergent materialism (whether weak or strong) leaves us with a physicalistic, mechanistic world-view that many see as altogether depressing. According to this view, all nonliving things and most living organisms are utterly devoid of phenomenal consciousness. Human consciousness, perhaps alone in the whole universe, owns the ability to not only *feel* its own existence (phenomenal consciousness) but also to *think about* it and *understand* it (reflective consciousness): to know its place and its sinister fate in the universe (self-awareness). The human subject's inner life is but a tiny, brief spark of feeble phenomenal light in a vast, black, nonconscious cosmos. Furthermore, every single conscious species lives in its own conscious reality, alien to other species, not knowing what it is like to be them – and most animal species not even caring because they are not able to represent in their small narrow minds that there is any such thing as consciousness in all the other creatures around them (Theory of Mind), or even in themselves. Furthermore, the individual human mind lives an isolated life within its subjective psychological reality, never able to merge together directly with another conscious being or to know another consciousness directly. We seem to be doomed to phenomenal loneliness of the most impenetrable kind!

Although the predicament of the human soul according to emergent materialism may be positively interpreted as a brave and exciting adventure in an alien world, it may equally well be asked what the point of conscious existence is if it is just a rare, brief, lonely phenomenal glimpse in an otherwise bottomless pitch-black space–time. (This problem, the problem of finding any meaning in a material world, has been coined the "*Really* Hard Problem" by Owen Flanagan, 2007.)

Another alternative that may contain a trace of plausibility is along the lines of neutral monism and panpsychism. Perhaps phenomenality and physicality are basically one and the same, or perhaps phenomenality is a very fundamental and widespread feature of the physical universe. Then we would not need to explain how the brain generates phenomenality, because phenomenality is everywhere and the brain only moulds and uses it to create a world simulation, a conscious representation of the world, to guide the behaviour of the organism in the physical world. Human consciousness is the sophisticated navigator system that evolution has built out of the qualitative ingredients that were hanging around in the universe anyway.

If panpsychism is on the right track, then we should see the world alive with conscious experiences everywhere. When we become unconscious or die, consciousness does not disappear but merely takes a simpler form, becoming once again one with the phenomenal background radiation of the universe, or a part of the cosmic consciousness. Mystical experiences and NDEs, in this case, would be glimpses of the true nature of consciousness. We would not be alone in the universe, merely one type of consciousness among the countless many surrounding us in every direction we look; most of the time we are just unaware of all the other centres of consciousness. The universe would turn out to be alive with conscious existence all around us!

However beautiful, inviting and consoling this view is, unfortunately there is no empirical evidence for such a view. It hardly seems to be a testable, scientific hypothesis at all, at least not until we have an objective consciousness detector available so that we know for a fact whether consciousness exists in any form at all outside the human brain. (In Revonsuo, 2006, I argue against the panpsychist view.)

Another exciting alternative for those who find materialism too depressing is the Buddhist view where phenomenal consciousness is believed to arise from the substrate consciousness – a state of radiant, clear consciousness beyond ordinary experience but reached in deep meditative states (see Wallace, 2007). It is not entirely clear to me which philosophical category the Buddhist view belongs to, apart from the fact that it is not any form of materialism.

Consciousness as an inner presence

For the time being, at least until there is stronger evidence for some more exciting alternative, my own theory of consciousness represents weak emergent materialism and is based on the multilevel framework of natural organization. Consciousness is a higher level of biological organization, therefore I call it the *phenomenal level of organization*. As with the lower biological levels of organization, the phenomenal level of organization includes a hierarchical order of levels where higher level phenomena emerge naturally from the lower level phenomena. The problem is that there are too many missing levels, too many gaps in our scientific knowledge, between what we know about the neural levels in the brain and the conscious levels in the mind to be able to connect them smoothly. The Explanatory Gap follows only from this ignorance of the intermediate levels, not from any fundamental metaphysical or epistemic inability to explain consciousness.

According to my model, pure phenomenal consciousness is the basic level of consciousness. It is a unified, spatial field or sphere where the qualities of experience come into existence. It is based on large-scale neuronal activities in the thalamocortical networks. In this respect, my theory is a holistic rather than an atomistic one. The phenomenal sphere or field, however, cannot be experienced *as such* – it does not in itself constitute an experience or include any phenomenal character. It is the level of organization that *mediates* between the nonconscious, purely neural levels and the conscious phenomenal levels in the brain. Thus, it should be called, more appropriately, the subphenomenal space. It is the system that reveals itself only indirectly, in the fact that all the phenomenal qualities that we do experience always appear to be spatially organized within a single unified overall context, the *world-for-me*.

The subphenomenal space must be activated for us to be in the conscious state – in the state where all kinds of experiences are enabled. When it is not activated, we are in an unconscious state and no experiences are possible. In its barest essence, phenomenal consciousness constitutes *an inner presence* – the simple presence or occurrence of experiential qualities, that is. No self is required – no representing, no intentionality, no language, no concepts – only the subphenomenal space in which phenomenal qualities may become present. At higher levels of phenomenal organization, the qualities form complex phenomenal entities. Some of them constitute our body image and others the phenomenal objects we see. The entire phenomenal level constitutes what I call a world simulation: a simulated world, or a virtual reality in the brain (here, my theory is in the same boat with Metzinger's and Lehar's theories, although subtle differences between our views also remain).

There is no separate subject or self who "has" the experiences or who inhabits the virtual world. What we call the self is the body image in the centre of the simulated world, and what we call the subject is simply the overall system of qualities that forms the phenomenal level in our brain. Thus, any particular experience is "had" by the "subject" simply because "having" is analysed as "being a part of" the phenomenal level. Your momentary total experience – you as "the subject" – simply consists of all the qualities that are simultanously present within the sphere of phenomenality in your brain. It is your subjective world, the world-for-you. You are both a part of the world (you as the "self" embedded within a body image and visual perspective) and the whole world (you as the subject whose experiences all the contents of the sphere are).

I have applied this "inner presence" and "world simulation" approach especially to explain dream experiences and other internally generated experiences. I have argued that the dreaming brain is in fact one of the ultimate challenges for consciousness science, but also a potentially useful model system, because in the dreaming brain the phenomenal level is brought about by the internal brain mechanisms alone, without any external stimulation or motor output going on. Thus, the dreaming brain shows us that consciousness itself – the entire sphere of experience – needs, for its momentary existence, only the internal activities going on in the brain. Also, dreaming presents us with the ultimate challenge in the measurement and detection of consciousness. Currently, we have no way of objectively verifying the existence or nature of a subjective experience. Nowhere is this deficiency clearer than in the case of dream experience, where complex and vivid experiences may unfold for the subject, but outsiders have no way of finding out their occurrence or precise content through objective measurements. The problem of measuring or detecting consciousness objectively should use dream experiences as the ultimate test case, because the subjective content of dreams cannot be indirectly inferred from stimuli or behaviour. Thus, if the content of dreams were to be successfully captured with an objective brain imaging method, the success must have been based on the brain data alone that were measured. This is the idea of the Dream Catcher test that I mentioned above. To pass the Dream Catcher test one will need to cross the Explanatory Gap and *derive phenomenology directly from neurophysiology!* In *Inner presence* (Revonsuo, 2006), I argue that it *can* be done, it *will* be done and that we can already now imagine the general outline of how it might be done.

The empirical theory of dreaming that I have built on the world-simulation metaphor of consciousness is called threat simulation theory (Revonsuo, 2000). I came up with this theory when I had first developed the idea that consciousness presents for us an "out-of-brain" experience and that dreams are a natural "virtual reality" system in the brain (Revonsuo, 1995). Consequently, the starting point for the threat simulation hypothesis was my view of dreaming as a natural virtual reality simulation in the brain. Next, I asked myself: If dreaming is essentially a simulated perceptual world, what *kind* of simulations might be particularly useful? I speculated that if flight simulators are used in order to safely train pilots to handle dangerous events that might arise during a real flight, perhaps the brain safely trains its own survival skills in *a fight-or-flight simulator*, specialized for extremely dangerous events that might be encountered in nature. Somehow I had always had the intuition that dreaming must be a biologically ancient state of consciousness, and when I got the idea of threat simulation I wondered how the dreaming brain would have behaved in the original evolutionary environment where our ancestors had lived and dreamed for millions of years: What did *they* dream about? It occurred to me that they must have had lots of recurring bad dreams and nightmares about all the threats to their survival that the natural environment presented to them every day.

Then I formulated in my mind the general prediction derived from the threat simulation function: that if such a function existed, at least in the human evolutionary history and in response to the survival pressures our ancestors went through, then the contents of dreaming should still today reflect this threat simulation function. I started to test this hypothesis in two ways: by looking at the results in the already published dream research literature; and by starting a research project of my own, collecting dream reports and analysing their threat content. Together with my then PhD student, now postdoctoral researcher Katja Valli, we have conducted and published several studies showing that threatening events are very common in dreams (e.g. in students' dreams, children's dreams and dreams after dangerous and traumatic events; for a review, see Valli & Revonsuo, 2009). I was at first actually quite surprised to discover that so many features of the contents of dreams and nightmares can be predicted and explained by threat simulation theory!

In a nutshell, my approach to consciousness can be summarized like this: Phenomenal consciousness is a higher biological level of organization in the brain that firstly enables the inner presence of phenomenal qualities and secondly organizes those qualities into a coherent world simulation, with a self or a body image in the centre of the virtual world.

This world simulation functions as an internal navigational system in the brain, playing a decisive causal role in choosing and guiding the behavioural trajectories that our physical body, the whole organism, goes through in the physical world. Dreaming is the biologically programmed, internally generated and stimulus-independent activation of the world-simulation system during REM sleep; the contents for the internally generated simulations are synthesized on the basis of emotionally charged memories, to rehearse dangerous and challenging events that we have encountered in the past and might encounter in the future as well.

Future of consciousness science

Whether the philosophical problems of consciousness are ever solved or not, the empirical science of consciousness will surely thrive – most likely its ascent has only just begun and the Golden Age of consciousness science is now dawning. The way I see it, consciousness scientists will have some background in all the three major disciplines that are involved in the study of consciousness: philosophy, psychology and neuroscience. The philosophical discussions around the Hard Problem, the Explanatory Gap and the "What is it like to be a bat?" problem will continue to energize the field. In addition, many new and more practical issues may emerge that consciousness scientists and philosophers have to deal with, such as the problem of possible "inverse zombies" among medically (behaviourally) "unconscious" patients (e.g. those in a coma or vegetative state or anaesthetized).

Animal consciousness is one of the problems for the future, along with the related question of animal treatment and suffering. If we can figure out which organisms are conscious and which not, and perhaps even what the conscious organisms feel in their subjective reality, does this change our relationship with those found to be nonconscious and those found to be conscious subjects? What justification can we give to actions that bring about pain and suffering in non-human subjects if we can objectively and exactly measure the suffering caused by our actions and know exactly how it feels? Should we treat all nonconscious organisms without any mercy and all conscious ones as basically in the same boat with humans?

If objective consciousness detection becomes a reality, we are at least bound to re-evaluate our views on these questions, because then at least we know for a fact what we are doing. Even with our current ignorance, I would strongly recommend giving the benefit of the doubt to animals and treating them as if they were feeling subjects akin to humans, with a value of their own, rather than as unfeeling objects whose purpose is to serve our needs only.

In cognitive neuroscience the search for the neural mechanisms of consciousness will undoubtedly continue to make progress. When we can narrow down the neural activities and brain electrical events that are directly responsible for phenomenal qualia, then things will start to get really exciting. Studying those activities in detail may let us approach the crucial interface where matter becomes mind: where bioelectricity sparks with phenomenal luminance. If we cannot see (or theorize about) anything there at all that could explain the magical connection, then we may have to give up the hope for weak emergent materialism and opt for the strong version. If we find out that our qualia are special modulations of an ever-present, universal electromagnetic field, integrated in a special way by our brain, then the unlikely marriage of neutral monism, information integration theory and Buddhist psychology may turn out to look feasible!

The prospects for an empirical solution depend largely on our abilities of consciousness detection. If consciousness remains invisible to all objective research instruments and direct consciousness detection remains just a pipe dream, then maybe we have to grant a point or two to our good old fellow Descartes: in that case maybe we have to admit that consciousness seems not to be of this physical world after all. Descartes would have predicted that *res cogitans*, the substance of consciousness, does not possess *any* physical properties whatsoever that our research instruments could get a grip of!

Scientific progress often depends on breakthroughs in theory, methodology and empirical observation. What kind of truly revolutionary breakthroughs might we expect to be forthcoming in the Golden Age of consciousness science? This is of course pure speculation, but here is my wish list of the greatest breakthroughs:

- We figure out exactly what the differences are in the brain between the conscious and the nonconscious state. For example, what happens when consciousness disappears or reappears due to anaesthetic agents, or what happens when dreamless sleep turns into vivid dreaming?
- We figure out exactly what the differences are between pure phenomenal consciousness and reflective consciousness. One crucial experiment would be the brain imaging of ordinary versus lucid dreaming: What happens in the brain when phenomenal dream experience turns into reflective, self-aware dream experience?
- We develop a method that can detect and monitor the presence versus absence of subjective experience with nearly 100% accuracy. Thus, with this device it would be possible to tell whether a sleeper is dreaming right now or not, or whether an unresponsive anaesthetized or a vegetative person experiences something – has a psychological reality.
- We develop a method that not only *detects* the state of consciousness, but also models or simulates the *contents* of consciousness in detail, so that by presenting the data collected from a conscious creature's brain we can know approximately what it was like to be that creature. (This is the Dream Catcher method that I describe in Revonsuo, 2006.)
- We get data about what happens in the brain and in consciousness during mystical experiences and during NDEs. The results will be decisive in finally ruling out (or perhaps confirming) dualistic or panpsychistic approaches to consciousness.
- We develop a Grand Unified Theory of Consciousness that explains, once and for all, what the place of the human inner life is in the universe. When this work is finished, we have answers to all the open questions that we have presented in this book.

Final word: At least we know that our consciousness exists but – what should we do with it?

Apart from the theoretical questions concerning the nature and the explanation of consciousness, there is also a pressing *practical* question: What are we supposed to *do* with our consciousness? What kind of conscious states are *valuable*, or *desirable*, and *meaningful*? These questions have already been raised by some consciousness researchers: Metzinger (2009) talks about "consciousness ethics" and Flanagan (2007) about the Really Hard Problem of the meaning of life in a physical world.

In the question of what makes a subject's life worth living, the science of consciousness might well combine its forces with another new field called the science of subjective well-being (Eid & Larsen, 2008). Subjective well-being is about the *positive quality* of phenomenal consciousness and self-awareness. When we possess high subjective well-being, we feel good and we evaluate our lives positively. Some overlap between the two fields – the science of subjective experience and the science of subjective well-being – already exists. It is most evident in the studies on meditation, flow and higher states of consciousness.

No matter what our subjective existence is based on metaphysically – or whether we are ever going to find out – it surely makes sense to aim at a pleasurable, engaging and meaningful quality of subjective inner life: that is, happiness and subjective well-being.

So, what should we *do* with our consciousness? We should *enjoy* being alive – in the sense of *inner mental life* – and we should have *a life worth living as subjects*. Furthermore, as we humans alone on this planet possess the capacity for a Theory of Mind, the capacity to *imagine* or *simulate* how *other* conscious subjects feel about *their* subjective lives, we should perhaps extend the goal of "having a subjective life worth living" to cover *all* subjects of experience, regardless of their bodily form or their biological closeness to ourselves.

That enterprise reaches far and wide outside the science of consciousness and is undoubtedly even more important than the questions probed in the present book.

Further reading

Eid, M., & Larsen, R. J. (Eds.) (2008). *The science of subjective well-being*. New York: Guilford Press.

Flanagan, O. (2007). *The really hard problem*. Cambridge, MA: MIT Press.

Metzinger, T. (2009). *The ego tunnel*. New York: Basic Books.

Revonsuo, A. (1995). Consciousness, dreams, and virtual realities. *Philosophical Psychology*, *8*, 35–58.

Revonsuo, A. (2000). The reinterpretation of dreams: An evolutionary hypothesis of the function of dreaming. *Behavioral and Brain Sciences*, *23*, 877–901.

Revonsuo, A. (2006). *Inner presence: Consciousness as a biological phenomenon*. Cambridge, MA: MIT Press.

Valli, K., & Revonsuo, A. (2009). The threat simulation theory in light of recent empirical evidence: A review. *American Journal of Psychology*, *122*, 17–38.

Wallace, B. A. (2007). *Contemplative science*. New York: Columbia University Press.

Glossary

afterlife hypothesis on NDE   The idea that near-death experiences are explained by the survival of consciousness after bodily death.

akinetopsia   Blindness to visual motion, caused by damage to the visual cortex (area V5 or MT).

amnesia   Disorder of autobiographical (episodic) memory, inability to remember events from one's own personal past.

anaesthesia   Loss of sensory experiences, especially of pain, usually induced by special drugs given before surgery.

anosognosia   Unawareness of deficit, specific inability to notice or understand that one is suffering from a disorder or from a medical condition, without any general intellectual decline.

artificial intelligence   Computers and programs that mimic or surpass human intellectual and cognitive abilities.

ASC   Altered state of consciousness. A state where the contents of consciousness are temporarily different from the normal state. The patterns of experience may be unusual or they distort or misrepresent reality in some way. Usually the subject and external observers are able to recognize that an ASC is or was present.

autobiographical memory   The part of long-term memory that stores our personal life history: all the events of our personal past.

autoscopy   An altered state of consciousness where a person sees himself or herself from an external perspective. A medical term for an out-of-body experience.

bad dreams   Very unpleasant or disturbing dreams that do *not* wake up the dreamer (if they do, the bad dream is called a "nightmare").

Balint's syndrome   A neuropsychological disorder characterized by the inability to see more than one object at a time (simultanagnosia), feature conjunction errors in visual perception and optic ataxia or visuomotor inability to accurately reach and manipulate perceived objects, typically caused by bilateral damage to the posterior parietal lobes.

behaviourism A dominating school of thought in the history of psychology, 1920–1950, according to which psychology is the science of behaviour, not a science of the mind or consciousness.

binding problem The problem of explaining how the unity of consciouness, especially conscious visual perception, is generated by the brain; how and where in the brain the different features of perceived objects are bound together to form coherent percepts.

binocular rivalry Two different stimuli are shown, one to each eye, and they compete for access to perceptual consciousness, so that only one is seen at any one time and the winning stimulus changes every few seconds.

blindsight Nonconscious visual perception in patients suffering from damage to the primary visual cortex and cortical blindness.

Buddha An awakened or enlightened person, a person who has achieved the highest state of consciousness. Siddharta Gautama, a prince who lived in India about 2500 years ago, is known as such a person and therefore he is called the Buddha, the founder of the religion and philosophy known as Buddhism.

Capgras delusion The persistent belief that family members have been switched to identical copies or impostors, although they still look exactly the same. Caused by brain damage affecting the emotional components of face recognition.

Cartesian theatre A term launched by the philosopher Daniel Dennett to indicate a special place in the brain where experiences happen and are presented to the subject. Dennett argued that many scientists intuitively think about consciousness as a Cartesian theatre, but according to Dennett the Cartesian theatre is a misleading idea and should be rejected.

cerebral achromatopsia Colour blindness caused by damage to the visual cortex at area V4.

challenge suggestion A hypnotic suggestion where the hypnotist first suggests that a body part has become impossible to move or control (e.g. eyelids are glued shut or arm is rigid as an iron bar), and then the hypnotists asks the hypnotized person to challenge the first suggestion (try to open your eyes, try to bend your arm).

cognitive neuropsychiatry A branch of cognitive neuroscience where cognitive models of information processing are used to explain psychiatric symptoms, especially when brain deficits have led to psychiatric symptoms such as delusions.

cognitive neuropsychology A branch of cognitive neuroscience where cognitive models of information processing are used to describe and explain the patterns of cognitive deficits in neuropsychological patients.

cognitive suggestion A hypnotic suggestion that aims to change some cognitive process (such as perception, memory), and thus creates perceptual hallucinations, amnesia or false memories, for example, that the hypnotized person experiences as real.

concentrative meditation The scope of attention is narrowed down to a single object and attempts to keep the mind focused on it so that everything else disappears from mind.

consciousness   Refers to the subjective psychological reality that we experience. Can be divided into different levels such as phenomenal consciousness, reflective consciousness and self-awareness.

content analysis of dreams   Systematic classification of the semantic content of dream reports (the meaning of the words and sentences) and the quantification of such content for statistical analyses. The best-known and most widely used dream content analysis system is the Hall–Van de Castle system of content analysis.

cosmic consciousness   A higher, mystical state of consciousness where consciousness seems to encompass or become unified with the whole universe and grasp the deeper meaning of life, the universe and everything.

delusion   An obviously false belief that is held with strong conviction in the face of no supporting evidence or explicit contrary evidence.

dorsal visual stream   A cortical pathway that goes from V1 to the posterior parietal cortex and processes visual information relating to spatial position, movement and visuomotor manipulation of perceived visual objects.

double-aspect theory   The metaphysical idea that there is a fundamental substance of the universe that has both physical and mental aspects.

double dissociation (of cognitive functioning)   Theoretically interesting, opposite patterns of cognitive deficits in two patients – one with brain damage who cannot perform one type of cognitive task but can perform another type, and the other who has the exact opposite abilities – showing that the two tasks are functionally and anatomically separate from each other in the brain.

dreaming   Complex, multimodal, dynamic and progressive conscious experiences during sleep that are organized in the form of a sensory-perceptual world or a world simulation.

dream-self   The character in the dream from whose point of view the dream is experienced. Usually this self-character is not significantly different from the waking self, but sometimes it can be a different person or very rarely even an animal character.

dreamwalking   The behaviour shown during REM sleep by patients suffering from REM sleep behaviour disorder. Their real physical body carries out the movements that they dream about doing, because their muscles are not paralysed as they should be in REM sleep. Do not confuse dreamwalking with sleepwalking.

dualism (Cartesian)   Philosophical mind–brain theory, the interactionist variety of dualism, developed by René Descartes (Latin: *Cartesius*). The material body and the immaterial mind are in two-way interaction with each other.

dying brain hypothesis of NDEs   The idea that near-death experiences can be explained by the physiological processes and pathological changes in the brain when its vital functions are seriously compromised or threatened.

EEG   Electroencephalography. A method that measures the electrical activity of the brain by placing electrodes on the scalp and showing the ongoing changes in the brain's electrical field as reflected on the surface of the scalp.

eliminative materialism   Philosophical mind–brain theory that eliminates the concepts "mind" and "consciousness" from science, arguing that such phenomena do not really exist and that therefore in future neuroscience such concepts will not be needed.

emergence The process where something new and unpredictable appears from a complex combination of simpler elements.

emergent materialism Philosophical mind–brain theory that says that physical matter is organized into lower and higher levels, and from the lower level physical entities new and unpredictable higher level physical entities or features can appear. Consciousness is precisely such a higher level, emergent entity.

endorphin A morphine-like chemical substance that the brain produces to remove pain and induce pleasure.

enlightenment The ultimate form of mystical experience and higher consciousness that awakens a person into seeing the true nature of the self and reality.

epiphenomenalism Philosophical mind–brain theory: brain activities cause changes in consciousness, but consciousness has no effect on the brain or anything else; consciousness is a superfluous epiphenomenon.

experience sampling method A method to collect representative and random samples of (reports of) subjective experience. The subject is signalled by a "beeper" at random intervals throughout the day to give reports of what he or she was experiencing just before the signal went on.

Explanatory Gap The gap between subjective experience and brain activity: We cannot give any intelligible account as to how subjective experiences could or why they should arise from brain activity.

false awakening An altered state of consciousness where a sleeping person has a realistic dream about waking up and getting out of bed, without realizing that he or she is still sleeping.

Fechner, Gustav One of the most important figures in the early history of experimental psychology; founder of psychophysics and the first scientist to measure and quantify the relationship between objective stimulus features and subjective experience.

flow experience Optimal experience is a higher state of consciousness when we are totally absorbed in doing something pleasant, challenging and engaging, and forget about everything else.

fMRI Functional magnetic resonance imaging, which measures changes in the blood oxygenation levels in the brain and thus indirectly reveals the localization of areas where neurons are active during different cognitive tasks.

functionalism Philosophical mind–body theory where the mind consists of functions or input–output relationships, such as a computer program, and the brain is the machine or hardware where the program is running.

Gestalt psychology An originally German school of psychology, launched in the 1920s, that emphasized the holistic nature of conscious perception.

hallucination A perceptual experience that occurs in consciousness without any corresponding external stimulus. If the subject knows or realizes that the experience is only a hallucination, then it is called a pseudohallucination.

Hard Problem The problem of explaining how any physical thing could produce any experiences at all.

heterophenomenology A term coined by the philosopher Daniel Dennett to denote a methodology for studying consciousness from the third-person point of view as purely objective behaviour, primarily using the verbal reports, texts or narratives produced by a person.

higher states of consciousness States of consciousness that are felt to be deeply enjoyable, meaningful and desirable and that involve exceptional cognitive, attentional or emotional phenomena.

hippocampus A seahorse-shaped structure in the brain inside the temporal lobes, crucially important for long-term episodic (autobiographical) memory and spatial memory.

homunculus problem The idea that to explain conscious perception we have to postulate a smaller conscious agent (homunculus, "little man") inside the brain who observes the contents of consciousness, and, in turn, to explain this internal agent's abilities we have to postulate an even smaller homunculus inside its head, and so on, in infinite regression.

hypnagogic hallucinations Altered states of consciousness that may happen at the borderline between sleep and wakefulness while we are falling asleep. We perceive at the same time both the real world and, mixed together with it, dream-like experiences (visual images or patterns, auditory voices or noises, etc.).

hypnopompic hallucinations Altered states of consciousness that may happen while we are waking up from sleep. We perceive at the same time both the real world and, mixed together with it, dream-like experiences (visual images or patterns, auditory voices or noises, etc.).

hypnosis "Hypnosis as procedure" is the interaction between the hypnotist and the subject that aims at making the subject more responsive to forthcoming suggestions. "Hypnosis as product" refers to the hypnotic state or changes in the subject's consciousness and scope of attention caused by suggestions given by another person.

hypnotic induction A procedure that starts a series of suggestions that aim to bring about a heightened state of suggestibility or "hypnosis". Typically includes suggestions to relax and to feel sleepy.

hypnotic suggestibility A relatively stable trait of a person, indicating his or her tendency to respond to suggestions given after a hypnotic induction. Normally distributed among the population so that most people are moderately suggestible, some are not suggestible at all and some are highly suggestible.

hypnotic virtuosos Persons who are very highly suggestible in hypnosis and who respond strongly to many different kinds of hypnotic suggestions.

idealism The philosophical theory opposing materialism and physicalism, saying that the world ultimately consists not of matter but of spirit or consciousness.

ideomotor suggestion A suggestion concerning mental imagery of motor actions. If the suggestion is realized, the person will actually carry out the suggested, imagined action but feels that the action happens automatically, without any voluntary intention or effort.

interactionism (or interactionist dualism) Philosophical mind–body theory, the variety of dualism saying that brain and consciousness interact bidirectionally: Brain activity causes changes in consciousness, and conscious mental activities cause changes in brain activity and thus also in behaviour.

introspection The mental process where we attend to some part of our own experience (in phenomenal consciousness) to verbalize and communicate our experiences (by using reflective consciousness).

James, William   American psychologist and philosopher, a prominent figure in the history of psychology and considered the grandfather of consciousness studies.

JND   "Just noticeable difference", the smallest physical difference between two stimuli that causes a recognizable difference in conscious sensation or perception.

Külpe, Oswald   A German experimental psychologist of the introspectionist era who found the controversial "imageless thoughts" in his laboratory experiments.

locked-in syndrome   A medical condition where brain damage has affected only motor functions and left the patient immobile and unresponsive to stimuli, but internally consciousness remains normal.

long-term memory   A memory system that lays down long-lasting memory traces. Divided into episodic, semantic and procedural subsystems, which store different types of information.

lucid dreaming   A dream during which the dreamer recognizes that the ongoing experience is a dream.

materialism   The philosophical theory that everything in the universe consists ultimately of nothing but physical matter.

meditation   Procedure that aims at calming the mind or creating positive states through the systematic training and control of attention and thinking.

MEG   Magnetoencephalography, which measures the tiny magnetic fields in the brain generated by the electrical activities of the brain.

mental causation   The idea that mind or mental phenomena have causal powers to change some purely material (e.g. biological or neural) processes in the brain.

mental health theory of dreaming   The idea that dreaming acts like an internal psychotherapist, making us feel better and helping to get rid of negative or traumatic experiences.

mental time travel   Ability to consciously think about, imagine or remember events from the past or the future of one's own personal life. Requires self-awareness.

Mesmer, Franz Anton   The discoverer of hypnosis in the 18th century. He called it "animal magnetism", and it has later been called also "mesmerism" after him.

mesmerism   An old term for hypnosis, referring to its discoverer, Franz Anton Mesmer.

microphysicalism   The ultimate form of reductive (or eliminative) materialism, according to which only the bottom level of elementary physical particles and forces really exists and everything else, the whole macroscopic world, is only an illusion created by the coarseness of human perception of reality.

mind–body problem   The philosophical problem concerning the relationship between the mind and the body, especially consciousness and the brain.

mindfulness meditation   A procedure that aims at widening the scope of attention so that we become vividly aware of all the sensations, perceptions and feelings that are currently present.

module   An information-processing mechanism that is limited to processing only a certain type of information, and handles its job rapidly and automatically, outside of consciousness.

monism   The philosophical theory that ultimately the universe consists of one substance.

monistic materialism The one and only fundamental substance is physical matter.

mystical experiences Brief, temporary, higher states of consciousness that are difficult to describe in words but are experienced as highly positive and significant, often with spiritual or religious meaning that may last throughout life.

NCC Neural correlates of consciousness. Neural activities in the brain that co-occur with conscious experience in the mind.

NDEs Near-death experiences. Mystical experiences reported by some people who have come very near to dying but have recovered. NDEs involve feelings of peace, out-of-body experience, a journey through a tunnel and seeing a light or an other-worldly realm.

neglect A disorder of spatial awareness caused by brain damage to the right posterior parietal lobe. The patient is typically unaware of the left side of perceptual space and/or the left side of his or her body.

neurophysiology The branch of neuroscience that studies the normal functioning of neurons and neural systems.

neuropsychology The branch of psychology that studies the relationship between psychological (cognitive) processes and the brain, especially in brain-damaged patients.

neutral monism The philosophical theory that ultimately the universe consists of one substance and the one and only fundamental substance is neither matter nor mind, but something even more fundamental.

nightmares Extremely unpleasant or distressing dreams that wake the sleeper up. They usually involve a long sequence of highly threatening or frightening events, vividly experienced.

night terrors Sudden panicky arousals from deep NREM sleep where the subject opens his or her eyes, may scream and appear to look around but is not in contact with reality. May involve brief frightening thoughts or images or feelings of imminent threat but never vivid, long, detailed dreams.

nirvana *See* **enlightenment**.

nocturnal wandering A long-lasting episode of sleepwalking where the sleep-walker may leave the house (and even drive a vehicle) and wake up several minutes or even an hour afterwards somewhere else, confused about what has been going on. An altered state that involves a mixture between wakefulness and deep NREM sleep.

nonconscious Not even potentially conscious: any processing, information or creature that has no phenomenal consciousness nor any access to phenomenal consciousness under any circumstances, but is totally devoid of subjective experiences.

NREM Nonrapid eye movement sleep. This consists of four stages (NREM stages I–IV), of which stages III and IV are the deepest stages of sleep (a.k.a deep sleep or slow-wave sleep).

NSC Normal state of consciousness, the baseline state against which an altered state of consciousness is altered according to some definable criterion.

occasionalism The version of parallelism that says that God synchronizes mental and physical events separately on each occasion when a mental event happens.

optic ataxia The patient can see visual objects but cannot point to them or reach them manually; a visuomotor disorder caused by brain damage to the posterior parietal cortex.

other-minds problem   The problem that we have no way of objectively knowing, measuring, detecting or perceiving the contents of other minds, thus we do not know with any certainty which creatures have a mind at all or what goes on in any other mind besides our own.

out-of-body experience   The experience of seeing one's own body from the outside, usually from above.

panpsychism   The philosophical theory according to which mind or consciousness is everywhere and in everything; all physical things have a mind or at least some kind of mental features or simple consciousness.

parallelism   The philosophical mind–body theory that says there is no causal interaction between consciousness and brain in either direction; they exist synchronized and in parallel without causal interaction.

PET   Positron emission topography. A functional brain imaging method that utilizes radioactive molecules and the signals they send when they decay in the brain to reconstruct an image of (some aspect of) the metabolic activity of the brain.

phenomenal consciousness   The most basic form of consciousness, which consists of subjective experiences and qualia but is independent of language and higher cognition.

phenomenalism   The theory that physical matter is dependent on perception and only exists as a potential object of perception.

phlogiston   A substance that was believed to be released from any burning material, but was never found and was discarded from science when oxygen was discovered to explain burning.

phosphenes   Brief flashes of light and visual patterns that are seen when the visual cortex is electrically stimulated directly.

phrenology   A mind–brain theory in the early 1800s that localized psychological traits in the brain and measured the external shape of the skull to determine the psychological profile of a person.

pineal gland   A nucleus in the centre of the brain that Descartes believed to be the gateway between the brain and the immaterial soul.

problem-solving theory of dreaming   The hypothesis that the function of dreaming is to find solutions to the problems we try to solve in our waking lives.

prosopagnosia   A deficit of visual face recognition.

proto-panpsychism   A variety of panpsychism, saying that simple physical things have a very elementary mind or consciousness, much simpler than our own consciousness.

psychophysical isomorphism   A mind–brain theory proposed by Gestalt psychologists, according to which the field of perceptual consciousness is based on an electrical field in the brain and both fields have the same overall shape or functional form.

psychophysical law   The hypothetical fundamental laws of nature that describe how consciousness is correlated with physical phenomena.

psychophysics   The branch of experimental psychology that studies the exact relationships between physical stimuli and the subjective sensations and perceptions caused by them.

qualia   The simplest components of phenomenal experience.

random activation theory   A theory of dreaming that regards dreaming as the byproduct of the random neuronal activity in the brain occurring during REM sleep.

reductive materialism   Mind–body theory that says that consciousness exists but it consists of only ordinary neurophysiological processes and therefore it can be exhaustively described in purely neurophysiological terms.

reflective consciousness   Contains a selected subset of experiences from phenomenal consciousness and applies concepts, language and working memory to process them further.

REM   Rapid eye movement sleep. This is a stage of sleep when the eyes move quickly under the closed eyelids, the brain is highly activated and the muscles are totally relaxed or functionally paralysed. This stage is also, most of the time, associated with vivid dreaming.

REM sleep behaviour disorder   A disorder where muscles are not paralysed as they should be during REM sleep, which causes the subject to act out the behaviours they are dreaming about.

res cogitans, res extensa   Terms introduced by René Descartes to denote the two substances (mind and matter) that the world ultimately consists of. *Res cogitans* is a substance that thinks and *res extensa* is a substance that has spatial extension.

runner's high   A higher state of consciousness induced by endurance training. It involves feelings of timelessness, weightlessness, powerfulness, joy and unity with surroundings.

samadhi   A meditative state of consciousness where the subject becomes one with the object of meditation; one-pointedness of mind.

self-awareness   Reflective consciousness that combines current self-related experience (e.g. self-image seen in the mirror) with the self-representation in long-term memory.

self-concept   The internal idea that we have of ourselves, expressed in the words we would use to define ourselves as persons.

self-representation   All the internal information we have of ourselves, including information about our own body, personality, history, future, etc.

semantic dementia   Progressive loss of semantic memory and semantic knowledge of concepts and words, due to a progressive disease in the brain.

semantic memory   The part of our long-term memory that stores information about the meanings of words, concepts, facts, categories and other knowledge about the world.

simultanagnosia   Inability to see more than one object at a time, typically caused by bilateral damage to the posterior parietal lobes.

sleep mentation   Any mental activity or experience occurring during sleep that is simpler than genuine dreaming.

sleep paralysis   The experience of having woken up but being unable to open one's eyes or move any muscles. May be accompanied by frightening imagery or feelings of panic. Caused by REM sleep mechanisms that paralyse muscles; these mechanisms are still working even though the rest of the brain has woken up.

sleepwalking   An altered state of consciousness where the person is partly awake and partly in deep NREM sleep. The sleepwalker has eyes open and usually carries out some routine behaviour or acts on an irrational idea without realizing that he or she is not awake and that the idea does not make sense.

solipsism   The philosophical theory that only my own conscious experience exists and the whole universe is contained within my consciousness; I alone exist.

somatoparaphrenia   A neuropsychological deficit where the patient denies ownership of a limb or body part.

split-brain   The condition where the cerebral hemispheres have been functionally separated from each other by surgically cutting the corpus callosum (and sometimes also the anterior commissure), typically to treat severe epilepsy.

strong emergent materialism   This theory states that even if we know everything that scientifically can be known about the lower and higher levels of emergent materialism, we still cannot understand or explain how or why the higher level phenomena (consciousness) emerge from the lower level (brain activity).

structuralism   The atomistic theory of consciousness supported by Edward Titchener: Consciousness consists of simple elements that are combined to form more complex mental contents.

supervenience relation   A dependency relation between two levels (e.g. brain and consciousness): the lower level features are more fundamental than higher level features; the higher level features depend on the lower level features; and changes in the higher level features are always accompanied by corresponding changes at the lower level. Consciousness depends on the brain and could never exist without a brain; any changes in the contents or states of consciousness must always be coupled with corresponding changes in the brain.

thalamocortical system   The neural system that combines the cortex and thalamus into one large network with very dense neural connections going both ways.

thalamus   A neural structure in the middle of the brain that connects to all parts of the cerebral cortex and is in constant interaction with it. Sensory information to the cortex travels through the thalamus.

threat simulation theory of dreaming   According to this theory, the evolutionary function of dreaming is to simulate threats, especially primitive aggressive and natural threats, because this was useful preparation for real threats during human evolution. This function is manifested most clearly in nightmares and bad dreams, especially following real threatening events.

Titchener, Edward B.   One of the leading introspectionists in the history of experimental psychology. He developed the ultimate form of introspectionism, called structuralism.

TMS   Transcranial magnetic stimulation. A method where brief magnetic pulses are sent through the skull to the cortex, to momentarily interfere with the normal cortical function.

unconscious   Potentially conscious: any processing, information or creature that temporarily has no phenomenal consciousness but has potential access to phenomenal consciousness under some circumstances.

V1   The primary visual cortex, which is the area in the occipital lobe where visual information first arrives at the cortex.

V4   A visual cortical area specialized in the processing of colour.

VAN   Visual awareness negativity. An event-related potential or negative wave in the EEG around 200 ms from stimulus onset that appears if, and only if, visual information enters subjective experience.

vegetative state   A state of unarousable unresponsiveness in a brain-damaged patient. However, the patient shows a preserved sleep–wake cycle and spontaneous eye-opening (if not, then the state is called coma).

ventral visual stream   A neural pathway going from primary visual cortex V1 to the temporal cortex.

visual agnosia   Inability to recognize visual objects.

weak emergent materialism   This theory states that when the lower and higher levels of emergent materialism are completely described, we can explain how the higher level phenomena (consciousness) emerge from the lower level (brain activity).

Weber-Fechner Law   A law about the relationship between physical stimuli and subjective experience, according to which subjective sensation is a logarithmic function of physical intensity.

working memory   The cognitive system that holds active information in the mind for a few seconds. Requires constant voluntary refreshing of the information to keep it from decaying. The contents of working memory are consciously experienced.

Wundt, Wilhelm   The founding father of experimental psychology and introspectionism in the late 19th century in Germany.

zombie   In philosophy, a creature that looks and behaves exactly as a normal human being but does not have any consciousness.

zombie systems   In neuropsychology, neural processing systems that take in sensory information and produce or guide behaviour but in the absence of any subjective experience or consciousness of the information.

References

Alkire, M. T., Hudetz, A. G., & Tononi, G. (2008). Consciousness and anaesthesia. *Science, 322,* 876–880.

Alkire, M. T., & Miller, J. (2005). General anaesthesia and the neural correlates of consciousness. *Progress in Brain Research, 150,* 229–244.

Aserinsky, E., & Kleitman, N. (1953). Regularly occurring periods of eye motility and concomitant phenomena during sleep. *Science, 118,* 273–274.

Baars, B. J. (1988). *A cognitive theory of consciousness.* New York: Cambridge University Press.

Banks, W. B. (Ed.) (2009). *Encyclopedia of consciousness* (Vols. 1 and 2). San Diego, CA: Academic Press.

Barnier, A. J., & Nash, M. R. (2008). Introduction: A roadmap for explanation, a working definition. In M. Nash & A. Barnier (Eds.), *The Oxford handbook of hypnosis* (pp. 1–18). New York: Oxford University Press.

Blackmore, S. J. (1992). *Beyond the body: An investigation of out-of-the-body experiences.* Chicago: Academy Chicago Publishers.

Blackmore, S. J. (2004). *Consciousness: An introduction.* Oxford: Oxford University Press.

Blackmore, S. J. (2006). *Conversations on consciousness.* New York: Oxford University Press.

Blanke, O., & Dieguez, S. (2009). Leaving body and life behind: Out-of-body and near-death experience. In S. Laureys & G. Tononi (Eds.), *The neurology of consciousness* (pp. 303–325). New York: Elsevier.

Block, N. (2001). Paradox and cross purposes in recent work on consciousness. *Cognition, 79,* 197–219.

Block, N. (2007). Consciousness, accessibility, and the mesh between psychology and neuroscience. *Behavioral and Brain Sciences, 30,* 481–499.

Block, N., Flanagan, O., & Güzeldere, G. (1997). *The nature of consciousness: Philosophical debates.* Cambridge, MA: MIT Press.

Borbély, A. (1984). Schlafgewohnheiten, Schlafqualität und Schlafmittelkonsum der Schweizer Bevölkerung: Ergebnisse einer Repräsentativumfrage. *Schweizerische Aerztezeitung, 65,* 1606–1613.

REFERENCES

Carruthers, P. (2007). Higher-order theories of consciousness. In M. Velmans & S. Schneider (Eds.), *The Blackwell companion to consciousness* (pp. 277–286). Oxford: Blackwell.

Cavanna, A. E., & Monaco, F. (2009). Brain mechanisms of altered conscious states during epileptic seizures. *Nature Reviews Neurology, 5*, 267–276.

Chalmers, D. J. (1996). *The conscious mind*. Oxford: Oxford University Press.

Churchland, P. S. (1988). Reduction and the neurobiological basis of consciousness. In A. J. Marcel & E. Bisiach (Eds.), *Consciousness in contemporary science* (pp. 273–304). New York: Oxford University Press.

Churchland, P. S. (2002). *Brain-wise: Studies in neurophilosophy*. Cambridge, MA: MIT Press.

Crick, F., & Koch, C. (1990). Towards a neurobiological theory of consciousness. *Seminars in the Neurosciences, 2*, 273–304.

Damasio, A. R. (1994). *Descartes' error*. New York: Putnam.

Damasio, A. R. (1999). *The feeling of what happens*. New York: Harcourt Brace.

Dehaene, S., Changeux, J. P., Naccache, L., Sackur, J., & Sergent, C. (2006). Conscious, pre-conscious, and subliminal processing: A testable taxonomy. *Trends in Cognitive Science, 10*, 204–211.

Dennett, D. C. (1976). Are dreams experiences? *Philosophical Review, 73*, 151–171.

Dennett, D. C. (1991). *Consciousness explained*. Boston: Little, Brown.

Dennett, D. C. (2005). *Sweet dreams: Philosophical obstacles to a science of consciousness*. Cambridge, MA: MIT Press.

Domhoff, G. W. (1996). *Finding meaning in dreams: A quantitative approach*. New York: Plenum Press.

Dretske, F. (1995). *Naturalizing the mind*. Cambridge, MA: MIT Press.

Edelman, G. M. (1989). *The remembered present: A biological theory of consciousness*. New York: Basic Books.

Edelman, G. M., & Tononi, G. (2000). *A universe of consciousness*. New York: Basic Books.

Eid, M., & Larsen, R. J. (Eds.) (2008). *The science of subjective well-being*. New York: Guilford Press.

Ellis, A. W., & Young, A. W. (1988). *Human cognitive neuropsychology*. Hove, UK: Psychology Press.

Engel, A. K., & Singer, W. (2001). Temporal binding and the neural correlates of sensory awareness. *Trends in Cognitive Sciences, 5*, 16–25.

Eriksson, J., Larsson, A., Ahlström, K. R., & Nyberg, L. (2007). Similar frontal and distinct posterior cortical regions mediate visual and auditory perceptual awareness. *Cerebral Cortex, 17*, 760–765.

Eriksson, J., Larsson, A., & Nyberg, L. (2008). Item-specific training reduces prefrontal cortical involvement in perceptual awareness. *Journal of Cognitive Neuroscience, 20*, 1777–1787.

Farthing, W. G. (1992). *The psychology of consciousness*. New York: Prentice-Hall.

Feinberg, T. E. (2001). *Altered egos: How the brain creates the self*. New York: Oxford University Press.

Feinberg, T. E., & Keenan, J. P. (Eds.) (2005). *The lost self*. New York: Oxford University Press.

Fenwick, P., & Fenwick, E. (2008). *The art of dying*. London: Continuum.

ffytche, D. H., Howard, R. J., Brammer, M. J., David, A., Woodruff, P., & Williams, S. (1998). The anatomy of conscious vision: An fMRI study of visual hallucinations. *Nature Neuroscience, 1*, 738–742.

Finger, S. (1994). *Origins of neuroscience*. New York: Oxford University Press.

Finney, J. (1976). *Invasion of the body snatchers* [film]. London: Sphere.

Flanagan, O. (1992). *Consciousness reconsidered*. Cambridge, MA: MIT Press.

Flanagan, O. (2007). *The really hard problem*. Cambridge, MA: MIT Press.

Fodor, J. A. (1983). *The modularity of the mind*. Cambridge, MA: MIT Press.

Foulkes, D. (1985). *Dreaming: A cognitive-psychological analysis*. Hillsdale, NJ: Lawrence Erlbaum Associates, Inc.

Freud, S. (1950). *The interpretation of dreams* (A. A. Brill, Trans.). New York: Random House. (Original work published 1900.)

Gallagher, S., & Zahavi, D. (2008). *The phenomenological mind*. London: Routledge.

Gazzaniga, M. S., Ivry, R. B., & Mangun, G. R. (2008). *Cognitive neuroscience: The biology of the mind* (3rd ed.). New York: Norton.

Gazzaniga, M. S., & LeDoux, J. E. (1978). *The integrated mind*. New York: Plenum Press.

Gazzaniga, M. S., LeDoux, J. E., & Wilson, J. E. (1977). Language, praxis and the right hemisphere: Clues to some mechanisms of consciousness. *Neurology, 27*, 1144–1147.

Goodale, M. A. & Milner, A. D. (2005). *Sight unseen: An exploration of conscious and unconscious vision*. New York: Oxford University Press.

Hall, C. S., & Van de Castle, R. L. (1966). *The content analysis of dreams*. New York: Appleton-Century-Crofts.

Heywood, C. A., & Zihl, J. (1999). Motion blindness. In G. W. Humphreys (Ed.), *Case studies in the neuropsychology of vision* (pp. 1–16). Hove: Psychology Press.

Hilgard, E. R. (1977). *Divided consciousness: Multiple controls in human thought and action*. New York: John Wiley & Sons.

Hirstein, W. (2005). *Brain fiction*. Cambridge, MA: MIT Press.

Hobson, J. A., & McCarley, R. W. (1977). The brain as a dream state generator: An activation–synthesis hypothesis of the dream process. *American Journal of Psychiatry, 134*, 1335–1348.

Hodges, J. R. (2003). Semantic dementia: A disorder of semantic memory. In M. D'Esposito (Ed.), *Neurological foundations of cognitive neuroscience* (pp. 67–87). Cambridge, MA: MIT Press.

Hothersall, D. (2004). *History of psychology* (4th ed.). New York: McGraw-Hill.

Jackendoff, R. S. (1987). *Consciousness and the computational mind*. Cambridge, MA: MIT Press.

James, W. (1902). *The varieties of religious experience*. New York: Longman, Green.

James, W. (1950). *The principles of psychology* (Vols. 1 and 2). New York: Dover. (Original work published 1890.)

Kallio, S., & Revonsuo, A. (2003). Hypnotic phenomena and altered states of consciousness: A multilevel framework of description and explanation. *Contemporary Hypnosis, 20*, 111–164.

Kanwisher, N. (2001). Neural events and perceptual awareness. *Cognition, 79*, 89–113.

Kapur, N. (1997). *Injured brains of medical minds: Views from within*. Oxford: Oxford University Press.

Kihlström, J. F. (2008). The domain of hypnosis, revisited. In M. Nash & A. Barnier (Eds.), *The Oxford handbook of hypnosis* (pp. 21–52). New York: Oxford University Press.

Kim, J. (1998). *Mind in a physical world*. Cambridge, MA: MIT Press.

Kim, J. (2005). *Physicalism, or something near enough*. Princeton, NJ: Princeton University Press.

Koch, C. (2004). *The quest for consciousness: A neurobiological approach*. Englewood Cliffs, NJ: Roberts & Co.

Koffka, K. (1935). *Principles of Gestalt psychology*. New York: Harcourt Brace.

Köhler, S., & Moscovitch, M. (1997). Unconscious visual processing in neuropsychological syndromes: A survey of the literature and evaluation of models of consciousness. In M. D. Rugg (Ed.), *Cognitive neuroscience* (pp. 305–373). Cambridge, MA: MIT Press.

Köhler, W. (1947). *Gestalt psychology*. New York: Liveright.

Köhler, W. (1971) An old pseudo problem. Reprinted in *The selected papers of Wolfgang Köhler* (pp. 125–141). New York: Liveright. (Original work published 1929.)

Koivisto, M., Kainulainen, P., & Revonsuo, A. (2009). The relationship between awareness and attention: Evidence from ERP responses. *Neuropsychologia, 47*, 2891–2899.

Kosslyn, S. M., Thompson, W. L., Costantini-Ferrando, M. F., Alpert, N. M., & Spiegel, D. (2000). Hypnotic visual illusion alters colour processing in the brain. *American Journal of Psychiatry, 157*, 1279–1284.

REFERENCES

Kuhn, G., & Findlay, J. M. (in press). Misdirection, attention and awareness: Inattentional blindness reveals temporal relationship between eye movements and visual awareness. *Quarterly Journal of Experimental Psychology*.

Külpe, O. (1895). *Outlines of psychology*. New York: Macmillan.

Làdavas, E., Berti, A., & Farnè, A. (2000). Dissociation between conscious and nonconscious processing in neglect. In Y. Rossetti & A. Revonsuo (Eds.), *Beyond dissociation: Interaction between dissociated implicit and explicit processing* (pp. 175–193). Amsterdam: John Benjamins.

Lamme, V. A. (2000). Neural mechanisms of visual awareness: A linking proposition. *Brain and Mind, 1*, 385–406.

Lamme, V. A. (2003). Why visual awareness and attention are different. *Trends in Cognitive Sciences, 7*, 12–18.

Lamme, V. A. (2004). Separate neural definitions of visual consciousness and visual attention: A case for phenomenal awareness. *Neural Networks, 17*, 861–872.

Laureys, S., Owen, A. M., & Schiff, N. D. (2004). Brain function in coma, vegetative state, and related disorders. *Lancet Neurology, 3*, 537–546.

Leahey, T. H. (1980). *A history of psychology*. Englewood Cliffs, NJ: Prentice-Hall.

Lehar, S. (2003). *The world in your head*. Mahwah, NJ: Lawrence Erlbaum Associates, Inc.

Leopold, D. A., & Logothetis, N. K. (1999). Multistable phenomena: Changing views in perception. *Trends in Cognitive Sciences, 3*, 154–264.

Levine, J. (1983). Materialism and qualia: The explanatory gap. *Pacific Philosophical Quarterly, 64*, 354–361.

Levine, J. (1993). On leaving out what it's like. In M. Davies & G. W. Humphreys (Eds.), *Consciousness* (pp. 121–136). Oxford: Blackwell.

Lippman, C. W. (1953). Hallucinations of physical duality in migraine. *Journal of Nervous and Mental Disease, 117*, 345–350.

Llinás, R. (2001). *I of the vortex: From neurons to self*. Cambridge, MA: MIT Press.

Lopez, U., Forster, A., Annoni, J. M., Habre, W., & Iselin-Chaves, I. A. (2006). Near-death experience in a boy undergoing uneventful elective surgery under general anesthesia. *Pediatric Anesthesia, 16*, 85–88.

Lutz, A., Greischar, L. L., Rawlings, N. B., Ricard, M., & Davidson, R. J. (2004). Long-term meditators self-induce high-amplitude gamma synchrony during mental practice. *Proceedings of the National Academy of Sciences of the USA, 101*, 16369–16373.

Lutz, A., & Thompson, E. (2003). Neurophenomenology: Integrating subjective experience and brain dynamics in the neuroscience of consciousness. *Journal of Consciousness Studies, 10*, 31–52.

Lyubomirsky, S. (2007). *The how of happiness*. New York: Penguin Press.

Mack, A., & Rock, I. (1998). *Inattentional blindness*. Cambridge, MA: MIT Press.

Malcolm, N. (1959). *Dreaming*. London: Routledge & Kegan Paul.

Marcel, A. J., & Bisiach, E. (Eds.) (1988). *Consciousness in contemporary science*. Oxford: Oxford University Press.

Mark, V. (1996). Conflicting communicative behavior in a split brain patient: Support for dual consciousness. In S. R. Hameroff, A. W. Kaszniak, & A. C. Scott (Eds.), *Toward a science of consciousness* (pp. 189–196). Cambridge, MA: MIT Press.

Marshall, J. C., & Halligan, P. W. (1988). Blindsight and insight in visuo-spatial neglect. *Nature, 336*, 766–767.

Marshall, J. C., & Halligan, P. W. (1996). *Method in madness: Case studies in cognitive neuropsychiatry*. Hove: Psychology Press.

Mashour, G. A., & LaRock, E. (2008). Inverse zombies, anaesthesia awareness, and the hard problem of consciousness. *Consciousness and Cognition, 17*, 1163–1168.

McGinn, C. (1991). *The problem of consciousness*. Oxford: Blackwell.

Metzinger, T. (2003). *Being no one: The self-model theory of subjectivity*. Cambridge, MA: MIT Press.

Metzinger, T. (2009). *The ego tunnel*. New York: Basic Books.

Murzyn, E. (2008). Do we only dream in colour? A comparison of reported dream colour in younger and older adults with different experiences of black and white media. *Consciousness and Cognition, 17*, 1228–1237.

Nagel, T. (1974). What is it like to be a bat? *Philosophical Review, 83*, 435–450.

Noë, A. (2009). *Out of our heads*. New York: Hill & Wang.

Noë, A., & Thompson, E. (2004). Sorting out the neural basis of consciousness. *Journal of Consciousness Studies, 11*, 87–98.

O'Regan, J. K., & Noë, A. (2001). A sensorimotor account of vision and visual consciousness. *Behavioural and Brain Sciences, 24*, 939–1031.

Owen, A. M., Coleman, M. R., Boly, M., Davis, M. H., Laureys, S., & Pickard, J. D. (2006). Detecting awareness in the vegetative state. *Science, 313*, 1402.

Palmer, S. E. (1999) *Vision science*. Cambridge, MA: MIT Press.

Phillips, K. A. (2005). *The broken mirror: Understanding and treating body dysmorphic disorder*. New York: Oxford University Press.

Ramachandran, V. S., & Blakeslee, S. (1998). *Phantoms in the brain*. New York: William Morrow & Co.

Rechtschaffen, A., & Buchignani, C. (1992). The visual appearance of dreams. In J. S. Antrobus & M. Bertini (Eds.), *The neuropsychology of sleep and dreaming* (pp. 143–155). Hillsdale, NJ: Lawrence Erlbaum Associates, Inc.

Rees, G. (2007). Neural correlates of the contents of visual awareness in humans. *Philosophical Transactions of the Royal Society of London, Series B, 36*, 877–886.

Revonsuo, A. (1995). Consciousness, dreams, and virtual realities. *Philosophical Psychology, 8*, 35–58.

Revonsuo, A. (2000). The reinterpretation of dreams: An evolutionary hypothesis of the function of dreaming. *Behavioural and Brain Sciences, 23*, 877–901.

Revonsuo, A. (2001). Dreaming and the place of consciousness in nature. *Behavioural and Brain Sciences, 24*, 1000–1001.

Revonsuo, A. (2005). The self in dreams. In T. E. Feinberg & J. P. Keenan (Eds.), *The lost self: Pathologies of the brain and mind* (pp. 206–219). New York: Oxford University Press.

Revonsuo, A. (2006). *Inner presence: Consciousness as a biological phenomenon*. Cambridge, MA: MIT Press.

Revonsuo, A., Kallio, S., & Sikka, P. (2009). What is an altered state of consciousness? *Philosophical Psychology, 22*, 187–204.

Revonsuo, A., & Tarkko, K. (2002). Binding in dreams. *Journal of Consciousness Studies, 9*, 3–24.

Sacks, O. (1985). *The man who mistook his wife for a hat*. London: Picador.

Sacks, O. (1995). *An anthropologist on Mars*. London: Picador.

Schwartz, S. (2000). A historical loop of one hundred years: Similarities between 19th century and contemporary dream research. *Dreaming, 10*, 55–66.

Schwitzgebel, E. (2004). Introspective training apprehensively defended: Reflections on Titchener's lab manual. *Journal of Consciousness Studies, 11*, 58–76.

Searle, J. R. (1992). *The rediscovery of the mind*. Cambridge, MA: MIT Press.

Searle, J. R. (1997). *The mystery of consciousness*. New York: New York Review Books.

Searle J. R. (2000). Consciousness. *Annual Review of Neuroscience, 23*, 557–578.

Silvanto, J., Cowey, A., Lavie, N., & Walsh, V. (2005). Striate cortex (V1) activity gates awareness of motion. *Nature Neuroscience, 8*, 143–144.

Simons, D. J., & Chabris, C. F. (1999). Gorillas in our midst: Sustained inattentional blindness for dynamic events. *Perception, 28*, 1059–1074.

REFERENCES

Simons D. J., & Rensink, R. A. (2005). Change blindness: Past, present, and future. *Trends in Cognitive Sciences, 9,* 16–20.

Smit, R. H. (2008). Corroboration of the dentures anecdote involving veridical perception in a near-death experience. *Journal of Near-Death Studies, 27,* 47–61.

Snyder, F. (1970). The phenomenology of dreaming. In L. Madow & L. H. Snow (Eds.), *The psychodynamic implications of the physiological studies on dreams* (pp. 124–151). Springfield, IL: Charles S. Thomas.

Solms, M. (1997). *The neuropsychology of dreams.* Mahwah, NJ: Lawrence Erlbaum Associates, Inc.

Spangenberg Postal, K. (2005). The mirror sign delusional misidentification symptom. In T. E. Feinberg & J. P. Keenan (Eds.), *The lost self* (pp. 131–146). New York: Oxford University Press.

Sperling, G. (1960). The information available in brief visual presentations. *Psychological Monographs, 74,* 1–29.

Strauch, I., & Meier, B. (1996). *In search of dreams: Results of experimental dream research.* New York: SUNY Press.

Strawson, G. (2006). Realistic monism: Why physicalism entails panpsychism. *Journal of Consciousness Studies, 13,* 3–31.

Stubenberg, L. (1998). *Consciousness and qualia.* Amsterdam: John Benjamins.

Tart, C. T. (2000). Investigating altered states on their own terms. In M. Velmans (Ed.), *Investigating phenomenal consciousness* (pp. 255–278). Amsterdam: John Benjamins.

Thompson, E., & Varela, F. J. (2001). Radical embodiment: Neural dynamics and consciousness. *Trends in Cognitive Sciences, 5,* 418–425.

Titchener, E. B. (1896). *An outline of psychology.* New York: Macmillan.

Tononi, G. (2009). An integrated information theory of consciousness. In. W. B. Banks (Ed.), *Encyclopedia of consciousness* (pp. 403–416). San Diego, CA: Academic Press.

Tye, M. (1995). *Ten problems of consciousness: A representational theory of the phenomenal mind.* Cambridge, MA: MIT Press.

Tye, M. (2009). *Consciousness revisited.* Cambridge, MA: MIT Press.

Uga, V., Lemut, M. C., Zampi, C., Zilli, I., & Salzarulo, P. (2006). Music in dreams. *Consciousness and Cognition, 15,* 351–357.

Valli, K., & Revonsuo, A. (2009). The threat simulation theory in light of recent empirical evidence: A review. *American Journal of Psychology, 122,* 17–38.

van Eeden, F. (1990). A study of dreams. Reprinted in C. T. Tart (Ed.), *Altered states of consciousness* (pp. 175–190). New York: Harper Collins. (Original work published 1913.)

van Lommel, P., van Wees, R., Meyers, V., & Elfferich, I. (2001). Near-death experience in survivors of cardiac arrest: A prospective study in the Netherlands. *Lancet, 358,* 2039–2045.

Vanni, S., Revonsuo, A., Saarinen, J., & Hari, R. (1996). Visual awareness of objects correlates with activity of right occipital cortex. *NeuroReport, 8,* 183–186.

Varela, F. J. (1999). Reply to Owen and Morris. In F. J. Varela & J. Shear (Eds.), *The view from within* (pp. 272–273). Thorverton: Imprint Academic.

Velmans, M. (1991). Is human information processing conscious? *Behavioral and Brain Sciences, 14,* 651–726.

Velmans, M. (1996). What and where are conscious experiences? In M. Velmans (Ed.), *The science of consciousness* (pp. 181–196). London: Routledge.

Velmans, M. (2003). Is the world in the brain, or the brain in the world? *Behavioral and Brain Sciences, 26,* 427–429.

Velmans, M. (2009). *Understanding consciousness* (2nd ed.). Hove: Routledge.

Velmans, M., & Schneider, S. (Eds.) (2007). *The Blackwell companion to consciousness.* Oxford: Blackwell.

Wallace, B. A. (2007). *Contemplative science.* New York: Columbia University Press.

Weiskrantz, L. (1997). *Consciousness lost and found*. New York: Academic Press.

Wilenius, M., & Revonsuo, A. (2007). Timing of the earliest ERP correlate of visual awareness. *Psychophysiology, 44*, 703–710.

Wilkes, K. V. (1988). –, Yishi, Duh, Um, and Consciousness. In A. J. Marcel & E. Bisiach (Eds.), *Consciousness in contemporary science* (pp. 16–41). New York: Oxford University Press.

Woody, E. Z., & Bowers, K. S. (1994). A frontal assault on dissociated control. In S. J. Lynn & J. W. Rhue (Eds.), *Dissociation: Clinical and theoretical perspectives* (pp. 52–79). London: Guilford Press.

Yu, L., & Blumenfeld, H. (2009). Theories of impaired consciousness in epilepsy. *Annals of the New York Academy of the Sciences, 1157*, 48–60.

Zeki, S. (2003). The disunity of consciousness. *Trends in Cognitive Sciences, 7*, 214–218.

Zeki, S., & Bartels, A. (1999). Towards a theory of visual consciousness. *Consciousness and Cognition, 8*, 225–259.

Zihl, J., von Cramon, D., & Mai, N. (1983). Selective disturbance of movement vision after bilateral brain damage. *Brain, 106*, 313–340.

Author index

Subject index